THE MAJESTIC TWELVE

THE
MAJESTIC
TWELVE

**The True Story of the
Most Feared Combat
Escort Unit in Baghdad**

Master Sergeant
Jack W. Lynch II
with
Rick Lynch

Thomas Dunne Books
St. Martin's Press   New York

THOMAS DUNNE BOOKS.
An imprint of St. Martin's Press.

THE MAJESTIC TWELVE. Copyright © 2009 by Jack W. Lynch II. All rights reserved. Printed in
the United States of America. For information, address St. Martin's Press, 175 Fifth Avenue, New
York, N.Y. 10010.

Library of Congress Cataloging-in-Publication Data

Lynch, Jack W.
    The majestic twelve : the true story of the most feared combat escort unit in Baghdad /
Master Sergeant Jack W. Lynch II with Rick Lynch.
                p. cm.
    Includes bibliographical references and index.
    ISBN 978-0-312-56121-5 (alk. paper)
    1. Lynch, Jack W.   2. Iraq War, 2003—Personal narratives, American.   3. United States.
Marine Corps—Biography.   4. Military convoys—Iraq.   I. Lynch, Rick.   II. Title.
    DS79.76.L94 2009
    956.7044'342—dc22

                                                                                    2009016946

Design by Sarah Maya Gubkin

First Edition: January 2010

10   9   8   7   6   5   4   3   2   1

Dedicated to the Majestic Twelve and those warriors of the United States Army and Marine Corps whose stories, though just as worthy as ours, have yet to find their voice

CONTENTS

THE MAJESTIC TWELVE

CHAPTER 1

Departure and Forty-Seven Dead

The hardest part of any deployment, peacetime or otherwise, is, of course, the leaving. Wartime deployments are harder still because, in addition to dealing with the knowledge that you will not see home, friends, or family for six months or longer, there is the specter of pending combat hovering about. Of the numerous and varied emotions one experiences when preparing for such a deployment, first and foremost for a Marine Corps infantryman of twenty years is excitement. Saying so in this politically correct age is, of course, verboten. The professional soldier is supposed to view combat with a cool, detached, and grim outlook. Excitement is for boyish amateurs who just don't know any better and who make cracks about how *Saving Private Ryan* is their favorite comedy. But if you've volunteered for twenty years to be an infantryman, and if you've endured the rigorous, punishing training and the misery and hardships that go along with it, well then, when the roll is called and your name is heard, you're excited. That rush is only slightly tempered by the dark side, by the threat of death or mutilation that combat represents. After all, the threat is at first a distant one and the adrenaline coursing through you easily overpowers any thoughts of your fragile body being ripped apart by steel, copper, or brass traveling at three thousand feet per second. Besides, my orders had me assigned to the safe and simple job of training soldiers of the New Iraqi Army in Kirkush, far from the dangers of places like Baghdad.

Still, safe orders or hazardous duty, combat or boredom, it is always hard to leave, and this deployment was no different. If anything, it was worse, for not only would I be leaving my three children, ages ten, fourteen, and eighteen, I would be leaving them without their mother, for in January 2002, my wife of nineteen years, Denise, had died of a blood clot. She had been in treatment for the blood clot since December 31, 2001, and according to medical records, her doctors had spent most of January 29, 2002 debating whether they should place a filter in her chest. In the end, they decided that her condition was not life threatening and they opted not to install the filter. By six the next morning, they had been proved wrong. My wife had passed.

Further complicating the situation, I'd remarried two years later and now I would be leaving my new bride after less than two months of marriage.

Those were the things going through my mind in early February 2004 as I spent my second day in Camp Wolverine, Kuwait. Wolverine was the layover before the final leg of my journey to Iraq. Family concerns aside, I could not help but notice that, as wartime deployments went, this one had pretty nice perks. Wolverine had an all-night Burger King, a Pizza Inn, and a coffeehouse. There were phones, Internet access, and a chow hall darn near as good as the one at Camp Lejeune, North Carolina. During my earlier trip to the region, in 1990, for the Gulf War, we lived in the holes we dug, there were no BK Broilers to be had, and my unit went eighty-eight days with neither a shower nor even a change of clothes. The second go-round started off much better. I slept in a tent and generally felt as if I were at Club Med.

Beyond the Wolverine, Kuwait City appeared immaculate and boomed with prosperity. When I had last seen Kuwait, the place resembled a large, stinking dump, the natural result of six months of Iraqi occupation and the war that had ousted them. Trash and the detritus of the Iraqi defeat were everywhere. Destroyed armored vehicles, spent artillery shells, and shattered cars and trucks of every type, military and civilian, covered the land as far as the eye could see.

Thirteen years ago, I had led a rifle squad in India Company, 1st Battalion, 6th Marines. Our mission had been to charge through the Iraqi defenses along the Kuwait–Saudi Arabia border and destroy the Iraqi army dug in between us and Kuwait City. The nature of the terrain, utterly flat in all directions, provided absolutely zero cover for attacking infantry. That landscape, combined with the large, densely seeded mine fields, which were covered by excellent Russian, French, and South African–built artillery, as well as the sheer numbers of Iraqi troops we would be facing (thirteen divisions of dug-in soldiers who had had six months to prepare their defenses), made our survival seem somewhat improbable.

"You know how we mark enemy units on maps with red symbols?" my platoon sergeant had asked, holding up a well-used map of the future battle-field. "Well, you might as well just paint this whole motherfucker red," he'd concluded with a short, bitter laugh. General Walter Boomer, the senior Marine Corps officer in the Gulf, had said the same thing, albeit with less colorful language, describing our "force ratios" as "horrible." No matter how you phrased it, though, it had all meant the same thing—more defenders than attackers. That is never supposed to happen, of course. Armies that choose the terrain and dig in, in advance of attack, have all the advantages. Theoretically, then, the attackers should at least be numerically superior. General Norman Schwarzkopf assessed that our losses could be as high as 50 percent just getting through the breech lanes. And that came *before* the expected fighting in Kuwait City. These things all made us just a little pessimistic about the immediate future. I remember looking around me as we got ready to cross the line of departure in our drive against the Iraqi army. I studied the faces of my friends, Crowley, Douglas, McDonald, Gaudet, Davis, Doc Wright, and so many more. How many of them would be dead by this time tomorrow? I also wondered how many of them were looking around and asking themselves the same thing about me.

As our vehicles lurched forward into the attack that day thirteen years ago, one of the new marines in our platoon played a cassette of the Kansas song "Carry On, Wayward Son." What is it about music, I had asked myself, that can so lift the spirit when combat is near?

Now many things were different. Chief of which concerned the fact that I did not deploy as part of a unit as I had back in 1990. In the war that would finish Saddam forever, destiny gave me no part; headquarters battalion and the rear lines called. Saddam was captured and his sons were dead. Except for the downing of U.S. Army troop helicopters, American losses in late 2003 and early 2004 had been very light, and it looked, for all intents and purposes, as if the war were over. At least that was what most people thought.

The tent in which I sat waiting for my flight into Iraq overflowed with about eighty people, all of whom were facing three large televisions. A different movie played on each set, and added to that was the background noise of forty conversations that made it pointless to try and watch a movie, so I simply waited to hear my flight, designated CHROME 33, called up. In the timeless way of the military, we'd all been awake since 0530 for a flight that might not leave until the next day. "Hurry up and wait" is a phrase that certainly has been known in the Greek phalanx, the Roman cohort, and in every army since.

Our flight received the go signal at 2300. About forty of us stood and shuffled outside to form a single file. An air force tech sergeant called off forty names from a roster and scratched out the names of those who did not answer up. He then counted the names remaining, counted the bodies standing in front of him, and had us follow him to a bus. In less than ten minutes we were on the flight line and being issued earplugs. We would be flying on a C-130. The aircraft, built for hauling troops and cargo, had little in the way of creature comforts, and the volume of noise thundering out of the turboprops could not be deadened by the sound-absorbing material between the passengers and the engines; hence the earplugs. I boarded the aircraft last, and as I did so I noticed some chalk writing on a door panel that told me the plane carried flares and chaff.

Flares are designed to decoy incoming heat-seeking missiles, like the Russian-made SA-7, as they are hotter than the deploying aircraft's engines. The SA-7 is a man-portable, shoulder-fired antiaircraft missile. While the design is quite dated and, consequently, poses little threat to high-performance combat jets, it is quite capable of bringing down less advanced aircraft like our pig. In fact, the enemy in Iraq had recently used them against U.S. Army helicopters to inflict heavy losses. In November 2003, seventy-three U.S. troops had been killed in action, making it the war's deadliest month up to that time. Thirty-nine of these soldiers had been killed when their helicopters were shot down. Though successful against helicopters, the SA-7 had failed to bring down any fixed-wing aircraft thus far in the war, and I had no fears that mine would be the first.

Chaff, used to defeat radar-guided missiles by flooding the radar with multiple reflections, is nothing more than tinfoil, released in strips that return radar signals and obscure the presence of the target aircraft. Chaff had been invented by the British during World War II and was first used with devastating effect on the night of 24–25 July 1943, when over seven hundred RAF bombers attacked the city of Hamburg. The fire raid, Operation Gomorrah, killed over 50,000 people. Largely thanks to the chaff, fewer than fifteen British bombers were lost.

I hoped, of course, that we would need neither the chaff nor the flares, and I really dreaded the air combat maneuvering that would certainly accompany their release.

Chaff and flares aside, the flight to Baghdad lasted only an hour and twenty-two minutes and passed peacefully. From the air, Baghdad looked like most cities at night, and nothing suggested that any great danger waited below—until we began our descent. Because of the threat posed by surface-to-air missiles and small-arms fire, we descended from the sky in a series of tight turns accompanied by stomach-churning drops in altitude. While exhilarating, all went well, and soon we were safely on the ground and taxiing to a stop. The hatch opened and I stepped out into the cool, refreshing night air.

After breaking down the pallet that held our baggage and collecting our gear, we settled down to sleep in the crowded tent that sheltered both new arrivals and departures. There were no cots, just chairs for watching TV. I found a spot on the floor and quickly fell asleep. The morning came suddenly and abruptly as a soldier tripped over me trying to navigate through the sea of sleeping men. After chow, those of us assigned, as I was, to the Coalition Military Assistance Training Team (CMATT) were told that the Coalition Provisional Authority (CPA), which was colocated with CMATT, had sent a bus with an armed escort to carry us to Hussein's Presidential Palace. None of us had ammo and many did not have the Small Arms Protective Inserts (SAPI) ballistic gear for our flak jackets. The SAPIs were an absolute Godsend and had saved many lives in Iraq. They will stop an AK-47 round at point-blank range, and they are, contrary to popular opinion, a relatively new thing. The inaccurately nicknamed "bulletproof vests" of old were effective at stopping shrapnel and handgun fire, but were absolutely no match for a rifle. Knowing of the SAPI's reputation, well earned on the battlefields of Afghanistan and Iraq, we were not happy about being without them. Of course, being without ammo produced even worse feelings, but the army ran things, and they were certain that we would need neither the SAPIs nor ammo.

When the bus finally arrived that afternoon it lacked the CPA-promised escort. When questioned about the lack of an escort, the driver of the bus merely shrugged and said one was not available and that since we were only going to the palace anyway one was not really needed. While the war was going well at that time, it seemed extremely foolish to me to send twenty-one unarmed men anywhere in Iraq. Incredibly, the lack of ammo, SAPI plates, and an escort did not bother anyone at the CPA. When Major Manning, the senior man with us, raised these concerns, he was assured that the route to the palace was perfectly safe. Because nobody, including the driver sent by the CPA, knew where we were supposed to go, we caught something of a break. We only knew that we were to go to "the" Presidential Palace so the bus driver simply took us to the nearest palace. Once there, it was obvious why our driver had not been worried about the lack of an escort. The palace he took us to was located on Camp Victory, which was colocated with the airport, which meant we never left U.S.-controlled facilities on our short trip to the palace. But this was the wrong palace.

When Major Manning asked the sentry at the gate where the CPA was located, he was told, "You guys are in the wrong place. There is no CPA here, just CJTF-7."

Major Manning then went in search of someone who might know where exactly the CPA was located. While things were sorted out, I went looking for some bullets. We got very lucky and found a small building housing both a supply section and an armory. From supply we were able to get SAPI plates, and from the armory we drew a full combat load of 210 rounds of 5.56 mm ammo for the M-16s and 45 rounds of 9 mm ammo for those of us armed with M-9s. The specialists and NCOs who hooked us up did so very graciously, in spite of the fact that we were all marines and not in any way attached to their unit.

By contrast, when I had tried to get SAPI plates from Quantico, I was told they were needed in security battalion in case the enemy attempted to open a second front in Virginia. The Marine Security Force at Yorktown had plates but refused to issue them without authority from their higher. In the end, I coughed up $1,500 of my own money and bought a set from a company in Harrisonburg, Virginia. I could not help but contrast the attitude of paper-pushing marines at Quantico and Yorktown with that of the fine soldiers at Camp Victory who gave me twenty sets of SAPI plates and all the ammo I needed with nothing but my signature for authorization. As we got the ammo and the plates, Major Manning found out where we were supposed to go—a little more than five miles away sat the Presidential Palace in Baghdad. I did not know it at the time, but the road linking the airport and Camp Victory to the Presidential Palace was the most important 5.4 miles of road in Iraq, and it would change my life.

The road to the Green Zone, the secured area of Baghdad surrounding the Presidential Palace, consisted of all high-speed blacktop. While the road spoke of modernity, the rest of Baghdad did not. Much of what could be seen from the highway consisted of trash and squalor, and the place reeked of decay when compared to Kuwait. Considering the oil wealth of both nations and comparing clean and modern Kuwait with the filth, poverty, and decay of Baghdad, I had to wonder what Saddam did with his nation's wealth. As we pulled into a large parking lot across from the gated grounds of the Presidential Palace, I noticed that things were much better in the Green Zone, the seat of coalition power in Iraq. The Green Zone was well maintained.

We quickly off-loaded and grabbed our gear from the baggage truck. Each of us carried just a ton of shit: Weapons, ammo, vests, two full seabags, a pack, and a carry-on bag completed the burden. Before we could begin to move our mountain of crap, dogs were brought in to sniff for drugs or other contraband. As I watched the dogs rut through our stuff, I was reminded of my last deployment, when the military police searching through our gear had found one penis pump. Abuse had rained down on its owner as the offending item was delicately removed by an MP.

We began the task of carrying our gear three hundred meters to the rear entrance to the palace. Marines from a Fleet Anti-Terrorism Security Team (FAST) were manning the gates. To get in we had to be issued new ID cards and be accompanied by an escort, one Sergeant First Class Mincie, the acting first sergeant of the CMATT. Mincie took us around for a quick check-in, after which we were shown our new home—a large but mostly empty tent. I found a rack near the door and dropped my gear. Near me were three men who would become very important to me later. They were Gunnery Sergeants Robert Josleyn and Hessen, and Corporal William Napier. Months later Gunny Josleyn would, in fact, save my life.

After dropping my gear, I walked back into the palace and reported to the C-3 operations section, also known as operations, ops, "the three," or simply "three," located in the palace's ballroom, to which I had been assigned. There I met Sergeant Major Robert Jackson, U.S. Army, the C-3 operations sergeant major. He told me that nothing further would be done that day and that we should just come back in the morning. He advised us to enjoy the down time, saying, "Walk around the palace and do some sightseeing, take some pictures, and relax. Just be here at 0800 tomorrow."

Robert Jackson was approximately forty years old and he stood 5'6" with a medium build. He wore his brown hair like an executive, well cropped, but longer than regulation, with a wave on top. He was both friendly and professional. His demeanor and the coveted Special Forces tab he wore on his shoulder impressed me. Before I left, Jackson introduced me to other members of the section, one of whom was Chief Master Sergeant Jeff Vorgang, U.S. Air Force. Vorgang was friendly and eager to please. Standing 6'0', Vorgang was in his late thirties and had the build of a Jenny Craig failure. As polite as he was fat, Vorgang always wore a friendly, less than military smile. Over time, I noticed that he almost revered Master Sergeant Jackson as a younger brother reveres an older, more accomplished big brother. I pulled myself away from the talkative Vorgang and went back to my tent. I told Gunnys Josleyn and Hessen everything that Jackson said to me and then we decided that we would take Jackson's advice and do some palace sightseeing.

The massive palace was as easy to get lost in as the Bermuda Triangle, and I quickly began to doubt that I would ever be able to find my way around the place. At a glance, it quite naturally impressed and awed, but in reality it was an amazingly tacky place, and an excellent lesson in the dangers posed by men of wealth but no taste. It was simply an abomination. If Saddam had somehow beaten the genocide rap hanging over his head, I am convinced we could have hit him with a crimes-against-humanity charge based on his palace decorating. The ceilings and floors were suitably grand and opulent, but everything between them screamed of poor taste. I found it hard to believe Hussein would spend millions of dollars on a building from which to rule his country and then start saving money by skimping on things like windows, window treatments, light fixtures, and paint. It reminded me of the home of that stereotypical, trailer-dwelling hillbilly who wins the lottery, buys a mansion, and then decorates it with the crap he had in his trailer. Around every corner, you just knew you'd be bumping into a revolving, pink, heart-shaped bed, flanked by mirrors and maybe a golden harp sitting in a corner. Tacky, yes, but amusing just the same, and it did help us while away the hours until chow.

Chow at the palace had been rumored to be a feast, and it didn't disappoint. The large and cavernous room in which our meals were served had also been a ballroom. Who knew that Hussein so loved a good party? Josleyn and Hessen were my dining companions that evening. Robert Josleyn was an imposing man at over six feet; he had the powerful build of a man who had lived and worked outdoors for most of his life. Though he was, at thirty-nine, two years younger than I, he looked much older. His face was Marlboro Man rugged. While Josleyn looked like the "typical" marine noncommissioned officer (NCO), he was actually very quiet and reserved. A sniper by trade, he was also a born-again Christian. He had been assigned to the marksmanship training unit in Camp Lejeune before being assigned to CMATT.

Gunny Scott Hessen could not have been more different from Josleyn. He was about 5′8″ and while strong, he was chubby. Hessen was like Josleyn in one way; both men were country boys with a corresponding love of guns, hunting, and fishing. Hessen, prematurely balding, had taken a shortcut and simply shaved his head, which further highlighted the Errol Flynn mustache he wore. He came from a very unique duty station, having worked in the Camp Lejeune brig's carpentry shop before shipping off to Iraq. It seemed an odd place for a combat engineer like Hessen to be assigned. Most of our time together went to discussing what jobs we were assigned to by our line numbers. Gunny Hessen had a line number that assigned him as the plans noncommissioned officer in charge or, simply, NCOIC. The line numbers listed on the Joint Manning Document had nothing to do with a service member's military occupational specialty (MOS). Rather, it designated a billet to be filled and the name of the person assigned to fill it. Often, but certainly not always, service members were assigned jobs that matched their experience and their MOS. Gunny Josleyn's number had him assigned the duties of the force protection NCOIC. Both jobs, especially the force protection gig, seemed better than mine, which, while still somewhat undefined, appeared to be shaping up to involve the mighty pen far more than the sword.

After chow we headed back to our tent and racked out. As I drifted off to sleep, I thought about the less than exciting job to which I had been assigned, and I was determined to do everything I could to change it. I had no idea that Al Qaeda in Iraq was about to take care of that for me.

At 0800 next morning, 11 February, I reported to the C-3. My first full day in Iraq and I was about to bear witness to a great deal of truly hideous violence, more than anything I had seen in the first Gulf War.

As I walked in, everything in the C-3 appeared in confusion. Sergeant Major Jackson was standing behind his desk, talking to his drivers and "shooters," and he was obviously excited. From what I could pick up, the Baghdad Recruiting Center (RC) had just been hit by a powerful car bomb and to Jackson fell the duty of attempting to get a team together to recover the Americans working there. He didn't have enough people to send a four-vehicle convoy, which I took to be the preferred method. In actuality, he did have enough people, but that would require that he go. I heard someone propose this course of action. Jackson was quick to answer.

"I can't leave the desk! Especially not now."

Not one to let an opportunity pass, I quickly spoke up.

"Hey, I'll go."

I then continued, giving my résumé, figuring that it couldn't hurt.

"I'm a twenty-three-year infantryman, and I don't have a job yet, so I can go."

The office suddenly grew very quiet as all eyes were turned toward the cluster of new arrivals that included me. Jackson looked at me and asked if I had body armor. I replied that I did; Jackson gave me the green light. I ran back to my tent and quickly put on my vest and grabbed my helmet. In the meantime, Gunny Hessen had also managed to get on the run. As we prepared to launch, a very large marine lieutenant colonel approached me, smiling broadly.

"Hey, I know you. You taught a staff course with that major at Lejeune."

The man's name was John Thomas and, while I was surprised that he remembered me, I had no problem remembering him. Lieutenant Colonel Thomas was as easygoing and funny as he was large, and at 6'5" and over 260 pounds, that was saying a lot. With crew cut, Thomas looked like a professional football player from the late fifties. Seeing him again, almost two years after our first meeting, I was immediately impressed by something I'd not had the opportunity to observe when we had first met in Lejeune: In a time of crisis, such as we were experiencing, Colonel Thomas acted just as he did in my class. While he was professional and serious, to be sure, he was not grave or agitated. He was to play a significant role in my life during the rest of my tour in Iraq.

Jackson had one of CMATT's intelligence analysts give us a threat brief. He warned us that on the way to the recruiting center we were to remain alert for small-arms ambushes. Once at the RC, our primary concern would be secondary vehicle-borne, improvised explosive devices (VBIEDs), or, to the laymen, more car bombs.

In addition to Gunny Hessen and me, Colonel Thomas, Gunnery Sergeant Vanegas, the intelligence analyst, and two other marines would be going on the run. Vanegas was the C-3's ground transport NCOIC, which simply meant that he controlled and coordinated all of CMATT's ground-based movement. He had less than two weeks left in Iraq when the car bomb hit the RC, yet he was going with us. I admired him for that. Looking around, I found it more than a little odd that everyone going to the RC was a U.S. Marine; in fact, every marine in CMATT's C-3 was on the run. In a joint unit, with fewer marines than soldiers, sailors, or airmen, you would have thought that maybe a soldier, sailor, or airman would have manned up for the trip. Well, a soldier anyway. Since CMATT lacked a full-time, dedicated quick reaction force (QRF) or convoy security team (CST) the makeup of these missions was often a matter of personal decision; and judging by who was going now, I could only assume that most of CMATT's soldiers, sailors, and airmen had better things to do. Maybe they, too, had desks that they could "not leave at a time like this."

As we walked to the lot where our vehicles were staged, Gunny Vanegas asked Hessen if he had a rifle. Hessen had only an M-9 pistol, which is a defensive sidearm and virtually useless in combat unless you're finishing off enemy wounded or any prisoners you may have collected, which was not what Hessen or I had in mind. As a quick fix, Vanegas offered him an AK-47, a weapon Hessen had had no experience with. Because I own an AK and am far more familiar with it than Hessen was, I gave him my M-16 and happily took the folding-stock AK-47. While I much prefer the M-16, the AK is shorter and lighter and far more easily employed within the tight confines of a vehicle. In the coming months I would end up fighting a long campaign to get my section issued mini M-16s. These weapons, more properly called M-4s, had shorter barrels and telescoping butts and were lighter and shorter than their full-sized cousins and far better suited to convoy work.

The run to the RC was the only time in Iraq that I did not have my issued rifle, in contrast with the large number of people at the Palace who routinely carried AKs. Some did it because, like Hessen, they knew they needed more than just a pistol. Others did it because they believed it looked really cool. It was not uncommon to see a large, Fatty Arbuckle–sized navy chief with an AK-47 slung over his shoulder and a doughnut in his hand as he walked to and from his trailer. We would come to call these people Palace Commandos or Pool Pansies.

I drew assignment as a shooter in a silver Durango driven by a marine corporal. The rest of our convoy consisted of two Yukons and a pickup truck. None of the vehicles had armor.

The weather fit the occasion, cold and bleak under a slate gray sky. While I would not call it ominous, it was less than inviting. We departed the security of the Green Zone via an exit called Assassins' Gate. Once we hit the Red Zone, which was what Iraq beyond the gate was called, the driver gunned the vehicle and we were doing eighty miles per hour on Baghdad's streets. The driver did his best to keep us moving forward as fast as he could, while I scanned the crowded streets for any threats. I could provide little value as I had no idea what to look for, beyond the obvious, like a guy with an RPG-7 or an MSNBC reporter with a camera.

The convoy went speeding around Iraqi vehicles that were stopped, we ran red lights and stop signs, and when traffic at an intersection became heavy, we went over curbs and sidewalks. Horns signaled our approach to Iraqi drivers, and weapons pointed out of windows told motorists and pedestrians to stay away. Vehicles that did not heed these warnings were "bumped," which meant that they were gently nudged by our bumper.

At the recruiting center we pulled into a large open area, an unpaved trash-strewn parking lot for buses. The lot was surrounded by an eight-foot-high iron fence set atop a wall of concrete eighteen inches high. Stepping out of our vehicles, we were greeted by an Iraqi army lieutenant colonel named Ahmed. This officer was the Iraqi whom C-3 relied upon to secure bus transportation to move army recruits between recruiting centers and training bases all over Iraq. As such, he was important, and since he worked for the C-3, he was a man I would get to know very well. Short and fat, with sinister eyes, and the cartoon villain's thin black mustache, Ahmed looked every bit the stereotypical powerful North African despot from some 1940s movie. He would be equally at home, or so it seemed anyway, twirling his thin mustache as he tied a damsel to the railroad tracks. Ahmed greeted Colonel Thomas warmly and expressed thanks for our safe arrival. Thomas thanked him and said that he was glad to see Ahmed safe. I was surprised by the evident close and warm relationship between Thomas and Ahmed. Like most Americans, I knew we were working with the New Iraqi Army, but I did not realize how warm and intimate that relationship had already become in many instances. After greeting Thomas, Ahmed turned to the rest of us.

"Listen, my friends, we are very worried about another attack, maybe another bomb or RPGs. I am most worried about RPGs, so look out for them. Now be very careful where you step."

This, of all the things Ahmed said to us, seemed out of place. Be careful where you step. Why? What could he possibly mean by that? His meaning became horribly clear in just moments.

Ahmed asked us if we were ready. Colonel Thomas said we were, and with that Ahmed led us around the barriers that had saved his life and separated us from the carnage on the other side. It sounds so very odd to say it, but before rounding the barriers, I really hadn't noticed the screaming, the smell, or the wail of sirens. The moment I turned that corner I descended into a world utterly different from the one I knew, and the relative calm and safety that had been ours were ripped away by the horror of mass slaughter.

"Words cannot describe it" or "Words fail me"—these are tired old clichés, and I feel almost disrespectful to the dead using them, but that's really all I can come up with. Shakespeare perhaps, or maybe Homer, could do justice to the nightmare spread before me, but I just don't feel up to the task. What can you say about the aftermath of a bombing that killed scores? Your mind can certainly dredge up horrors aplenty; you perhaps *expect* to see a severed head here, a stomach and intestines there, a chest cavity ripped open and showing heart and lungs, even a face—a human face neatly skinned from a skull and deposited in the gutter—your mind can imagine these things, certainly, but to see them, to actually *see* them, is something else entirely. But see it I did. We all did.

The sights that lay before us were easily the most horrifying thing I had ever beheld. The carnage and devastation were of such extremes that it would make a director of Hollywood slasher films ashamed at his inability to recreate such mind-numbing destruction. Human debris lay everywhere. It covered the ground like a rug. Looking down, I understood what Ahmed had meant when he said be careful where you step. Large pools of blood gave mute evidence of the places where men had died. The walls of the recruiting compound were covered with small fragments of human tissue. In other spots large red-and-black smears told where a body had been slammed into the wall with terrific force. The stucco-covered walls had acted like giant cheese graters, stripping flesh from the dead as they slammed into them. Everywhere one looked were the remains of the forty-seven men killed in the attack. Bodies lay in incredibly contorted shapes, which would have been incomprehensible to me had someone described them but looked frighteningly and almost cartoonishly twisted in real life. Below the body-impact splatters on the walls were clumps of red, pulverized meat. Most often you couldn't even tell the parts were human, let alone identify what the part actually was. In the trees and chain-link RPG screen above the gated entrance to the RC, you could see limbs and smaller, impossible-to-identify gobs. Often, the larger parts looked like clumps of thick Jell-O. Scraps of clothes, shoes, and used bandages added to the sea of blood and human fragments on the ground. The most horrific sights could be seen in the concertina wire. Concertina wire is designed to deter direct attack by catching and ripping the clothes and flesh of advancing infantry. That day I learned that it catches other things very well. Wrapped round and round, and shredded by the concertina wire, were long strands of disgusting pinkish yellow ribbons that were unmistakably human intestines. They oozed from the concertina wire in sickening, stringy masses. The wire also caught a man blown into it with such force that the steel tore deeply into his horribly mutilated, eviscerated body. In fact the wire had wrapped so thoroughly around and in his body that he had to be cut out. Even then the wire caught the man one last time as medics attempted to gingerly and respectfully remove him from its coils. Snagging on something in his torn abdomen, the wire pulled out what remained of the man's stomach. Rather than pull the organ from the wire, the medic simply cut the wire and threw the stomach and wire into the body bag in which the corpse had been placed.

The concertina, though, wasn't the only thing making an almost unimaginably nightmarish scenario even worse. The Hesco barrier did its part, too. A Hesco barrier is a prefabricated, burlaplike material that is placed in steel netting approximately four feet square. This steel frame interlocks with other frames to create a wall, and the barrier is then filled with earth. The completed work is very effective at stopping shrapnel, small-arms fire, or human beings blasted into paste. Splashed against the barrier that would not yield were the distorted bodies of several slaughtered Iraqis. What I saw was a mass of pulverized goo from which protruded arms, legs, and heads at impossible angles. Heads were twisted completely around but still attached. Crowning this wretched mess was the neatly removed head of a man. The dead man's eyes were wide open, and he seemed to be wearing an expression of absolute terror. As much as I wanted to avoid eye contact with the dead man, I could not help but to stare at the horrible mass atop which his head sat. Arms were torn from torsos and protruded from the revolting mass where legs should be. Beneath the recognizable parts lay thick gelatinous muck that made me want to turn away. Intestines seemed to spread in all directions from beneath this horror. All of these men were burned to some degree, some worse than others. Together they looked like hell's version of a multiheaded octopus with twisted human limbs and stringy masses of intestines for arms.

Not far from this mass of suffering lay a man who appeared to have died hard. Most of the victims never knew what hit them. This man had no such luck. His clothes were gone, burned or torn off by the force of the explosion, I could not tell. But he had been burned and broken. His head was propped up on the curb and he lay on his back. His right hand rested across his chest and his left lay at his side. His right leg had been pulled up so that his knee was in the air and his face wore a mask of suffering. Spent bandages and other bloodied medical gear offered mute testimony to the valiant, yet ultimately futile, fight to save this man's life. I hoped that he had died quickly and not alone.

I was assigned security for the intelligence team as they took pictures of what remained of the car and the crater the bomb had created. According to witnesses, the car, a Chevy Caprice carrying an estimated three hundred pounds of explosives, had plowed into the dense crowd of men before it exploded. The explosion blasted a hole about two feet deep with a diameter of about seven feet. As the intel team did its work, I became aware of how vulnerable we would be to a secondary attack by any VBIEDs that might be in the ambulances that were pulling up to the scene; the soldiers on the perimeter had neither the numbers nor the time to thoroughly search them. Only a month before I arrived in Iraq an ambulance had been used to deliver a secondary attack following an earlier VBIED. I did not really feel fear as I stood just four feet from one of these ambulances, but I remained aware that I could be killed. Looking around me, I also realized just what it meant to be killed by a car bomb. Neither the words nor the pictures I had seen on TV and in print adequately described what it meant to die in such a way, and I found myself wanting the intel team to hurry up and finish. Working side by side with us were dozens of armed Iraqi soldiers and policemen. I knew they weren't all "good guys," and that some of those men were, in fact, the enemy.

But considering that the ultimate objective of our efforts in Iraq was to transfer responsibility for the security of the nation to these very men, you had to trust them. If you didn't, then the war was already lost.

Once the intel team had completed its task, we went into the recruiting center itself, and the nightmare that simply would not die threw up fresh horrors for our inspection. Mutilation and horror were everywhere. One body had smashed into the wall of the recruiting center, leaving only a red-and-black spatter to tell the tale. A trailing red-and-black smear pointed to the spot where the body came to rest. On the ground lay a man, facedown, with his chest peeled open and lying out at his sides like a butterfly-cut steak. His body had been torn in half across the abdominal cavity, and his intestines snaked out from this horrific wound like rivers on a map. As I walked, I became aware of the fact that I was stepping on something other than pavement, something bad. I knew by how it gave way beneath me—soft, rubbery, and resilient—that it had to be human remains. But I couldn't help it. Looking at the ground for a place not covered in gore seemed largely futile and took time, so I just kept moving and forgot about what I was walking in. It was shortly before that point, when I was still trying to look before I stepped, that I saw the shaved-off human face lying in the gutter. I would rather step in that and not know what it was than look at it. I will never forget that face. The face of man reduced to caricature.

Permeating everything were the odors. The odor of blood, burned flesh, and guts hung on the air and could not be escaped. Even after everything I had already seen, I could not help but be amazed at the vast amounts of human debris covering every square inch of the recruiting station.

I made my way to the station commander, a retired marine colonel, who now worked for the Department of Defense as a civilian contractor, identified myself, and asked how many people we needed to evacuate. He said that he had nine he needed to pull. There were five civilians, one marine, one navy chief, and two airmen. The marine going back, one Major Fitzpatrick, had flown from Tampa to Kuwait with me, and I had actually teased him in Florida about being assigned to recruiting duty in Iraq, the most unlikely of places for such a job.

Fitz, as he was called by the officers, was about 6′3″ with a very large and powerful build only slightly smaller than Colonel Thomas. He did not look anything like a pilot; which is what he was. Fitz was also one lucky marine. He had just left the recruiting station with the station's translator, an Iraqi national, and was headed toward the gate when he stopped to take a picture of the building. As Major Fitzpatrick took his picture, the translator continued on toward the gate. Seconds later, and before Major Fitzpatrick had resumed walking toward the gate, the car bomb struck. The translator, being at the gate, was killed instantly, his clothes torn off except for his underwear and T-shirt. His body was thrown atop a Hesco barrier. The man's back, which was facing us, bore no obvious wounds, but blood covered the Hesco barrier he was lying on, indicating he had suffered massive injuries to his chest or abdomen. The blast threw Major Fitz to the ground, while pieces of the car, the gate, and people flew past him. He was close enough to the blast to feel the heat wave wash over him. I found him to be very composed considering what he had just endured.

After a few minutes talking with the major, the recruiting team was ready to be pulled out. Loaded into the middle seat of my Durango were Major Fitz and the two airmen, a captain and a tech sergeant. Before departing I secured an AK-47 for the captain and gave him a quick lesson in its use. I gave a brief to my passengers, essentially the same as the one given me earlier that morning. As we rolled out, an Iraqi police officer, who I think must have been in shock, actually tried to pick up the small pieces of flesh scattered on the ground in front of us. He soon realized that his efforts were futile and he stood up and waved us through. As we moved forward he studied the ground in front of our tires. With tears welling in his eyes, he glanced up at us as we drove by. A dejected and heartbroken man, he realized that there was nothing he could do on this day, not even protect the dignity of the dead. He turned his face away as we left the compound.

On the ride back, Major Fitz and the captain began talking and I reminded them of the need to stay focused and alert. Much of what they said was nervous banter, almost celebratory. I understood that. They had just survived an ordeal that had left forty-seven people dead. I would have acted the same way, but we needed their attention on the road so we could get back in one piece. The trip back resembled the one out—an uneventful, yet pulse-pounding, high-speed demolition derby with automatic weapons.

Safely back in the Green Zone, Hessen and I, along with the rest of the new joins, were informed that we had to sit in on a CMATT mission brief given by Lieutenant Colonel Finchley Cuddlesworth Roddington of the Australian army. Roddington was about 5'9" and thin with a bald head and with a long neck which sat stooped upon his shoulders in such a way as to resemble a sulking vulture. He had been an artilleryman in the Australian army. He seemed both professional and intelligent and was not at all as formal as his appearance made me think he would be. Colonel Roddington's brief was heavy with a bunch of political and strategic information that nobody in attendance really needed. I was just minutes from the most horrifying blood-bath I had ever witnessed, and am still amazed that I retain anything from the brief. In excruciating detail, Colonel Roddington explained that our mission in Iraq boiled down to recruiting and training soldiers, noncommissioned officers, and officers for the New Iraqi Army. This had to be done as rapidly as possible but without going so fast as to compromise the integrity and ability of the new force. Originally, the recruitment and training of the army was to have been a much slower and more methodical affair. This time-consuming plan would have produced a better-trained (and better-led) army, but the realities of the growing insurgency forced the original plan to be scrapped for the model we were now being shown. Colonel Roddington glossed over this unpleasant reality.

"The first plan seemed just too slow, but when we looked at the rapid growth of the American army from 1940 to 1942, we realized that there existed a proven model for doing the same thing in Iraq, only faster."

I found Roddington's statement a tad troubling, for while it was certainly true that the explosive growth of the American military after Pearl Harbor represented a truly phenomenal achievement, it should be remembered that it took place in a unified nation whose mainland was virtually invulnerable to serious attack by any of the Axis powers. Cultural differences aside, attempting to do the same thing in a nation fighting a civil war and dealing with terrorism seemed to be a stretch. What I had just seen at the Baghdad recruiting center gave a horrible lesson in the reality of the war in Iraq, and I knew the Iraqi military and security forces were not as well trained as they should be; furthermore, the Iraqi government, military, and police facilities were not as secure as they should be. Iraqi "soldiers" were being killed before they even had a chance to enlist and, I felt, this was due in large part to the failure of the Iraqi security forces. While I believed that we were moving too fast, I did not see that we had any other choice. Americans were already growing tired of the war, and Democrats were demanding that we pull out of Iraq. Contrary to what the situation required—slow, methodical, and comprehensive training—we were being forced to go with America's favorite solution to any complex problem: fast and easy. Trouble was, we were rebuilding the government and security forces of a nation of 26 million people, not selecting a date.

The brief, weighed down by an excessive amount of marginally useful information, was rather dull. What highlights there were came from our distinguished guest, a German diplomat. He appeared to have graduated from the Von Ribbentrop School of Charm. He was also an utter ass. His demeanor switched effortlessly between arrogant and condescending, and for almost every item that Colonel Roddington briefed, the Reich's diplomat had something negative to say. While there were certainly legitimate concerns about the plan for building the Iraqi army, it became clear that what the German really had problems with was our being in Iraq in the first place. Furthermore, he exuded utter contempt for our chances of success in Iraq. A marine next to me slipped me a note: "Maybe he thinks we'd be more successful if we threw all of the Iraqis into 'special' camps."

For a man whose people had a rather impressive history of conquering, enslaving, and murdering their neighbors, the German seemed awfully touchy about the use of American military power in the world outside of Europe. I recalled that when American military might was expended in Kosovo, the Germans saw it as a good thing. After all, in that conflict American power had been used to bolster European security. In the eyes of our German and French friends, it always seemed that the only lawful use of American power lay in the defense of Europe. American blood existed as a currency to be spent only to save the flower of European "manhood" from the horrors of war. Sixty

2004/02/11 10:25:33

Aftermath of the suicide car bombing at the Baghdad Recruiting Center on 11 February 2004. Gunnery Sergeant Scott Hessen is in the foreground, and to the right **is Lieutenant Colonel John Thomas, both USMC.** *(From the collection of Jack Lynch)*

years in Germany and Japan or fifty in Korea was great, but eleven months in Iraq was already too long. For the United States to use its awesome strength against a sworn enemy of our nation was, to many of our allies, reprehensible. I am sure that it did not help that the ouster of Saddam came as bad news for German chemical companies that had made millions of dollars in business deals with the butcher. I left the brief wishing that the United States picked its friends better.

That night, as I slept, the diplomat and his silliness were far from my thoughts. I could not help but relive the horrors I had seen at the RC.

Not surprisingly, I had a nightmare about the bombing. In it, I entered a large and dark, almost black, room. Someone in the shadows, I think the Iraqi lieutenant colonel whom I had met at the bomb site, handed me a big bottle of champagne which was covered with gore. Floating within the murky liquid in the bottle were bits of red and black material that appeared to be viscera. In the darkened room only the colonel's face and hand and the bottle were clearly defined. But within the black background, like a part of it, were several faces, maybe dozens. The faces were shadowy and indistinct, but they

The author, between partially destroyed barrier and ambulance, with raised AK-47, at the Baghdad Recruiting Center after the suicide car bombing.
(From the collection of Jack Lynch)

seemed very pissed or mocking, perhaps both. Later, after I woke up and sat thinking about it, I concluded that they were indeed pissed. Maybe they were pissed because the last day of their lives, a day in which they died so horribly, would turn out to be one of the best of my career. With their deaths I saw an opportunity to make more of my war than simply training Iraqi soldiers. The haphazard way in which we had formed a QRF to reach the site was unacceptable. CMATT, I was convinced, needed a dedicated CST/QRF team. Sooner or later the half-assed way of doing business was going to get someone killed. Whether CMATT liked it or not, believed it or not, the war was not over. As I lay there I decided that I would build a convoy security and quick reaction team. While the idea was nothing more than a concept, it would lead to the creation of the Majestic Twelve. The gore-filled bottle seemed to have been offered in mock congratulations by the men whose deaths had provided me a way out of a dull job pushing Iraqi recruits.

CHAPTER 2

Kirkush and the Convoys

My second full day as a member of CMATT was unremarkable except for my discovery of the swimming pool immediately after breakfast. Unlike the rest of the cheap and tacky palace, the pool area did not disappoint. It really was quite beautiful, with superb landscaping that included several mature trees and vine-covered pagodas and trellises. I imagined the pool became very popular during the summer, but it was too cold for swimmers in February. I had forgotten how cold and wet the region got in the winter. It rained my first two days in Iraq and I doubt that the temperature climbed out of the low fifties, making it hard to imagine the 120-degree temperatures that I knew were coming once the summer arrived. Still, I preferred the heat to the rain, as I hated the rain. *All* infantrymen hate the rain, and hate it with a passion. I have heard people describe the rain as romantic, which I'm sure it is in the right setting. But if you're soaked to the bone and sleeping in the mud for days on end, it is as romantic as Michael Moore in a bikini spreading suntan lotion on your back.

In December 1990, I deployed to Saudi Arabia for Operation Desert Shield. Like all the marines in my battalion, I carried very little in the way of rain or cold-weather gear, disparagingly called "snivel gear" by seasoned infantry. We had down-filled sleeping bags, and that was about it. Of course, tents were something *no* marine infantry battalion would even dare think of bringing to the field. You do that and you might as well make Michael Jackson the commandant of the Marine Corps. Tents were for the weak, and besides, we were going to the desert, not the arctic or some exotic rain forest.

On 12 January 1991, Tariq Aziz, the Iraqi foreign minister, and James A. Baker, the U.S. secretary of state, failed to reach an agreement that would avert war, and fittingly it started to rain. It kept raining. Sometime at about 0200 the next morning, I awoke to find that because my poncho was as waterproof as the *Titanic*, I was soaking wet from my knees down. In an effort to stay as dry as possible, I pulled my legs up into a tight fetal position and fell asleep. Within the hour, I awoke again, positively awash. I crawled out of my wet and worthless bag of feathers, tossed my poncho aside, and spent the night talking with other soaked and miserable marines. Rarely have I been as wet and cold as on that night and the three days that followed.

This time, some thirteen years later, the rain wasn't quite as bad. While it had been constant, it didn't come down nearly as hard and, besides, I now had an entire presidential palace to shelter me.

Later that day, Master Sergeant Jackson informed Gunny Hessen, Staff Sergeant Glakin, Sergeant West (two marines who had checked in with the gunny and me) that we were all headed for Kirkush the following day, 13 February. Glakin and West were being sent to stay, as they were assigned to the CMATT training team located there. They were both disappointed at what they saw as a boring assignment, one unlikely to let them see any action. Gunny Hessen and I were sent to "babysit" (Master Sergeant Jackson's words) some Iraqi soldiers who were already there and awaiting the arrival of their U.S. Army trainers. I did not like this at all. I did not come to Iraq to be used as an odd-jobs guy. Besides which, there was no war in Kirkush, and there were even fewer things to do in one's limited time off duty than in Baghdad. On the plus side, we were told the trip would take about three hours. Now that represented good news, for it was on the road that you found the enemy in Iraq. To be more correct, it was on the road that the enemy came to you. What I did not like, once again, was the apparent lack of structure with which the CMATT portion of the convoy ran. People were being assigned to convoys almost as haphazardly as they had been on the run to the Baghdad RC the day it got pulverized. Unbelievable! Convoys, the most frequent target of enemy attack, seemed to be treated as an afterthought rather than the serious combat missions they were. As I saw it at the time, this could be blamed on the shortage of personnel and the lack of mission-essential equipment. These factors could be somewhat excused, as they were beyond the immediate control of CMATT, and there were simply not enough resources to go around. But the complete lack of training given the soldiers and marines riding these convoys was inexcusable.

The brief we got from the C-2 was, thankfully, more thorough and polished than the hurried one we had been given when we were rushed out to the Baghdad RC. My assignment on this run had me as the shooter for a retired army lieutenant general, then employed by a civilian firm that had been contracted by Department of Defense (DOD) to do much of the training at Kirkush.

Behind the general, who did the driving, sat a British army paratrooper returning to Kirkush after a few days at home. The para was a corporal of the world-renowned Gurkhas, and, as expected, he was every inch a bright, professional, and competent soldier. His Brit comrades called him "Ish," a shortened version of his true name. The Gurkha carried the standard British infantry rifle, the SA-80. Looking more like a *Star Wars* gun than anything else, the SA-80 was sexy in appearance, but underwhelming in performance. Like our M-16, the SA-80 fired the 5.56 mm round, but that's where the similarities ended. The SA-80 has a shorter barrel than the M-16 and is much shorter overall thanks to its "bull-pup" design. The bull-pup design, among other things, has the magazine well placed behind the trigger housing. This unconventional layout contributes to both the weapon's exotic appearance and its short length. The rifle also incorporates a 4× telescopic sight, with backup sights being woefully inadequate iron affairs that are no better than those found on a pistol. Even with the scope, the weapon is not as accurate as the M-16 and lacks both power and accuracy beyond 300 meters. It also had the bad habit of dropping parts off here and there.

When introduced, the SA-80 replaced the beloved, respected, and battle-proven 7.62 mm SLR. Known as the FN-FAL or simply the FN outside the United Kingdom, the SLR is a Belgian rifle that continues in service around the world. Older Brits, and almost all the Royal Marine commandos I have spoken to, hate the SA-80 with a passion. The Royal Marines much prefer the M-16A2, which they simply call the Colt. Still, I appreciated that the SA-80 had at least one advantage for convoy work—like the AK-47, its compactness made it much easier to employ from the vehicle than the M-16A2.

The general was unarmed because DOD policy did not allow nonsecurity contract personnel to carry weapons. This is simply madness. On a convoy that might be as small as four men in two vehicles, you positively needed everybody armed, and armed to the hilt. There is no such thing as too many guns and bullets, both of which are worth their weight in diamonds when things get nasty. Conventional wisdom was that it took at least ten magazines per man to break contact on the street, that is to say, to get away from a fight you will lose if you linger in the area too long. None of us carried more than seven magazines, and they were simply not enough even if we had all been armed.

Other vehicles in the convoy were two SUVs and one pickup. We had four armored Hummers of the U.S. Army providing escort. Two of these were armed with medium (7.62 mm) machine guns, and two had light (5.56 mm) machine guns. I preferred that they carry heavies, such as the 12.7 mm M-2s. The lighter weapons just did not have the power to stop a VBIED in its tracks as the M-2 could. But the army preferred the lighter weapons because they reduced the potential for collateral damage in heavily populated Baghdad.

In addition to the machine guns, one of these vehicles was equipped with an electronic jamming device called a warlock. The warlock was used to defeat signals sent to detonate IEDs remotely. We were told that it did not work all the time, but it was certainly better than nothing. The weather was heavily overcast with a light rain—good news, said the general, in that the insurgents (in what must surely be their only display of normal human behavior) were said to dislike fighting in the rain.

The convoy departed the Green Zone along the same route we had taken on the morning the RC got hit. Again, I marveled at just what a dirty and wretched place Baghdad was, without a doubt the filthiest and most disgusting city I had ever been in. Piles of trash, dead animals, and abandoned vehicles lay everywhere one looked. Earlier we had been briefed that all of these things—trash, animals, and abandoned automobiles—could be used to conceal IEDs, so we were to be leery of them, and to look ahead and attempt to detect and then avoid these hazards. What a joke! The only possible way to avoid these potential bomb sites would be to fly to our destination. As such, I quickly gave up trying to scan the roadside for the IED hidden in a dead dog. Instead, Ish and I looked for the things we might have been able to detect and do something about—things like armed men or vehicles closing on the convoy rapidly, for example. The general, on the other hand, was very relaxed; he just talked and drove. I was very thankful for Ish's company.

I quickly learned that scanning Baghdad's streets for potential bombers was taxing work. Traffic was very heavy, and the Iraqi drivers were frighteningly inattentive. How do you detect the suicide bomber among the snarled throng of vehicles? Which vehicle closing on you is a VBIED? How do you tell the difference? If you guessed right and shot the driver before his vehicle detonated in your convoy, you'd never know for certain, because you definitely weren't going to stop the convoy to check and see who you had just blasted. The enemy in Iraq was very cunning, and most often there was a backup trig-german in case the suicide bomber decided seventy-two virgins of unknown quality and minimum experience (being virgins) were not as much fun as a tethered and well-worn goat. The insurgents sometimes had a chase car follow the bomb car. If things went awry, the chase car could remotely detonate the bomb and ensure a successful attack. Obviously then, you would not be stopping and checking to see if the guy you shot was a real threat. On the other hand, if you did not shoot, and it was a suicide bomber that you had let close on the convoy, *everybody*, or at least the survivors, would know it. It was a lot to think about.

All of these considerations raced through my mind as I scanned the area looking for threats, and with each passing mile I became acutely aware of how ill prepared I was for this type of operation. Searching for anything that might be a threat, I felt as if I would never see it coming until too late, if at all. My lack of training and experience in this type of operation left me feeling very exposed, and I knew this defect needed to be fixed. If I, a veteran infantryman of twenty-three years, felt unqualified for this type of mission, what did that imply about the twenty-somethings riding with me? Worse, observing the occupants of other vehicles in our convoy, I could see that many of them were not looking at anything except the inside of their eyelids. They were as relaxed as if they were cruising the block back home. Those awake were busy talking to and looking at each other instead of concentrating on staying alive. To many Americans in February 2004, the war was over.

My thoughts were interrupted by the heavy crash of an armored Hummer colliding with an Iraqi's car. In the intersection ahead, the hapless Iraqi lost virtually the entire front end of his car to our lead Hummer. The convoy continued without stopping. We kept moving, not because of any lack of compassion on our part, but because stopping could have been lethal. It was unlikely the car was carrying a bomb, as it did not explode when we hit it, but it was possible. Or maybe the car had perhaps been driven into the convoy in the hope that we would stop in a kill zone covered by the ubiquitous and deadly RPGs and Russian machine guns. Either way, stopping to exchange insurance information was out of the question.

Minutes later, we cleared the city and the general told me to roll up my window and relax. Against my better judgment, I complied. Outside the city we zipped past mile after mile of empty desert; soon, though, the barren desert floor gave way to a landscape littered with destroyed and abandoned Iraqi tanks and armored personnel carriers, all of Russian and French manufacture.

One of these tanks, a T-72, was lying on its back, a gaping hole blown out its bottom. Not five feet away was the tank's turret.

I glanced back at the tank and felt pretty sure I knew what had happened to it. A small hole was neatly punched into the left front side of the turret. Radiating out from this hole, in a sunburst pattern, were small gouges in the armor, characteristic of a HEAT (high explosive, antitank) round impact. HEAT rounds can be delivered by antitank guided missiles or by cannon, most commonly a tank gun, and they rely on the explosion of a shaped charge lined with copper to focus the blast with enough resulting speed (up to twenty-five times the speed of sound) to push a high velocity jet of metal through armor. This metal then sprays the inside of the tank, burning to death anyone unfortunate enough to be there. Worse, if the ammunition stowed in the cramped confines of the tank is hit with this molten metal, it will detonate as well. The near simultaneous explosion of forty-five 125 mm shells consumes the entire tank, reducing the crew to DNA. The sound is not unlike the roar of a powerful jet engine as the propellant charges cook off, interrupted by the muffled whump of exploding projectiles.

In the case of this T-72, the HEAT round did indeed touch off secondary explosions of onboard ammunition. This blew out the bottom of the tank, lifted the forty-three-ton beast in the air, and flipped it over. The turret, weighing more than twelve tons, had been cast aside. I had seen tanks destroyed in this manner before. For the crews, death, while horrible, comes quite quickly. The tank is rolling along and suddenly there is an explosion on the outside. Almost instantly it loses power and begins to slow to a halt. If the crew is still alive and not disabled, the hatches pop open. Most often, they never make it that far. Within a second or two of being hit, the onboard ammo will blow off the turret. If the ammo detonates in a chain reaction, rather than all at once, the hatches will blow open but the turret will stay on. I did not know whether this tank's crew had even been in the machine when it got blasted, as the Iraqis often abandoned their equipment without fighting.

None of that mattered, anyway. This tank and its crew were from a war that seemed very distant now. The gallant and quick charge through the desert, which terminated in Baghdad, had seemed to end the war. Obviously it had not. This destroyed tank stood as a relic of that swift victory, which many of us realized had been nothing more than the first battle of what was turning out to be a longer and more costly war. This slaughtered beast might as well have been one of the bronze cannons sitting on the Manassas battlefield near my home. It was ancient, alien, and useless.

We arrived in Kirkush, and it was not long before I realized that my earlier premonitions about the place were true. Not only was it far removed from the war, but my reason for coming was as bogus as a three-dollar bill. There were no Iraqi recruits to mind. But I did not complain. The seclusion and lack of formal duties would allow me plenty of time to study and analyze convoy operations in Iraq.

Before departing from the palace, I had taken several hundred after-action reports from attacks on American convoys as well as a copy of CMATT's convoy standard operating procedure (SOP). The quiet time in Kirkush, very near the Iranian border, allowed me to examine not only how CMATT's convoys were run but what other units were doing when they got hit and how, exactly, the enemy was attacking American convoys. Some things became very clear. Many American units in Iraq were failing to inflict losses on the enemy when he foolishly exposed himself by engaging convoys with small-arms fire. Most often, this type of engagement was a static ambush. But, in something of a surprise, Iraqis were frequently doing drive-bys on our convoys. These attacks, whether static or via the drive-by, rarely killed anyone, as the Iraqis were almost universally inept with small arms. What was disappointing was that we were not killing many Iraqis in these attacks, either. Presumably, the U.S. Army had taught all of its soldiers how to shoot, and we had a definite advantage in firepower, and yet we were not getting the results we should have when the enemy was there for the killing. Looking a bit deeper into the after-action reports it became obvious why: Our guys were simply interested in surviving the contact and then breaking off as fast as possible. There were no reports of army units dismounting and going after their attackers or running a drive-by down and killing him. This needed to change, and it needed to change now. While the Iraqis could not consistently hit anything at that time, I was fully aware that eventually they were going to figure out how to kill effectively with AKs and PKMs. We needed to kill them before they became more effective, and we could not do that by running away. If I was to fix the system, I needed to get myself a job as the ground movement NCOIC. In that role, I believed, I could control exactly how CMATT's convoys were run, who went on those convoys, and how these people were trained. It would not win the war, of course, but at least no one was going to shoot at a CMATT convoy and live.

I knew that in order to sell command on my still developing vision, I needed a good pitch, so I decided to call the concept "Kopfjäger," which is German for "headhunter." I borrowed the concept from the British Q-ships of World War II. During that war, the British navy sought to bait U-boats by heavily arming some merchant ships; they left the ships' external appearance unchanged, so that the vessel still looked like an unarmed merchant ship just begging to be blown up. German subs would surface to engage these "unarmed" ships with the submarine's deck gun. By using the deck gun to finish off cripples and to engage defenseless ships, they could spare their limited supply of torpedoes for more heavily defended targets, which required stealthy attack. Once the sub had taken the bait and surfaced, the merchantmen would drop its sides, revealing the previously hidden guns. The heretofore defenseless "victim" was now, in fact, a heavily armed hunter, bristling with guns and dealing death on a grand scale.

Selling the concept was merely the first step in a plan. Next, I would have to change the SOP. There were a great many things in the SOP with which I had issues, but the most significant of these was the policy that CMATT convoys, if engaged by the enemy, were, as seemed to be the case with many army units in Iraq, to break contact and flee. Yes, you read right. The army was like the Girl Scouts: They both wore uniforms, both were venerated American institutions with long histories, and neither had much interest in close combat. The only difference between the two was that the Girl Scouts could get Thin Mints cheap and in bulk.

That had to change. One need not be a demented, warmongering psychopath to see that we should have been engaging, with decisive force, the enemy whenever and wherever he presented himself. I believed it was the army's failure to go after the insurgents that was allowing them to grow in strength and ability. The Marine Corps had one policy for all units, and it was quite simple: When the enemy hits you, you are to run him down and kill him. That's what I had been trained to do. Fleeing would be no part of any mission I led. My first task, therefore, was to rewrite the convoy SOP so that we would not only be *allowed* to go after the enemy, but would be given a core mission to do so. By failing to kill the enemy when we had the chance, we were allowing him to grow stronger and smarter. He might miss us once, twice, even three times, but with each miss he was gaining the knowledge and experience with which he would, in time, be better able to kill us.

The next problem was CMATT's lack of armor and crew-served weapons. I envisioned four SUVs sporting one 240G, three SAWs, seven M-4s (an M-16 with a shorter barrel, telescoping butt, and rails for mounting optical devices), and three additional M-4s with attached M-203 grenade launchers. The SAW is a light machine gun that fires the same round as the M-16, but the SAW fires from a belt at an incredible rate of a thousand rounds a minute to a maximum effective range of 1,100 meters. Both the range and the rate of fire are far superior to the M-16's. The M-249 squad automatic weapon, as the SAW is officially christened, also has a quick-change barrel that allows it to sustain this high rate of fire longer than would otherwise be the case. Three SAWs would give the team an incredible volume of firepower, which, coming from a small, four-vehicle convoy, would also have some shock value.

The M-203 is a 40 mm grenade launcher with a maximum effective range of 150 meters on a point target or 350 on an area target. It is nearly useless when employed from a moving vehicle, but quite lethal when employed from the ground.

Additionally, we would need at least one 240G, a medium machine gun firing a more powerful round (7.62 mm) than the SAW. The 240 has superior range and penetration to the SAW, with a maximum effective range of 1,800 meters, and a rate of fire of 950 rounds per minute. The only real advantage the SAW has over the 240 is its lighter weight and shorter barrel. The size and weight of the 240 make it difficult to employ from within a vehicle and more fatiguing to use once dismounted.

If I could get Hummers, it would be divine, as the armor offered some protection from IEDs, and the vehicle comes equipped with a weapons station that can take the mighty M-2 .50 caliber heavy machine gun or the Mk-19 automatic grenade launcher. For well over sixty years the heavy, slow, and methodical whump, whump, of the M-2 has commanded the respect of anyone who has ever heard it. Affectionately known as the "Ma Deuce" or simply the "fifty," the M-2 has been around since before World War II, and can be either ground mounted or placed in armored vehicles or aircraft. Throwing its heavy slugs at a rate of 550 rounds a minute to a maximum effective range of 1,830 meters, the venerable .50 is a powerful weapon. The chief advantage of the fifty is the penetration of its heavy bullet, which can cut clean through light armored vehicles with ease. There was nothing between that slug and the driver of a VBIED that was going to spare his life. In fact, using a fifty on an Iraqi suicide car bomber would be like using a twelve-gauge on your parakeet as he perched sleeping in his cage.

The Mk-19 is also classified as a heavy machine gun, though it is really an automatic grenade launcher. Firing 40 mm high-explosive shells out to a maximum effective range of 1,500 meters for a point target and 2,012 for an area target, at a rate of 325 to 375 shells a minute, the 19 can reduce targets to pulp or parts within seconds. The rate of fire and the lethality of its exploding rounds make the Mk-19 a real crowd-pleaser.

So configured, we would have three fire teams of four men each plus a leader, a corpsman-medic, and a two-man crew for the 240. But what my sixteen-man team would need more than anything else was training. From everything I had seen, CMATT's personnel were not even properly trained to defend themselves, let alone go after the enemy. Before I could rewrite the SOP into something more aggressive, therefore, I had to train the people we had to fight as infantrymen. Better still, I would be allowed to select and train who I wanted on my team rather than simply make do with whoever, if anyone, was given to me.

The time in Kirkush made me more determined than ever that once I got back to Baghdad I would become the "convoy guy." I did not want to spend the next six months of my life pushing Iraqi recruits. Now, with my theories formed and the ideas in place, I had to get back to the palace and make it all happen. Each additional hour spent at Kirkush was an hour wasted.

Finally, the day of my departure from Kirkush arrived. I was talking to one of the Royal Air Force instructors when Gunny Hessen came in with the news.

"Top, our ride is over at the Commandant's Office. They sent two vehicles to take you, me, the corpsmen, and some sergeant back to the palace."

"Awesome, man. When do we leave, Gunny?"

"They said we should stage our shit now, go to chow, and be ready to roll by 1300."

Gunny and I grabbed all of our shit and humped it down to the parking lot where our vehicles were staged. We then headed off to chow with some of the Brit and Aussie trainers we had gotten to know during our brief stay at Kirkush. After chow the Gunny and I said our goodbyes and linked up with our ride, which was then staged in a lot adjacent to the Commandant's Office.

"Which one of you is driving lead?" I asked the assembled drivers.

"Master Sergeant Lynch, Private Pennington. I am your driver, and my vehicle is already in front."

I walked over to Pennington's vehicle and put my gear in the front passenger seat before heading off to the Commandant's Office to get anything they wanted us to take back to the palace. When I got back to where our vehicles were staged I noticed that everybody was present except for the sergeant we were taking with us.

"Pennington, do you know the sergeant going with us?"

"Yes, Top. It's Sergeant Williams, he is going home in two weeks."

"Well, where the hell is he?" I asked.

"At the barracks, Master Sergeant," Pennington answered.

"Let's go," I said.

I was a little agitated as we took off to find Sergeant Williams. While I did not know the man, I knew that he had delayed our departure and that he might cause us to miss our linkup. When Pennington and I arrived at the CMATT barracks where I had been a guest, I got out of the vehicle and went upstairs looking for the tardy sergeant. Sergeant Jason Williams was about 5′11″ with a medium build, dark eyes, and black hair. Standing in the pigpen that was his quarters, hands outstretched at his sides, he whined, "I told them not to let anyone fuck with my stuff." He had the voice of a foulmouthed, pissed-off kid who needed a good ass whipping or Ritalin or both.

To me he was nothing more than a nasty little dirt lord. Thinking to myself "How typically army" as I eyeballed his filthy quarters, I stood amazed that anyone could live in such filth.

Disgusted, and losing my patience, I said, "Hurry up and grab your shit. We have been waiting for you and we are running late."

"Yes, Master Sergeant."

As he gathered his gear I walked back into the Commandant's Office to call the palace and report that we would be departing Kirkush later than expected, but soon. By the time I returned to my vehicle, I could see that my gear had been moved to the backseat and someone else's placed up front.

"Pennington, whose shit is this?"

Pennington stammered, "I'm not sure, Master Sergeant."

It was obvious that Pennington was a little nervous. Ignoring Pennington's discomfort, I moved the offending gear to the backseat and placed mine in the front again. When I returned to my vehicle, after checking on the status of vehicle two, I was astonished to see that once again my gear had been moved.

"Pennington, whose fucking shit is this?" I asked.

"That's mine, Master Sergeant. I'm his shooter."

It was Sergeant Williams. Then I knew why Pennington had been nervous; he had been caught between a sergeant and a master sergeant. I hid my bemusement at the difficult position Pennington was in.

On the verge of losing my mind with the belligerent sergeant I commanded, "Yeah? Well, you can pretend this is a B-17 and you're the tail gunner. Now move your shit."

Sergeant Williams's answer, which I will never forget, dripped with sarcasm and loathing.

"Roger that, *Master Sergeant.*"

Williams, obviously disgusted, moved his gear. As he did so, I noticed that he wore a ranger scroll on his left shoulder and had the Combat Infantryman's Badge, a coveted award given only to combat grunts, on his chest. I knew that he deeply resented having to move his gear so that this palace cherry (as he later admitted thinking about me) could ride in the front seat and feel self-important. He did not know me, and so, like most veteran grunts with a natural suspicion of unknown leaders, he did not trust me, and he certainly did not like me. Could I blame him? My potential incompetence was a threat to his survival. Rank is a wonderful thing. The more you have, the more money you make, and the more privileges you get. But rank cannot earn you the trust, confidence, and respect of jaded, veteran infantrymen. I understood exactly how Sergeant Williams felt because I had certainly felt that way about more than one superior myself.

Weeks later, as Sergeant Williams, Sergeant Kevin Facemyer, and I talked about this event, Facemyer would say, "Top, Will was so hoping you would get killed." Williams laughed hysterically as he said, "Oh, man, I so did, too. I was like, 'Fine, fine! Take the front seat. I hope you die. Die!' But I'm glad you didn't."

So was I, actually.

Our convoy back to Baghdad was a long and very dull affair, and the only fight I had was with the sandman, who was trying to kick my ass. That was not good. If I, a man who had made convoy escort work his new mission in life, could be so bored as to have to fight to stay alert after just four convoys, how hard was it going to be for the average grunt after twenty? Or fifty? Our survival, I felt certain, would depend in large part on our ability to look like people you do not want to screw with. If I got my team up and running, I suspected that in the beginning, at least, we would lack armor, crew-served weapons, and backup; all we would have would be posture. Like the declawed house cat that, when threatened, arches his back and hisses to look bigger and appear mentally unstable, we needed to look more lethal than we in fact would be. Fighting the sandman was no way to project such a posture. That was akin to giving Richard Simmons a knife and telling him to carjack Mike Tyson; chances were Mike was gonna keep the car and Richard's next video was going to be about his painful rehab and recurring nightmares. The initiative was almost always going to be with the enemy, no matter how alert we were. But we could work with that; we accepted it and planned accordingly. But if we got caught napping it would all be over in seconds.

While the trip provided no excitement, it did, like the time spent in Kirkush, provide learning opportunities. Watching our escort, call sign "Wolf Pack," I could see that they were a highly professional team. They knew the trade very well. Every time we stopped, no matter how briefly, they dismounted and pulled security around the vehicles. By doing so, they presented an aggressive and alert posture; if attacked, they would be far more capable of defending themselves than if they had simply stayed in their vehicles. The same could not be said of the CMATT convoy team. CMATT boys stayed in their vehicles no matter how long they were stopped; they were nothing more than victims, guys looking for chalk outlines to fill. I had my work cut out for me.

CHAPTER 3

The Team Forms

When we got back to the palace, I immediately compiled my notes on the CMATT SOP and the various after-action reports into one paper arguing the need for a dedicated convoy security team within CMATT. I presented this paper to Colonel Thomas. He was impressed with the data I had amassed in so little time and so soon after my arrival in Iraq.

"Where did you get all this, Top?" Thomas asked.

"Well, the SOP is ours, and all the after-action reports came from Libby, the air force guy in intel. The concept I based on the Q ships of World War II."

Thomas replied, "I'll pass this to Colonel Buchanan when he gets back here and let you know something as soon as I know anything."

Colonel Jeffrey Buchanan was the operations officer and, as such, all of us in the operations section worked for him. He would have the final say on my ideas. A few days later Gunny Hessen and I were told to report to him. My paper was about to pay off.

At 1015, on February 17, Buchanan sat down with Hessen and me to explain what our CMATT duties would be. As he spoke, I was impressed by his professionalism and his command presence. He was every bit the professional warrior, even when out of uniform. He was utterly unlike most of the officers in the palace, who could easily be mistaken for social workers. Now he continued. Gunny Hessen was to be the ground movement NCOIC, and as tight as the gunny and I were, that meant that *we* would be the ground movement NCOIC.

As noted earlier, securing this billet was the first step toward controlling what happened with CMATT's convoys; only the operations sergeant major could interfere, and having observed the current holder of that billet, Sergeant Major Jackson, we were sure we could work around him. The only problem remaining was that he would be leaving at the end of the month. The next guy might be a control freak, or worse, and as he would be the man with Colonel Buchanan's ear, he could undo anything we had been able to put in place prior to his arrival. Buchanan, however, was only seconds away from relieving our minds of any concerns about any operations sergeant major.

"Do you have any questions, Gunny?" he asked.

"No, sir. None that I can think of at this time."

"Okay, then, you are dismissed."

After dismissing Hessen, the colonel turned toward me.

"Master Sergeant Lynch, your orders say that you are here to train Iraqi soldiers, but I think we can make better use of you around here. Sergeant Major Jackson is leaving at the end of the month and I want you to be his replacement as the operations sergeant major. Now that is an army billet, and it calls for an army E-9 and we already have a few inbound, but I will worry about that when the time comes."

I'd have felt greedy even secretly wishing for such good news. Not only had we secured the ground movement NCOIC billet, but with the operations sergeant major post in our bag, we could now take our ideas directly to the top without having them filtered or halted altogether by some risk-adverse fat-ass just trying to punch his ticket and go home. I already suspected that we had a strong ally in Colonel Thomas, and while I was unsure about Colonel Buchanan, I did know that his handing me a job identified as an army billet said a lot. It did not matter that I might get replaced by a sergeant major at some point, for by the time that happened I would have established a great and invulnerable working relationship with the only two men who mattered, Buchanan and Thomas. Or so I hoped.

Buchanan was not yet done, though. Pulling up my paper concerning the need for a CMATT convoy security team he continued. "You also have my permission to start putting together a convoy security team. You need to scale it back a bit from the concept, and even still you will have to be a little creative here, but get with Lieutenant Colonel Thomas for the details."

I struggled to find the right words. I had just been given everything I had dared hope for.

"Thank you, sir."

"Do you have any questions, Top?"

"Not right now, not for you anyway, sir, but I have a few for Top Jackson," I answered.

"Very well then, Master Sergeant, you're dismissed."

I could barely contain my glee on leaving the meeting. I had left Quantico merely to train Iraqi soldiers, but in scarcely one week, I had been promoted to operations sergeant major and given the task of building a convoy security team from scratch and leading it. Instead of sitting on my ass in Kirkush, I would be on Iraq's roads, an active player in the war, as often as I liked. I did not have a team yet, or the firepower I wanted; and I had not fully developed my concept, but this obviously represented a significant first step.

The only bad news I received that day was from Colonel Thomas: Gunny Josleyn would soon be shipping out to Tal Afar. Josleyn had been Hessen's and my constant companion before we went to Kirkush, and in that brief time I had learned enough about him to know that I wanted him on my team. I knew I had to figure out a way to get him back, and being the new operations sergeant major, I was sure I could make that happen; it just might take a while. Even in the Marine Corps, men like Josleyn are rare; not only did he possess a skilled sniper's résumé, but he also displayed maturity and high intelligence. His quiet and reserved nature were perfect counterbalances to my own personality. I knew I could rely on him to keep me rooted in reality and rein me in when required. I coveted the gunny's services as much for his qualities as his résumé.

After leaving Colonel Buchanan, I went looking for sergeants Williams and Facemyer. Sergeant Williams, the aforementioned dirt lord I had met when heading out of Kirkush, had changed his mind about me in the few days we had been back at the palace. He even introduced me to his good friend and constant sidekick, Sergeant Kevin Facemyer. Both were army rangers and both were extremely intelligent. While very close to each other, they were in fact very different. "Face," as Facemyer was known, tended to be less serious than Will. Nothing ever seemed to get on Face's nerves, whereas Will was almost constantly in a state of agitation about something. Over the week or so that we were back at the palace, I explained to both what I wanted to do with the CMATT convoys, and they were in total agreement with me on all points.

I really wanted to get these two guys on my team, but my early intelligence gathering had begun to make that look impossible. First of all, both men were due to rotate out of the country in just weeks, having already done six-month tours. Now, asking a man to extend at the beginning or middle of his tour was hard enough, but when a soldier, sailor, airman, or marine deploys, his countdown clock starts immediately, and the projected date of return is circled on the calendar. The anticipation of the reunion with loved ones builds with each passing day. Often this date of return helps maintain the morale of the deployed service member. Extensions that push that date back into the Twilight Zone can kill morale. Asking Williams and Facemyer to extend at the end of their tours, as I was doing, was understandably a hard sell.

On top of that, Facemyer's wife was eagerly anticipating his return to North Carolina. How do you call your wife after doing six months in a war zone and tell her, two weeks before a long-awaited reunion, that you have *voluntarily* extended another six months? In most cases you'd better call a lawyer first.

Sergeant Williams seemed to be a tougher sell, for he was not returning to the army life that he had left in the States; he was getting out of the army, and was already scheduled to begin college courses that summer.

I knew it was selfish of me to ask them to stay, and I knew Facemyer's wife would kill me if she and I ever met, but I needed Will and her husband. I needed Facemyer more than his wife did, and I needed Williams more than he needed to go to school. While I doubted that I would get either man, I had to try. I hoped I would be able to break both men in the two weeks I had left with them.

My attempts to recruit Will and Face aside, much of what was left of February was spent in the futile search for gear, weapons, and equipment. While armor was nowhere to be found, we were able to trade four folding-stock AK-47s for two antiquated Russian RPKs. The RPKs are long-barreled, bipod versions of the AK-47. With the exception of the buttstock, bipods, and long barrel, the AK and the RPK are identical. The longer barrel gives the RPK greater range and, with the bipod legs, greater controllability and accuracy on automatic, but that's about it. The weapon is fed by either the thirty- or forty-round box magazine or a seventy-five-round drum, same as the AK. The RPKs are little better than the AKs, and are far inferior to the SAW in firepower, range, and, lacking a changeable barrel, sustained fire. But they are better than nothing. I was learning that you could get a lot for a weapon that was different and therefore sexy, such as the folding-stock AKs, which I had plenty of, if you could find the right palace commando. Palace commandos craved the attention that an exotic weapon could get them as they walked from their trailer to the palace and back again. Now, if I could get MP-5s, I was sure I would be able to trade those for an M-1 tank. As things were, however, the acquisition of the two pitiful RPKs represented my only success in an exhaustive search for weapons, armor, radios, and other mission-essential gear as February wound down. I had barely gotten started and I was already frustrated. Fortunately, my efforts at recruiting proved to be more successful.

During the last week in February more marines were checking in to CMATT. One of these turned out to be someone I knew, Sergeant Chris Schroeder. Schroeder and I worked at the same building in Quantico, and I had known him for about ten months, and while those ten months had been spent in an office, far removed from the field, I had liked what I'd seen in him. I believed he would fit well into what I was attempting to put together. Schroeder was about twenty-five and, like so many prematurely balding marines, had taken to shaving his head. He was 5'8" with a medium build. He was also quite a hothead in Iraq, which was very different from what I had seen in Quantico. He reminded other members of the team of the character in the movie *Stripes* who threatens bunk mates with violence if they touch his stuff. Schroeder became my third recruit. While he was all for joining my budding team, getting him was to prove difficult. Schroeder was to be assigned to CMATT's C-4, and they were proving reluctant to part with him.

Even with the "new joins" now checking in, I still wanted Will and Face. Initially, both men continued to say no, of course. Williams was adamant that he was going home. Not only did he have school waiting, but he was sick of the army. Facemyer, while not as blunt, said that he, too, would be going home. I explained to them that I wanted to recruit, build, and train a dedicated convoy security team that would operate under a different and far more aggressive SOP than the one currently in place. I further explained that we would also be used to augment the security of vulnerable sites belonging to CMATT. Furthermore, I told both that I wanted killers not afraid to dismount and take the fight to the enemy when I gave the word.

Compounding my recruitment problem, Sergeant Major Jackson was busy telling Will and Face that they should not, under any circumstances, extend. Weeks later both Will and Face would tell me that Jackson had repeatedly told them how fucked up things were going to be now that the marines were "taking over." If by fucked up he meant no more beer runs to the Red Zone, no more all-nighters before a convoy, and no more sleeping on convoys (as both Will and Face had said was the norm before I arrived), then Jackson was indeed right: Everything would soon be fucked up now that marines were on board. Blissfully ignorant of all of this, I continued hammering away, saying everything I knew to say in what seemed to be a vain attempt to appeal to their warrior hearts. But warriors they were.

Facemyer cracked first. In the days before his capitulation, Face had started asking me specific questions about what I wanted to build. What tactics would we employ? How, exactly, would my SOP be different from what was now in place? Would I be going out with the team? How would we get the proper equipment? While Williams often asked questions as well, and even expressed enthusiasm for what we were trying to do, he seemed set on getting out. One evening I remembered telling him that if he stayed, I could guarantee that he would see more combat than he had seen in Afghanistan. He looked at me and smiled as if he were thinking about it and then said, "Get away from me, you evil temptress."

This went on for just over a week, and gradually I began to accept that we would not get Williams. Facemyer maybe, but not Williams. Then one morning, as we were preparing to escort a convoy of army trainers to Kirkush, Facemyer approached me and said, "Top, I'm all yours. I've already called my unit and they have no problem with me extending for six months as long as Colonel Buchanan says it is okay."

Within minutes of Facemyer's joining the team, and before I could fully appreciate this bit of wonderful news, Williams came in.

"I'm in, Top. I've already turned in my weapon, so I'll need an AK."

While Will never explained why he changed his mind, I suspected it had a lot more to do with Facemyer's decision than it did with anything I said. Face and Will were inseparable, and where one went, the other was sure to go. I also knew that Will was not yet satisfied with his part in the war, and I am certain that he felt he needed to stay on if there was even the slightest chance the team would see combat. Combined with Facemyer's decision, Will's own desire to kill the enemy ended up outweighing any desire to go to school.

Just like that, we had two new members for the team. I looked over at Gunny Hessen and half expected him to hold up four fingers, like Yul Brynner in *The Magnificent Seven*, signifying that we were now four. Being utterly devoid of theatrical flair, however, he merely grunted and returned to his comic book.

At a time when the army was offering young men and women thousands of dollars just to enlist and thousands more in college incentives, the only inducement offered to these two men for their voluntary extensions was a chance to kill America's enemies. That this chance came with a great deal of risk (after all, Iraq is a two-way rifle range) did not deter them at all. Those were the kind of men I was looking for, men who were smart enough to know the risk but who wanted the action anyway. Williams and Facemyer (known by their call signs, Hollywood and Rock Star) would eventually end up being my constant companions. While they were no more valuable to the team than any other member, these two, by virtue of riding in my vehicle, would always have my six whenever I dismounted.

Chris Reed, staff sergeant, U.S. Army, came to us almost by accident. Reed had orders for a billet which, in typical military fashion, was already filled. First Sergeant Fullard, knowing that I needed people, came over to see me. Fullard was a powerfully built marine, with coal-dark skin and a background in intelligence. He was carrying his omnipresent cigar, which was something of a personal trademark.

"I have an army staff sergeant, 11B [infantryman], for you. He doesn't look like the type you want, but if you like, I can send him over," Fullard offered.

Interested, I said, "Sure. Send him over so I can have a look-see."

At first glance I agreed with Fullard's assessment; Reed did not look the "type." But looks are just as deceiving with gunslingers as with anybody else, it seems. Check out photos of the real Sergeant Alvin York, and everybody's favorite Georgian dentist, Doc Holliday, for proof of this. Neither man looked anything like Gary Cooper or Val Kilmer, but both were extremely lethal in spite of their less than intimidating appearance. Reed was about 5'7", with darting, nervous eyes, and thinning red hair, busily retreating faster than the French army. I spoke with Reed for only a few minutes, and that was all I needed. I explained, as I had with all the other candidates, that we were forming a convoy security team made up of volunteers. I told him what we would be doing and what I was looking for. Like Williams and Facemyer before him, Reed appeared thrilled at the prospect.

"Top, I would fucking love to do that, and I think I can help with the driver training and maybe some other stuff as well, and I would really love it if you could get me moved to the team."

Reed impressed me as an intelligent and intense man. He also seemed quiet and reserved. Over time, a very short time actually, I would learn that Reed was neither quiet nor reserved. Eventually, he would evolve into my de facto second in command, and his contribution to the team would prove to be invaluable.

"We do not yet have dedicated vehicle teams, staff sergeant. The crews rotate as we shake things out to get the right mix, but for now I am going to assign you as vehicle one's driver. Your shooters are two rangers, sergeants Facemyer and Williams. Both are great guys, and they can help you get settled in."

"Thanks, Top, I really appreciate this and look forward to working with you."

"No problem, glad to have you. Make sure you stop by the get-together this evening so you can meet the rest of the team. If you don't have any questions for me, I am done with you."

Because of his arrival at about the same time as two other new joins, sergeants Jason Algarin and Edward Boeringer (call signs Starsky and Hutch, respectively), Reed was tagged with the call sign "Huggy Bear." Sergeants Boeringer and Algarin were our two marine pickups. Like Face and Will, in that both men were inseparable, they became our second "team" within the larger team. Their cohesion and intuitive knowledge of what was going on in the other's head at all times would make them an integral and indispensable part of the team. I assigned both men to vehicle two of my three-vehicle team, Algarin as the driver and Boeringer as his shooter.

Sergeant Edward (Ed or Eddie to his friends; Bo or Hutch to us) Boeringer was 5′10″ with a large build. Bo hailed from New York City, a fact easily discerned from his accent and mannerisms. Almost outrageously gregarious, Boeringer exuded the stereotypical tough guy New Yorker image. Though a sergeant, Bo was thirty-eight years old, and he had previous combat experience as an artillery marine during the Gulf War.

Though they were close, Algarin was nothing like Boeringer. Sergeant Jason Algarin, often called "J" by Boeringer, was a short Puerto Rican with a small build. Unlike Reed, who grew what little hair he could as lovingly as an English gardener tending to his roses, Algarin had given up trying and shaved the scant survivors of his hair holocaust from his scalp daily. Always with Boeringer, Algarin was frequently teased for being like the small dog always chasing after the much larger dog in the old Warner Brothers cartoons. Yipping in this ear, "Which way do we go, Bo? What do you want to do now, Bo? Ya thinks we should eat something, Bo?" That was their gimmick, their bit. In fact, both men had a deep and abiding love and respect for each other and were an excellent complement. Where Bo could be abrasive and sometimes even surly, Algarin could always be counted on to keep Bo rooted to the ground. Both men played off and relied on the other, perhaps even more than did Facemyer and Williams. With Boeringer and Algarin on board I suddenly had seven full-time members, and we were just getting started.

While I saw Gunny Hessen, Will, Face, Reed, Boeringer, and Algarin for what they were as soon as I laid eyes on them, I am quick to admit that I'm not always that intuitive. In fact, sometimes I am far too opinionated and

Sergeant Edward Boeringer, USMC, commander of vehicle 3, or "Rear D." *(From the collection of Jack Lynch)*

bullheaded for my own good. Sometimes I allow my preconceived perceptions about certain kinds of people to blind me to a person's individual qualities.

I had been told that Private Pennington's replacement had just checked in. While we were indeed expecting a replacement, I could not have been more surprised if the army had sent me Osama Bin Laden. Specialist 4 Isis Delacroix was a *female*! Despite the fact that I had gotten used to the idea that women had a place in the service, and despite knowing competent women in the Marine Corps, I had never fully accepted that they *belonged* in the service. The last thing I wanted on the convoy security team was some chick who thought an empty magazine was *Cosmopolitan* without the ads, who would expect a Bronze Star for being knocked unconscious when her vehicle crashed, à la Jessica Lynch, and who, I felt certain, would flee at the first sign of trouble. When word reached me that she eagerly anticipated being on the team, I made it quite clear to everyone within earshot that under no circumstances would she be joining us.

I did not count on Delacroix's tenacity. Hearing that I would not assign her to the team, Delacroix confronted me. I was throwing on my flak jacket one morning when I saw Fullard approaching me with a young woman in tow.

Fullard introduced her, saying, "Master Sergeant Lynch, this young lady wants to talk to you."

I quickly studied her features. She was 5'6", and attractive. She kept her long dark hair in a bun at the back of her head and did not wear much makeup, but her large, dark brown eyes were framed with eyeliner and eye shadow. Looking at her, I could plainly see that she was angry.

I thanked Fullard and turned to Delacroix. "You'll have to walk and talk, Specialist, because I'm heading out."

"Why don't you want me on your team, Master Sergeant?"

Annoyed that she even thought I owed her an answer, I nevertheless gave her one. "It's nothing personal, but I don't think women belong in combat units, and contrary to what you see around the palace, that is what I am trying to build. I sincerely doubt that you have what I am looking for. Besides, I do not need another Jessica on my team."

I saw Jessica Lynch as nothing more than a victim of bad navigation. Her convoy had gotten lost, been hit, and she had been rendered unconscious by her injuries. She woke up a hero. I had not forgotten how the first press reports had credited her amazing "fight" before it was revealed for the feminist fantasy it was. I remembered how the pilot of her medevac flight, an air force officer of some stature, had said how superlative a warrior Jessica was and how he doubted he could have done what she did.

"I am over six feet tall and I doubt I could have done what she did." The problem with that analysis is that, next to Jessica herself, an air force pilot was the last person who should be commenting on ground combat; 4'11" or 6'8", he had no idea what he was talking about.

It was immediately obvious that my remark, casting Delacroix and all female soldiers in the same role as Jessica Lynch, pissed her off. "I am not Jessica Lynch, and I do not need any special favors. I am a driver and mechanic by trade, and I came here to do what you guys are doing. I have read your SOP and I know I can meet the physical demands placed on the drivers. I know what I am asking for, I know the risks, and all I am asking you is to give me a chance to prove myself. I want to be on the team, Master Sergeant."

I looked at her for a few seconds and quickly realized that I really didn't have much reason to keep her off the team. One of my primary objections to women serving in combat units like the infantry was their inability to perform at the same physical levels as men. But Delacroix's chief duty would be to drive, and in the event that she had to dismount, it appeared highly un-likely she would have to cover more than a hundred meters on foot. Unless the rest of the team was incapacitated it was also highly unlikely she would have to carry one of us. She was, therefore, more than capable of meeting the physical demands of convoy escort duty.

However, I also believed that the presence of women in a combat environ-ment was a distraction. But there were already dozens of them in the pal-ace, and while they were a distraction, they were not going away. Delacroix had been forceful without being confrontational, and her argument for why I should at least give her a shot—the fact that I did need a mechanic and that within the confines of my SOP she would be able to meet the physical de-mands placed upon her—was well reasoned. She was smart, and intelligence was something I long ago learned to value greatly. But more than that, there was something about Delacroix herself which made me *feel* that she was worth taking a chance on. She had all the qualities I was looking for, and it seemed awfully small of me to not give her a chance simply because those qualities came with long hair and eye shadow.

Looking at her, I said, "I do not want you on the team, you need to know that. But I will take you. You're a mechanic-driver and we need one. The other stuff I will teach you. Do you have any questions?"

She seemed shocked at my sudden capitulation but quickly replied, "No, Master Sergeant, and I promise you, you won't regret having me on the team."

No truer words would I ever hear in Iraq. Specialist Isis Delacroix would more than prove herself in the coming months, and by doing so change for-ever some of my longest held beliefs about women in the service. Known as "Del," "Della," "Deadly," or simply "D," Delacroix quickly became an equal and indispensable part of the team. Instead of bemoaning women in the ser-vice, I should have appreciated them for having the "balls" to do what thou-sands of young and fit men refused to do. But, hey, my mother had not called me a chauvinist piglet for nothing. With Del we were now eight in number, but that would quickly change.

Soon, Fullard was bringing me another misfit. Corporal Kelly Meggison was thirty-eight years old and had been in and out of the army five times. Short and plump, with a block for a head, Meggison did not fit anybody's pic-ture of a soldier; in fact, he looked like an older, somewhat sinister Barney Rubble. Picture Barney in a police lineup, suspected of some horrible crime; add a dangling cigarette and a sinister laugh and you've got Meggison. Meggison practically begged to be on the team, explaining that he had been assigned to the engineering section but that they had no use for him since he was an infantryman. That was fine with Meggison; he really wanted to ride convoys anyway. "Meggi" was something of a gun nut, which may have scared off other potential employers within the palace walls. In fact, I had never met a man who knew more about small arms and ammunition than Meggi, and that was saying quite a lot after my more than two decades in the infantry. Many of us would come to suspect that Meggi never had a girlfriend he was not related to, or hadn't paid for, as it seemed that the only thing he knew anything about were guns. When Meggison arrived in Iraq, he had never sent an e-mail, he had never surfed the web, and he did not own a credit card. But Meggi could tell you the exact weight and muzzle velocity of the 7.62×39 round and the history behind the development of that round. While Meggi may have had poor social skills for the real world, he was a perfect fit with us. Funny and brutally honest, Meggison would become a source of great fun, both as the object of our humor and as a man quite capable of dishing it out as well.

Meggison was assigned as a shooter. Like Del he had no designated vehicle and roved between different crews as we shook things out. Eventually, once the crews were formalized, Meggi would be assigned as the machine gunner in vehicle 1 (All Star One) and, cramped in the cargo area of our Nissan, caked in dust and grime, sweating in the 130-degree heat of an Iraqi summer, Meggi would get tagged with the call sign "Trunk Monkey." His enthusiasm and morale would have made him an awesome addition by themselves; weighed with his courage and skill, they made Meggi nothing short of a force multiplier for the team.

We also recruited another marine at about this time. Lance Corporal Charles Dann had just begun checking into CMATT when Hessen spotted him and quickly snatched him up. Hessen had worked with Dann at the Lejeune brig, where Dann served as a guard. Hessen made a very strong pitch to get Dann on the team. I was not enthusiastic about Dann at first, as I had been hoping to fill some of my remaining spots with infantrymen. But the gunny really went to bat for the guy, saying that I would not regret putting him on the team. I respected the gunny and trusted his judgment, and we took Dann on board. Time would prove Hessen to be correct.

Like Del, Dann was twenty-two. Standing at about 5'9" and weighing less than 160 pounds, Dann looked like a marine is supposed to look—fit. Though his hair was not thinning, he shaved his head anyway. In spite of his youth and comparative lack of experience, he would frequently "outsoldier some sergeants," as Staff Sergeant Reed would later say. Alert, motivated, and intelligent, Dann quickly mastered the skills required for serving as a member of a small convoy security team. Initially he was assigned as a roving shooter. The team had rapidly grown to include ten members, split evenly, with five marines and five soldiers. But more were on the way.

Staff Sergeant Michael Patterson, U.S. Army, checked in as the operations section admin NCO. He was, by trade, a secretary, which meant that in terms of skills, training, and experience he had nothing of value to offer the team. Patterson nevertheless made it very obvious that he wanted to be assigned to us. In desperation, he had even prepared a résumé for me to read. It not only listed his military skills but also highlighted his service on a prison incident-response team. A reservist, he had a full-time job as a North Carolina corrections officer. Irritated, I quickly read the résumé and handed it back to him.

"What am I supposed to do with this? You know we're not subduing unruly prisoners out there, or doing body cavity searches, Patterson. We're basically killin' fuckers. But I will tell you what, if we start arresting people instead of shooting them or I need someone's asshole examined, I will let you know."

But I was wrong about Patterson because, while he possessed no skills of any value to me, in that he had no infantry training and was not a mechanic, he had the most important virtues, which at first I did not see. A mature, thinking man, he had a warrior's heart. He could have stayed in the palace and simply done the job the army sent him to do. Mission accomplished, duty satisfied. But he could not sit on his ass in the palace if other guys were going out and risking their lives. It was not ambition for glory won that drove him, but obligation. He felt that he should be sharing the risks. It took a few weeks and a lot of pushing on his part before I saw his true qualities instead of simply his qualifications. Eventually his relentless determination won me over.

The transition from admin NCO to reliable killer came hard for Patterson, though. He was not allowed to ride with the team until he had finished all the training I felt the job required. He picked up the driving pretty quickly and eventually became a good driver, steady, calm, and mature. His shooting skills were not nearly as developed as his driving skills, though. He took a great deal of time to master the function of the AK and even longer to learn how to hit a target with the thing. But he never quit, even when a barrage of abuse descended on him from the team with each folly at the rifle range. Next to myself, Will was the toughest on Pat, and Pat's difficulties on the range always provided Will with fresh material.

"What the fuck, Top, I don't think Pat could even kill himself with the damn thing."

Frequently Pat would have to shoot an exercise over and over before he mastered it. All the while, the team, having already completed the course of fire, would rain insults on him as they grew impatient. Like Will, Facemyer was quick to add to Pat's misery.

"Hey, Pat, maybe you can throw your keyboard at them."

"Fuck you, Facemyer!" Pat would wail in his defense.

Pat would patiently endure. With time, he would get good enough that we could count on him to hit a target consistently. If it had been up to him, or me, he would have ridden with the team every day, but his admin duties sometimes tied him to his desk.

Patterson was 5'9" and weighed 175 fat-free pounds. But he had not always been so fit. In fact, at one point he had weighed over 230 pounds. Patterson had battled the pounds most of his life. In a moment of sincere reflection (and almost incomprehensible stupidity, given his audience), he once told us that kids used to call him "Fatterson" and that this name had even followed him into the army. You need not possess the visionary powers of Nostradamus or even be an unemployed Psychic Friend to know what Patterson was thereafter known as. His official call signs, however, were "Admin Bitch," "Paper Cut Patty," or just "Paper Cut."

Patterson was a floater with the team, which meant he served as either a driver or shooter and with all three crews when we needed an extra hand to fill a hole. Patterson would serve in this capacity even after the crews were formalized a month later.

A second mechanic joined the team in mid-March. Specialist James Brackin was a young soldier with a terrible speech impediment that masked a very sharp mind. He served primarily as a driver-mechanic because of his MOS. His youthful enthusiasm—at twenty he was the youngest member of the team—would sometimes result in reckless driving; it got him pulled from behind the wheel on more than one occasion. Once, while barreling down a cramped Iraqi street at something like ninety miles per hour, he, in all sincerity and near somnambulistic calm, looked over at me and asked, "Did you ever see that chase scene in *Bullitt*? This reminds me of that."

Fortunately, he possessed smarts enough that we were able to plug him in elsewhere as a gunner. Like Patterson, Brackin would frequently float from one vehicle or billet to another. Because of his speech impediment, Specialist Brackin was known simply as "Fudd." Brackin looked nothing like the cartoon character, however, with thin build and dark, receding hair. In off-duty hours he could frequently be found chasing black women, for Brackin loved jumping the fence. For him, the old adage "Once You've Had Black You Never Go Back" was a way of life. As Patterson was, at that time, still weeks from formally joining the team, Brackin became our eleventh member.

Specialist James Brackin, USA, and Lance Corporal Charles Dann, USMC.
(From the collection of Jack Lynch)

I rounded out the team by "borrowing" two soldiers who were to be sent south in a few weeks. The first of my borrowed soldiers, Sergeant First Class Steven Shenk, was a fifty-one-year-old army reservist who had been a marine for two years just after the Vietnam War. Back in the States, Shenk worked as an eighth-grade biology teacher. At 5'11" and weighing 180 pounds, he had the appearance of a very fit grandfather. The avuncular look, combined with his profession, would allow him to pass for a respectable pillar of any community. In fact, "Shenky," as he was often called, was as much of a social misfit as the rest of the team. His soft-spoken ways only served to mask the gunslinging lunatic lurking within. During his brief time with the team he served as a floater.

Joining the team with Shenk, and on an equally temporary basis, was Sergeant Dave Balan, a regular army infantryman of Russian descent. Standing at 5'7" and weighing 170 pounds, Balan was tagged with the call sign "Closet Diesel" because of his well-hidden yet impressive build. Closet Diesel was one of the most modest men I had ever met, and he was easily the quietest member of the team. Like Shenky, he fit in very well.

We had more bodies than I ever thought I would have, but we still did not have the man I felt we needed. Gunnery Sergeant Josleyn was still in Tal Afar, where he was working for a Major Kesterson, U.S. Army. The small CMATT staff to which both men belonged was busy trying to establish that place as a base for the new Iraqi army. I called the major and asked what it would take to pry the gunny away from him. He said he would be more than willing to give me the gunny so long as he got a good replacement. It just so happened that two soldiers, a master sergeant and a specialist, whom I had no use for, had just checked in at CMATT. Major Kesterson agreed to trade the gunny for the two soldiers, but he had one condition—Josleyn had to stay on long enough to teach his replacements his job. If I agreed to that, I could expect to see the gunny in mid-April. That was more than agreeable, and I quickly accepted, thanking the major for his willingness to part with a man he clearly thought of as "shit hot."

One person not assigned to our group, but who nevertheless made a significant contribution to the team, was Corporal William "Bill" Napier. Napier was assigned as the chief of staff's driver. As such, he played gofer for the chief of staff and the sergeant major. As often as he could, he not only drove for the team, he allowed us the use of the chief's Chevy Suburban when he himself could not drive with us. Corporal Napier was 5'8" and weighed 140 pounds dripping wet. His shaven head and sinister appearance made him look something like a vampire. In fact, some members of the team took to calling him Nosferatu. He was a very easygoing and fun-loving guy who was always ready to share his last beer with his friends. Quick-witted and quick to laugh at someone else's shitty joke, he was all the rage at parties.

Other people would join the team, but as March drew to a close, the core of the team was firmly established. There were eleven full-time members: Gunnery Sergeant Hessen, Staff Sergeant Reed, Sergeants Williams, Facemyer, Boeringer, and Algarin, Corporal Meggison, Specialists Delacroix and Brackin, and Lance Corporal Dann, as well as myself and two temps, Sergeant First Class Shenk and Sergeant Balan, and two part-time, yet full-fledged members, Sergeant Schroeder and Corporal Napier. The team was a diverse group. Including temps and part-time members we had seven marines and eight soldiers. Within weeks we would add Staff Sergeant Patterson and Gunnery Sergeant Josleyn as full-time members. Many of the soldiers were infantrymen, and two were rangers, while a third had a very different background. Of the marines, I was the only infantryman. The mixed bag was rounded out by soldiers and marines who served in a variety of support MOSs from "data dink" (computer geek) to motor transport. It was my job to teach all these people to fight as a team.

Corporal Kelly "Trunk Monkey" Meggison, USA, holding
his beloved mini AK, which he had affectionately named
"Prom Date." Behind him is a Russian-made PKM
machine gun. *(From the collection of Jack Lynch)*

But with the successful recruiting drive we were on our way to building a
cohesive and dedicated team of killers.

What had, just weeks earlier, seemed like a wild fantasy, was a reality. I
had been allowed to recruit, select, and organize my own combat team. One
more time, probably my last, I would be allowed to lead men into combat. All
that remained for me to do now was to rewrite the conservative SOP, get
higher to okay it, and then get the weapons and armored vehicles that would
make us unstoppable. Of all these, I expected the most difficult task would be
getting higher to sign off on the new SOP. Most people at the Palace were all
about avoiding combat. Colonel Buchanan and Lieutenant Colonel Thomas
were my only hope.

Gunny Hessen and I were justifiably very happy. The world seemed like a
perfect place in March of 2004. One finishing touch was needed to complete
the assembly of the team. We needed a name and it had to be good and unique
at the same time. World War II had had its "Black Sheep" and its "Abbeville
Boys," so why should this war be any different? Finding a cool name that had
not been used before would be the hard part. Names like "Rough Riders" and
"Road Warriors" had been used more times than a Norfolk hooker during
Fleet Week. It was the creative Sergeant Williams who came up with the
team's name one evening as Corporal Napier was driving us to chow. "We are

the Majestic Twelve," he said. The Majestic Twelve, he went on to explain, was a select group of twelve men who secretly run the world. According to conspiracy buff Williams, these men even knew of the existence of alien technology in the hands of the United States. These men, he continued, control the slow and methodical introduction of this technology into our daily lives. While I did not buy the story behind the name, and fretted that a man with access to full automatic weapons did, the name itself was perfect. When someone pointed out to Williams that the team had only eleven full-time members he responded, "Yeah, well, I was counting the gunny [Gunny Josleyn] Top is waiting for."

Napier asked, "Well, what about me and Sergeant Schroeder? Don't we count?"

"You guys are part-time and both of you actually belong to other sections," answered Williams, who was growing irate.

Unable to resist, Napier added, "Okay. Well, what about Staff Sergeant Patterson? He does belong to operations, and unlike the gunny Top is waiting on, he is here now."

Williams answered, "Well, he may be here now but he is not yet on the team, and besides, Majestic Twelve sounds a lot cooler than the Majestic Thirteen or the Majestic Thirteen plus two temps."

In Will's defense, at the time we chose it, there were, indeed, only eleven full-time members of the team, but the arrival of Gunny Josleyn would give us twelve, and full-time, part-time, and temporary, as far as we were concerned, we were all majestic.

CHAPTER 4

Training

On 13 March we made a run to the Tadji Military Base to drop off some airmen being assigned there as trainers. We also took the opportunity to do some training. Tadji had great ranges which we could use to zero our weapons and conduct familiarization training on the AK-47 assault rifle. Zeroing the weapons was critical to accuracy. Unlike movies, where a man can pick up any rifle and start dropping targets by the score at any distance, each rifle must be sighted or "zeroed" to the man who actually carries it. This is because we are all built differently, hold a weapon differently, and even sight the thing a little differently. Even the way a man wears his body armor and gear will greatly influence how he fires the rifle. Zeroing the weapons synchronizes the rifle with its owner. It is a time-consuming process but absolutely critical to accuracy.

The first step in the process is to return the weapon's adjustable sights back to what is known as mechanical zero. In other words, the previous owner's adjustments are removed and the rear sight is returned to its center position. The front sight post is put back flush with zero adjustment up or down. From zero, the shooter will adjust his weapon to his shooting style. This is called "battle sight zero," or BZO, and is different from mechanical zero in that it reflects the adjustments made by the shooter to ensure he is accurate

with the weapon. BZO is cal-
ibrated for targets at 300
yards. Simply stated, once a
shooter has zeroed his weapon,
he should be able to pick it up
and consistently hit targets
300 yards away, dead center,
without making any adjustments to the weapon's sights,
provided there is no significant crosswind. Targets closer
or farther require adjustment
to the rear sight, but these adjustments are easy to make
even under stress. If there is a
strong wind, he will have to
give it a "value" and make a
corresponding adjustment, left
or right, to ensure a hit.

**Staff Sergeant Michael "Paper Cut"
Patterson, USA.** *(From the collection of Jack Lynch)*

Because of the line-of-sight
difference between the barrel
and the sight, the point of im-
pact for a bullet on a target at 25 yards is the same as at 300, so zeroing is
always done at 25 yards. In other words, if you aim center mass at a target at
25 yards or 300 you should hit both targets dead center without making any
adjustments to your sights. By zeroing at 25 yards it is easier to get a shooter
on target and, because of the short distance, reduce the effect wind has on the
bullet's flight to nothing.

Familiarization training on the AK-47 was important because some members of the team had to carry one, and while the AK-armed members of the
team would zero them, all members of the team, including those armed with
M-16s, needed to know how to use the weapon, hence the familiarization
training on the AKs for everybody. The AK is the favorite weapon of America's enemies around the world, and its very name has become synonymous
with Communist revolutionaries and terrorists of all stripes. Cheap, easy to
use and maintain, and brutally effective out to ranges of 300 meters, it is indeed a potent killer, if not quite as awe-inspiring as its reputation.

The trip to Tadji only took about forty minutes, though almost the entire
route is through Baghdad and its heavily populated suburbs, making the trek

one of the city's more dangerous runs. While there were ranges located nearby on Camp Victory, they did not meet our needs. They were static line affairs that allowed for no fire and maneuver training or engagement of any targets beyond fifty meters. Plus, we—meaning CMATT—did not own those ranges; they belonged to Victory Base, which meant we had to play by their more restrictive rules, which, while great for safety, inhibited effective combat training. CMATT owned Tadji, and as the operations sergeant major for CMATT I could use the ranges there as I wanted and as often. The distance could be traveled in twenty-five minutes if not for two heavily congested and dangerous intersections and a really nasty traffic circle, which was an ambush just waiting to happen. The congestion forced us to travel very slowly and even stop at times. These man-made choke points were obvious to everybody, including, certainly, those who wanted to kill us. As noted earlier, our unarmored vehicles' only defense against roadside bombs was speed. Robbed of this, we were easy meat for an IED. Dedicated insurgents would certainly follow up the IED with a barrage of RPG, PKM, and AK fire on the convoy's survivors. Moving slowly was bad enough, but we never wanted to be stopped on Iraq's roads if we could avoid it.

We were able to push and plow our way through the intersections and the traffic circles, and that kept us moving. Soon enough, we found ourselves stopped at the gate leading into the Tadji Military Base. After being cleared by the sentries, we pulled off to the right shoulder, where five or six clearing barrels were lined up. Clearing barrels are fifty-five gallon oil drums buried in the soil at a forty-five-degree angle and filled with sand. A hole is cut into the top of the barrel. Their only purpose is to make sure that your weapon is safely cleared and empty of all ammunition. Standing in front of the barrel, you first remove your weapon's magazine, and then pull the charging handle or slide, depending on your weapon, to the rear, ejecting any live rounds. Then you release the charging handle or slide and place the muzzle of the weapon in the barrel's hole and pull the trigger to ensure that the weapon is clear. If your weapon is not clear, then everybody will know you are a dumb ass when you launch a round into the barrel but nobody will be hurt by your negligence. Clearing barrels are set up at the entrances to military facilities considered secured. We did not clear our weapons. We were professionals, and I saw no reason to clear my weapon *anywhere* in Iraq. (Our policy of not clearing our weapons was vindicated years later when four U.S. soldiers were captured and later killed by Iranian agents or Iranian-trained insurgents in an attack on a military base at Karbala. While tragic, the attack is a fine example of why you do not clear your weapon just because you are on a "secure" base.)

Tadji was a vast facility that closely resembled a junkyard and a used-car lot all rolled into one. Driving down the main road you could see several large warehouses off to the right. In front of them was a large field covered with destroyed armored vehicles of every type. These included some old American M-109 self-propelled artillery systems. Self-propelled artillery resembles a tank in that it is armored, fully tracked, and has a large gun sticking out the front of a turret. Self-propelled systems, though, lack the thick armor of main battle tanks and are therefore very vulnerable. These M-109s appeared to have been captured from Kuwait during Iraq's invasion of that small nation in August 1990. Hundreds of French vehicles of numerous types, including self-propelled guns, armored personnel carriers, main battle tanks, and even armored cars, covered the ground. As numerous as the French weapons were, there were far more of Russian manufacture, self-propelled guns such as the M-1973 and the M-1974 as well as infantry-carrying BMPs and BTRs, and of course main battle tanks. Most of the tanks were the older T-55s and T-62s, with a few of the more modern T-72s sprinkled among them. The T-72s, self-propelled guns, and troop carriers all had one thing in common, though; they had been reduced to wrecks on the battlefield. The fate of their crews was less certain. In most wars, destroyed armor usually means that the crew or members of the crew have been killed or wounded. That was not so in Iraq.

Whether it was the Gulf War or this war, the qualities of the Iraqi soldier had remained constant: He would not stand and go toe-to-toe with American firepower, and much of this armor, indeed most of it, was probably destroyed after having been abandoned by the crews. Viewing the ruthless efficiency of the precision American weaponry that had destroyed these armored vehicles, I almost felt pity for the men who had been asked to man them. I almost could not blame them for just quitting. Almost.

After checking into the Coalition Military Assistance Training Team headquarters at Tadji, I was given my range assignment. The range had a 25-yard BZO range and a 300-meter range. My iron sights were already zeroed, so I took this opportunity to zero my new advanced combat optical gunsight (ACOG) with Bindon aiming concept (BAC). The ACOG with BAC is an excellent combat optic. In my opinion it was the best available, and I put my money where my mouth was. The sight cost me $1,300 at a gun store in Virginia and I considered it well worth the cost. The ACOG with BAC allows you to keep both eyes open and still engage targets as the aiming reticle is superimposed on the target. This allows for the quick and precise engagement of multiple targets. There were many open-eye gun sights like the ACOG available on the market. What I liked about the ACOG was the four-power magnification it provided. Most open-eye sights did not provide any magnification, and that, while ideal for close quarters combat, was not optimal for combat in open spaces. Having zeroed my sight, I decided to see just how precise I could be with the ACOG. I took a unit coin, about the size of a dollar coin, and emblazoned with a red cross, and taped it to a target. In nine seconds I was able to put seven rounds into the center of the coin. The rapid target acquisition and accuracy of the ACOG were impressive.

Others were having a more difficult time. Sergeant Facemyer had problems zeroing his weapon. He claimed the rifle, a folding-stock AK-47, was defective. Taking the weapon myself, I fired it as rapidly as I could while still maintaining accuracy. Facemyer and I walked down range and checked the target.

"Fuck, Top, how did you do that?"

Handing Face his weapon, I teased him about what it must feel like to see his girl (weapon) being more satisfied in the arms of another man. I continued berating Facemyer. "If you screw like you shoot, I guarantee you your wife has a boyfriend, Face."

My other ranger, Sergeant Williams, was also having difficulties, not with hitting the target—he was tearing it up—but with reloading magazines into his AK. Williams vented his frustration on his weapon's magazines.

"Damn it, these fucking magazines suck."

Facemyer had no problem reloading his weapon and was actually quite adept at it. That was a good thing, because he needed to empty two magazines just to ensure he got a hit. It made for an interesting contrast with Sergeant Williams, who had no problem hitting the target but was as thumb-fingered reloading his AK as a male adolescent attempting to unhook a bra for the first time. I could not resist poking fun at my two rangers.

"Hey, Gunny, if we could just combine these two we would have us one super soldier. As things are now, they are useless without each other."

Gunny Hessen answered. "So, Top, if I read you right, what you are saying is that if we combine our two rangers into one, we will have us one marine?"

I continued to harass Will and Face. "I used to think you guys hung out together so much because you were queer, now I know it's because Face can't shoot worth a shit and you, Will, can't even load your own weapon. Face, maybe you should invite Will over to your house and introduce him to Mrs. Facemyer and maybe, just maybe, between the two of you, you guys will figure out how to keep her satisfied. Or you could just ask a marine to do the job for you, sort of like you're doing today. I am available by the way. What about you, Gunny? Care to have a go at Mrs. Face?"

The original vehicle 3. Left to right **are Sergeant Jason "Starsky" Algarin, USMC; Sergeant First Class Steven "Trick Shot" Shenk, USA; Gunnery Sergeant Robert "Gate Keeper" Josleyn, USMC; Sergeant Ed "Hutch" Boeringer; Lance Corporal Charles "Four Shot" Dann; Sergeant Dave "Diesel Dave" Balan, USA; and Corporal Kelly "Trunk Monkey" Meggison.** *(From the collection of Jack Lynch)*

"Top makes a joke, take two," Facemyer answered as he mimicked hitting drums in a ba-ra-bump manner.

Williams defended himself. "I don't know what Facemyer's problem is, but my fucking magazines are not worth a shit, Top."

"I'll be with you in a minute, Will," I answered as I continued to help Facemyer.

Since Face was still not convinced that his problems with the AK were his, and not the weapon's, I took it from him and handed it to Hessen.

"Here you go, Gunny, but be gentle. I was rough on her and she is still in recovery mode."

"I hear she likes it that way, Top," Hessen answered.

To Facemyer's dismay, Hessen had no problem hitting with the AK.

Displeased, Facemyer said, "Fuck, gimme that thing, Gunny."

Hessen handed the weapon back to Face, saying in his slow drawl, "Here ya go, but ya better give her some recovery time because I think the Top and I done wore her out for a while."

(Ultimately, Face found an M-16 and stuck with it until we got U.S.-manufactured machine guns in June, at which time he was issued a SAW.)

I walked over to Williams and asked, "So, Will, what's the problem here?"

"These fucking magazines, Top. They suck."

Taking his weapon, I showed Will how to feed a magazine into the AK by using the index finger to guide it into the weapon's magazine well. With this simple instruction and more time practicing reload drills, Williams quickly mastered the art of reloading the AK. Will and his AK became inseparable.

As I watched the team shoot, I was very proud of them and yet painfully aware that none of them would ever be known to their countrymen unless they committed some horrible crime. To me, my soldiers and marines were heroes just for volunteering for the job of convoy security. Each one could have stayed safe in the palace or, in the case of Will and Face, just gone home. Most had volunteered just to come to Iraq in the first place. It saddened me to think their bravery, service, and determination would never be known to anyone outside our own little family. But if they made some mistake, or did something the media considered wrong, the world would certainly know their names. My soldiers and marines were not unique in this. Most Americans had never heard of Sergeant First Class Paul Smith, U.S. Army, who won the Medal of Honor for his actions at the Baghdad International Airport in April of 2003. But they knew how to spell Abu Ghraib in their sleep. Everybody on the planet knew who Lynndie England was.

Worse, peace activists are frequently characterized as heroic when they hold "die-ins" in Washington, D.C., while real heroes are denigrated by Democratic senators and congressmen as mere dupes serving in an illegal war, forced to do so because of a lack of education or because they are victims of the poverty draft. Real heros had their conduct likened to that of Genghis Khan or were libeled as murderers. Of course, not even I would have dreamed that within a few short years my comrades and I would be identified as potential threats to the nation we were fighting for.

None of those in the team fit the liberal stereotype of the all-volunteer military as being made up of poor, uneducated "victims." Intelligent, thoughtful, and dedicated, they could just as easily have gone to college as did most of their peers. Instead, they joined the army or the Marine Corps to serve their country and to test themselves as warriors. The need to test themselves was, I suspect, a big part of the reason they volunteered for convoy duty. Watching and listening to them as they interacted with one another, I was aware that they were rapidly building the cohesion and élan that they would need to survive. Ultimately, the love of country and of service, and the desire to test yourself, are only good enough to get a person into trouble. To fight and win, you have to love the person next to you more than you love life itself. We were quickly building that kind of camaraderie. I pulled myself away from my thoughts and moved on down the line and helped shooters who needed the help.

Bo, Algarin, and Reed had, like Hessen, checked in with M-9 service pistols, so I issued the four men AK-47s. All did surprisingly well with the new weapon, especially Boeringer, who had a standard AK-47. Algarin, like Reed, was issued a folding-stock AK-47. The folding-stock model would be easier for the drivers to use if they had to get busy with the rifle while driving. Not the ideal situation to be sure, but possible nonetheless. Gunny Hessen quickly zeroed his weapon and was able to help me work the line. Dann came to Iraq with his own service rifle, which he had zeroed long before leaving the States. After confirming his zero, Dann spent most of the morning improving his accuracy. Shenk, Balan, Brackin, and Schroeder also had their service-issued rifles, and like Dann they spent most of the morning working on their accuracy. Del was having a more difficult time. The army had provided her with an M-16A2 service rifle, but as with many soldiers, sailors, and airmen assigned to CMATT, they had not bothered to have her zero the weapon, let alone train with it. Though it took some time, we were able to get a good zero on Del's weapon, and while she would never be compared to Carlos Hathcock, the marine sniper who during the Vietnam War killed ninety-three enemy soldiers, she became competent in the weapon's use and could be counted on in a fight.

Once everybody had a good zero on their weapon, we conducted familiarization fire with the AKs. This consisted of engaging targets from twenty-five yards to a hundred. We fired single shots and we fired on full auto. Full automatic fire from a rifle is viable in some situations, as in room clearing and when the desire is to suppress or pin down the enemy. You pin the enemy with automatic fire and you kill him with well-aimed single shots. Firing the rifles on full automatic, the marines and soldiers quickly learned how difficult it was to hit even a stationary target. On the positive side, they could easily see why a sudden burst of automatic fire would cause a man to look for cover. Sustained automatic fire from a rifle would buy time, I told them, but it was not an effective killer outside of certain situations, such as the aforementioned room clearing. I explained that they should think of automatic fire at the cyclic rate (the theoretical rate of fire for a weapon free of malfunctions and with unlimited ammo) and the sustained rate. Because of the heat generated when a weapon fires, it can only maintain fire at the cyclic rate for a short period of time before the heat causes the weapon to malfunction or cease functioning entirely (known as a "stoppage"). To avoid this, the rate of fire at some point has to be reduced to a rate that can be sustained indefinitely. This slower rate of fire slows the heat buildup and reduces the chances of a malfunction or stoppage, and is known as the sustained rate. For practical purposes, the cyclic rate is pulling the trigger and holding it down until the weapon is empty and then reloading as rapidly as possible and repeating. We would use this only to gain fire superiority at the start of a fight.

I continued. "We will need to get the enemy to start thinking more about his own safety than about killing us. We will use automatic fire at the cyclic to drive him to ground so that we can maneuver against him while he is look-ing after himself. We call this gaining fire superiority, which simply means that we are doing more shooting than he is. We must gain this superiority before we can maneuver. Once we have gained fire superiority, we must ex-ploit it quickly, especially more so in our case since we do not have machine guns."

Ideally, fire superiority is gained and maintained by machine guns. As we lacked these most important infantry weapons, we would have to gain and maintain that superiority with our rifles. Firing rifles at the cyclic, there was the danger that they would overheat and malfunction. Even if they did not malfunction it was certain that the fire would be wildly inaccurate, especially when compared with the automatic fire that far more stable machine guns could deliver. After gaining fire superiority we had to maintain it. That was done by dropping down to a more sustainable rate of fire. While the support-ing element provided this cover fire, the assaulting element would maneuver on the enemy and rely on semiautomatic precision rifle fire to actually kill him.

We ran several fire and maneuver drills, and while they went well, I was more than a bit concerned about our lack of machine guns. Malfunctions caused by overheating, inaccuracy of rifle fire in full auto, and ammunition consump-tion rates all left me feeling uneasy about our half solution. We needed machine guns and we needed them now. The obvious solution was to have U.S. weap-ons issued to us, but we were not be able to get them because these items were not in the CMATT inventory. We would have to look at getting Russian weapons to fill this critical need. Ultimately, we would end up trading the "sexy" and exotic weapons in our mini armory for the far more useful Russian machine guns. The weapons traded were submachine guns like the MP-5 and the Sterling. They looked great but were of limited use for actually killing someone in the conditions we operated in. As mentioned earlier, another big hit on the trade market was the folding-stock AK-47. Like the more sexy sub-guns, the folding-stock AK was in high demand among Green Zone ninjas because it was different and it looked cool. As to where the people we traded with got the Russian machine guns I never knew, and I did not ask. I was certain we were breaking some law, rule, or regulation somewhere, and the less I knew the better.

The final course of fire was quick-kill drills. These drills involved the engagement of multiple targets at short ranges. Three-by-five cards were placed on the center of the silhouette target's heads, and larger, five-by-five cards were placed centered on the target's chest. Targets were engaged one at a time and in pairs with the emphasis on accuracy and not speed. To emphasize this, shots that missed the cards but hit the target did not count. There were eight targets, and each shooter had four shots on each of these. We used two magazines, one with twelve rounds and the other with twenty. This forced each shooter to change his magazine once, which added stress. For those who were not infantrymen, this was something new. While everybody enjoyed the training, it was a wake-up call for our noninfantrymen, who were not as good with their weapons as years of static line firing had led them to believe they were. With practice we would all, infantry and noninfantry, improve. We wrapped up our day at the range and headed back to the palace.

Back in the Green Zone, the team turned to refueling and securing the vehicles while I walked back to the three to get briefed on the next day's missions. Colonel Thomas told me that there were no runs scheduled and asked me what I would be doing with the team.

"We will run some immediate-action drills, sir."

IA drills were nothing more than practicing tactical scenarios and observing how the team reacted to the changing situation. Each drill was then critiqued by each member of the team to ensure that they all understood the SOPs and knew why they did what they did in response to a given threat. When required, corrections were made and drills were rerun until they were properly executed. We did this over and over until all mistakes were eliminated.

This training was critical to the survival of the team. The drills taught the individual members of the team to respond and act as one. By changing things and adding variables, the drills also taught them to think.

Training space in the Green Zone was at a premium. The only place in the Green Zone large enough to allow IA training, and where we conducted ours, was an area known to Americans in Baghdad as the Crossed Sabers. They were Saddam's version of France's Arc de Triomphe, complete with conquering troops marching under them, and they were located at opposite ends of what was known as Martyr's Square. It was this "square" that we used for our IA drills. The area was interesting for many reasons. Located very near this parade ground was the Iraqi Tomb of the Unknown Soldier, which consisted of a domed open-air building in front of which was an ugly spire covered with colored tiles matching the Iraqi flag. Near this eyesore was a large clamshell-looking structure that was meant to be a falling shield, representing fallen Iraqi soldiers. Nearby were restaurants, movie theaters, and shops that had all served the elite of the ruling Baath Party.

Colonel Thomas asked me a few questions about the SOP training and then said, "Sounds good, Master Sergeant. What do you have them doing now?"

"They are waiting for the word, and then I was going to secure them unless you want to talk with them, sir."

He had no information to pass to us, so I headed out to the smoking area where we held our daily debriefs at the end of the day. The debriefs were informal affairs and, in addition to passing required information, served as a way of letting off steam and providing one and all with a forum in which they could verbally abuse one another for some minor infraction of road etiquette or some perceived act of stupidity. Once I finished passing the word, I asked if anyone had questions. Today there were none, and I dismissed the team for chow.

For evening chow (dinner to civilians and airmen) most of us, and frequently all of us, went to the KBR dining facility. While chow within the palace itself was better than anything served to me by any Marine Corps chow hall, it was nothing compared to what KBR served at the dining facility used almost exclusively by their employees. From the outside, the dining facility looked like little more than a "West Virginia mansion" (two doublewides placed together with plastic covering the joint). But once you entered this hillbilly Taj Mahal you could not help but be amazed at the incredible chow KBR was serving its own employees. Bastards! The dining facility (DFAC) in the palace was known to all uniformed personnel, but this one, less than half a mile away, was not. Here they served food that could be served in any three-star restaurant in the United States: shrimp, lobster, and steak. The desserts were something one would kill for. But it was destined to not last. About a month after we had been going to the KBR DFAC, I overheard one of the KBR employees, upon seeing all the uniformed people eating there, say, "Well, I guess the secret is out." Unwilling to continue the expense of their extravagance for such a large clientele, the chow at the KBR facility soon became little better than that at the palace. But it was nice while it lasted.

CHAPTER 5

The Fight

We did not run any immediate-action drills on the following day, 14 March, because the operations section, more commonly referred to as "the three," had received a call from the Baghdad RC saying that hundreds of Iraqis were rioting. There was not a lot of info, but Colonel Thomas passed what he had. It seemed that the Iraqis were angry because they were not being allowed to enlist. They did not understand that they were being turned away for their own safety. The RC had remained closed after the bombing as security was improved. For some reason, a large group of Iraqi men thought that the center was open and they were upset to find out that it was still closed. It was also reported that shots had been fired at the RC, though it was unclear who fired them or why. More ominously, some sort of verbal threat had been made against the RC by two men in a car. Very little is known about what, if anything, this had to do with the rioting. The man who "owned" the RC was Jeff Baxter, a retired Marine Corps major who did something in Vietnam. Just ask him, he would tell you. As he told you about his stellar service in Vietnam, he always made sure that he threw in a barb or two about the questionable value of your service to the nation as compared to his when things were "really bad." While he did not have a great deal of respect for the team, we were more than good enough to be his 911.

Hoping for more information, I asked Colonel Thomas, "Do you have anything else, sir?"

"No, Top, that's all I have."

I turned to Gunny Hessen, who had been standing next to me, and told him, "Gunny, go tell the team that we are not training today. Pass what the colonel has just said, and I will be out in a few minutes. I am going over to the two and see if the intel has changed since yesterday."

Staff Sergeant Libby told me the general situation in Baghdad remained unchanged from the day before. While he knew about the situation at the RC, he had nothing to pass that I did not already know. I thanked him and left for the staging area. I walked past the Gurkha guard at the rear entrance to the palace and then quickly past the marines on the palace gate.

The team was already assembled by the time I arrived in the parking lot. Going on the mission were Colonel Thomas, Hessen, Reed, Williams, Facemyer, Algarin, Boeringer, and Schroeder, Napier, Delacroix, Brackin, and myself. I asked the colonel if he had passed anything new.

"Just what I passed to you, Top. They know where we are going and why."

I gave the team a premission brief that consisted of the route we would take to the RC and the known threats in the area. Nobody had any questions.

"Okay, then, let's mount up," I said.

We quickly loaded our vehicles, and as we did so, I got radio checks from each vehicle commander.

"Huggy Bear, Huggy Bear, this is Stonewall, radio check, over?"

"Stonewall, Huggy, I've got you Lima Chuck, over." "Lima Chuck" was slang for loud and clear.

"Huggy, I have you the same, out," I answered.

This process was repeated two more times with the other vehicle commanders. As we pulled out of our lot and into the staging area, we did so in an orderly, slow, and calm fashion, nothing like the demolition derby that would follow.

Driving in Baghdad always reminded me of the bizarre and deadly races on Speed Racer. Crazy stuff like racing around the rim of an erupting volcano, against each other and against violent racing gangs who killed the unwary driver. It also reminded me of *Death Race 2000*, but without all of the attractive women. Once we hit the gate that marked the end of the Green Zone and the beginning of the Red, the end of safety and the beginning of the great game, I keyed my handset and passed "Eyeballs." This single word served as a gentle reminder that we were now in a different world and that all casual conversation was at an end; it was now life and death, a game played for blood, and the game was on. Most of my people never needed this reminder. As soon as the syllable "eye" left my lips, Chris "Huggy Bear" Reed, in the lead vehicle, punched the accelerator on his Ford Expedition through the floorboard. Each driver trailing him followed suit.

The ride out was a wild affair. Darting in and out of traffic, jumping curbs, sidewalks, and medians, running stop signs—doing whatever we had to keep moving. Move, move, move! At all costs, keep the convoy moving. In less than five minutes we were at the gate to the RC. I quickly dismounted and was followed by my team, minus the drivers. The dismounts and I stopped all traffic and formed a protective cordon around our vehicles as they slowly pulled through the vulnerable gate. Stopping traffic was critical to protecting the convoy from potential VBIED attacks. The gate to the RC was narrow and required each vehicle to negotiate a 90-degree turn. These two factors slowed them to a crawl as they entered the compound. After the last of them had finally cleared the gate, we collapsed our protective cordon and entered the relative safety of the Baghdad Recruiting Center compound. The building in which the recruiters worked and lived lay some 150 meters from the gate, so we quickly remounted our vehicles for the short trip to the inner gate to the RC itself.

The boys were already bitching, Gunny most of all. We couldn't help but notice that there were no rioters. Where was the mayhem that had gotten us out here?

Gunny gave voice to what we all thought. "This is fucking bullshit, Top. Just another fucking wild turd hunt."

We all felt like the little boy who got a goldfish on his birthday when he had asked for a puppy. I was certain that many of us wanted to kill Colonel Thomas. Not that it was his fault. All he had done was repeat what he had been told, and I am sure he was as disappointed as any of us. Things were about to get much worse. As we dismounted from our vehicles, Mr. Baxter, filled with the self-importance of his lofty position as a grizzled veteran, began to explain to us that we were in the Red Zone now, the "very heart of it!" After explaining to us the dangerous position we were in, he walked away.

Facemyer, disgusted with Mr. Baxter's attitude toward the team, said to no one in particular, "Yeah, this is the first time I have been let out to play."

"I know how you feel, Face. I think he has forgotten how he first met the Gunny and me," I answered.

To me, Mr. Baxter was an arrogant and thankless bastard. Gunny Hessen and I had not even checked in when we made our first run to the Red Zone, the "very heart of it," on that horrible day barely more than a month earlier when the RC was attacked with a VBIED. Mr. Baxter was not so dismissive of the Gunny and me then, and that *was* our first in the Red Zone. Dipshit!

Disappointed and pissed off, we loaded the vehicles and waited to begin the ride back to the palace. As the boys were loading up, the colonel told me that we would be escorting Mr. Baxter and four of his staff back to the palace. Because he did not have room enough in his vehicle, two of Mr. Baxter's staff would be riding with us. We would be packed in pretty tight as a result. Colonel Thomas and I were discussing the order of movement when Mr. Baxter interrupted.

"Driving here is not like anything you've experienced before. I've trained my Gurkhas, and they are very good at it, so do your best to keep up."

What the hell? Did this guy think we teleported out to his location?

"That won't be hard, sir," I answered. "We will be leading you, and I will have vehicles behind you as well. Fall in behind the Suburban. That's my lead."

Mr. Baxter was not happy, but he was professional about it and said nothing. I told the team that we had additional troops and another vehicle in the convoy. I briefed the order of movement and the bump plan to accommodate our unexpected passengers. Once the team was loaded and staged, I cautioned them to forget what had just happened.

"I know we are all pissed off, but forget about this false 911 and just focus on getting back alive."

As we approached the outer gate, I could see there was something of a brawl between two of the Iraqis guarding the gate and two other Iraqis dressed in civilian attire. Four other Iraqi guards stood by, just watching. The uniformed Iraqis were losing. Colonel Thomas told us, incredibly, "Wait here," as he alighted from the vehicle and ran toward the gate, now less than twenty meters away.

Under most circumstances, telling us to wait while something was going down would be like telling a fat kid not to eat the last Ho Ho. The fat kid was going to eat it anyway. But today we were all feeling a little resentful about having been called out for nothing, and now, here was a golden opportunity to make something out of nothing. It was as if these two assholes had just fallen right out of the sky. This was very unfortunate for the two Iraqis.

"What the fuck did he just say, Top?"

Napier looked as dumbfounded as I felt.

"Fuck that. Let's go, Nape," I answered quickly.

I keyed my handset and ordered "Dismount, dismount!"

Immediately, we all dismounted our vehicles and ran toward the trouble, all but two of us anyway. Algarin and Boeringer, because of the increase in passengers, had to ride in the cargo area of the Suburban. From the inside, you cannot open the rear cargo hatch of a Suburban. With all of their gear on, it was impossible for them to climb over the seat to exit the vehicle. They had to wait for someone to open the rear hatch and let them out. In the excitement of the moment everybody had forgotten about them, and nobody had let them out. Trapped as they were, both men became quite worried that they were going to miss what was about to happen. None of us knew what that was, but each of us knew we did not want to miss it. Boeringer and Algarin did what any man would do in the same situation. They began to scream.

"Hey, you assholes, let us out! Somebody please let us out!"

Their pleas were frantic, their faces like those of a child left in the school office as he watches his classmates board a bus for a field trip to some exotic and exciting destination. As funny as it was, it was also to serve as a very sobering lesson about the liabilities of our equipment. Opening the rear cargo hatch, when we had people in the cargo area of our SUVs, would have to be added to our SOP and incorporated into our IA drills. After freeing Boeringer and Algarin, we rushed the gate. Will, Face, Brackin, and Schroeder covered the gate while Thomas, Hessen, Algarin, Bo, Del, and I converged on the two Iraqis. What happened next would have made the LAPD green with envy. Compared to the ass whipping these two men were about to get, Rodney King merely received a warning not to run from an elementary school hall monitor. Thomas grabbed one man and tried to restrain him with as little force as possible. Nicknamed "Hesco" because his large frame reminded us of the large and stout Hesco barriers that surrounded American facilities in Baghdad, Thomas was nevertheless one of those very large men who knew how easily he could hurt someone and showed tremendous restraint even when provoked. But the Iraqi, in an incredible act of stupidity, given both the size of the man grabbing him and what was bearing down on him and his friend, resisted. In hindsight, that alone should have told us that there was more going on with these two than it appeared. The Iraqi attempted to twist free of Hesco's grasp. Thomas simply ratcheted the man's arm behind his back and into a position that Houdini would have envied. I will never forget the unearthly wail that bellowed out of that man. It was an ear-piercing and unholy scream, which left no one in Baghdad in doubt that the animal or person who made it was suffering intense pain. Hearing the man wail, I was reminded of my own screams of pain and shame when I got my first prostate exam. The searing pain quickly reached the thinking part of the brain, and the Iraqi went as limp as a hand puppet without the puppeteer's hand up its ass.

Seeing what was going on, some Iraqis outside the gate started moving toward it. Will, Face, Brackin, and Schroeder leveled their weapons at the crowd and ordered it to disperse, which they quickly did. Four of us, myself included, closed on the one Iraqi who was still fighting with the Iraqi guard. Looking over my left shoulder toward the commotion at the gate, I turned back just in time to see the Iraqi I was closing on dropped to his knees with a quick rifle butt to the face. Algarin then fell on the man and wrestled him to the ground. The Iraqi continued to fight.

Something was not right. If this was just a simple dispute between locals, these guys would have quit as soon as they saw us coming. The fact that they had not, and that one was continuing to resist even after having his face tattooed with a rifle butt unnerved me. Algarin placed his knee in the man's back and pulled his arms behind his back in an attempt to tie them. The man still fought. Growing more alarmed, I placed my boot on his back, between his shoulders, and stuck my rifle into the side of his head. I told him not to move or I would kill him. With each word, I jabbed my rifle a little harder into the man's head for added emphasis. He was not impressed and continued to struggle. He was not fazed by anything I said or did. He defiantly turned his head away. Algarin wigged out. He grabbed the man's hair and twisted his head toward me. He then shoved the side of the man's head into the dirt and as he did so he said, "Listen to him, you fuck."

With the muzzle of my rifle pushed firmly into the side of the man's head I told him, "If you keep pissing us off, I am going to put your head on that fucking wall. Now stop moving and you will not get hurt. Do you understand me?"

My tone was even, maybe even deadpan. The Iraqi nodded his head yes. The Iraqi guards on the gate were not happy with how violently we had quelled the mini disturbance. Lost on them, for the moment at least, was the fact that nobody was dead and these two guys were just not right. More was going on here than it seemed. The man did not move as Algarin completed his search and tied the man's hands behind his back. Again, something just did not seem right about these two. I was not sure why, but I had a very uneasy feeling about them. The little voice in the back of my head was growing frantic and louder: *Do Something, You Dumb Bastard!*

Looking at Algarin I said, "Starsky, strip search that piece of shit."

As Algarin started to remove the man's shirt, the Iraqi tried to roll away.

Algarin punched the man repeatedly in the side of the head, and as he did so he said, "Hey, fuckhead, you move again and I am going to fucking kill you."

His shirt was not even completely removed when we saw, taped to the man's left forearm, a large knife with a six-inch blade. Knowing what these fucking people can do with a box cutter, I needed no explanation of what he had planned to do with the concealed knife. It was immediately obvious that the men had wanted to get past the Iraqi guards and into the recruiting center where they would have been able to stick some of the Americans working there or another guard and take his weapon.

In hindsight, I am almost certain that these men had detailed plans of the interior of the recruiting center. Why else would they try to sneak past the gate guards with just one knife? Sure, if all they wanted to do was gut an American or maybe two, the knife would do the trick, but to do that you only needed one guy. But with two guys you could gut one guard and immediately have access to several rifles and even a belt-fed machine gun, and with these you could kill far more than one or two Americans. To me it seemed that the only reason two men, with one knife between them, would try to get into the RC was because they knew how easily they could get weapons once inside the building. Inside the building was a mini armory that sat on the floor of Mr. Baxter's office. It included AKs and PKM belt-fed machine guns. The door to this office was always open, and the weapons were clearly visible. Either they themselves had been in it before or had simply gotten the information from a recruit they fed into the system. If these two could have grabbed just two AKs, they could have inflicted heavy casualties on the unarmed recruiting staff as almost all of their security was geared toward perimeter threats. External security at the RC was heavy, but internal security at the RC was as soft as Rosie O'Donnell's thighs. Holding the knife inches from the Iraqi's face, I grabbed a fistful of his hair and pulled his head back so that he could see my face.

"And what the fuck is this for, asshole? You want to stick one of our guys with this, you miserable fuck. Huh, you motherfucker."

He pulled away and was immediately beaten. Algarin punched him repeatedly in the side of the head as he shoved his face into the dirt. The Iraqi stopped moving.

Looking at the knife, I told Algarin, "Starsky, finish undressing this bastard."

Whereas before Algarin had been careful not to tear the man's shirt, he now took the man's own knife and used it to cut off his belt and pants. Having undressed the man down to his underwear, Algarin jerked the man up to his feet and asked me,

"Hey, Top, let me do a cavity search on this guy here."

Ignoring Algarin, I called Boeringer over and told him to load the guy into the pickup. I should have been more specific. As Boeringer grabbed the detainee, my attention was called to the gate, where there was more trouble. A red car similar to a VW Jetta, but called a Brizilla in Iraq, had stopped at the gate. Inside were two men who, despite all urging by Will and Face to move on, refused to do so. The passenger seemed to be trying to see who was being led away in custody. With six rifles leveled at them these two men simply scowled at us. They were taunting us. They only pulled away when they were ready to. That these men were there and so curious about what was happening at the RC was not damning by itself, but their refusal to move on when it was obvious that the RC was a bad place to be, and their disdain for us, were certainly cause for concern. Further, innocent civilians did not poke their nose into places where there was a high likelihood of its getting shot off. But with no obvious hostile intent, we could not simply kill them because we felt they were "dirty." Not in March anyway. In April or anytime after that we would have killed them, but in March we were too new, myself included, to know when the rules of engagement required a liberal interpretation.

As the car pulled off, I heard a large and heavy thump, like what a sack of potatoes might make if thrown into the bed of a pickup truck. Boeringer had literally heaved the detainees into the truck.

I called Del over to me.

"Yes, Master Sergeant?"

I took Delacroix to the truck with me and had her sit at the head of the truck bed by the cab. I pointed to her and made sure the two Iraqis could see her.

Looking at them I said, "If either one of you moves, *she* will kill you."

No virgins in paradise, just a one-way ticket to hell with an "infidel" and "inferior" woman as the travel agent. In jihadi heaven that probably meant they would get passed around as two of the seventy-two promised virgins. It was as if I had just neutered both of them. I told Del to watch them and then discreetly told Algarin to back her up.

Turning to Hesco, I asked him what he wanted to do with the two holy warriors. He talked it over with CMATT and they told us to take them to the forward operating base (FOB) located only a hundred meters from the RC's gate. We took the two detainees to the FOB and gave them water while we waited for the army interrogators to come and get them. One of the men remained defiant and said nothing while at the same time refusing the water we offered him. But the other, the one who had fought and got his ass kicked for his efforts, was running his yap more than any host on *The View*. One of the Iraqi translators working at the RC who had accompanied us to the FOB was questioning the talkative and suddenly repentant man. The translator finished talking with the detainee and walked over to me and explained what the man had said.

"The one with the knife is crying about his mother, father, sisters, and brothers and how poor they are. He says that all he wanted to do was join the army so he could better provide for them all. Liar! Now tell me, my friend, when you look for a job in America, do you tape a knife to your arm?"

"No, not if you want the job anyway," I answered.

"Foolish man," muttered the translator as he walked away.

The "fool" was now sobbing and saying in English, "Me mother, me father, we are so poor."

"Shut the fuck up, shithead!" I blurted out.

The other man remained silent and sullen. Within minutes the army arrived, and after getting filled in on what took place at the gate they took the two prisoners.

Libby was waiting for me when we got back to the palace.

"Top, take a look at this, I think you will find it interesting."

He handed me an intelligence report that raised my eyebrows. The report listed some potential VBIEDs. Brief descriptions of each potential VBIED were given. Sometimes these descriptions included the license plate. While the report identified several vehicles of various types and models, my eyes focused on one in particular: "Red Brizilla, possibly in Baghdad." This alone was not too alarming, as there were hundreds of these in Baghdad. Any one of them could be a VBIED, so what? What were you going to do? Shoot everybody in a red Brizilla that day? Obviously that was not a course of action available to me. But what Libby shared with me next made my jaw drop.

"I just got this, Top. It is a translated copy of what the Iraqi guards say happened earlier, before you guys got to the RC."

Two men in a red Brizilla had stopped at the RC's gate that morning before the altercation between the guards and the two Iraqis we detained. One of the two men in the car had said to the Iraqis guarding the gate, "You did not learn your lesson the last time. Today we will teach you again." If all of this information had been made available to me before we got to the RC, the two men in the Brizilla would have been detained or killed. Immediately, I deeply regretted that we had not killed them, and to this day I still regret it. I would later come to believe that these two men were with the two we had detained. I believed that they had been in some sort of overwatch position. Again, in hindsight, I felt it possible that the intent that day had been not only to kill some Americans but capture one or two as well. The two in the car would have helped in this and obviously been the means by which a knife-wielding pair escaped. Some three months later seventeen people would pay with their lives for my mistake.

Fortunately, I did not know that at the time, and I was able to consider all of the day's events without the burden of knowing the future. On the positive side, I had now been able to observe my new team actually do something that had not been scripted and several valuable lessons were learned. The team was very aggressive, and that was certainly something to be valued. But in our rush to the gate we had exposed ourselves to attack by a suicide bomber. If one of the two men we detained had been so inclined, we would have lost a few people. We should have had fewer people dealing with the two men we detained and more securing the perimeter. That was my fault. I had allowed too many of us to be pulled into a fight, and by doing so I had left us vulnerable; that would not happen again. We also learned that we needed to have someone designated to open the rear of our SUVs if we ever again had people riding in the cargo area. The next time it might not be so funny.

March 14 had netted us two detainees and some very valuable lessons, but it also left us wondering what was next. We did not have long to wait.

CHAPTER 6

Vorgang

The next few days were quiet as the team conducted quick runs to Baghdad International Airport (BIAP) and Camp Victory and longer ones to Tadji. The BIAP and Victory runs were viewed as training runs, rather than combat runs, because nothing ever happened on that route, officially designated Route Irish. Because this was a milk run we had secondary drivers operate the vehicles under the supervision of our regular drivers. While the route was traveled quickly, and there was a lot of traffic, nobody was shooting at us or setting off IEDs, so it was a good place to get the team some training to augment that which they got in the Green Zone.

While things were quiet on the road, something was in the air. That something was mortar fire, and a lot of it compared to the norm in Iraq. It started on the night of 18 March with several rounds impacting around the palace. None of these were very close, but they did get our attention. It felt odd to walk around almost like we did not have a care in the world but knowing, just the same, that people were throwing mortars and rockets at us. While I was not afraid of these weapons, as the insurgents were as adept in their use as is the French army with their rifles, I nevertheless was aware that these types of attacks were increasing in frequency if not effectiveness. These attacks continued with little change until the twenty-fourth of March.

At 0408 on that day I was awakened by a powerful blast that sounded as if it had come from only a few feet away. Close enough to shake my trailer and rattle my windows, the blast jolted me upright. This round was far more accurate than all those that had proceeded it. While it landed short, impacting in front of us, it was quickly followed by three or four more that landed behind us. As I lay there, terrified, listening to the impacts, I had vivid thoughts about the side of my trailer being ripped open by steel splinters microseconds before I myself was eviscerated. What if we took a direct hit? Would it be a blinding and painless flash followed by death? Or would it be a flash followed by searing heat and pain as I was engulfed in flames and torn to shards of flesh and pink mist by blast and steel? They had us bracketed; they had landed short and they had landed far, now all they had to do was split the difference. If these guys were worth a shit the next rounds were going to be on target. For a few seconds a thousand thoughts flashed through my mind, and none of them were good. For the first time in Iraq I was genuinely afraid.

But these guys were not worth a shit, and there was no follow-up to the first attack. As quickly as it had started, the attack ended. After first checking my shorts for terror poo, I went and checked on Gunny Hessen and Corporal Napier, who lived in the trailer adjoining mine. Both men were fine. While we all laughed about the near miss I was certain that we were all in fervent agreement in our hope that there would be no more such nonsense for the rest of the night. After checking on the other team members I headed back to my rack and tried to sleep, but sleep did not come easily.

In a few hours we would be escorting a convoy to Kirkush, and I really needed my sleep for that long and dull journey, but my mind kept racing back and forth. I thought about the mortar attack and the increase in these attacks over the past few days, and I wondered if that meant anything. While we had not seen an increase in convoy attacks over the previous few days, there had been a dramatic increase in mortar and rocket attacks. As alarming as this recent near miss had been, it was not what troubled me the most. Conditions on the roads were changing. The populace, which had been mostly friendly or, at worst, indifferent, was now at best indifferent but most frequently openly hostile. Worse, civilian pedestrian and motor traffic had dropped way off, so much so in fact that parts of Baghdad resembled ghost towns. Civilian activity at the RC had also greatly diminished. My uneasiness at the general situation was raised by the increase in rocket and mortar attacks. I wondered how long it would be before we saw more action on the roads.

As bleak as things were in Baghdad, the picture outside the capital was not much better. Those of us on the team could see it. Being in the Red Zone almost daily afforded us a great chance to observe and learn, firsthand, what passed for normal and what was abnormal. We talked about it among ourselves and in e-mails home to our families. If Iraq going down the drain was obvious to us, we were almost alone within the palace in seeing it.

Because of my growing concern that "something" was coming, I had been stressing the training even more than before. I was harder on the team, and they, understanding that the war had changed, responded as professionals with a greater intensity and determination not to be some rag-wearing shithead's next victim. Noting this and growing concerned about the new direction the team was taking, Chief Master Sergeant Vorgang, U.S. Air Force, felt compelled to address the issue with those working in the office. "Somebody needs to tell him [meaning me] the war is over, and if I have to, I'll step up."

When Napier repeated to me what Vorgang had said, I confronted the air force sergeant. Vorgang explained himself by saying that he was upset and said things he should not have said. However, he added that he did not understand why I was bringing so much stress to the office. Then he got to the real source of his problem.

"I would also like someone to explain to me why I was never considered for your job [operations sergeant major] because I am senior. What, does Colonel Buchanan think an air force guy can't lead?"

I did not answer that question for the sergeant; the answer was already obvious. He was senior to me in time in grade, and he had even been in Iraq longer, but like most airmen he was not trained for ground combat leadership. He was a manager and a technician and, while no doubt very good at what he did, no more qualified to lead men in combat than a competent airline ticket agent. He was effective in his box, a small box, and needed to stay there. I ended the conversation by telling him to stick to what he knew and I would do the same. Chief Master Sergeant Vorgang was not alone in his the-war-is-over attitude. It permeated the palace in late March of 2004.

As I finally drifted back to sleep, even I had no idea how violently that shortsighted attitude would be revealed for the fool's fantasy it was.

CHAPTER 7

Deadly April

April started off with attacks on the road from the palace to BIAP. The first victims were CIA contract employees whose Chevy Suburban was destroyed by an IED less than a mile from the Green Zone. Four men were reportedly wounded, and one of them was not expected to survive. Things only got worse from there. The third of April was a day of heavy losses, by the standards of this war, for us. Several marines were killed in action in combat ranging from towns just west of Baghdad all the way to the Syrian border. Soldiers were killed in multiple attacks on convoys in and around Baghdad. In fact, it was so bad that our mission to provide additional security at the Baghdad Recruiting Center on 4 April was almost scrubbed by higher. Higher, in fact, suspended all but mission-critical travel on 4 April. (This ban lasted all month.) There was also a rumor that the marines were getting ready to launch the largest offensive since the fall of Baghdad. The target was said to be the city of Fallujah, which in March was the site of a brutally effective attack on a four-man Blackwater security team. The team was destroyed, and their charred bodies dragged through the streets while howling mobs cheered. Two of the dead were then strung up on a bridge over the Euphrates. While tragic, it did not surprise anyone.

Many of the contracted security companies operating in Iraq were filled with some of the most arrogant and overconfident men I had ever met. They loved khaki and sunglasses. They looked like they had just walked off a Hollywood set filming *Navy Seals II, Bad Ass and Baghdad Bound*. Because of the nearly uniform wearing of khaki, expensive shades, and seemingly mandatory goatees, we would dub them Task Force Obvious. Later I would be told by a Blackwater medic, himself a former special forces medic, that the team leader on the ill-fated mission was a shoot-from-the-hip guy who never took the time to properly plan anything. There were rumors the company did not even know for several hours who was hit and why the team was where it was when it was hit. The rest is history.

Now good marines were going to die in an ill-conceived and politically motivated attack on the city to avenge the loss of men who would have loathed their avenging marines as "stupid grunts." This formed the backdrop to our mission to the RC on the morning of 4 April 2004. We left the palace at 0630 and by 0640 were inside the perimeter of the Baghdad RC. The ride out had been the routine, if mad rush. Nothing about the rest of the day would be routine, however.

We could hear gunfire erupting across the city. While there had always been gunfire in Baghdad, this was more intense, widespread, and sustained. This was not the sound of small ambushes but of pitched battles in the streets of Baghdad. This was the heart of Coalition rule in Iraq, not some distant town on the Syrian border, and the United States was locked in a death struggle to maintain control. The fire intensified as we took up our positions within the RC compound. At one point, shortly after 0900, we took some small-arms fire at the RC. The fire was wildly inaccurate, and I was not even sure we were the intended target. Unable to locate the source, we did not return fire.

While gun battles continued to rage across the city, the rest of the day at the RC passed uneventfully, and soon enough it was time for us to head back. This time I was riding lead as Hesco insisted on riding in the rear vehicle. Just outside the gate to the Green Zone, and on the right side of the road, was an Iraqi police station. As we pulled up alongside it, I noticed that the police had strung concertina wire across the road. While that was out of the ordinary, I did not dwell on it for very long. I should have. As my vehicle eased to a stop, I dismounted and began pulling at the concertina wire blocking our path.

The gate was now only fifty yards distant from us. As I pulled the concertina wire aside, I looked to my front and only then noticed that the crowd at the gate was much larger than the normal crowd of Iraqis seeking work with the Coalition. Many men among the crowd of several hundred wore black clothes adorned with green and red headbands. The significance of these "uniforms" would become evident in a few days. At about the time that I noticed the crowd, they noticed us and turned their attention from the gate and began moving toward us. I quickly jumped in my vehicle and got on the radio.

"Hesco, do you see this up here, over."

"I see it, Top," he replied.

Keying my handset again, I said, "I think we can get into the gate if we go around the crowd to the left."

Hesco wisely killed that idea.

"Negative, Top. Turn us around and head back to the RC and we can try again later."

As we turned around, the crowd made a rush for us. My vehicle was now the rear vehicle and the vehicle that had been pulling rear now had lead as we all turned around in place rather than maintain the order we had been in. Lead immediately hit heavy traffic. The driver for lead was my Royal Marine commando, Corporal "Tug" Wilson. Tug had only recently joined the team. Working out of Basra, he had been sent to Baghdad for some job that did not exist. Since they didn't need him back in Basra for the rest of the month, he offered his services to us, and I gratefully accepted. Tug was 5'9" with a stocky build and light brown hair and beard. He could easily have passed for Brett Favre even among the most ardent of Packer fans. He did not much care for wearing a uniform, and most often he wore a ball cap and T-shirt with his Royal Marine cammie bottoms and body armor. As his issued weapon remained in Basra, I provided him with an AK-47. Skilled, mature, funny, and smart, Tug quickly won his place on the team.

Encountering the heavy traffic to his front, Tug bumped the first two vehicles out of his way before becoming completely locked in traffic. To our rear the crowd, now some 150 yards away, continued to close. I told Gunny Hessen, my driver, to shoot around and into the oncoming traffic lane. We, too, quickly became engulfed in the traffic jam. In addition to the crowd closing on us, we were trapped in a sea of cars, any one of which could be a VBIED. Stopped, we were also highly vulnerable to an ambush like the one that had destroyed the Blackwater convoy in Fallujah. The gates to the Green Zone were well known, and very symbolic of Coalition rule in Iraq. The enemy knew that there were very few entrances to the Green Zone, and these choke points were natural places to target American convoys. On a good day we were always aware that there could be VBIEDs loitering about. But on this day, with the large crowd and the situation across Iraq going to shit, I knew I did not want to be stuck in traffic anywhere near the gate. If a VBIED was going to target the gate, with the crowd as cover or as a target, today was as good a day as any. Being stuck, we were a potential target of opportunity. The sound of constant gunfire ripping across Baghdad only further emphasized that we were in a shitty place. We were in a situation that in seconds, even under "normal" conditions, could prove disastrous. Today, we all knew, was not normal. Today was a day in which the stupid, the slow, and the plain unlucky could quickly find their ticket home punched by an AK-47 or an IED.

My mind raced as I scanned the area around me, looking for a way out of the mess we were in. I dismounted my vehicle and ran forward to the jammed intersection. My adrenaline was pumping as I got there. Pounding on the trunks of the vehicles I wanted to push along, I was able to get them to squeeze forward. While painfully slow, they were moving! Turning around, I got the cars traveling behind them in the intersection to stop. Within seconds the intersection was cleared and we were moving again. We pulled into the RC and dismounted our vehicles. Algarin dropped his helmet and wiped the sweat from his brow.

"Wow, Top, did you see that shit, man? Who are those fuckers anyway?"

"Not sure, Starsky. Nobody said shit to me about guys in black PJs and green shit rags."

Tug put his hand on my shoulder, and said, "Master Jack looked like Moses parting the Red Sea, he did." We all enjoyed the laugh. Tug's accent was as funny to us as anything he said.

Hesco called the palace and got in touch with force protection. Force pro told Hesco that the gate was being cleared and that it should be passable within thirty minutes. Playing it safe, Hesco waited until the time had passed and called force protection again and was assured that the gate was cleared. We headed back to the supposedly clear gate. Nearing the gate I saw that it was still impassable. I gave the bad news to Colonel Thomas.

"Hesco. Force pro screwed us. The gate is not, repeat not, passable."

As I passed this information to Hesco I saw something I found hard to believe. An Iraqi man placed a small child of about six years of age in the street. The child sat with his legs crossed Indian style. Next to the child were several others, similarly placed, all in a line. These fucking animals built a roadblock with their children! To our Muslim enemies, disciples of "the religion of peace," a child was just another weapon to be exploited. Children could be used to stop us in kill zones. If we did not stop and ran the child over, then that was okay, too, because then Al Jazeera and their allies at CNN and MSNBC would be sure to show the grim footage, complete with anti-military rhetoric, nonstop. Fortunately for these children, there existed another way for us to get back to the Green Zone.

Looking around and considering how inaccurate the information being given to us by force protection was, I decided to give the other gate a try. "Hesco, I am going to turn around and try the other gate, over."

"Okay, Top, but force pro says that gate is closed, over."

I answered, saying, "I think they have their gates mixed up, and we do not have a better option anyway."

"Roger that," said Hesco in response.

Keying my handset again, I addressed the team. "Vehicles two, three, and rear, maintain your positions and follow in trace of lead, over."

All vehicles rogered up as we turned around and headed back to the intersection that had been so congested before. This time, instead of turning left and having to cut across oncoming traffic, we got in the far right lane, turned right, and went down two blocks before turning right again and sailing through the open gate known as "Baby Assassins."

That night, during our daily debrief, the mood of the team was more somber, reflective, and serious than was normally the case. When the time for questions came, Bo asked one that I knew he did not like having to ask.

"Top, if it had been our safety or those kids, and I am asking this with an eye to the future, what do you want us to do if you're not lead or you're dead?"

Bo was like a big brother to the kids at the RC, and I knew he did not relish the thought of hurting them, let alone killing them.

"I think I know what your answer is, Top, but I think we all need to hear it from you."

"If it ever comes to us or a child, then we will do what we have to do," I said, trying to avoid using the word "kill."

"What exactly is that, Top?" Boeringer pushed.

"If, to save the life of any one of us, you have to kill or run over a kid, you do it. We will all deal with the price later. I would much rather deal with the pain of having killed a child than the pain of losing one of you because I did not act when and how I should have." The war was not only turning more violent and deadly, but it was also turning uglier.

On 5 and 6 April we conducted quick and uneventful runs escorting officers on the suddenly dangerous Route Irish. On 7 April we drew another run to the Baghdad RC. The run was the easiest we had ever made, as the roads were virtually cleared of all traffic. We had all been trained to look for things out of the ordinary, and at the top of the list was the absence of locals. Missing locals almost always preceded an attack. The roads were almost empty of both vehicular traffic and pedestrians.

Not thirty minutes later a man approached the gate separating our positions from the road. He turned toward us and held up a sign in Arabic. He then bowed toward Mecca twice and prayed. He left only to return a short time later and do the same thing. This got our attention. Survivors of suicide bombings report that sometimes there is some sort of prayer said by a bomber or one of his confederates before an attack. The prayer is said to be part of a ritualistic purification process. This process may include the bombers being dressed in white and clean-shaven. But most often the bomber just looks like another Iraqi. Still, the whole incident was unsettling. We also saw numerous buses filled with men in the same black uniforms we had seen at the gate on 4 April. When they drove by the RC, they would look at us like a cat eyeing a mouse. This went on throughout the day. Later we would learn that these were members of something called the Mahdi army, a militia unit loyal to the radical cleric Muqtada Al Sadr. When we got back to the Green Zone, we conducted immediate-action drills at the Crossed Sabers. The drills were endless and marked an attempt by us to train for every imaginable contingency. We all knew, however, that these drills were just a start. In a real fight we very well might see something that we had never anticipated. If that happened, we would be relying on our training, our bravery, and our esprit, our belief in and love for each other. No matter what happened, if things went really bad, we knew we had each other.

After we had completed our drills and secured our vehicles and weapons, we returned to the operations center. It was obvious that something had gone very wrong. There was a lot of discussion between the battle captains about something of a disaster in Fallujah. At first I was very concerned about the marines fighting there, but I could not imagine anything these people could do to marines that would precipitate a disaster. I asked Colonel Thomas what was going on. Details were sketchy. What he did know was that a convoy was taking an Iraqi infantry battalion to Fallujah to help in the fight to clear that city. The convoy included a small number of marine advisors assigned to the battalion. En route the convoy had been hit very hard by insurgent forces, and there were both American and Iraqi casualties. Nothing else was known.

What we learned later would sicken us. Major General Paul Eaton had decided to push this Iraqi battalion into battle though its marine advisors did not think it was ready. Eaton claimed that this decision was his to make alone, but I have always suspected he was under some pressure to make the bloody fight for Fallujah an Iraqi and American fight for political reasons. The war was not popular at home, and now marines were dying in an effort to liberate an Iraqi city from the insurgent and terrorist forces that held it. Americans wanted to know why their marines were doing all the fighting. Where was this new Iraqi army they had heard so much about? Wherever the decision was made, whether by Eaton or much higher, the result was a disaster. When the insurgents hit the convoy outside Fallujah, most of the new Iraqi army soldiers fled. One marine, Sergeant Oscar Powers, who would later become a part-time member of the team, said that all the Arab Iraqi soldiers on his truck fled. The Kurds did not. They were manning a PKM machine gun, and they were burning down lots of people. If it moved, Powers said, they shot it. But while the Kurds, marines, and some of the Arab members of the new Iraqi army fought, they were not enough. The battalion suffered light casualties, but the psychological damage was severe. The unit never reached Fallujah and was, in fact, destroyed as an effective fighting force. There was one more attempt to get the battalion into the fight. That night commanders tried to force the remnants of the battalion onto helicopters for a night insertion outside Fallujah. The battalion had *never* trained for helicopter operations, let alone night ops in helicopters, and they understandably refused to do it.

Eaton would later, manfully, take all the blame for the disaster, but I am not sure that it was all his to take. In the end it really did not matter. Not only had that Iraqi battalion lost its resolve, so, too, had the president of the United States. Mercifully for ourselves, and especially for the marines fighting in Fallujah, we were unaware of all of this as we bedded down on the night of 7 April. Next day we had a cargo escort mission scheduled to Quervo, a forward operating base just outside Baghdad. None of us knew what to expect.

CHAPTER 8

Gunfight

The eighth of April 2004 is a day that will live in the collective memory of the Majestic Twelve for the rest of our lives. A small part of Islam was destroyed, wiped from the earth in a matter of seconds, just as easily as one would kill any vermin. The day was to prove to be one of the best of my life.

The morning started like any other in Iraq. I got up, shaved, put on my uniform, and went to chow. While there, I overheard a conversation between two army officers. They were talking about new rules of engagement (ROE) and how they were radically different than what had been in force. In fact, it sounded too good to be true. The ROE outlines the conditions under which we can use deadly force, and are different from operation to operation. Sometimes they are absurdly restrictive, like the ROE with which the marines operated in Beirut in 1982–1983, when they could not even carry loaded weapons while on guard duty. Other times they are extremely complex, like the ROE for Kosovo in 1999. The best, from the grunt's point of view, are those that are simple and allow him to protect himself when he feels threatened. We had that kind of ROE in Iraq.

But this morning I was hearing that the ROE had changed to one of the most aggressive employed by U.S. forces in some time. I quickly left chow and ran to ask our J-2 (intelligence section) to check the rumor out. Lieutenant

Colonel Vic Sarna, the J-2 officer, was not in, but Staff Sergeant Libby was. I asked him to confirm what I had heard and then rushed off to ops, where Huggy Bear and Gunny Hessen were waiting for me. I told the two of them and Hesco what I had heard, and we all agreed that it was too good to be true. We also agreed that if the ROE had actually changed, then it represented a big shift in how we were going to fight this war.

While I was still discussing the implications of all of this with Huggy and Hessen, Libby returned with Sergeant Melissa Garate, U.S. Army, and Sarna. They confirmed that CJTF-7 had issued a new ROE that reflected what I had overheard earlier. Pushing aside my concern that nobody, incredibly inexplicable as that was, in my chain of command was aware of the change in ROE, which was of a strategic magnitude, until I made them aware of it, I quickly had Reed gather the team so that we could brief them on the change. Within twenty minutes Reed had assembled the team in the vault, where we could brief them on the new ROE without fear of being overheard by our Iraqi counterparts.

First we told them that this was not to be mentioned outside the office because we did not want the Iraqis to know about it. There always existed the possibility that some of them were not the good guys they appeared to be, and we certainly did not want them letting their friends on the other side know that it was now open season on them and that there was no bag limit. Secondly, we did not want the new ROE mentioned to other shops, because sometimes Americans have big mouths and the guys not going on the road did not need to know about the new ROE. After telling everybody that this was classified, I turned the floor over to Libby and Garate. The two intelligence specialists then gave us the ROE verbatim. They then gave us an ROE class, which presented various scenarios. For example, you are riding in a convoy when you notice a man holding an AK-47 standing on the sidewalk: Do you shoot or not? In this example, the answer is no, for many Iraqi companies employ guards armed with AK-47s to protect their businesses from crime. In still another scenario, a man wearing an Iraqi army uniform points an AK-47 at you: Do you shoot or not? The scenarios could be endless and further complicated by variations. At the end of each scenario, the Maji were asked a simple question: "Shoot or don't shoot?" The correct answer to some problems was "Shoot," and to others it was "Don't shoot."

My Maji Knights and I felt like we were unleashed Dogs of War. Someone was going to die today, and we were going to be the instrument of that death.

We had a run to pick up two Coalition officers scheduled for 1400 to Camp Quervo, which is just east of Baghdad and barely outside the city limits. The trip should only take twenty minutes there and twenty back. The hours between the ROE briefing and our 1400 run passed very slowly. I spent the time thinking about all the Mahdi we had seen just days before. If the same thing happened today, we were going to be up to our knees in spent brass and blood. The more I contemplated what might happen, the more disgusted I became with what had not happened over the past few days. Had I been given the new ROE immediately, we would have killed hundreds of Mahdi militiamen at the RC and just outside the gate to the Green Zone. That they had so freely strutted about told me that either the ROE was so secret as to be useless or, as I strongly suspected, most army units in Baghdad simply refused to follow it. My guys looked at the ROE as a gift, and we had every intention of following it ruthlessly. Baghdad, indeed most of Iraq, was embroiled in the heaviest fighting of the war.

No place in Iraq was worse than the road to the airport. Route Irish, once so secure, was now a shooting gallery, with several attacks on it every day. They came in every form, from complex multi arms (IEDs or VBIEDs followed by RPGs, and machine gun and AK fire) to simple drive-bys. It lacked reason, and it just seemed that the violence exploding across Iraq had as its focus Route Irish. Maybe it was because the route was an important link between the Green Zone and the airport. Maybe it was because the enemy knew important men traveled the route. We were not sure why Route Irish was so hot, but clearly it was no longer a mere training run for us. This increased enemy activity in our own backyard made it seem certain that it was only a matter of time before we had a run-in with the enemy. Maybe today would be our day!

At 1300, we began prepping our vehicles and weapons. On any run, this is always an exciting time. Pistols and rifles are given a once-over by their owners and then a quick functions check is performed to ensure that every weapon is operating as it should. No detail is too small or insignificant. While I was a recruit at the Parris Island Recruit Depot in beautiful, sunny, South Carolina, I learned the value of making sure my weapon functioned properly. My platoon had been assigned the task of defending a perimeter during a field training exercise. It was a miserable time. It rained every day and it was extremely hot and humid, as August in the Carolinas always is. Late one night we were attacked by one of our sister platoons. I engaged a few targets and then, as I attempted to pull the trigger again, I got a loud metallic click instead of the expected bang. The click serves as a very audible, unmistakable notice that your weapon has malfunctioned. Even in training there is no more heart-sinking sound than that of a metallic click when the trigger is pulled.

I immediately dropped down in my fighting hole and attempted to clear my weapon and get it back in firing order. Unfortunately, the recruit in the hole with me took cover as well, so nobody was defending our position. Within seconds, a drill instructor was standing on the edge of our fighting hole spraying both of us with a burst of automatic fire, and telling us how fucking stupid and useless we were. It was a very miserable feeling. When a weapon fails to fire in training, no warrior ever forgets it. That same simple failure in combat could cost you your life. It is a lesson that has never been lost on me since that humiliating moment on a sultry night in a Carolina pine forest so long ago.

Once the weapons check is done, everybody inserts a magazine into the weapon and chambers a round. After chambering a round, the soldier or marine will check to ensure that the weapon is on safe. On this day I was more acutely aware than normal that the round, a 5.56mm lead projectile sheathed in copper and capable (when fired) of traveling at over 3,150 feet per second, might lay waste some shitbag with an AK. I hoped so. With every part of my being, I hoped so. For every insult not addressed, for the murder of every innocent not avenged, I hoped that today was our day.

At 1330 we linked up with the armored gun trucks provided by the 1st Cavalry. This unit was new and had only been in country for about two weeks. The commander of the detail was a very young second lieutenant. He gave his brief, which included tactical details, formation, routes, radio frequencies, and the ROE. To my surprise, the ROE he briefed was not the current ROE. Pushing, I asked him if there were any changes to the ROE. He replied, "No, none that I am aware of." I then told him that we had been briefed on a new ROE and that the portion of his brief that covered the ROE was incorrect. At that moment a first lieutenant, a member of the junior officer's unit, stepped in and said to the younger lieutenant, "You know what this is about." The two officers then told me that, yes, in fact, they were aware of the new ROE but that they would not be operating under it because of the nature of their mission. I reminded both men that the commander of CJTF-7, Lieutenant General Ricardo Sanchez, issued the ROE and that the ROE clearly stated that it was not to be modified, in any way, for any reason, by subordinate units. In fact, the commander of CJTF-7 had once said that when you see the enemy, you have two choices, "Kill him or capture him."

While the commander of CJTF-7 was an army general, it seemed that he was an army of one. That day would not be the only time I would observe a total obsession on the part of some army units with *avoiding* combat at all costs. Now I knew why the Mahdi strolled about Baghdad wearing their uniforms as if they hadn't a care in the world. The ROE was not reduced to being useless by its secret nature; it was useless because some army officers flatly refused to follow it. Time and again, 1st Cavalry units would use the "unique" nature of their mission as a reason to avoid dismounting and killing the enemy wherever and whenever he was seen. In fact, I believe that obsession went almost army wide. The insurgents the marines were in combat with on a daily basis in Ramadi and Fallujah did not just appear in April. They had been operating in those areas for nearly a year before the marines returned to Iraq, but the U.S. Army preferred to remain on its FOBs and send the occasional armored patrol down a street or two. The army's famed 82nd Airborne, which had responsibility for the Anbar Province before turning it over to the marines, did little to secure it, and contrary to remarks by their commanding general about the marines finding few enemy in Anbar, they had found thousands.

The largest battle fought in the year that the marines had been out of Iraq was an ambush on a convoy that left dozens of Iraqis dead. After the marines returned, clashes in Fallujah, Ramadi, and Najaf claimed the lives of thousands of Iraqis. Marines locate, close with, and destroy the enemy. We do not let him shoot at us and run away. We do not let him plant IEDs with impunity. But the army is very different. The units of the U.S. Army we operated with were representative and dispelled any doubts we may have had about the nature of the army in Iraq. I am not alone in my assessment. A CIA officer quoted in an April 2004 issue of *U.S. News and World Report* would say, "What is going on now [April 2004] in Fallujah should have happened a year ago." In the art of avoiding combat, the Cav had no equals, and today they would demonstrate their mastery of that art. The two army officers remained adamant that they would not follow the new ROE.

"That's fine, gentlemen," I answered, "but I have every intention of following the ROE, and you need to understand that."

The two officers exchanged a quizzical look but said nothing. It was not a good thing to have two elements operating in the same mission with different ROEs. It was a potentially lethal flaw, but I was not going to run away simply because that was what these guys were determined to do. While my people loaded our three SUVs, I walked past each vehicle and asked some questions about the ROE to ensure that they still fully understood the CJTF-7 rules we were going to be operating under. As I asked these questions, I also ensured that I gave each member of the team "love." Algarin never accepted the simple expression of love offered in our now traditional, premission fist-to-fist greeting. He would rock back, place both hands on his hips, and say, "I know you can do better than that." Then he would lean in for a hug. In reality the premission ritual was very important to us. The fist-to-fist was always accompanied by some words of encouragement. Taken together, the greeting told each member of the team that we were all in it together, and no matter how bad things got, someone would always have their back. Finally, we all knew that each premission greeting might be the last act of friendship and love we would ever receive on this earth. As such, the ritual was as profound as it was sincere. After walking the line, I returned to my vehicle. Before departing the Green Zone, we did one final radio check and then I addressed my people.

"You guys all volunteered for this job. You have earned for yourselves a reputation that would be the envy of any unit operating in Iraq. That you have done so with almost no support from higher, that you have done so without even the most basic gear, that you have done so without armor or proper weapons, is all a testimony to your courage and skill as warriors. But if you fuck up today, if you fail at the decisive moment, none of that is going to matter. Remember, it's always about us. We win and they die. We come home and they don't go home. How we live the next thirty minutes will say everything about who and what we are. You might not have any choice in when you die, but you sure as shit do in how you die." With that, I looked at my driver, Corporal Napier, and said, "Roll."

With me that day were Sergeant First Class Shenk, Staff Sergeant Reed, Sergeants Boeringer, Algarin, Williams, Facemyer, and Balan; Corporals Meggison and Napier, as well as Lance Corporal Dann. In the lead vehicle was Reed; the driver, Facemyer; right-front passenger, Williams, who was behind Reed, and Meggison, who was seated next to Williams. Algarin was behind the wheel of the second vehicle, known as vehicle 2. Riding shotgun in vehicle 2 was Boeringer. Behind Algarin sat Balan, and next to him was Shenk. In the rear vehicle with me were Napier and Dann.

At approximately 1430 we departed the safety of the Green Zone and headed toward Quervo. It was a perfect day. No clouds in the sky and temperatures in the mid eighties. While more tense than most trips, nothing out of the ordinary occurred until the lead vehicle, a Cav gun truck, made a wrong turn off the freeway and back into Baghdad. I keyed my handset and asked my lead driver if the lieutenant had just missed his turn.

"Huggy Bear, this is Stonewall. Did we just hit a wrong turn, over?"

"Negative, I think we are okay, Stonewall," Reed replied.

"You sure?" I asked.

It soon became clear to us all that the lieutenant leading the way was lost. More important, we could see very large crowds gathered in the streets.

We passed dozens of people who showed their contempt and loathing of us. This was different, and because it was, it was alarming. While many Iraqis were very friendly to us, they were most often indifferent. But openly hostile crowds had not been seen until a few days before. How was it, I wondered, that our intel didn't know of this? Or if they did, why were we not warned? Considering that most if not all of us, from lance corporal to master sergeant, saw it coming, how was it that the people paid to see these things did not? We knew something was coming simply because things had been so very different in late March, and in Iraq we knew that anything different was not good. We lacked the ability to put the pieces together; the people who got paid to do that, our intelligence professionals at the national level, had failed us. With each passing yard it became increasingly apparent that we were in a bad part of town. Or maybe every part of Baghdad was now a bad place to be if you were an American. I thought back to the jubilant crowds when we hauled down Saddar's statue and I wondered, how did we get here? For several minutes we drove into parts of the city that I had not seen before, and we appeared to be going ever deeper into "Indian country."

Eventually, the lieutenant figured out he was as lost as Amelia Earhart, and he turned the convoy around. As we slowly maneuvered in the busy street, more angry people gathered. Some of these people were shouting at us, but we could not understand what they were saying. It was obvious that they hated us, and it was just as obvious that we were extremely vulnerable. Our vehicles, unlike those of the Cav, lacked armor. Our only protection from enemy action was speed. Stopped as we were, waiting for the lieutenant to get everything turned around, we had *no* protection. If we were going to be stopped for a long time, I would have ordered the team to dismount, but as I did not anticipate the turnaround taking long, I got on the net and said, "Pop hatches." With those words, everybody opened their doors and got ready for whatever might come. If we took fire, we would now be able to more easily identify the source of that fire, dismount, and kill everyone who needed to be killed. The simple act of opening our doors and readying ourselves for action also let the enemy, who was surely watching us, know that unlike the victims in waiting, sitting snugly in their armored Hummers, we were not to be fucked with. At the same time, if the need to dismount did not materialize, we would not have the delay of recovering our dismounts once we got turned around. It was a half solution, which I felt best addressed the tactical situation. Tactics are always about trade-offs. Finally, we were turned around and headed back toward the highway, but everything remained very tense. More people seemed to have gathered. Off to the right, I noticed something that I had not seen earlier, a large tent that appeared to be a Mahdi army recruiting center.

The tent, about fifty meters off the road, was set in the center of a large vacant field littered with trash. (Every square inch of Baghdad not occupied by a building was covered with reeking piles of garbage.) Gathered outside of this tent were vendors of every type and large numbers of young men. Green, black, and red flags fluttered, by the dozens, in the afternoon breeze. A loud-speaker blared. While I could not understand what was said, from the volume and the intensity of the man's voice I was certain the man was encouraging the locals to kill Americans as he damned both our president and our nation. In actuality, however, nothing about what the man was saying or how he was saying it was really that unusual. Loud speakers blared constantly in Iraq and they almost always carried the voices at seemingly angry men. But when considered with the banners having Al Sadr's image plastered on them, and the three lines of men outside the tent, I thought we might have stumbled on a Mahdi army recruiting center. Each of these lines was neatly covered down on a desk at which sat a man. I suspected that these men might be Mahdi army recruiters. The Mahdi army is a militia loyal to Muqtada Al Sadr, a cleric who hated the United States. Saddam's forces killed his father and it is a shame they missed his Jabba the Hutt–like son. Muqtada was a very ugly man, a fat ball of humanity with the raggedy beard of a hobo. He was never going to make the cover of *GQ*. I was not sure if he was fond of wearing his trademark long black man dresses because they were the traditional garb of his faith and position in that faith or if he simply wore them for the reason fat men wore muumuus. The motto of the Mahdi army was "Serve and Die." Young Mahdi militiamen were not paid, there were no commissaries or medical benefits, and clearly, judging by Muqtada's British-like smile, there was no dental plan. We were determined to help these eager young recruits fulfill their terms of service by killing them. Maybe "Serve and Die" meant to serve, retire, and *then* die of old age, but as any American knows, you had better look at the fine print before you sign.

As we passed the tent, my radio came alive with reports of sightings of enemy personnel. Reed was the first to spot them.

"What do I do?"

"Huggy, if you see them, you fucking kill them, over."

"Roger, Top."

With each second, things only grew more tense as we pushed our way back toward the highway. Napier was eyeing the large and hostile crowds but seemed more bored than alarmed. "Top, look at all these fucking jokers. Jokers look like they want to play. I'll play with these bitches."

"Yeah, Naps, I think these people want our asses."

We were now barely moving forward.

"Top, we have Mahdi up here on the left, about a hundred meters out. What do you want us to do, over?" It was Reed again.

I hesitated. I knew that after I made the call to engage, especially since the two armored Humvees in the lead were content to leave the enemy alone, a lot of people safely locked away behind the walls of the palace were going to have questions. "Why did you shoot them?" "Why did you dismount?" "Did you consider how they felt about being shot?" What I did not know then was that some of these people would end up hating all of us, in part, for what I was about to do. I also realized that it was I who had brought my people to this point and that any course of action contrary to what I had given them every reason to believe they could expect from me would represent a betrayal of trust and confidence of incredible proportions. In the end, that trust and confidence meant more to me than any fears about my career. At no point did I worry about return fire. Being sent home in a box seemed a far more remote possibility than being sent home in handcuffs.

Reed was waiting for an answer. I keyed the handset and said the words I wish could be my epitaph. Very slowly and deliberately I said, "Take them."

Now only fifty meters ahead of vehicle 1, I could see several Mahdi army personnel. Sergeant Williams, sitting in the left side of the lead vehicle, would be the first person to engage unless the soldiers in the armored gun trucks, who, by virtue of being in front, would have the first chance to engage, opened fire first. I doubted they would do so, as killing the enemy seemed to be far less important to them than avoiding trouble. They reminded me of the cowering men seen in some western movies. They were like the character who said, "We don't want no trouble." Not wanting trouble, the Cav rolled by the Mahdi without firing a shot. Will would not give them the same break. He had picked out his target when his vehicle was still some fifty yards away from the Mahdi "soldiers" and tracked him as he drew closer. Weapon in his shoulder, weapon off safe, and finger on the trigger, Will lined up his sights on a man's chest. In what seemed an eternity to him, Will maintained his sights on his target as the meters between the two of them melted away. As soon as Reed heard me give the green light to engage, he brought his vehicle to a stop. The sudden screech of the tires gripping the hot asphalt in their drive to stop the forward momentum of the vehicle caught the attention of Will's intended target and some of his friends. In one of life's ironies, the targeted hadji (a derisive term used by soldiers and marines to refer to enemy personnel) looked up just in time to see Will's rifle pointed at him. At that moment, I suspect he knew that today there would be no jihad. His eyes locked on to those of Sergeant Williams in a wordless plea for his life. It did not work. As Reed stopped his vehicle, he screamed, "Engage your targets." The first round was already on the way.

Everything in our professional and personal lives would be different from this moment forward.

Sergeant Williams rocked back into his seat when the SUV stopped. Leaning into his weapon, he slowly squeezed the trigger of his AK-47 one time. It was enough. The rifle functioned as designed, and a single 7.62 mm bullet left the barrel at about 2,600 feet per second. In no time, it crossed the distance between Will and his target and smashed into the left side of the man's chest. The bullet smashed through ribs and muscle and pulverized the soft tissue of the left lung before exploding the heart and punching its way through the right lung. The hadji was dead before he hit the ground. By the time he fell I had pulled within fifteen yards of him and the look on his face was one I shall never forget.

When the bullet that killed him hit, the hadji's face contorted with the agony of having been shot, but something other than pain was also clear on his young face—fear and surprise. Only moments before, he was a proud jihadist, wearing a black shirt and pants and a green headband, with a green sash about his waist, the "uniform" of the Mahdi army. He carried an AK-47, and he strutted with an arrogance and contempt for American might, born of the belief, false as it turned out, that he was perfectly safe. The Americans, after all, had no stomach for killing eyeball to eyeball, and as long as he played it cool, he could flaunt his uniform, his weapon, and his hatred of the United States without fear. Don't do anything too outlandish and the Americans will tolerate insults and murders heaped one on top of another. His was the face of jihad.

Next to him, another man carried their battle flag high above his head. On this day they had the misfortune of having a convoy take the wrong turn and, by so doing, bring them into direct contact with men who wanted to kill them. There would be a reckoning, and when the bell tolled, it would not be for the hated Americans. The dying would all be on one side. Will's kill would only be the first of many. The look on the hadji's face was a look shared by all of his comrades. Suddenly, to "Serve and Die" did not seem as romantic as the recruiter had made it sound. Suddenly, all those virgins waiting in the afterlife looked a lot less enticing than the most wretched Baghdad slut or the tried-and-true goat. This was the shock and awe the air force always talked about but liked to deliver only from afar. Fear, surprise, and then nothing. Will's man pitched forward in the filth of his beloved Baghdad.

Sergeant Williams screamed, "I got him! I got him!" It was only the beginning. Just prior to giving the word to engage the enemy, Colonel Thomas had called me on my cell phone. I provided him with a quick report as our situation developed. Hesco was still on the line when the shooting started. I threw the phone to Napier and said, "Here, you talk to him," as I dismounted. Instead, Napier also dismounted, leaving my phone, still open, in the front seat. Hesco heard the first shots ring out and, turning to the rest of the C-3, said, "Oh my God, they're in a firefight." My phone stayed open during the entire fight.

As we dismounted our vehicles, all Iraqi traffic moving in the opposite lanes stopped, providing no cover for the enemy. The traffic on our side of the road stopped behind us. The "arena" was cleared. Nothing lay between us and the enemy except fifteen yards of road.

While there was no cover for those men directly in front of us, there was some behind them. Less than thirty meters behind the small cluster of men to our direct front was a small field covered with high grass, which exceeded the height of a man. Behind this grass, and all along that side of the road, were several buildings. Most of these buildings appeared to be family dwellings. First we engaged those targets to our direct front as these men were both the most obvious targets and, potentially, if allowed to recover from the shock of our action, the most dangerous to us. We put out a heavy volume of fire, most of it directed at this small group of men. We had some fire coming in from our front, but it was not from these men. Whether this came from the buildings behind the grass or somewhere else, I never knew. It all happened very quickly, but I remember thinking that the incoming fire was not as heavy as I expected it should be.

When that first shot struck their friend, the survivors had stood, in stunned silence, around the dead man, as if trying to figure out what had happened to him. Slowly, far too slowly, the horrible truth seemed to dawn on them. As we dismounted, they looked up, and they saw what was coming just as their now dead friend had. They, too, knew that today they were going to die. Eyes fixed, mouths agape, most offered very little resistance as they were cut down in a cyclone of American lead. Pathetically, they had attempted to hide behind a guardrail. Other men fell behind the guardrail after having been shot, and this group of dead, dying, or simply cowering men drew our full attention as there was no one left standing in front of us. We continued to pour fire into this group, and as we did so the sound of our rounds ripping through the steel guardrail sounded like a pinball machine, *ping, ping, ping, ding, ding, ding*. There, standing in the middle of a Baghdad highway, wearing our cammies, body armor, and distinctive kaffiyehs (Arab headdress) around our necks, and with only our vehicles for cover, we, in the words of Facemyer, dispensed justice. Unlike the farce that American justice has become, our justice was swift. We cut down every man in front of us within seconds. The men who had only moments before been enjoying a walk with their buddies now lay dead or dying. I can only imagine how we must have looked to the dumbfounded Iraqi motorists. Here were heavily armed Americans destroying a Mahdi army squad coolly and methodically. Using the engine block of my Suburban for cover, I had fired over the hood of my vehicle into the human mass directly in front of me. To my immediate right, Sergeant Williams was still "dealing it" with his AK, which he had, sometime earlier, affectionately named "Crazy Ivan."

Farther to my right, Face, Reed, Algarin, Boeringer, Meggison, Balan, and Shenk did the same. All were using the cover provided by their vehicles. Only my driver was different. Standing dangerously exposed on his side of the Suburban, with no cover except that provided by his open door, Napier emptied his M-9 Beretta pistol at the enemy. He looked more like a gang "banger" than anything else. But he was lethal. Watching the men in front of us die was like watching a hurricane blow down trees but without the pity you feel for destroyed trees. They went down in mass with multiple impacts from powerful weapons fired at a range of fifteen meters. Contrary to Hollywood special effects, I did not see great geysers of blood explode with each impact.

Blood was not apparent until the dead men hit the ground and it oozed or sprayed out of them. Headshots caused the body to jerk, drop like a rock, and go stiff with exaggerated movements. Within seconds, all movement to our direct front had ceased, but we were now taking fire from the right. This fire was increasing in intensity. Multiple impacts bounced off the street, and some shots zipped through the air. The fire seemed to be coming from the field of tall grass. I shifted my point of aim to a spot in the tall grass that seemed to be "waving" as a weapon was fired from behind that spot. I fired off a few rounds at this spot and this seemed to reduce the fire coming from the field. Whether I hit the man or not, I did not know; I was not even certain anyone was in the area I was shooting at. After suppressing the field, I rolled to the rear of my Suburban and engaged targets on our left.

Minimum fire was coming from our left, and there were no targets in the open. I believed that the incoming might have come from the buildings near the road. At one point I lined my sights up on a man who had just been felled by fire. As he hit the dirt, he lay on his side with his back to me. He was still moving, trying to roll over onto his back, when I acquired him as a target, but he stopped moving before I fired at him. I quickly scanned for other targets, and seeing none, I shifted my position once more, this time to the Hummer behind my vehicle, and assumed a firing position over its hood.

It was only then that any member of our escort opened fire. The effort was too late, and too little as well. Only the two soldiers on the left side of the Hummer fired their weapons. At no point did any member of the escort dismount. They all seemed content to remain under armor. The enemy fire from the left continued, but it was high, with several rounds hitting a light pole, which the Hummer was parked next to. Still other rounds, coming from somewhere I could not locate, impacted the street we were standing in. I heard two rounds crack by my right shoulder, and then I saw a man wearing a white shirt break from the scant cover provided by the shoulder of the road and run, as fast as he could, for the safety of the tall grass behind him. In his left hand he carried an AK with a folding stock or maybe no stock. I lined my ACOG up on his right shoulder as he ran away from me, crossing from my left to my right. I fired three rounds and he went down. By this time, however, he was the only target visible, and I am certain that I was not the only one shooting at him. As soon as he broke cover, there was a significant increase in the volume of our fire. Given the ruthless efficiency with which my Maji had killed this man's friends, I was certain they were all locked on to him. It was like dropping chum into shark-infested waters. It was a feeding frenzy. Everybody wanted a piece of this guy. He died in a hail of gunfire, falling forward heavily. If he had been the subject of an autopsy, the variety and number of projectiles that found their way into this guy's body would have impressed the coroner. There was probably some 9 mm and 7.62 mm in addition to 5.56 mm. If we had been equipped with RPGs and AT-4 rocket launchers at the time, I am sure we would have let fly with these as well. When all incoming fire had stopped and there was no longer any movement to our front, I gave the order to cease fire. I shouted the order and gave the corresponding hand and arm signal. A few more shots rang out, and then everything was perfectly quiet and still.

I moved forward of the Humvee and observed the scene to my front. The ground was covered with Iraqi dead. Pools of blood spread beneath the crumpled forms. Nothing moved, no one spoke, or if they did, I did not hear them. For a moment, a very brief moment, I thought about searching the dead, but I quickly abandoned the idea. Turning back to our convoy, I asked the occupants of the Hummer nearest me who the senior ranking soldier was.

"I am, Sergeant."

The soldier, a black staff sergeant, stepped out of the front seat of the lead Hummer.

"Are all your people accounted for?" I asked.

"Let me check," he replied.

The staff sergeant yelled back to his trail vehicle, asking if they were up on people. They were. I then got on the net and confirmed that all of my personnel were also accounted for.

"Huggy, Huggy, are you up on all personnel and equipment, over?"

"Stonewall, this is Huggy. All personnel are up and gear accounted for," Reed answered.

"Roger, Huggy. How about you, Starsky?" I asked Algarin.

Algarin answered, "We are up and up, Top."

"Huggy, haul ass until we catch the rest of the gun trucks," I instructed Reed.

We had not gone very far, maybe a mile, when more shots rang out from the right. One of these rounds struck my second vehicle, almost dead center of the windshield. I could see two individuals almost standing by the side of the road. One of them had what looked like a pistol, and the other appeared unarmed, but he was wearing the distinctive headband of the Mahdi army. By the time the second vehicle was hit, lead was already on top of the two Mahdi militiamen. Reed gently slowed his vehicle to allow Face to drill both men with surgical precision. The man with the pistol was hit twice, dead center of his chest, and his comrade was shot once very high in the chest. Both dropped immediately and were already down when my vehicle pulled to a stop at the point where both men had dropped out of sight. Reed had brought the lead vehicle to a stop only a few yards distant and sideways, across the road. I dismounted and quickly ran to the spot where I had seen the men fall. Looking down, I could see small drops of blood on the ground were the two men had been standing. Looking farther down the steep embankment, I could see two men, apparently dead. Beneath them, the ground appeared to be dark with what I assumed was their blood.

I wanted to go down and examine the men more closely, but we were taking more fire from the right by this time. I attempted to locate the source of this fire, but I could not. It appeared to be quite distant, and I did not hear or see any impacts in my area. I quickly remounted and told Reed to hit it and to not stop until we caught the gun trucks. I was tempted to abandon them and just get everybody else back to the Green Zone. It was the gun trucks that left us, so why did I owe them anything? Why attempt to catch them as they fled? No matter how pissed I was at the lieutenant, it just seemed wrong to abandon them even if they had done it to us. After several miles we finally caught up to lead. I keyed my handset and told Reed: "Huggy, that's them, pulled off to the right. Pull us in behind that asshole."

Once he had pulled off, I got out and went to go see the young lieutenant. Reed accompanied me.

"Hey, sir, how are your guys?" I asked the young officer.

"We're fine, we're all fine. How about yours?"

"We're up sir," I answered. I continued, "Sir, what do you want to do now? You want to head back to the palace or continue the mission?"

He was unsure how we should proceed. I told him that I felt we should turn around and go back to the Green Zone. He ultimately decided that we might as well continue the mission since we were very near Quervo anyway. That was fine. What was not fine and in fact very disquieting was the officer's demeanor. He was clearly shaken and it appeared that he had been crying. It was so bad and so obvious that I felt compelled to ask him a simple question.

"Sir, are you all right?"

"Yes, yes, I am. I am fine."

He did not look fine at all. He was a wreck, and as things turned out, he would be of no use to us today. As I walked back to my vehicle, Reed could not resist poking fun at the poor lieutenant. Putting his thumb in his mouth and rocking his head back and forth, Reed mockingly intoned, "This is not happening. *This* is not happening."

Not willing to let a chance at taking a shot at the army slip by, I teased Reed. "Hey, 'an army of one.' "

Feigning hurt feelings, Reed answered, "Oh man, Top, that shit really hurt, man."

We remounted our SUVs and followed the lieutenant into Quervo. There we left the lieutenant and his boys in the exchange parking lot while we went to pick up the two Coalition officers, a Spaniard and a Brit. Once we located the CMATT building where the two officers were quartered, a wild and spontaneous celebration broke out among us. It all seemed so very incredible. We were *alive*! We were alive, and ten men lay dead in our wake. It was a feeling of euphoria that I had never felt before, or since. We hugged each other, and we shouted obscenities about our enemies while at the same time praising ourselves for having killed them.

Combat is a very primal thing. War is the greatest of all human experiences. In war a man will know and experience joy, fear, love, hate, and courage in a way that nothing else but war can show him. War is exciting. War is the source of the greatest adrenaline high known to man. We had known fear, and yet we had acted in spite of that fear. We knew the soul-cleansing power of courage overcoming fear. We had exercised the ultimate power given to man, that of life and death. We had killed. We had killed efficiently and ruthlessly, without pity or mercy. But none of these elements, by themselves or taken together, is what made our war one of such great joy. What made this an incredibly joyous moment for us was that it had come free of charge.

Most often, a man's natural love of war is tempered by the loss of friends. Just as surely as war causes a man to inflict great violence on his fellow man, it also teaches him more about love than any relationship formed outside combat ever will. In combat, men survive, units function, and nations stand, not because of a soldier's blood lust, but because of the soldier's love. Concepts such as "country" become very distant when a man is thrown into combat. Patriotism is good enough to get a man into uniform, but what sustains him through the danger and dehumanizing violence of war is love. The love of comrades is the greatest love known to man. We were in a state of euphoria not simply because we had killed but because the people who meant the most in the world to us were alive. We had won! Whoever said that in war there are no winners, only losers, is a liar. At its most visceral, war is all about winners and losers. Today we survived, and we were, thus, the clear winners. The ten men who died were the losers. They lost everything they knew, family, friends, pets, *everything*! The only thing worse than being killed in a war is to be killed in a war your country does not win. For the moment, all of that did not matter; all that mattered was that all of us were still breathing.

Once the wild celebration died down and the team stopped debating who killed whom, we got back to business. I sent Corporal Meggison to locate the two officers we were sent to retrieve while I attempted to find a phone from which I could call the palace and let them know that we were okay. My own shit-ass cell phone could not reach the palace even though we were just outside Baghdad. I had asked the lieutenant to do this before we left him at the exchange, but his radio was down, too. Quervo had a satellite phone that I was able to locate, but it had no charge. Some sack of shit had used the phone to call his loved ones back home and failed to recharge the thing. I had no problem with the phones being used this way, but you really should make sure you recharge your only means of voice communication with the world outside. I would not be able to raise the palace until we were back in Baghdad, and even then my ability to communicate with them was hit-or-miss.

Everybody had known for some time that our communications gear was a total joke, of questionable reliability on their best days. The problem was that there simply was no money for real communications equipment. We ate very well and lived in air-conditioned trailers complete with TVs, DVDs, and re-frigerators, but we did not have the money for armor, crew-served weapons, M-4s, or radios. It was a joke! From the top down, everybody in CMATT just hoped it would never become an issue.

After we picked up our two Coalition officers we linked up with the lieu-tenant. One thing became an immediate concern: The two officers were driv-ing a vehicle that had much less than a quarter of a tank of gasoline in it. This would not be a problem so long as we did not become lost. But given what I had already witnessed, I thought it highly likely that we would lose our way. I was so concerned that when we linked up with the Cav, I offered the lieuten-ant the option of letting my lead vehicle take over the navigation.

The young officer, now seeming much more composed, said that he did not think that would be necessary as his platoon sergeant was familiar with the way back. I pulled out my map and laid it on the hood of the lieutenant's Hummer.

"Which route are we taking back, sir?"

The lieutenant called over his platoon sergeant and had him show me the route. Both men pointed out the route we most often took, and both seemed confident that they knew it. If all went well, we would be back within the Green Zone in about twenty-five minutes at most.

"Okay, sir," I said. "Looks great. Give me a few minutes and we will be ready to go. By the way, I have one additional vehicle with two packs, both Coalition officers. Their vehicle has less than a quarter of a tank of gas, but they are sure it is more than enough to get back to the palace."

"Okay, just let me know when you are ready to go," the young officer an-swered.

Before we left the safety of Quervo, I reminded everyone that we needed to forget the shooting and focus on getting home or the next celebration might not be ours. I also passed the word that the British vehicle had very little fuel and that it might become necessary to abandon it and cross load the personnel and weapons as well as classified material that the British officer, a colonel, was carrying.

I told my team: "If we have to cross load the Brit vehicle, my vehicle will conduct the cross load while one and two pull security."

Lastly, I assigned Sergeant Balan to the British vehicle so that they would have additional firepower. As we left Quervo, I gave one more warning for everybody to remain alert and pay attention to what was going on around us. As it would turn out, this was sound advice. The trip started out fine. We left Quervo and crossed the small bridge in front of the FOB before turning left on what should have been the route home. Less than half a mile from this point, the highway splits. Go straight and you end up in Sadr City, a fact clearly indicated on the highway sign that is written in both Arabic and English. Turn left and you are going the right way.

I keyed my handset and said, "Huggy, ten to one he misses the turn."

No answer from Staff Sergeant Reed. My anticipation built as I watched the lieutenant approach the turnoff. I had no reason to fear that I would lose my bet. The lieutenant continued straight ahead, missing the turn and taking us on a tour of Sadr City and its environs.

Sadr City was extremely dangerous, not a place that you wanted to get lost in. It was a Mahdi army stronghold, and I was certain that we would not be welcome there. Going into Sadr City with a unit equally determined to kill Mahdi men could have been fun, but blundering about blindly, with no purpose and with a unit you knew would leave you if anything happened, was not a comfortable feeling. Looking up ahead to where the road split, I keyed my handset again.

"What the fuck did I tell you. These fucking guys are useless. All stations, all stations, listen up. If you do not know it, we are now heading into Sadr City. Dipshit took the wrong turn. Look sharp and pay attention. Acknowledge."

One by one each vehicle checked in and acknowledged receipt of my last transmission. We continued down the highway toward Sadr City. Part of me, the small part that still believed in things like hope, patriotic Democrats, and unicorns, believed that maybe, just maybe, the lieutenant knew a different way of getting back to the palace. After all, he had the best navigation gear, and he had assured me he knew the way back.

I basked in the warm glow of hope until we were stopped by a roadblock. It was not a checkpoint manned by U.S. or Iraqi government forces, just a bunch of crap thrown on the highway to make it impassable. This was never a good sign. Often such roadblocks are the first hint of an impending ambush. This roadblock was perfectly placed for an ambush. It was set over a rise so that it could not be seen from afar. By the time we saw it, we were almost on top of it. Stopped in a potential kill zone as we now were, we made very easy targets. It was critical that we extricate ourselves from what was a bad situation before it got much worse.

I looked around for a place from which we could gain some meager cover and defend ourselves. Our options were limited. To my right there was a significant dropoff from the road to the ground, perhaps as high as fifteen feet. To our left, less than twenty-five meters away, was an exit ramp that sat higher than the one we were on. That bothered me the most. Fire coming down from the ramp could rake the entire convoy. We would be easy targets, and it would be difficult for us to engage our attackers effectively. To our right was an open field, and that was bordered by some buildings maybe 125 meters away. These buildings were at a lower elevation than our overpass exit, so I did not worry too much about them. Fire coming from below us would have very little effect on us if it had any at all. To our direct front, a hundred meters away, were buildings from which we could be engaged by effective fire. Worst of all, a VBIED could come sailing over the rise we had just come over and slam the rear of the convoy almost as soon as we could see it. I passed much of this to my guys as we slowly, almost painfully so, turned our convoy around. No ambush came, and we were able to get ourselves sorted out more quickly than I thought we would. That was the only good news.

The situation within the Cav section operating with us was beginning to deteriorate. You could see the stress and fear on many of the Cav troopers. Some just looked disgusted. As they passed, one fed-up soldier looked at me and threw his hands up in disgust and embarrassment. I felt his pain; we all did.

After turning around, the lieutenant took an off-ramp that I assumed he felt would lead us back to the safety of the palace. It did not. I tried to tell him that all we needed to do was go back a few hundred meters and pick up our exit, but he was sure he could get us back without doing that. At one point, after sitting on an off-ramp for several minutes for no apparent reason, I had my men dismount and assume defensive positions around our vehicles. Several more minutes passed before the lieutenant turned the convoy around again!

Discipline within the gun trucks began to falter as fear and panic took control. The lieutenant's soldiers began to yell at each other about the clumsy driving and what was going on with their leadership. It was not a good place to be. Half of the element we were traveling with was at war with the other half, and nobody had any confidence in the officer leading the mission. Eventually, the lieutenant found yet another exit to take. Like the turns made earlier that day, like the one that had brought us into the enemy's midst, and like every attempt to get "home" that followed, it was a wrong turn. It would have been a real hoot had we not been in Iraq! Watching it all unfold, I wondered if I were not witnessing the opening stages of some truly tragic event that was yet to be realized. In many ways what was happening reminded me of the Bermuda Triangle's famous Flight 19. Listening to historical recreations of radio communication between the pilots of the doomed flight, the flight leader, and ground stations, anyone could see that at first nobody knew how serious the problem was. I was sure that none of those men had any idea they would all be dead soon. But as things continued to deteriorate the leader became more shaken, and with his own loss of confidence, men in the flight lost confidence in him, and things only got worse. Watching events unfold for us, I felt that we might well be the beginning of another myth, the Baghdad Triangle. Soon we found ourselves knotted up in the middle of a very busy Iraqi intersection somewhere deep within the city. Not far from us a banner hung from an overpass, and it read, "America is finished."

"Napsalot, you see that fucking thing, man," I asked Napier.

"Yeah, Top, I see it. That joker is going to get us all killed, Top."

If there were any doubts that we were not in one of the better parts of Baghdad, the banner dispelled them. The echo of nearby gunfire ensured that even those among us who could not read knew they were in a shitty place. Extracting ourselves from this mess was complicated, and as we slowly did so, people began to gather and watch us. It seemed that many did so almost in anticipation of something happening to us. Some of them looked at us as if they knew we were living on borrowed time. If we were, theirs was just as borrowed, and a lot more of them were going to die than us if anyone of them went OK Corral on my team. Many within the crowd grew bolder as their numbers grew, and some of them began shouting at us. While we could not understand anything these people said, their hostility toward our presence was as unmistakable as a fart in a posh restaurant. Looking back at them I thought to myself, "One shot from anywhere, you grinning bastard, and you die, and so do you and so do you," as I eyeballed several men in turn.

"All stations, stay cool, pay attention, and be ready for anything."

Reed and Algarin both answered, "Roger, Top." Things with the lieutenant and his boys were nearing the critical stage. I wished that I had decent comm so that I could talk with the lieutenant and reassure him and, through him, his soldiers. With each mistake, with each passing minute, with no word or explanation from the lieutenant, I grew more disgusted with my lack of comm. I also felt that it was only a matter of time, maybe only minutes, before this lack of something so basic and essential as comm cost someone his life. Finally, inevitably, one of the lieutenant's drivers panicked and rear-ended Reed's SUV in a pathetic attempt to ram the convoy out of danger. While both vehicles remained operable, the force of the impact was great enough to send three of my men to the hospital upon our return to the Green Zone. Seeing the accident, the platoon sergeant began berating the errant driver, who simply ignored him, staring out his windshield as if the man did not exist.

The Iraqis saw it all, and they thought it was very funny. They were laughing at us!

This only added to the danger we were in. Instead of fearing us as they should have, they saw us as pathetic, and each sign of weakness on our part increased the likelihood that we were going to get hit. If that happened, given the state of the soldiers with us, I had little hope that they would, as a unit anyway, be worth a shit to us. The Iraqis could smell the fear and see the panic. Psychologically, they held the advantage, and that advantage was growing by the minute. As we attempted to extricate ourselves, I began looking for a building from which we could defend ourselves if things went sideways. Years before, I had served in a rifle platoon that became part of the Urban Warrior exercise. The purpose of the exercise was to experiment with different tactics, techniques, weapons, and equipment in a variety of urban scenarios, from full-on room-to-room urban combat to police and civil operations. For six months, six days a week, eighteen to twenty hours a day, we practiced clearing, capturing, and defending buildings. We became very good at it. Now, I knew that if I could just get my boys out of the street and into a solid building, there was not enough dirt in all of Iraq to bury the people we would kill trying to get us out. I quickly found a building that would suit my purposes. It was on the corner and had excellent fields of fire down several roads. In urban combat the roads are kill zones. The building was also taller than those near it and of sturdy construction; the walls looked like they could absorb rifle and machine-gun fire and maybe even RPG fire. It had the added virtue of being small enough for us to defend effectively. I quickly passed directions over the net so that my people could locate the building. Once everyone had identified the building, I told my guys to be ready to move quickly if we had to abandon the vehicles, and I explained what I intended to do.

"Listen carefully. If we get hit hard and pinned down in this street, we are all rushing that building. Do not allow anything to get in our way, period! When you reach it, we will have to quickly clear a room, maybe more. Napier and I will do that. The rest of you will defend the perimeter and then we will take it from there. Any questions?"

Clearing the building while holding the perimeter would not be easy, but it was a lot better than standing in the street believing that your vehicle was real cover. We would quickly need to move up a floor or two so as to cover fewer points from which our perimeter could be violated. In other words all buildings have fewer stairs than they do windows or doors. By moving up we would not only have fewer entry points to defend and watch, but by having fewer of these to cover, more of us would be free to engage targets in the street below. Urban Warrior had also taught me that it was nearly impossible to clear a stairwell held by people who did not want to give it up. There was no way in hell these people would ever be able to take a stairway we held. As it turned out, we did not need to worry about it. With excruciating slowness, we extracted ourselves from the mess we were in.

At some point, as we drove about Baghdad aimlessly, I considered just taking over from the lieutenant. I relayed as much to Colonel Thomas via my cell phone. He felt I should not take over unless it became apparent to me that there was an immediate threat to the security of the convoy. If that happened, he said, he would support me no matter what I did. Eventually, however, the lieutenant found his way and we made it back to the Green Zone. I had never been more relieved to see the gate. Once inside the Green Zone we pulled off to the side so that the two gun trucks in the rear could catch up to their lead. The platoon sergeant's vehicle pulled in behind mine, and the sergeant dismounted and walked over to my vehicle.

"I do not know what we would have done today if you had not been there."

I thanked him for his kind words and said that I hoped he got a new platoon commander soon.

"You know, sergeant," he added, "out there it is always us and them. We better be one team with one fight or we ain't going home."

I agreed with the soldier. "I hear you, and if you ever need anything, man, let me know—extra trigger pullers, anything."

He smiled and walked back to his vehicle.

A motto of the 1st Cav was "One Team, One Fight." It should have been "One Team, One Flight." But I admired some of their soldiers very much. Like the sergeant, there were soldiers who wanted to fight every bit as much as the best marines I knew. I needed to look no farther than my own team to be reminded of that. I had more soldiers than marines, and they were just as dedicated, skilled, and courageous as my marines. I could not understand why the army wasted such motivated men by tying their hands. While my loathing for the army was to grow day by day, my admiration for the soldierly virtues of many of its soldiers would continue to grow.

Once we were back in our own parking lot, the British colonel whom we had picked up at Quervo approached me. Colonel Harvey Finchley was pissed. He thought that the officer commanding should be cashiered from the service. He wanted me to make sure that my higher was aware of what had taken place. He added that he would write whatever I needed about what he had witnessed to support what I passed to higher.

"That man needs a new job," he said. "It is only a matter of time before he gets someone killed."

After the colonel and the Spanish officer left, we all headed toward the palace. I wondered what was waiting for us. What would I be asked? Who would be asking the questions? Had this been a marine infantry battalion, I would simply be viewed as having done my job, nothing more, nothing less. But here at the headquarters of the Coalition Military Assistance Training Team I was sure that there were going to be a lot of people who would be looking for a chunk of my ass. Considering how reluctant I knew many of my superiors were about actually following the new ROE, I began to consider the possibility that I might be on my way home or, at the least, barred from going on the road, exiled to my desk. We cleared our weapons at the clearing barrel next to the gated entrance. After having our badges checked by the marine guard, we walked toward the rear doors of the palace where we always entered. This time things were a little different. Gathered on the steps of the palace was a large group of people, officers and enlisted men. Up until this time our conversation had been subdued. It picked up a little bit as we approached the group of people gathered on the stairs. Shenk was the first to notice the large crowd.

"Oh boy, Top, looks like some people are going to want to talk to you."

Looking ahead and still pondering the potential outcome, I answered somewhat tersely, "No shit, Shenk . . . You think so?"

I tried to read their faces, but I could detect neither approval nor disapproval. While my team said very little, they all wore very broad smiles. Nobody standing on the stairs said anything to us as we entered the palace. They looked at us like we were from another planet, but nobody said anything. Colonel Thomas came out and congratulated me with a broad smile and a handshake as he said, "Good job, buddy."

"Thanks sir," I answered, grateful for his support.

Hesco continued, "Have your people go ahead and head directly to the conference room. Colonel Sarna is going to conduct a debrief, and then you guys are done."

We all filed into the conference room and slowly took off our heavy flak jackets, helmets, and web gear. We gathered around the large table that dominated the room. I sat at the head of the table. To my left were Sergeants Libby and Garate. To my right, but seated at the middle of the table, was Colonel Sarna. Seated to my left, but away from the table, were Thomas and the deputy C-3, Lieutenant Colonel Roddington. Colonel Sarna began to ask us questions. It was nothing like what I expected. I had walked into the room half expecting the questioning to be adversarial, something akin to what you see on TV cop shows when the dreaded internal affairs begins to go after the hero in some misguided attempt to get a murderer released from custody. It was nothing at all like that. While Colonel Sarna asked many highly detailed and well–thought-out questions, he was in no way combative. He was extremely professional and only sought from us, in our own words, the details of what had happened. The questions lasted for about twenty minutes. We were finished so soon that I was caught off guard when Colonel Sarna said he had nothing else for us.

"That's it? We are done?" I asked almost in disbelief.

"That's it unless you remember something else. I have nothing more for you."

Before we could celebrate, though, Colonel Roddington had some questions of his own.

"Who gave you the authority to use the CJTF-7 ROE? This is CMATT, mate, not CJTF-7."

Before I could answer, Colonel Sarna spoke up.

"The new ROE, put out by CJTF-7, applies to all subordinate units, which includes CMATT."

Roddington was quick to answer, "Right, I understand that, but did anyone clear this with the general or the deputy?"

I wondered if Colonel Roddington had any idea what the new ROE was. It was very clear that he felt I should have gone to the commanding general or his deputy first and asked them if I could follow the ROE issued by higher before doing anything else. That neither the commanding general nor his deputy ever spoke to me about the ROE seems to indicate that they did not feel the need to address an issue that CJTF-7 had already addressed. To Roddington's question, I replied, "No, I did not check with them. That is not my job."

Thomas said that he had checked out the ROE and that there was nothing wrong with what we had done.

But Roddington continued. "Don't get me wrong, mate, I am not saying that you did anything wrong. I am just making sure we were in the right here."

Roddington's questions, his tone, and his body language spoke volumes, however. Like most Coalition soldiers from England or Australia, he was all about being nice. If we were just nice to the Iraqis, they would like us. I am certain that he thought I was not at all a gentleman and possibly even a war criminal. As we left the conference room and headed toward the office to lock up all of our gear, Roddington went the opposite way in search of the deputy commanding general, Brigadier Nigel Alwin-Foster. Alwin Foster, of Her Majesty's Royal Army, was certain to lend a sympathetic ear.

(Five years later, in May of 2009, Colonel Vic Sarna would forward to me an e-mail that he had sent to General Eaton on 8 April 2004. While the colonel was effusive in his praise for my team, he also addressed Roddington's displeasure. So upset was Roddington that we had freed the souls of ten locals that he first protested our actions to Colonel Sarna. Not getting any support there, he decided to accompany Sarna when he turned his after-action report in to the joint battle staff. Sarna handed his report to the senior officer on duty, a U.S. Marine Corps major. The major, having grown disgusted with the less than assertive approach some units in Baghdad were taking with the Mahdi army, asked sarcastically, "And what did your guys do when they saw them?" Meaning what did we do when we saw the Mahdi men. Sarna replied, "They closed with and killed them!" The major, elated, replied, "About fucking time someone did!" This reply left Roddington "red in the face and visibly shaken." Still not satisfied, Roddington then went to CMATT's senior legal officer and expressed his belief that my team and I were guilty of war crimes. The legal officer told him that we were not. Roddington said that he was going to formally protest our actions to the Austrialian Forces Headquarters. Shortly after this, Roddington was replaced without explanation by another Austrialian. That man lasted less than a month. I was later told that he left in protest over the conduct of American forces.)

As we stored our gear, I did not think the magnitude of what had happened had yet dawned on us. I felt utterly invincible as I put away my gear and exchanged small talk with my killers. I do not remember most of what was said, but I know we were all incredibly high and I know much of it was both congratulatory and celebratory in nature.

Boeringer was already feeling the post-high crash. "You know, after a good fuck some people like a smoke. This feels like that, except I just want to eat, man."

Algarin, always quick to support Bo in his quest for food, quickly added, "Bo, no shit, man, I am as hungry as hell. Where we gonna eat, Top?"

"KBR, Starsky, KBR!" I answered.

Meggison added, "If you guys don't want to go to KBR, I know where we can get some fresh roadkill."

While I had no problem killing the locals, I certainly did not want to eat them. "If you want to kill and then eat 'em, and or fuck 'em, Meg, that's okay. Just keep it to yourself."

"C'mon, Top, live a little," Reed said.

"You wear a dress for us, Huggy, and we will all do some living," I said.

As I slammed my locker shut and turned to leave, I noticed that many in the office were looking at us in utter disbelief. One of the operations officers, Major Stacie Ricks, who was a USAF C-130 pilot, seemed disgusted and Chief Master Sergeant Vorgang appeared to be shocked. Hesco called me over to his desk and told me to cut the boys loose for the rest of the day. Out of the entire C-3, only he and another captain, also a marine, had any words of congratulation for us. As we got ready to leave for chow, the ops officer of "Steel Dragons" (a call sign we derisively changed to "Still Running") came in. He was extremely agitated by what had happened with our convoy. Not wanting to hear any more shit in one day, my team and I quickly left.

The conversation at dinner was dominated by the retelling of the day's events and discussing what might come next in what was obviously, to all of us, a very different war from what it had been when most of us arrived in Iraq. None of us had realized how hungry we were until we sat down. The food at the KBR chow hall was always first rate, but today it seemed especially so. We ate like condemned men. I can honestly say that I'd never had a more enjoyable meal in my entire life. The company was tops as well. After chow we all met for our nightly ritual of casual banter, insults, and storytelling. Of course, this night was different! Whereas much of the conversation was normally spent on a combination of things, from Patterson's childhood obesity and the issues stemming from it, to women, to the war and our part in it, and a myriad of other nonsensical issues, today the conversation was solely about what had happened. At first it started formally, with me asking everyone to relive the day's events from his perspective and to do so in detail. "What did you see? What did you hear? And what did you do?" These were the questions put to everybody. After everybody had his turn, and all the important lessons learned were committed to memory, the gathering turned into a great celebration. After all, we had won. We were alive and ten Mahdhi army guys were left dead. We had not lost one of our own, and we were entitled to celebrate.

In the flickering light of our bonfire, men told animated tales about the day's events with the enthusiasm of a child telling his friends about a fantastic birthday present. Frequently the storyteller was interrupted by someone adding some detail the teller had missed in his telling of the story.

Sometimes it was humorous, as when Dann spoke, and was quickly reminded that his weapon had jammed after only four shots.

"Yeah, Dann, tell them what you did after your weapon shit itself," Algarin suggested.

The author and Sergeant Kevin Facemyer, premission. *(Photo courtesy of Sergeant Jared Zabaldo)*

"I don't know what you're talking about, Sewer Rat." "Sewer Rat" was Dann's favorite nickname for Algarin.

Algarin continued, undeterred by Dann's defense. "Top, this sorry bastard comes running up to me asking if I got an extra rifle, pistol, anything."

This prompted howls of laughter and added commentary. "Yeah, he did the same thing to me," Reed added.

Then somebody, I do not remember who, called Dann "Budda, Budda, Jam," which is the sound soldiers and marines make to simulate firing their weapons when they do not have live ammo. Since Dann had only gotten off four shots before his rifle jammed, we all agreed that from this day forth Dann would be called "Four Shot." Dann was not the only person to get a new name after the shooting.

"Yeah, well, if he is 'Four Shot,' what the fuck are we gonna call Meggison? He emptied, like two magazines, crazy bastard."

Meggison challenged Will's assertion.

"Aww, now you know that's fucking bullshit, Will."

"So, Meg, how many rounds was it?" I asked.

"Top, thirty-nine exactly. You know you can't believe his sorry ass."

"Shit, Meg, that's still a lot more than anybody else fired," I asserted.

"Yeah, but, Top, you don't understand, I also killed more guys than any of you."

Sergeant Jason Algarin and the author. *(From the collection of Jack Lynch)*

This claim caused many in the group to cry bullshit and issue claims for their own kills.

Will's protest was the loudest. "You know that's fucking bullshit, Meggison. I killed three before you even got your fat ass out of the car."

It was almost like when we played war as children. My guys were shouting things like "No way! I killed that guy. He was already dead when you shot him." This went on for a while as some of us debated what to call Meggi. Someone suggested "Machine-gun Kelly," and while this was used sometimes after the shooting, it was never as popular as Meggi's "official" call sign, which was to become "Trunk Monkey." If you ever saw Meggison, stuffed into the cargo area of a Nissan Patrol, covered by miles of Iraqi road dirt, and armed with a large machine gun, you would know why he was called Trunk Monkey. You would also know why no Iraqi ever fucked with the crazy bastard.

One more man would get his call sign that night. Corporal Napier, who had stood in the street firing his 9 mm pistol like he was back on the block, would forever be known as "Street Monkey." Many of those gathered around the fire that night had not been on the fateful convoy. Among them was Patterson. All of those who had not been there were disappointed they had missed the trip. Most of them were happy for us but just wished that they,

The Majestics returning to the palace. *(Photo courtesy of Sergeant Jared Zabaldo)*

too, had been there. We felt sorry for them and assured them that they would get their chance. Nothing we said, however, could console Patterson.

"I hate you fuckers."

He was kidding about hating us, but it was obvious he felt like he had been screwed.

"Fuck, Pat, you forget that we have all seen you shoot, so it's not like you would have hit anything anyway."

"Fuck you, Boeringer," Pat responded.

Algarin, joining Boeringer, said, "C'mon, Bo, maybe he could have hit a couple. It just would have taken him longer, that's all."

Patterson glowered at Algarin even though he had tried to cut him a break.

After the party broke up and I was alone, back in my trailer, I thought about my family. After chow I had sent them word of the shooting via e-mail. Now I was afraid that had been a mistake. I was certain that they would worry more than ever.

I felt guilty about leaving them. I worried about what my kids would endure if I were killed. Today was a great day, but what said that the next, or maybe the following week or month, would not see us lying dead in a Baghdad street like some of our less fortunate comrades?

Somewhere in all this, my thoughts wandered away from my family and centered on just how badly I wanted sex. The desire was as strong as it was sudden. In fact, I had never wanted it as badly at any other time, not my first, not my honeymoon, not ever, as I wanted it then. I knew that this passionate craving had something to do with the fight, but I was not certain what. Perhaps I just wanted to reaffirm that I was alive! I felt so powerful, so invincible! I was then reminded of something Reed had once said to me when I had made a passing remark about needing some "things" from Robin.

"Top, all you have to do is sit on your left hand until it falls asleep. Then jerk off with it. Your hand being asleep will leave it free of any feeling, and since you are using your left hand it will *totally* feel like Robin is doing it."

At the time, I thanked Staff Sergeant Reed for sharing his creativity with me and told him I would try it. I fell asleep before my hand did, though, so the passion faded into a very sound sleep. So much for creativity.

CHAPTER 9

Our Own People Want Us Dead

Next morning I quickly got up and rushed off to chow. We would be going back to FOB Quervo again, this time to pick up equipment and personnel for the palace. As I ate, the boys, who always got up ahead of me, were busy loading and staging our vehicles for the day's run. I considered the potential for trouble. We had just killed ten people in the same area less than eighteen hours earlier. I was certain that we were not very popular in that part of Baghdad, or anywhere else in Iraq for that matter. The entire country had erupted into widespread violence that exceeded anything seen in the war so far. It was hard to believe how fast the war had changed. The quiet boredom of February and March now seemed a lifetime ago.

Finishing chow, I hurried to the ops center and pulled on my gear. As I did so, Chief Master Sergeant Vorgang and Major Ricks looked at me as if I had just eaten some Iraqi children. They were not the only ones. With each passing day it had become more and more obvious that we were looked at by some in the office as bloodthirsty monsters, and this attitude was evident *before* the eighth. This attitude was easy to understand. Most of them were merely in Iraq to do their time and go home, and they sincerely hoped that their tour would pass in quiet and safe boredom. That we were in Iraq to hunt down and kill our country's enemies, that we actively sought combat, and that we absolutely enjoyed killing were things they just could not come to grips with. To them, men who killed were to wear an eternal look of sadness that matched the invisible scars of war that killing had left on them. To them, we should have regretted that we had been *forced* to kill, and the fact that we *chose* to kill, and enjoyed it, unnerved them. Now that we had relieved ten souls of their mortal coils, it was sure to get worse.

Ignoring the hostility, I quickly grabbed my weapons and started to leave. Hesco, who was going with us, joined me. As we walked to the staging area, I told him I would love to nail half the office. He reminded me that my attitude did not reflect well on my faith and that I needed to master the Christian tenet of forgiveness. Though I knew he was right, I did not give what he said the thought that it merited. The spiritual awakening I had experienced after my wife's death was now very distant, and though I regretted it, I did nothing to change it.

Libby was waiting for me when I reached the lot. Whenever the intelligence differed greatly from that of the day prior, and when Libby's duties permitted, he would give the team the updated brief. After Libby gave his brief, it was my turn. My brief covered the route we would take and included things like what we would do if we were hit or a vehicle went down with a mechanical problem. If we were escorting personnel, they would be introduced to the team at this time, and the team would be briefed on where these people were to be located within the convoy. Most of what I said was the same as it always was, but this time I addressed events of the day before.

"I know we are all feeling a little bit of a letdown from where we were yesterday. I feel it, too. Forget yesterday, and forget it now. You guys all know the quickest way to get killed here is to lose focus and start thinking about shit that is not important here and now. That means your wives, kids, all the things that can distract you. Yesterday is nothing more than a potential distraction. But before we roll out of here, I want you to think about yesterday one more time. I don't want you to think about the fight; I want you to think about what it felt like to celebrate. Then I want you to think about someone acting that way after they have killed you. It makes me sick to think of these shits dancing in my blood. You all know we are going back to Quervo, and you probably have given that some thought. You know that those guys we killed had friends and that their friends are mighty pissed right now. You also know the whole country is going nuts. Lots of things have changed in the last few days, and nothing is what it was barely two weeks ago. Pay attention and think about what you are doing. If we are lucky, we can get ten more, but if any of us are off in our own thoughts, we are all in deep shit. Any questions?"

I looked at each man and each shook his head. They all wore the look of serious professionals. Gone were the carefree and happy expressions they wore just moments before. Each understood our deadly game, and each had his mind in the right place.

"Okay then, mount up," I instructed.

We mounted our vehicles and fell in with the armored Hummers of the 1st Cav. I listened to the brief, and it was evident that the Cav was sticking by its runaway approach to convoys. But that was okay with us. They had left us once, and I was sure they would do it again. Once we cleared the Green Zone, it was immediately evident that, just as had been the case the day before, the streets were filled with people who seemed to hate us. I did not know where they had all been just two weeks earlier, and that did not matter. More than ever before, we were encountering Iraqis who were openly hostile to us. Where we had often been greeted with warmth or, at the worst, indifference, now we were treated to scorn and ridicule. The people we passed frequently flipped us off or screamed at us in their native tongue. A few broken words of English did manage to make it to our ears, though. "You damned!" "Down with Bush!" As background, we could still hear gunfire all over the city. That used to happen only at night, and it never lasted long. Now it was all day every day, and the intensity was greater than anything before. As tense as convoys had always been, they were getting worse. Teams were being hit all over Baghdad, and sometimes more than once on the same run. Frequently, teams suffered casualties, and as a result, we began to look at everyone as a threat. I gripped my rifle tighter in my hands and continued to gaze out at hostile faces while also looking forward in an attempt to anticipate potential ambush sites. The best places for setting up a traditional ambush (small arms and RPGs) had one thing in common with good spots to set an IED; the natural terrain, road conditions, or traffic would combine in such a way as to force us to slow down or stop in the ambush's or IED's kill zone. On any given trip there were dozens of such places. All you could do was try your best to determine which kill zones were the most likely. It was never easy, and it amounted to little more than educated guessing. Still, you had to try.

Other than the increased stress, the trip to Quervo was uneventful; the trip back to Baghdad was not to be as nice. As incredible as it may seem, the 1st Cav had us lost *again*! Not once, but several times. As we prepared to leave Quervo, I went to the 1st Cav's senior man, a lieutenant, and asked if he knew the way back, just as I had the day before. He called over his lead navigator, and they both went over the route with me using my map.

I offered to help. "You know, sir, if you want, we can take lead. I know the way, and it is only a twenty-minute trip."

As before, pride got the better of judgment.

"No, I think we've got it. And my guys need to learn the roads," the lieutenant answered.

Though I was a little uneasy about this, I told myself I was being an ass. Holding yesterday's fiasco against these guys was not fair, as they had not been a part of the disaster. Besides, they had gone over the route with me, and they seemed to know the way. On top of that, they had something I would have killed for. Their vehicles were equipped with Blue Force Trackers. Where I had to navigate with good old-fashioned maps and satellite photos, these guys had the military version of OnStar, and a navigation system found in all the best cars, only better.

They might as well have been navigating by the sun for all the good their high-speed gear did them. Once we cleared the gate leaving Quervo, we were only a few hundred yards away from the exit that led to home and safety. I watched as, incredibly—given the previous day's events, the subsequent debrief that must have taken place at the Cav, and our own just completed review of the route back—this team, like its predecessor, sailed right past the exit. As shitty as this was, shittier still was my lack of comm. I had no way of telling the Cav to stop.

Then things got worse. It was a repeat of yesterday's lost convoy. Aimlessly, we blundered from one Baghdad roadblock to another. As before, I did not know whether these obstacles had been left by us or by insurgents, but it did not matter. If they had been erected by the insurgents or merely discovered and manned by them, we were in trouble.

Each one we hit occasioned great confusion with the soldiers in the gun trucks. It was not long before the stress of being lost in a hostile city, blindly blundering from one roadblock to the next, or going down yet one more dead end, began to take its toll on their discipline and combat effectiveness. Something akin to panic was starting to set in.

As we drove deeper into what was Sadr City, it became evident that *everybody* in this part of Baghdad hated us. Some of the walls were painted with anti-American graffiti written in English. "Down with the USA," "Damn Bush," "Damn you." Posters featuring Sadr as well as his militia hung everywhere. While none of these posters were in English, their meaning seemed clear. Many had images of Sadr and his militia superimposed over pictures of burning American vehicles. Others featured American soldiers and crying Iraqi women and children. Other posters featured Sadr's father, and while these were not anti-American, they made it very clear that we were in a Mahdi army stronghold. On the surface, Sadr had many reasons to be pro-American; after all, we had ousted Saddam, the man responsible for his father's death, but we had stayed in Iraq after doing so, and that was counter to Sadr's own ambitions and those of his Iranian allies.

As with the previous voyage of the damned, I offered to take the lead several times, and each time I was rebuffed. Whenever we stopped to turn around or to figure out where we were, I offered to take over the navigation. Each time I was assured that would not be necessary. Pride can be a great thing, but misplaced pride can get a lot of people killed.

It was not long before we found ourselves sucked into the black hole of a Baghdad slum. The 1st Cav drove down the most congested alley I had ever seen. The road was packed with vehicles at a virtual standstill. Above us on both sides of the road were buildings as tall as five stories. To the front the road was filled with vehicles, all stopped, and held firmly in place by the worst traffic jam I had ever seen in Baghdad. All around us were hundreds of pedestrians. Shops lined the street. Smoke filled the street as all manner of things were cooked by sidewalk vendors. Soon we realized we were stuck in one of Baghdad's busy markets. Before we could back out, vehicles pushed in from the rear. It did not matter, anyway, for the Cav was hell-bent on getting through the market. I immediately had my team dismount and take what cover was available in the alley. I keyed my handset as I dismounted my own vehicle: "Stay sharp, guys."

I noticed that most of my men were eyeballing the balconies, rooftops, and upper-floor windows.

As I walked by them, I pointed out the different dangers. "Watch the cross alleys and these people!"

Corporal Tug Wilson came up next to me.

"Black Hawk down, mate."

Tug's reference to the ill-fated mission to snatch some of Aideed's warlords in Somalia was easily understood. While we were not trying to rescue downed helicopter crews, we were lost in a heavily populated city where the people wanted to kill us. Cut off, isolated, and lost as we were, Tug's reference to that long-ago mission was more than a bit appropriate to the situation we were in. As I checked on each of my men, I thought about the potential for a very heavy loss of civilian life if we were fired upon by gunmen hidden among the crowd. We would return fire, the insurgents would continue to fire, and everything between us would be shit-outta-luck. Once the people were out of the way, the insurgents, too, would be out of luck. I continued to push to the front of the convoy, looking for the senior officer present with our army unit.

Many Iraqis, perhaps sensing my concern, said, "Mister, mister, no problems here." "Mister, here is good, very good, mister." Still, given the vulnerability of our position we could not help but be apprehensive. Colonel Thomas came up alongside of me. "Top, are you sure this isn't the same guy from yesterday?"

"Yes, sir," I answered. "Different element, same unit, but these guys were not with us yesterday."

Hesco pushed forward with me. The navigator and his lieutenant were trying to figure out what to do and it was taking them a long time to reach a consensus. The minutes kept slipping away. The longer we remained stuck, the more vulnerable we became. At first, our predicament seemed to amuse the Iraqis, but as we remained there, stuck among them, they, too, began to grow concerned. They knew that the insurgents would not give a shit how many Iraqis they killed so long as they were able to kill some of us, too. Our continued presence was not only making us more vulnerable, it also put the Iraqis around us at great risk. Their newfound apprehension only increased ours.

"Mister, you must leave now. It is no good."

Looking over at Hesco, I asked, "Sir, you listening to this shit? These guys are more worried than we are. That should be telling us something."

"Yeah, Top, I hear them. We are getting the hell outta here *now*."

I do not know how long we were in the alley when Colonel Thomas grabbed the 1st Cav's lieutenant and ordered him to back us out of the alley, but I know we had been stuck there far too long. I do not know what intimidated the young officer more, a marine colonel or the massive, hulking size of that colonel, but whatever it was, the lieutenant immediately ordered his team to back out of the ally. While my team was apprehensive, they were not overcome by fear. That was not the case with the 1st Cav. Knowing that we had been stuck way too long and were only going to be more vulnerable as we attempted to back out of the mess we were in, fear grew into panic, and panic led to chaos. Two of the 1st Cav's Hummers collided, causing minor damage.

"Fucking First Cav, man, they haven't been cool since Nam," Face moaned.

Will was more direct. "Hey, you fucking asshole, you got a license for that thing!"

The driver looked at Williams sheepishly as he pulled into his position in our reassembled formation. Face and Will were giving voice to how we all felt. To us, it seemed incredible that we could get so lost twice in two days, both times heading back from the same FOB and with two different elements from the same unit. What did that say about the parent command? It all seemed like a very bad nightmare that just kept repeating.

Hesco had had enough. "If that asshole gets us lost again, you take our section home. If they are smart, they will follow you, and if they don't, then they will wish they had."

"Yes, sir, I will pass that to the team."

As Hesco walked back to his vehicle I told Reed and Algarin that we might be pulling ourselves out and heading back on our own. Slowly we began to sort ourselves out of the mess we were in once we were back on the main road. I considered how best and when to pull my guys out and take them home when should we get lost again. As I considered this I was suddenly surprised to see we had arrived at the large traffic circle that pointed the way home. The circle was one of the largest in Baghdad, and it was marked with a very large billboard upon which was a massive ad extolling the virtues and benefits of service as an Iraqi police officer. Well known to all road-bound Americans, surely the Cav would not miss this large traffic circle with its distinctive billboard. I held my breath as they approached the circle and was mildly surprised when they took the right exit. In less than ten minutes we were back in the Green Zone. Once back in the staging lot, the team dropped off Hesco and me while they went to refuel and secure the vehicles. Hesco ran off to find the Cav's operations officer, and I headed back to our own operations section.

As I entered the palace I noticed how much it felt like I was entering a wind tunnel. The air-conditioning was now running full power, twenty-four hours a day, and the large open entrances created a powerful wind as cold and hot air fought over their boundaries. I was aware, for the first time, just how hot it was getting, and I could not even imagine what it was going to be like in the summer. I grabbed a bottle of ice water from the refrigerator kept in ops and went over to my desk. As I pulled off my body armor and secured it and my weapon in my locker, Chief Lewis approached me and said he had something he needed to tell me.

"I am getting ready to go to chow with the team. Can it wait?"

"No, Top," Lewis replied. " This is pretty important, and I think you will want to hear it."

It already sounded like another issue that I was not going to like, and certainly did not feel like dealing with, especially after the lost patrol.

"Okay, let's go to the debriefing area," I answered.

"Hey, Top, where you going? What about chow?" the eternally hungry Meggison asked.

"Give me a minute, Meggi," I answered.

Lewis led the way.

Once in the briefing area I asked, "Okay, what's up, Lewis?"

"About three hours ago, I don't know how it started or with who, but Major Ricks and Vorgang were talking about you and the team, and they were talking a lot of shit, Top. Anyway, at some point she says, 'If they had all gotten killed they would have deserved it.' "

It did not take long for the gravity of what was said to sink in, though I must admit I was surprised by the matter-of-fact way Ricks had said what Lewis was quoting her as having said.

Shocked, I asked, "You're fucking kidding me, right?"

"No, Top, she said that shit."

Incensed, I replied, "Fucking bitch! Was she married to one of the guys we smoked? What did the candy-ass say to her when she said that?"

"Nothing."

"Bitch! Okay. Thanks, Lewis. I'll take care of it."

While I knew that there were many people in the palace who did not approve of our shooting the life out of the Mahdi army guys, I did not know how much they disapproved of it. As I walked back toward the office I met Vorgang in the hallway and immediately questioned him about the incident.

"Hey, Chief Master Sergeant Vorgang, did Major Ricks tell you my team all deserved to die?"

"No," was all he said, though clearly the question had unnerved him. I went and saw Colonel Thomas, who had returned. I told him what had been reported to me. He said that he would take care of it.

"Can we kill her?" I asked, only half kidding.

"Top, I'll take care of it," Hesco replied.

Pushing, I asked, "That means we can't kill her?"

Hesco, always on an even keel, joked, "Well, not yet anyway. Just let me deal with this."

As I walked by my team, still waiting to go to chow, without breaking stride, I said, "You guys are not going to believe this." Walking out of the office, we passed the two fine airmen, Vorgang and Ricks, and it was obvious that they were deep in conversation. It was just as obvious that she was extremely upset. Once outside, I told the team what had been said.

Reed was the first to register his displeasure.

"Fuck her! What the fuck does she know anyway? What has that bitch done since she has been here?"

Will answered, "I'll tell you what she's done, Chris. Very fucking little.

When she is not scheduling a flight or two, she is whining about how much she misses her boyfriend."

Will continued, saying, "Yeah, and what the fuck are they going to do her, because she is a fucking officer. She is pissed at us because we killed those people and she wishes we had gotten killed instead. What would have happened if it had been one of us saying that about anybody in that office, but especially an officer? Fuck it, the next thing I kill might just be wearing an air force battle dress uniform. What the fuck do they wear BDUs for anyway? Man, that *bitch*!"

"Just let me fuck her first, Will!" Meggison requested.

I attempted to dissuade Meggison, saying, "You don't want any part of that, Meg."

Meggison, though, was not about to be put off so easily. "Oh, Top, that might be true but we are in Baghdad and my options are limited. C'mon over here, Stacie, and let Meggi love on ya before Will kills ya."

We all laughed, not just at what Meggi said, but at the mental image (in my case anyway) of Meggi, "loving" anyone. Meggi of the Barney Rubble body and head, with the voice and mannerisms of Ernest Borgnine.

When we returned from chow, we discussed the composition of the team. For the first two months of our existence we had largely moved from vehicle to vehicle as the team sorted itself out. The only exceptions to this were that sergeants Williams and Facemyer were always together, as were sergeants Algarin and Boeringer. People rotated in and out of the rear vehicle, with myself being the only constant in the rear. I had remained in vehicle 3 (a.k.a. Rear D) because experience had shown it to be the one most likely to be hit by enemy fire or IEDs. Before I asked others to ride in 3, I wanted to set the example. But there were problems with that. The fast pace of convoy escorts meant that I should have been in vehicle 1 so that I could better make decisions based on what I saw ahead of us rather than what someone reported to me. Our situation could change rapidly, and I needed to be where I could better observe and control our reaction to any situation. But I was reluctant to stick someone else in vehicle 3 because of the dangers of that position.

As I hemmed and hawed about what to do, Algarin spoke up. "Top, me and Bo have been talking about this for a while with the rest of the team and we do not think you should be in the rear vehicle anymore. I mean, we know why you do it, and we appreciate it, but we really think you should be in lead."

"Well, who is going to take rear then?" I asked.

Boeringer, speaking for himself and Algarin, answered. "Me and J will, Top."

Because of the rear vehicle's ability to attract lead, rockets, and IEDs, it had long been less than affectionately known as the Hearse. Wanting to make sure both men understood what they were asking for, I said, "You guys sure about that, Hutch?"

"Yeah, Top, we're sure," Boeringer said.

Vehicle 3 was now set. Algarin was the driver, and Boeringer would serve as the vehicle commander. For the time being, "Diesel Dave" Balan and "Trick Shot" Shenk would serve as their dismounts. When he arrived later that month, Gunnery Sergeant Josleyn would serve as their trunk monkey; until then they would make do with whoever was available. When Balan and Shenk left in May, Specialist Brackin would take Balan's place, and floaters would replace Shenk.

Sergeants Boeringer and Algarin fully understood how dangerous the Hearse could be. Their willingness to place themselves at the center of the storm was a tremendous testament to their courage. By the time the two sergeants made their request to be assigned to the rear vehicle, they had displayed an aggressive yet appropriate understanding and application of deadly force within the confines of the rules of engagement. This was critical, as Rear D was responsible for the detection and decisive engagement of threats coming from the rear. I needed smart, aggressive warriors back there, and I had them.

Next up was vehicle 1, more properly known as "Lead," pronounced "leed."

Looking at Reed, I said, "Huggy, you will be my driver. Face and Will, you will be my dismounts and, Meggie, you will be my trunk monkey."

Facemyer, who had said nothing to this point, quickly added, "Well, Top, if you are joining vehicle one we will need a new call sign for us. Something which reflects our status."

I had never considered myself a status symbol, but apparently Facemyer felt otherwise.

Seemingly knowing what was coming, Boeringer moaned, "Oh, here we fucking go."

Enjoying Boeringer's agitation, I encouraged Facemyer. "Go ahead, Face, what is it?"

"Well, given that vehicle one already has Hollywood and Rockstar"— Will's and Face's rarely used call signs—"Huggy, and now you, I think All Star One is appropriate."

Boeringer looked over at Algarin and said, "See, J. I fuckin' knew it, man. These motherfuckers are going to get all the breaks now."

I held my hand to my chin and tapped my cheek with my index finger as I pretended to mull over the suggested call sign before answering. "You know, Face, I like it. I like it a lot. All Star One it is."

"Fucks," murmured Boeringer.

Moving on, I said, "Okay, on to vehicle 2. Del, you are 2's driver. J-Lo, you are the vehicle commander, and for now Fudd and Paper Cut, when he is ready, will be your dismounts."

Thus toward the middle of April the team organization was formalized.

After we had finished with our meeting I returned to the operations section. Major Ricks, not surprisingly, was not in the office and remained away from it for about two hours. When she finally did show up, she appeared to be upset. Eventually, she walked over to my desk.

"Top Lynch, can I talk to you?"

"Sure," I answered as I set aside what I was doing.

Major Ricks followed me out of the office, and when we were out of earshot of the CMATT area she started.

"I want to apologize for something I said. I was wrong and I know that I should have supported you and not said anything in front of the troops that would cause them to not respect you. I don't know why I said it; maybe it was all the stress in the office."

She then spoke about how "nice" things used to be in the office before I arrived and changed "everything." When she had finished lamenting the way things were I asked, "Are you done?" She was.

"Well, just so I know what we are talking about, ma'am, when you say that you want to apologize for *something* you said yesterday, that something wouldn't be saying that my team and I deserved to die, would it? Because if that is what you are apologizing for, shove it! Every time we hit the road, we know there are thousands of people out there that want to fulfill your wish. That you wish us dead does not make it any more or less likely to happen, but I am shocked and disgusted that an American, let alone a member of the military, would share such a thought. You do not need to worry about how my soldiers and marines view me because of what you said. There is not a damn thing you or *anyone* else in this fucking palace can say that would reduce or change, in any way, the way my guys feel about me. As to how they feel about you, on the other hand, you can rest assured that every one of them knows what you said, and to whom you said it, because I told them. The only person they look at differently now is *you*! I want you to know that my kids also know your name, and they know that you, a major in the *U.S. Air Force,* wished their father dead. They know your name and so will my grandchildren. I am really sorry that you miss Rob. I know you guys enjoyed a close working relationship in the office. I did not come over here to be your friend, and I do not give a shit what you or anybody else in that office thinks of me. I came over here to do *exactly* what we did yesterday, and I will do it every time I get the chance. Ma'am, I cannot accept your apology, but I can promise that you and I will never talk about this again. You know what was said and so do I, so let's just leave it at that."

As we turned to walk back to the office Major Ricks said, "I just want things to be like they used to."

Disgusted with her, I answered, "Ma'am, that is never going to happen."

I was still seething.

While I fully expected that many in the palace would not approve of what we had done, I never suspected that any of them, let alone someone who knew me and my guys as Ricks did, would actually verbalize the belief that we all deserved to die. It was especially shocking, given that we could be killed quite easily doing what we were doing almost every day on Iraq's roads.

Not everybody saw things the way Ricks did, however. Hesco told me that he was putting the team in for the Joint Service Commendation Medal with V device for our actions on 8 April. The V device, a small anodized letter V, was placed on the ribbon of medals that could be awarded for either valor or merit. It denoted that the wearer had won his award for valor. Medals such as the Silver Star, Navy Cross, and the Medal of Honor did not come with V devices since they were awarded solely for valor. I did not know how I felt about the award. Part of me felt like we were only doing our job, which was true. It was equally true that while we were "just" doing our job, that job was one that most people flatly refused to do, including those members of the 1st Cav who had been with us that day. Not too many people stand and deliver punishment when part of the unit takes off. Most often that fear spreads and everybody takes off.

The sad fact is that there are a great many men who will do what we did, or even do more, who will not get anything for their actions. Nothing we did would even rate mention in any battalion I had ever been in. While we were going to be decorated, marines fighting and dying in the Al Anbar would be lucky to just go home. Here at the palace, on the other hand, all senior enlisted, senior warrant officers, and senior officers would receive a Bronze Star just for showing up and eating chow. That was the "end of tour award" for senior members of CMATT. When I say senior members I include myself. Chief Master Sergeant Vorgang, like Sergeant Major Jackson before him, would get a Bronze Star, while young soldiers and marines riding convoys or patrolling streets will get nothing more than a compliment. I had even witnessed one senior army NCO writing himself up for a Bronze Star. To my obvious surprise the NCO had answered, "What, you don't think these officers are doing the same thing in an attempt to justify his actions?" Still, I was glad that my team, unlike most doing the same job, would not be leaving Iraq without some small token of thanks for their selfless courage. I just wished that the system was fair.

The situation across Iraq continued to grow worse by the day. Route Irish was getting worse by the hour. Multiple attacks were recorded all along the route. It was hard to believe that we had ever used Route Irish to train secondary drivers. Now, when you traveled the road to BIAP, you better have your game face on. I believed the attacks on the BIAP road caught higher completely off guard, as we did not get any intel briefs saying the road was about to become lethal. You certainly did not need a brief *now* to tell you the BIAP road was suddenly very dangerous. The roadside was littered with destroyed American vehicles. Most were large cargo carriers, but every now and then one saw the charred remains of an SUV just like the ones the team rode in. It was getting so bad that many of the contracted drivers refused to haul their loads because they claimed the escorts kept leaving them. While I did not know for certain that contracted drivers had been abandoned to their fates by their escorts, I did know it had happened not only to my own team but to other CMATT elements as well. One of CMATT's logistic convoys had been left when they hit an IED. The convoy, consisting of a flatbed truck with two thousand AK-47 rifles and a million rounds of ammo and a bus carrying sixteen newly arrived soldiers, was escorted by elements assigned to the 1st Cav. A few miles outside of Kirkush they were hit by an IED that damaged one of the Hummers and wounded one soldier. The escort took off, leaving the flatbed and the bus to make their way to Kirkush alone. They simply hauled ass, leaving behind a cargo that could have caused us much grief had the enemy followed up his IED hit with a ground attack, not to mention twenty lightly armed American soldiers and airmen, most of whom had been in Iraq less than seventy-two hours! By a stroke of luck, one of the drivers had been to Kirkush before *and* had paid enough attention to know the way; otherwise they would have been lost. To me it was simply incredible, beyond belief, that any American wearing a uniform would leave another to his fate. The big picture in Iraq continued to go to shit as well. Even within the Green Zone you could hear the sounds of firefights raging across the city day and night. Mortars and rockets were hitting the Green Zone and Camp Victory almost daily.

From official reports coming in to the operations center and those in the media, it was clear that this was the way things were in most of Iraq, the exceptions being southern and northern Iraq. Yet, other than our own intuition, we never received any warnings that something was up. We just woke up one morning to find that the war was suddenly different. Nowhere was the violence greater than in Fallujah. In response to the attack that killed four Blackwater employees in March, the White House decided to send in marines to clean the city up. We received very little in real info about that fight, but it dominated the news. It was obvious that many marines had been killed in action and that many times more diaper-headed hadjis had as well. For me, one image from the fighting in Fallujah will remain the most vivid. It is a picture of a squad of marines gathered outside their armored personnel carrier. They are kneeling and standing over the body of a friend who has just been killed in the fighting. The men are praying for their fallen comrade in an image as old as war itself. General Conway, the marine commanding the forces reducing Fallujah, said the terrorists had two choices, surrender or die. I sincerely hoped that the marines were allowed to obliterate that troublesome city.

As disturbing as the violence was, what seemed to be most worrisome for the policy makers was the apparent cooperation between the largely pro-American Shiite population and the pro-Saddam Sunni population. Nobody seemed to know whether this cooperation represented the start of a new and unified effort against the Coalition or was simply a matter of temporary convenience: The enemy of my enemy is my friend. For those of us who rode, it really made no difference. Who was trying to kill us and why was not as important for us to understand as how they were trying to kill us. Who and why were strategic concerns, far beyond us.

For us the war ground on, and as it became more deadly, our missions evolved in nature. On 9 April a large and heavily escorted U.S. Army–KBR convoy was hit in Baghdad. Several vehicles were destroyed, with a significant loss of life. Two soldiers were reported missing and presumed captured. Contract drivers were among the dead and the missing as well. Ominously, many of the KBR drivers said that the army escort left them, and they refused to make any more runs unless we provided them with additional protection. In fact, it was rumored that while army and KBR truck drivers suffered casualties in the ambush, the escort did not have a single man killed. Something just did not seem right about that. The protected suffered while their protectors sailed through without loss?

To us it simply meant more to do with the same shitty equipment, as we were directed to provide additional protection to the vulnerable KBR convoys. This was a big change for us. Up until now, we had only provided escorts for CMATT assets and personnel. While we were certainly honored to be asked to do something a far better equipped and larger unit had failed to do, we were, nevertheless, concerned about the vulnerability of these large and slow convoys. Accordingly, extra care was taken with every detail. First the team assembled in our staging area where we conducted the now routine premission briefs and gear, weapons, and vehicle checks. Once all that had been accomplished, we left our staging area and went to the KBR heavy vehicle lot. Here we picked up our package, which normally consisted of from five to seven KBR eighteen-wheelers and one KBR control vehicle. To my dismay I saw that none of the KBR employees was armed—at least not openly. I imagine that many of them were packing pistols at the very least, given what had happened to some of their coworkers. Five hundred dollars a day is hard to spend if you are dead.

"Huggy, pull your vehicle into lead. Starsky, put yours behind number three heavy." ("Heavy" was what we called the semis.) I then turned to Napier. "Pull us in to the rear behind the last heavy."

Once we formed up for the escort, we pulled the KBR drivers in for a brief. The brief explained threat tactics and techniques, but, more important, I also explained what the drivers should do if their vehicle was hit and they could not move it. I attempted to assure the drivers that we would do everything to protect and recover them should their vehicles become disabled.

"No matter what is going on, no matter how bad things get, if you are unable to drive because of wounds or your vehicle is disabled, you are to remain in the cab, if possible, or exit the vehicle and hide, next to the engine block, on the side away from the fire. You must wait in one of these two areas or within a few feet of them. You will stay put until my vehicle comes to get you."

Pointing at my vehicle I asked, "Does everybody see the white Suburban at the end of the convoy? That is my vehicle, and it will act as a recovery vehicle for any casualties or stranded drivers. Remember, be where we expect you, because we will not look all over the place for you. Does everybody understand?"

One of the drivers asked, "Sergeant, what if your vehicle is hit, then what do we do?"

"If that happens, you are fucked until one of my vehicles up front realizes that there is a break in the convoy and can come back and get you. That might be a few minutes, given what passes for comm and the size of the convoy."

"They will come back though . . . Right?"

It was obvious that this guy did not want to be left behind. I wondered if he had been on the convoy hit on the ninth.

I tried to lighten the mood. "They better come back for me if nothing else."

"How much money you got, Top?" Del teased.

"Damn, Del, you're as bad as Will," I answered.

Boeringer answered the driver's question. "We will come and get you, me and this little Puerto Rican motherfucker. We are driving that blue Ford."

Boeringer pointed at his vehicle and the KBR drivers nodded.

I resumed the briefing.

"Now, if sergeants Boeringer and Algarin are killed or wounded on the way to you, or if we lose more people than we can evacuate, then nobody is going anywhere. We will make do where we are and fight it out. But no matter what happens, you have my word and the word of every man on my team, we will not leave you, not one of you, so long as you follow my instructions. Any questions?"

The drivers, most often, did not have any questions. Frequently they would thank us for our help and draw a distinct line between how we conducted escorts and how other units did. Most spoke of having been left behind before and not wanting to ever have that happen again. None had *ever* been told what to do if they were ambushed other than simply drive through.

Following the brief, we all mounted up and moved out. We had one other duty on these runs in addition to those of escort and casualty recovery. Any vehicle to be abandoned would first be destroyed. For that purpose we carried thermite grenades. Any classified documents or gear would be recovered. Most often these runs did not have any classified gear or documents, but when they did, I had to detail someone to ensure their recovery. We did this by introducing the soldier or marine assigned the job to the custodian or caretaker of the classified stuff. The owner of the classified then showed the designated soldier or marine where on his body or in the convoy the classified material was kept. This ensured that nothing was left behind that could hurt us later.

About thirty minutes after I had completed my brief we rolled out of the KBR heavy lot and were on our way. We were not even out of the Green Zone, and we already had a full appreciation of just how slow these trucks were. It was going to be a difficult run. Once we cleared the Green Zone, the slow speed of the lumbering trucks made us extremely vulnerable to the only weapon we all dreaded, the IED. Winding our way through Baghdad's congested streets was never easy, but with such a large and slow convoy it was many times more difficult. The roadsides, once littered with destroyed Iraqi army vehicles of Russian manufacture, were now littered with the burnt-out remains of Hummers, SUVs, and large trucks. These silent sentinels served as a not so gentle reminder that we were now fighting a different war. The Iraqis we passed in these areas smiled at us, not friendly smiles but knowing smiles, as if they were responsible for the destroyed vehicles. Some of them no doubt "pulled the trigger" that left these wrecks. Each burnt-out hulk was a graphic reminder of our own mortality. Seeing these shattered wrecks in which some of our countrymen had lost their lives made us all hungry to deal some suffering of our own. We were more determined than ever to kill as many of these people as we could.

Most often the KBR runs involved two stops, and this run was no different. Our first stop was in Baqubah. Baqubah was just north of Baghdad and almost as dangerous. Unlike most of Baghdad, which had been relatively quiet until April, Baqubah was always known as a bad place to be. Now, of course, it was much worse. While the soldiers there had their hands full, for us there was a sense of relief in reaching Baqubah; four of our seven semis were to be left there, which meant we would have a much smaller convoy to control and defend.

Time on the road was extremely stressful, and we really did not realize *how* stressful until we pulled into a "safe" place. As with most stops we quickly staged our vehicles and found a base exchange or fell into a deep sleep. These naps, whether they lasted twenty minutes or two hours, were a welcome relief. I never slept more soundly than I did during these "road" naps. Algarin shook me awake.

"Top, the KBR guys will be ready to go in fifteen minutes. I already sent Bo to go grab Will and Face. Everybody else is here."

I pulled my helmet on and did a quick head count to make sure everybody had returned from the head or the small PX, both popular stops anytime we pulled in anywhere. All was as Algarin had said. Once we were up, we pulled into formation and waited for the convoy to start rolling.

From Baqubah we escorted the KBR trucks to Kirkush, which was more than an hour away. Once we cleared Baqubah we were able to relax a little since most of the area between Baqubah and Kirkush was nothing more than a vast expanse of sun-baked desert populated by the occasional goatherder and his flock. Mile after empty mile rolled by our windows in a mind-numbing and sleep-inducing nothingness. It was like the background in a Fred Flintstone cartoon; it repeated endlessly. Almost like time travel, we arrived at Kirkush before we realized we were even close.

We were on the ground just long enough to check in with the CMATT Commandant's Office. We picked up personnel scheduled to go to the palace as well as outgoing mail. Major Manning, the commanding officer, informed me that things had been very quiet in his area. Captain Dan Barrett, his deputy and a coworker of mine at Quantico, came in as we were getting ready to depart and asked me how things were in Baghdad. When I told him, he seemed to sincerely wish that he was going back with us. Even in the best of times, Kirkush was little more than a backwater, with none of the amenities that life in the Green Zone offered. Now, for anybody who wanted to get in the war, being assigned to Kirkush had to be painful. I had never envied the men assigned there; I did so even less now that the war was hot, and I was mindful that had it not been for the bombing at the RC just two months ago, I very likely would have been assigned here as well. Bad luck for the victims, just as bad for the recently harvested Mahdi, but great for me. Sometimes, if a person just looks hard enough, he can find the good in a really bad situation. I did not have to look very hard. Of course, I also knew that fate could be a fickle bitch, and what seemed like a great deal now might end in a blinding and searing flash as I became someone else's great opportunity.

I said goodbye to Captain Barrett and walked out to my convoy. The trip back would be a snap, as only the KBR control vehicle would be returning with us. In comparison with the trip out, the return trip seemed almost tranquil, but that semitranquility melted away as we approached the gate to the Green Zone. Just yards from living another day, we suddenly became more vulnerable. All military vehicles entering Coalition facilities were subjected to a quick ID check. Though the process was done as rapidly as possible, most often the delay, combined with heavy traffic entering the Green Zone, caused long lines to form outside the gate. While the check was necessary, it did not make us feel any easier as we sat waiting for the vehicles in front of us to crawl through the gate. If we had Hummers, we could enter via a different gate, which was reserved for tactical vehicles. Tactical vehicles were "field" military vehicles such as tanks, APCs, Hummers, trucks, and so on. Free of Iraqi pedestrian and vehicular traffic, these gates were far safer than the one we were forced to crawl through. Parked outside the gate were dozens of Iraqi cars, many cabs, which I presumed carried Iraqis to and from work in the Green Zone. Any one of these could be filled with explosives. Still another group of Iraqi cars sat in a line next to the entrance used by Coalition personnel. Like us, they were waiting to be cleared by soldiers manning the gate. It made for a very uneasy feeling. We were all sure, to a man, that it was only a matter of time before one of the gates guarding the entrance to the Green Zone was hit with a VBIED again. This had happened just before my arrival in Iraq.

Entering large fixed locations via a few well-known and highly visible choke points made you little more than a potential victim; like an innocent man walking up to an ATM at two in the morning, you were a victim just looking for a crime scene. While this system had kept weapons and explosives out of the Green Zone, it left returning convoys highly vulnerable to any suicide bomber sitting in his car waiting for a target to blunder by. Time was on his side. He did not care who he killed; he just wanted to kill Americans and their Iraqi "puppets." Hell, for that matter, they did not even have to be Iraqi puppets. For his purposes a child would do just fine. A body is, after all, a body, one more nail, however small or innocent, in the coffin of American resolve. Maybe he detonated his car while you are still five miles away at Camp Victory, causing you no more damage than the inconvenience of having to go to another gate while army medics slowly policed up the remains of fellow soldiers or Iraqi civilians killed. But maybe, just maybe, he detonated his bomb as you pulled alongside, not because of who you were or anything you did that made you a target, but because God told him, "*Now!*" The only consolation, if that happened and you were "lucky," is that you would not know it. You would be gone in a flash, reduced to a number duly reported by the press and at most an inconvenience to those forced to make a detour because of the wreckage your untimely death was merely a small part of.

If we came to a complete stop, even just outside the gate, we always dismounted and formed a perimeter around our vehicles. No vehicles, except those that were obviously U.S. military, were allowed to approach the rear of our convoy while we were stopped. While many thought this was overly cautious, we did not. More than one American convoy had been hit while sitting outside a FOB. Dismounts were the best protection in this situation. All of us accepted that we might be killed; that was fine. But none of us was going to *let* it happen because we had become lazy or complacent. Slowly, painfully, the long line of Coalition vehicles snaked its way through barriers, past the sentries and into the safety of the other side. There are no words to describe what it felt like to clear the barrier. No matter how "easy" the convoy had been, they always ended the same way, with a mad dash to the gate.

Sometimes, no matter how fast we went, the gate never seemed to get any closer until we were actually through it. Clearing the gate led to something of a ritual for us. Once we had cleared, Facemyer would always ask, "What do you say, Mayor of Kpotinstan, do we take them off?"

"K-pot" is an army term for the helmet. While the helmet is a critical piece of gear that has saved many lives, it is also uncomfortable. In the heat of the Baghdad summer it was so uncomfortable that you had to fight the temptation to remove it. Since I never let the boys remove them unless we were inside a secure facility, I was derisively referred to as the aforementioned mayor or sometimes "Kpotowicz."

Answering, I said, "Sure, tell 'em to drop 'em."

Reed would key his radio. "Top says take off the brain buckets." Taking off the helmet became the physical acknowledgment that, barring the extremely rare hit with a mortar or rocket, we were safe. Safe until the next run, anyway. Things were getting so bad that many days in April were listed as no-go days. No-go days meant that no CMATT personnel were to be on the roads except for the most critical of missions. Units across Iraq suspended road travel altogether, restricting their movements only to those that could be made by air. This was done in an effort to reduce casualties. It was effective at doing so, but it was a reaction that was akin to accepting defeat. We were surrendering control of the cities to the enemy!

For the team, however, nothing changed. We were making more runs than we ever had, no-go day or not. Now if a staff officer was going to the Water Palace, he would simply call on us as his escort, whereas before he would have just grabbed a vehicle and a couple of friends and made a day of it. The same men who viewed us as little more than lowbrow thugs were calling upon us almost daily. Better yet, if something needed to be picked up at the Water Palace, then they could just send us to get it without risking a valued officer. This was all new. Before Route Irish turned so deadly, everybody looked forward to any excuse to get to Camp Victory or BIAP. BIAP had the most prized of all American cultural icons, a fast-food establishment. Not some generic knockoff, either, but a real live, albeit trailer-bound, Burger King. Yes, Camp Victory had a West Virginia Burger King! Camp Victory also had the largest exchange in Iraq. Thus both the BIAP and Camp Victory runs had been very popular until people started getting killed on Route Irish. Somehow a Whopper with cheese, hold the pickles, and give me a heavy dose of IED and AK just did not seem worth the trip.

The Water Palace was located at Camp Victory, near enough to the Baghdad International Airport and the exchange that you could hit all three as long as you had an hour on the ground. The palace served as the headquarters for Combined Joint Task Force-7 (CJTF-7). It was a large, stately building that sat in the middle of a small lake. With large windows set in its sand-colored walls, the Water Palace looked much more like a resort than anything military. Other than by boat, the only way to get to the palace was through a gate at the end of a causeway which ran about 150 yards. The effect was not unlike that of a moat around a castle. From the outside, this palace, though smaller, was as impressive as the Presidential Palace. The surrounding lake also had several man-made islands upon which were buildings that appeared to be opulent homes for the ruling elite of prewar Iraq. Saddam and his ruling Baathists had it pretty good.

Now these homes housed the privileged few of the Coalition military.

Large balconies overlooked the lake, and many homes had small boat docks. The best of these homes sat on their own islands while others, just off the road that wound through the complex, still had the lake as their backyard even if they did lack the seclusion of their own private island. The entire complex, surrounded by clear blue water, was incredibly beautiful. It all seemed so totally out of place in Iraq. I wondered how beautiful it had been before the war or how much more so it would be after Hilton, Ramada, and others came in and developed the place. As it was, sitting under the bright sun of the short Iraqi spring, the complex was the most beautiful and tranquil place I ever saw in Iraq. While getting to the palace was no longer easy, and the effort potentially fatal, once you were there, you felt that it was worthwhile.

With the increased demands placed upon us, we were on the road twenty-six days in April, and the strain of making multiple runs, almost every day, while always being under the gun, was beginning to take its toll. Corporal Napier began to pull away from the team and draw closer to people who spent a lot of their time enjoying the Green Zone party scene. As odd as it may sound, the Green Zone was a mecca for the party animal, and there was an active social scene at night. Parties could be found at trailers, the pool, the "secret" Central Intelligence Agency compound, and other places too numerous to mention. The CIA compound was not so secret, because nothing was quite so sexy as telling a woman that you worked for the CIA.

It was not long before Napier quit riding with the team altogether. Napier never explained his reasons and I never asked. Sergeant Schroeder, barely in Iraq for two months, made it clear that he wanted to be reassigned to a desk job in the palace. It was hard to be critical of either man. Both had done far more than most would ever do, and every man has his limit. Maybe they just reached theirs earlier than the rest of us. But for most of us the strain showed in the tired, almost hollow expressions some wore after every mission. Our return home started to look more and more like a fantasy, which, for some, I was certain, would never be realized.

So it was in April that the team's humor turned blacker than ever. While everybody was a victim of this at one time or another (the team argued over who would get my scope when I was killed, for example), the most frequent targets were those whom I saw as having nothing to live for anyway. Using this criterion, three of us stood out as being the most likely to be killed. Chris "Huggy Bear" Reed led this group of dead men walking. He made the list because he was, as he would frequently say, "a short, fat white guy, with thinning hair and no game." Of course he was joking, a little, anyway. The additional burdens of being thirty-eight and single, firmly secured his place at the top of the "least to live for" list. Kelly "Trunk Monkey" Meggison was another member of the nothing-to-live-for team. There were so many reasons he was on the team it was difficult paring them down into a short list. In the end, Meggison was placed on the "not going to make it home team" because he had absolutely *no* social skills, and could only engage in intelligent conversation if the subject was weapons and killing people with them. Actually, Meggison was very intelligent, but he chose to limit his conversation to weapons and killing people. In hindsight we all kind of did the same. Charles "Four Shot" Dann was on the list because his fiancée had just dumped him. Frequently, I would tease the three as we sat around shooting the shit at the end of another day.

"You three are like the security detail beaming down with Captain Kirk, Spock, and McCoy. You don't know how or when, but you know they're as dead as Elvis before the first commercial. You three are the guy in the World War II movie showing his buddies a picture of his girl, who is no doubt cheating on him, and saying, 'Isn't she just swell? We're going to get married when this crazy war is over and start a family.'"

As anyone who has ever watched a World War II movie knows, the minute a guy shows a picture of his kids or his girl, or talks about his plans after the war, he is as good as dead. Reed, who had a beautiful daughter, whom he was completely smitten with, would frequently show us the newest picture of the child.

I continued. "Huggy will be showing us a picture of his daughter one day and he will say, 'Ain't she a swell kid, Top? Yeah, Top, when I get home, I am going to take her to Kings Dominion'"—a large amusement park located between Richmond, Virginia, and Washington, D.C.—"but then his voice is going to trail off and you know that Huggy, just like the guy in the World War II movie, has serious doubts about getting home. Finally Huggy, true to the World War II character, will perk up with false optimism and say, 'Yeah, sure, we will go to Kings Dominion, just me and her.'"

His last words lack any emotion as if they were just being said to finish a sentence. In a movie a harmonica always plays when the "dead man" is talking; that was the one effect we were lacking in our bashing of the team's walking dead until one mail call in late April when Shenk received his harmonica. We decided not to let Reed and his fellow Star Trek red shirts know about this until later that night. That evening, at our nightly gathering, we all waited for Reed to say something, anything. We did not have long to wait. As Reed spoke, Shenk pulled out his harmonica and began to play a soft, mournful tune. Reed grew silent, and with a grin on his face looked over toward Shenk. We all started laughing with Reed, who could only say, "Damn."

For the rest of the night whenever Reed, Meggi, or Dann spoke, their words had the soft background of Shenk's harmonica; their very own theme music! It was a good time, and we all needed the relief. We needed it more than we knew, for April was to end very badly for the United States and its Marine Corps.

The twenty-ninth of April had the team on the road in the morning and again in the afternoon. On the afternoon run we were to take Colonel Percy Woolworth Smythington IV to the Water Palace. Colonel Smythington was tall, blond-haired, and in fact, looked like a fair-haired Adam Sandler. His demeanor was typical of so many British officers, smug and contemptuous of almost everything around him, certainly anything and anyone American, but most of all enlisted personnel of the U.S. armed forces. Like most of the British and Australian military in Iraq, I was certain that he was of the opinion that things would be so much better if only the "bloody Yanks would give us a listen."

In their eyes, we were what was wrong with the war. Of course, this was an arrogance that forgets the senseless carnage of World War I where the jolly ol' empire wasted men by the tens of thousands in a *day*! Now, after fifty years of U.S. domination that has seen Europe more at peace than at any other period in that continent's history, our allies did little more than prattle about how we were what was wrong in Iraq.

As we assembled in the parking lot and waited for the designated briefing time, I sat in my Ford Explorer and turned on the radio. The news that came over Armed Forces Radio made me ill. The United States was suspending all combat operations in Fallujah. What the fuck! Why did we go in if we lacked the courage, resolve, or resources to finish the job? Why had U.S. Marines been thrown away for nothing? Four contractors roll into Fallujah, get smoked, and now the Marine Corps must conduct combat operations simply to avenge the deaths of men who would have looked at those marines as little better than the enemy. Everything from the attack itself to its sudden end seemed to be motivated by politics. Obviously, or so it seemed to us so far down the totem pole, as April grew bloodier and bloodier with no end in sight, the president lost his nerve and halted combat operations in Fallujah. For the first time since the war began, I wondered if we had the resolve to win it.

When I say "we" I do not mean the warriors fighting the war, I mean Americans in general and the president in particular. Our resolve was fine, and all we needed was for our country to leave us alone and let us fight. After all, what effect did the war have on the average American? None! The average American was still going to work, still sending *his* kid to college, and enjoying the freedom we maintained. He did not have to support us or the war, all he had to do was shut up and let us win. Maybe the president knew that the resolve of Americans at home was less than solid and that if he wanted to win in November he had better find a way to avoid a bloodbath in Fallujah. So the president gave in to the worst part of America and called it quits. Those of us in the war were incensed at his decision. I knew that the battle to take the city would be rejoined, if Bush was reelected, immediately after the November elections. But that would come later. As things stood, we had lost good marines, and for what? President Bush had blinked and I was certain we would pay a high price for it now and later.

First, Fallujah would be reinforced by the enemy. He would pour men, material, and weapons into the city. He would fortify the city against attack. He would use the victory cry "Remember Fallujah" to rally new recruits to his cause. Just as the news had crushed our morale, it was certain that it had raised that of our enemy.

I began to wonder if this war would end just as the war in Vietnam ended. In Vietnam we became the first country to win every battle and lose the war. We lost the war on the only battlefields that mattered, in the media and Washington, D.C. We were not losing this war in Baghdad, Fallujah, Tadji, or Ramadi, we were losing it back home. It was a bitter realization. Why fight at all if a bunch of cowards sitting safely at home can throw away your hardearned victory and with a cavalier attitude dismiss the war as "wrong," "impossible to win," and "too costly," and thereby make a mockery of the deaths and maiming of friends? I was disgusted! I turned off the radio and walked over to the assembled team and colonels Beemer and Smythington.

Colonel Bruce Beemer, an air defense artillery officer, had only recently been assigned as the J-3 operations officer, replacing the respected Buchanan. Air defense artillery guys shoot down incoming enemy aircraft. Since no enemy aircraft had been shot down by U.S. ground fire since the Korean War, that meant Colonel Beemer had spent the greatest part of his career in the army collecting a paycheck for learning a skill he might never use. Short, slightly pudgy, and with a receding hairline, Colonel Beemer looked exactly like Captain Kangaroo. I liked Beemer, though my experience with officers had taught me not to trust any of them until they had earned that trust. Sergeant Williams, ever suspicious of everything and everybody, was not willing to give the new colonel any breaks.

"I don't like him. He is just like that fucking asshole Owen."

Owen was an army officer who always chided Will on his less than regulation uniform appearance and his less than respectful attitude. That Owen, a major in the U.S. army, lacked the courage to tell Will what to do spoke volumes about him as a man and an officer. I reminded Williams that there was a time he wanted me dead.

"Will, if I remember right, you wanted to see me get killed when you first met me."

"Yeah, well, that was different, Top. I am telling you, this guy is bad news."

Will was not alone in feeling uneasy about our new boss. Meggi, blunt as always, said, "Well, look at it this way, Will, if we don't like the fuck at least it's good that he is riding with us. Anything can happen out there and 7.62 by 39 is 7.62 by 39 no matter who fires it."

Our enemy's rifle of choice was the AK-47, which fired 7.62 mm by 39 ammo, and Meggison's statement was an obvious play on the fact that some of my guys carried AKs.

Meggison laughed to himself as he mulled over the possibilities and then placed his cigarette back in his mouth. I briefed the two colonels on what we would do if we made contact and reminded the team that unless we lost a vehicle, we would not dismount if we were fired upon since we had two colonels with us.

"The job today is to get these two from here to the Water Palace and back again. That's it."

In Maji code for "Top, can we go to BK and the exchange?" Algarin asked, "Top, how long are we going to be on the ground?" Colonel Beemer answered for me.

"Two hours, marine."

The answer satisfied Algarin. Two hours was more than enough time to visit the exchange and BK. We loaded up and hit the road. Traffic was light, and we had no problems reaching our destination. After dropping our passengers at the end of the causeway leading to the Water Palace, we continued on to the exchange and Burger King. As we sat in the parking lot eating our chow, we discussed our new boss.

Will was his friendly self, saying, "I am telling you, Top, that fucker is bad news! Asshole!"

Remembering again Will's initial dislike for me, I said, "Will, not everybody is an asshole."

"Well, this guy is. You mark my fucking words. You'll see."

Boeringer and Algarin walked up as Reed, Will, Face, Meggi, and I continued to eat and discuss the merits of our new boss.

Boeringer asked, "Hey, Top, what are you guys talking about? Our new boss, Captain Kangaroo?"

"Yeah. Believe it or not, Will doesn't like him, Hutch," I answered.

"Yeah, well, that fuck doesn't even like his own mother, but I gotta tell ya, Top, I think Will is right on this one," said Boeringer, agreeing with Will.

Algarin, as could be expected, agreed with Boeringer's assessment of our new boss. "No shit, Top, I get along with everyone, but I gotta agree with Bo and Will here. That guy is bad news."

"Listen to this fucker. Even disagreeing with you he has to kiss a little ass, Puerto Rican fuck."

Algarin defended himself. "Bo, it's not like that, I'm just saying is all."

Facemyer added, "You watch, that guy is going to try to fuck us before the week is out."

"I think you guys have been in the palace too long. Not everybody is trying to fuck us. I think he will be okay, Face," I said.

Del came up, laughing with Dann and Brackin, "You guys are talking about the new colonel, aren't you?"

Boeringer, quick to enlist Del's support, said, "He is a prick, isn't he, Del? Tell Top. Top seems to think the guy is going to be cool."

Delacroix answered, "Top might be right, Bo. Then again, Top likes anybody shorter than him."

Wiping the remains of my Whopper from my face, I stood. "You guys might all be right but give the guy a chance. Remember, none of you wanted Boeringer or Algarin on the team because you thought they were queer, and look at them now. Everybody accepts them for *who* and not *what* they are. We should do the same here."

We finished our lunch with no agreement between those of us who wanted to give the new colonel a chance and those who wanted to sell him to the insurgents. We picked up our charges and a bus with three American colonels and six Iraqi officers on it. Now we were a big fat target. We had limited firepower, and we were escorting senior officers, many of them riding in a bus. Buses draw attention, and they slow you down. Insurgents look at buses as high payoff targets because of the possibility that they can inflict far heavier casualties with an IED than is normally the case.

We no longer had speed as a defense against the VBIED or IED. Things only got worse. Before we even left, I made a critical error, and it was to have serious repercussions. I assigned Colonel Smythington a seat in the lead vehicle. I did this because lead is the least likely to be hit in an IED attack. I should have strapped his sorry, ungrateful, tea-drinking, fish-'n'-chips-eating ass to the bumper of our rearmost vehicle instead. On the way back to the Presidential

Palace the team encountered heavy traffic. At one point an Iraqi driver switched into our lane, cutting lead off. Reed high-beamed him and honked his horn, and when those gestures failed to get the driver to move, he bumped him. The driver got out of the way, and the convoy continued moving. As always, rifles bristled from every window in the convoy, warning, in very visual and certain terms, all vehicles to stay away from the convoy. Shortly after the errant Iraqi driver got out of our way, a gray BMW sedan closed on the rear of the convoy at a high rate of speed. The car maneuvered through traffic and made for our rear vehicle, which I was in, since I had placed the mutton-eating Coalition speed bump in my seat.

Gunny Josleyn, manning the rear machine gun, said, "Top, we got a fast mover closing back here."

"What's it look like, Gunny?" I asked.

"Gray BMW with tinted windows. Looks like a man driving, and he has a passenger who may be a woman."

Looking for further clarification I asked, "Is it in a convoy?"

"No, Top."

Satisfied that this was at least a potential threat, I told Gunny Josleyn, "Don't let it pass." I then passed what I knew to the rest of the team, saying, "All Maji, listen up. We have a BMW sedan, gray, closing on the rear of the convoy at a very high rate of speed. Acknowledge."

After everybody had "rogered" up on the radio, I passed that we were holding the vehicle to our rear.

"Top."

It was Gunny Josleyn again, "Yeah, gunny."

"The driver is waving an American flag and wants to pass."

"Fuck him. Do not let him pass," I replied.

"Just letting you know."

I keyed my handset and said, "All Maji, if the BMW goes around and makes it past us, engage immediately."

Everybody acknowledged that they understood. Lacking speed and escorting the package we were, I saw few other options. There was no way we could afford to let an unknown vehicle pass up the rear of our convoy. If they were intent on doing us harm they would pass us, wave, and detonate when they were next to the bus. Why waste five guys in an SUV when instead you can waste perhaps dozens in a bus, and those important enough to rate an escort? The driver of the BMW now had two choices, stay put or die. All of this information flowed over the radio, and all of it was heard by Smythington. According to Reed, Smythington was already in a foul mood because of the way he was driving. "Far too fast and damned aggressive." He almost went mad with rage after Reed tapped the vehicle that had slowed in front of him.

Hearing my orders to engage the gray BMW should it shoot past my vehicle only further discomfited the English officer. To those who have never spent a great deal of time on Iraq's roads, my orders no doubt would seem very harsh. I had, in reality, just signed a death warrant for the occupants of the BMW should it do something as simple as attempt to pass my vehicle—an occurrence that happened every day on highways the world over. But to allow a vehicle to overtake your convoy was a lethal mistake made by dozens of Americans in Iraq, and it was not one I was ever going to make. Shooting and killing one or two people who may or may not pose a threat, simply for driving in a manner that indicated they could be a threat, was far easier on my conscience than it would be to allow that vehicle to pass and then watch it take out my friends in a blinding flash.

While Iraqi drivers could be terribly inattentive, they were not stupid. Often they would close on the rear of a convoy at a high rate of speed, oblivious of the weapons, until suddenly, and normally at less than twenty-five yards distance, they would see the weapons and back off. A few of the more unwary would draw even closer. These you would signal with hand and arm motions to back off, and if that failed, you would point a weapon at them in an aggressive manner. The Iraqi, his attention now fixed on you, would open his hands by extending his fingers while they were still on the wheel, in an apologetic manner, and slow down. Frequently, the Iraqi driver would raise one hand, hold it up as if to swear, and then wave it as if he were apologizing for his inattentiveness. Male drivers who did not do these things were always presumed to be a threat. Male drivers who continued to close and try to catch the convoy were in danger of being shot. Our aggressive posture was not something we did just so we could harass the Iraqi driver. Our posture helped us separate the threats from the regular guys who just were not paying attention. It kept us alive, and it lessened the chance that we might kill a driver who was simply not paying attention.

Smythington, who did not spend a lot of time on Iraq's roads, like so many palace commandos, just did not understand this. In his ignorance he could not see how our actions helped ensure not only our safety but also that of the average Iraqi driver by allowing us to have clear and escalating signals that a driver's intent was hostile. Only a man who wanted to kill you would continue to close on such an obviously aggressive formation. Only a man who wanted to kill you would ignore the weapons, the hand gestures, and, finally, the weapons pointing his way. Smythington did not see any of this. All he saw was dumb American grunts abusing the local populace. Nor could he begin to understand, let alone appreciate, what kind of nerves it took to wait, as a vehicle closed to under seventy-five meters, fifty and still closing. Wait, wait, maybe he is just not paying attention. Signal him, hope he acknowledges the signal. He doesn't. Closing rapidly . . . forty . . . thirty . . . twenty-five meters! Point the weapon at him and make him stop! The trunk monkeys, especially Gunny Josleyn, had an extremely difficult job. Torn between their desire to live and not to kill the innocent, they made life-and-death decisions without the benefit of hindsight or a panel discussion. Men like Smythington were highly critical of those of us who had to make these decisions, but I bet he thanked God that they were never his to make.

The driver of the BMW wisely stayed behind the convoy. As we approached the gate and slowed to a stop, we dismounted as we always did. This time however, we dismounted and immediately leveled our weapons on the gray BMW.

The driver, an American contractor as it turned out, opened his car door and began screaming at us.

"You guys are fucking dangerous. I was giving you all the signs, and that asshole wouldn't let me pass."

"What fucking sign was that?" I asked.

"I was waving a flag, flashing my lights, and still you guys wouldn't let me pass. You're scaring the shit out of my passenger. Hell, you're scaring the shit out of me now. Can I please get around you assholes?"

I answered, saying, "First, I was never briefed that the running password or signal was waving an American flag. Face, anyone ever pass that one to you?"

"No, Top, never heard that one before," Facemyer replied.

I continued, turning my attention back to the contractor. "Second, just because you're in a hurry and waving an American flag does not mean shit to me. You are not traveling in a convoy, and you are driving an unmarked sedan. Your driving fit the profile for a car bomber, and there is no fucking way we were going to let you close on us. Besides that, we are uniformed U.S. military, and we, not you assholes, have priority."

Almost frantic now, the contractor answered, "Okay, dammit, just let me get in front of you fucking assholes. Do you know how dangerous it is out here?"

Looking around as if surveying the dangerous environs around the gate for the first time, I answered, "Yeah, I do, and it is no more so for you than it is for us or anyone else coming through this gate, and you, just like everyone else, just like us, will wait until everyone in front of you has gone."

The man grew extremely irate and even appeared to reach for a pistol before, wisely, thinking better of it. After we were through the gate, the BMW turned off into the secret CIA compound. I should have known—another dipshit security contractor. Like many Americans making a lot of money in Iraq, the driver seemed to regard himself as critical to the war effort while disdaining the common grunt as little more than some dumb bastard getting in his way.

Once we pulled into the staging area, Smythington stormed over to me. "Master Sergeant, this convoy was an absolute disgrace."

Not at all sure what he was talking about, I asked, "How's that, sir?"

The social worker in a uniform told me that our aggressiveness and speed were excessive. He added, "You are, in fact, creating more terrorists and costing the lives of Coalition soldiers."

Smythington was obviously of the "blame America" school of thought. If we only showed more understanding, we would win the hearts and minds of Islam. This school of thought stumbled to explain how we provoked September 11, but was, nevertheless, certain that somehow American policies were to blame. It never dawned on them that we were at war with an enemy who wanted to kill us just because we did not see the world as he did. It was a school of thought that could not explain why Daniel Pearl had been decapitated or why Russian schoolchildren would be murdered. But somehow, if we just did not point our rifles at Iraqi vehicles closing on the convoy, terrorism in Iraq would die.

I attempted to explain to the Coalition officer why we operated as we did. "Sir, you do understand that we lack armor, jammers, and other basic equipment. You do understand that speed is our only protection against IEDs. You do understand the principle that a hard target, that is giving the appearance of an alert, determined, and aggressive unit makes us look like a hard target, and if you look like a hard target, you are, in fact, a hard target. You understand those things, right, sir?"

Her Majesty's officer was not satisfied. "I have been on numerous convoys with the brigadier, and his people do none of that."

Pushing back, I asked the Queen's officer, "Sir, do you know the terrorists' TTPs [tactics, techniques and procedures]?

The gentleman from England said, "Yes I do."

Not one to let an opportunity pass, I challenged him, "Okay, sir, what are they?"

The man could barely contain himself. He was incensed.

"Master Sergeant Lynch, is it?"

I nodded. "Yes, sir."

He answered, "Right, then, have it your way. I have been in Northern Ireland and in Basra, and our forces in those places do not conduct themselves this way, and we have none of the problems you are facing here, in Baghdad and elsewhere."

The comparison was a foolish one. The south, where Basra is located, was dominated by Shia Arabs. Long oppressed by Saddam, the Shia, like the Kurds in the north, were very supportive of the Coalition, and that made life easier in places like Basra and the Kurdish north. But Baghdad, Ramadi, Tikrit, Hit, and Fallujah were dominated by Sunnis. Saddam was a Sunni, and they had prospered under Baath rule. The ouster of Saddam left them a suddenly powerless minority, and they were not happy about it, and they expressed their displeasure by trying to kill you. The Sunnis also held sway in the best units of Iraq's army, and Sunni insurgents were far more lethal than the untrained Shia. The Sunnis also brought in scores of foreign fighters, making the cities they populated even more deadly. Incredibly, Smythington could not seem to understand that Northern Ireland and Basra were not Baghdad and Fallujah. His statement was akin to Sheriff Taylor, of Mayberry, North Carolina, asking a D.C. cop why he felt the need to carry a gun.

Refusing to let the man's foolishness go unchallenged, I answered, "Sir, you do know that Americans run the Kurdish North and have fewer problems there than you have in Basra? It's not us. It's a difference in who you are dealing with in the Sunni Triangle as opposed to places like Basra. The tactics we use are not designed to torment or harass the Iraqi. They are designed to protect us and the Iraqis, and I am not changing them until someone senior to you and in an American uniform tells me to."

"Sergeant, alright then, you can rest assured that I will make it my personal business to see to it that you are told to change your tactics, do you understand me?" the Queen's colonel threatened.

I answered, saying, "Sure, good luck, sir."

Before this could degenerate any further, Colonel Beemer pulled Smythington aside, effectively ending our pointless exchange. (As an interesting postscript to my exchange with the English officer, *The Times* of London would report in August 2008 that a "secret deal" between the Mahdi army and the Brits in Basra kept the Mahdi from attacking British forces in exchange for those forces not interfering with the militia's activities in Basra. As a result Basra became a hell on earth for Iraqis living in the city. When the Iraqi army moved against the Mahdi in the spring of 2008, the four-thousand-man British force sat and watched, which necessitated U.S. Marines going down to Basra to support the Iraqi army. One highly placed British source was quoted as saying the secret deal had "dealt a huge blow to Britain's reputation in Iraq." He continued, "You can accuse the Americans of many things, such as hamfistedness, but you can't accuse them of not addressing a problem when it arises. While we had a strategy of evasion, the Americans just went in and dealt with the problem." I almost wondered whether Colonel Smythington was one of the architects of the deal.)

April ended with Iraq appearing to descend farther into anarchy. American leaders wondered what was next; all expected casualties to rise as we drew nearer to the formal transition of power in June. As it was, April was bad enough. April turned out to be, as of September 2009, the second most deadly month for the Coalition. No fewer than 139 Coalition soldiers died. Those killed in action numbered 127, still the highest monthly total for KIAs in the war. Of course, the vast majority of the Coalition's dead were American soldiers and marines. Worse, April had seen the United States back down in Fallujah, a defeat that was sure to have serious repercussions. Closer to home, April saw greater numbers of palace commandos sleeping on cots in the basement, rather than in their far more comfortable trailers. This was done to avoid the rocket and mortar fire. Believe me, when you make a rear area commando give up creature comforts for safety, you have struck that man's psyche a mortal blow.

For the team, life got significantly better with the arrival of Gunnery Sergeant Robert Josleyn, whom I was able to pry away from Major Kesterson in exchange for two soldiers, one master sergeant and one specialist. I felt like an NFL general manager on draft day. I had just traded two draft picks for a proven veteran, and I was sure I got the better end of the deal. Time would prove this to be the case. Major Kesterson knew what he was losing, but he was a good man, and while he would not have harmed his own command to give me the gunny, he would not stand in the way of a soldier or marine wanting to fight so long as he had an adequate replacement. Gunny was a warrior, and he was happy to be joining the fight.

In palace politics the convoy security team was holding its own, largely due to the unwavering support of men like colonels Thomas and Sarna and Major Drury. But the team was also making prominent enemies. April left all of us wondering if we would make it home in one piece, and we all felt certain that not all of us would. As the war grew hotter and the atmosphere in the palace grew more hostile, we drew more into ourselves and became even tighter. No matter what happened, we would ride it out together.

May started with a bang, and I very nearly became our first casualty. On 2 May we were told that we would be making runs to the Ministry of the Interior, or MOI, for short. Not sure how to get there, I decided that we would recon what appeared to be good routes on the map. For this purpose we took Colonel Ahmed with us.

"Lunch, Lunch, yes, I know the way. I will show you."

Ignoring his now customary butchering of my name, which was probably less than my butchering of his anyway, I asked him if he was sure. Colonel Ahmed assured me that he knew a very good route through the market. When I questioned him about the heavy traffic in the market, he told me it would not be a problem. Much to my regret, I accepted what Colonel Ahmed said. Almost to my eternal regret, I took him with us for our route recon that afternoon. As Colonel Ahmed only had a pistol, I instructed Sergeant Facemyer to give him an AK-47. This seemed to make sense, as Colonel Ahmed had carried an AK-47 before. Facemyer locked and loaded the weapon, placed it on safe, and handed it to Colonel Ahmed. As Ahmed took the weapon, Facemyer and explained to him basic safe weapons handling and made sure the colonel knew where the safety was. "Here you go, sir. Now remember, she is loaded and ready to fire, so keep her on safe until you see us shooting."

While Facemyer's instructions to Colonel Ahmed were not what one would expect at a range, they were clear enough. At least I thought they were. We were just clearing the gate and had not even turned into traffic when there was a sudden and terrific blast behind my head. I felt the blast wave pass over my right arm, and the right side of my face, neck, and head. It was immediately obvious that Colonel Ahmed had accidentally discharged his weapon and almost killed me. For whatever reason, I did not react as others expected. In fact, I had almost no reaction at all. Face screamed, "Top!" I looked back at Ahmed and then Face and said, "I am okay. Perfectly fine."

"You stupid motherfucker," Facemyer admonished the colonel. Meggison, in his slow Maine drawl, just said, "Ha, ain't that some shit, boss." Will and Face proceeded to dress down Colonel Ahmed like he was a private.

"Give me that fucking rifle," Will ordered.

As soon as the shot was fired, vehicles 2 and 3 were on the net.

"What the fuck was that?"

"Are you guys hit?"

I answered, "We had an ND [negligent discharge] in vehicle one. Everybody is fine, out."

"Who the fuck was it?" asked both vehicles.

I keyed my handset. "Never mind. Pay attention, out!"

Someone answered, "Check, Top."

While the verbal abuse continued unabated in the backseat, Reed looked over and very quietly said, "Top, really, are you okay?"

"Yeah, Huggy, but I think we got damn lucky that vehicles two and three didn't smoke everybody on the street."

I did not know then, and I do not know now, why I did not shit all over myself or lose my mind on Colonel Ahmed. Certainly part of the reason I did not lose it was that I respected him because of his courage. At a time when many Americans were hiding and even sleeping in the palace in fear of their lives, he had volunteered to ride out into Dodge City with us. I also felt sorry for him. Iraqi soldiers wanted to make a good impression on Americans; they tried very hard to be as professional and competent as they viewed us. They were very sensitive to how we perceived their courage and professionalism, and they wanted to be seen as equals. I knew that Ahmed was humiliated, and though he had good reason to be, he was not alone in having almost killed a man in a moment's carelessness. Repeatedly, Ahmed apologized to me.

"Lunch, Lunch, I am sorry, Lunch. It is my duty and I am sorry."

I think I was more aggravated with him for screwing up my name than I was for having almost killed me.

The trip to the MOI, was uneventful after that except for the transition through the heavily congested market. Ruling that route out, we were able to find safer and quicker routes to the MOI, which we designated as primary and alternate. When we got back to the palace, and after Ahmed had gone inside, Sergeant Boeringer asked about the ND.

"So, Top, you gonna tell us what happened in your vehicle? Will and Face get into it with each other over whose turn it was to be on top? Or did you and Chris get in a fight about whose turn it was to make the bed? C'mon, give us something here."

Bo always spoke with a moderate New York accent and everything he said had a New York attitude. He was like a big kid with a new toy whenever he had something on somebody, and it was obvious that he was hoping that one of us (Meg, Face, Will, Reed, or I) had been the person responsible for the negligent discharge.

Looking at him, I said, "Ahmed almost shot me."

Boeringer replied, saying, "What? You gotta be fuckin' kidding me. You guys didn't shoot him or anything? I mean the important thing is that you're all okay, especially *you*, Top, but still, somebody should have shot him."

"You know, Top," Reed chimed in, "think about how ironic it would have been to get killed by a friendly Iraqi."

Not all the shots came from friendly Iraqis however. Two days later, on 4 May, while traveling to BIAP, the left passenger window of my Ford Explorer was blown out by an apparent rifle shot. Staff Sergeant Leroy Waters, newly assigned to operations, was seated at the window. He screamed, "Ahhhh, someone just tried to kill me."

Gunny Hessen, my driver on this run, did not even flinch. I told Gunny to stop three hundred meters ahead and then keyed my handset and told the team that we had shots fired from the left side of the highway, just past the second overpass. We dismounted and scanned the area we thought the shot came from but could not see anything. Since it was a single shot and had been fired either with some skill, given our speed at the time of impact, or tremendous luck, I weighed the possibilities. If the shot was in fact not the byproduct of just dumb luck, then it might have come from a Dragunov SVD.

The SVD is a Russian sniper rifle firing a 7.62 by 54 mm round. Though well made and accurate, the weapon can be used by only the very best shooters at anything approaching its maximum effective range of eight hundred meters. Assuming that this guy was anything but the very best, we scanned the area in front of us out to five hundred meters. The heat of the day was already well over 110 degrees, and the black asphalt made it feel like we were kneeling in a skillet. As I continued to scan, I decided that our speed and the limited field of view available to a guy peering through the optic of an SVD seemed to rule out a guy shooting at us with a Dragunov. It was far more likely that the shot was nothing but an extremely lucky round fired by some ass spraying rounds with an AK. Still, it was difficult to get a fix on where the shot came from, as none of us heard it. This was not unusual, as previous experience had taught me that you almost never heard shots fired at you when you were moving at high speed. You only knew you were being shot at when the bullets impacted your vehicle or objects very near it. After several minutes of fruitless searching, I had the team remount and move out.

Once we had dropped off our cargo at the airport, Colonel Thomas and I inspected my vehicle. Waters's window appeared to have been blown in after being struck with an object of some velocity. Glass was blown out, in a radial pattern, from his window, across his seat, and into the right front floorboard. The window across from Waters was rolled up and did not have any holes in it. The door across from Waters was also free of any bullet impacts. That left one place for the bullet to go, one place it could go without doing any additional damage to our vehicle, and that was over my right shoulder, just as had the bullet fired by Colonel Ahmed. It seemed too incredible to be true. Twice within a span of two days I had a bullet pass over my right shoulder. Del finished looking around the inside of the vehicle for an impact, and finding none, she said with a laugh, "Hey, what can I tell you, Top. You're just lucky."

Schroeder looked at Waters and said, "Bullshit, this fat fuck broke the thing somehow."

"Hey, you know what? Fuck you, Schroeder! This fat-assed hillbilly will kick the hell outta you."

I was growing disgusted with the display. "Both of you shut the fuck up and get back in the vehicles."

As the team loaded up I approached Colonel Thomas about checking the area from which we believed the shot to have originated.

"Hey, sir, looking at how low that thing hit the window, it had to have come from that grassy area next to the road—"

Hesco interrupted me, "I was already thinking it, Top. Let's go back and see if we can find the guy."

We all loved and respected the colonel. Not just because he did his best to get us critical gear and keep the palace pansies off of us but because he really cared. He put his ass out there with us as often as his duties would allow. He was not the typical staff officer who hid behind words like "duty."

When we were about 300 meters short of where we believed the shot had come from, we dismounted, leaving drivers and machine gunners with the vehicles. The drivers would move slowly down the shoulder, keeping just 100

Vehicle 1, a.k.a. "All-Star One," and crew, left to right: **Staff Sergeant Chris Reed, USA, the author, Sergeants Jason Williams and Kevin Facemyer, both USA, and Corporal Kelly Meggison** *(From the collection of Jack Lynch)*

meters behind the dismounts, as we swept the tall grass on the shoulder. The area was surprisingly swampy and offered numerous concealed locations from which a man could take a shot or two before escaping into the town through this grassland. We swept the roadside for over 600 meters without finding anything. Frustrated, we remounted our vehicles and arrived at the Green Zone within a few minutes.

One of the C-4 soldiers was waiting for us when we returned. The C-4 was the logistics section, and they controlled CMATTs vehicles.

"Top, KBR wants the vehicles. They are overdue on maintenance."

All of our vehicles were leased through Kellog Brown and Root, more popularly known as KBR, a subsidiary of Halliburton.

Concerned, I asked, "Did they say they would temp some vehicles to us while these are serviced?"

The soldier answered, "Yeah, no problem. They just gotta get to these."

I turned to Reed.

"Hey, Staff Sergeant Reed, have the drivers take these over to KBR and drop them off and exchange them for some temps."

While the drivers saw to the vehicles, the rest of us went into the palace and stowed our gear. The weather was terribly hot now, well over one hundred degrees on most days. The cool Iraqi spring was a distant memory, and the cold Iraqi winter was a mirage. I grabbed a water bottle out of the fridge kept in the operations section and sat behind my desk to check up on the latest news. What I saw sickened me.

CHAPTER 10

KBR Protects Its Profits

Adherents of the religion of peace have an American, wearing an orange jumpsuit, bound before them. The masked disciples of Muhammad are armed with the tools of religious conversion, as called for by their faith; they hold AK-47s and other weapons. One man, believed to be al-Zarqawi, reads a manifesto calling for holy war against the west, the United States in particular. This man then takes a large knife and cuts off the head of the man bound before him. The victim screams in terror and pain while his head is slowly cut off. The blade saws back and forth across the defenseless man's neck. The minister of peace then holds the severed head up for the camera. Another "infidel" served the justice of Allah! Both during the brutal murder and in its immediate aftermath you can hear the savage subhuman sons of Muhammad shout *"Allah Akbar."*

Our new enemies are not like us in any way. We have no shared culture. The Christian faith does not demand that we kill those who will not convert or that they accept our domination over them. For that matter neither does Judaism, Hinduism, or any other faith. These people look at all of us as beneath contempt and deserving of only the most horrific death. And while we are wringing our hands over waterboarding and Abu Ghraib these people are singing the praises of Allah as they remove our heads. We should be fighting this war with all of our might and wrath! But America, I feared, no longer had the will to fight total wars. Looking at the dancing animals on the screen in front of me shouting *Allah Akbar* as they carried their grim trophy aloft, I had no doubt that they were willing to fight a total war. While I knew I would never forget any of this, I was certain that my fellow country-men would forget it by morning. I did not have long to digest any of this when the phone rang in the operations center. Major Ricks answered it. "Top Lynch," she said as she held the phone out for me, "It's Chris Reed for you." I ignored the fact that she forgot Chris had a rank and thanked her as I took the phone.

"What's up, Staff Sergeant Reed?"

"Top, KBR says they are not giving us any more vehicles because of the condition these are in."

More than a little shocked, I asked, "What the fuck do you mean they aren't giving us any more vehicles?"

Reed answered, "Top, they refused to issue us any temp loans while these are serviced because they are all banged up and shot up."

I was barely able to believe what I was hearing. I said, "Ask them if we can just have those back after they are serviced."

"I already did, Top. They said they could not do that because they were a hazard."

"A hazard, a hazard? Ask that asshole if he knows where we are. You're kidding me, right?"

"No, Top, I wouldn't kid ya about a thing like that."

"Can I talk to them?" I asked him.

"Sure, hold on."

I heard Reed tell someone that the operations sergeant major wanted to talk to him. I heard someone, apparently the man Reed was passing the phone to, say, "Yeah, I'll talk to him, but it isn't gonna do any good."

"Hello."

Doing my best to be both polite and professional, I answered, "Hey, my name is Master Sergeant Lynch and I am the operations sergeant major for CMATT and the convoy security team commander. I understand that you will not release my old vehicles back to me nor will you issue us new ones. Is that correct?"

"Yes, it is," the disinterested, disembodied, bureaucratic voice responded.

"Why not?" I asked.

"These vehicles are a mess. They are overdue on maintenance. Two have significant damage from hitting something—cars, trees, deer, I don't know what. One is missing a bumper, and two have holes in the windows and windshields."

I abandoned my attempt to be both polite and professional. I answered, "Those are fucking bullet holes. The dents and missing bumper are from collisions with Iraqi vehicles. You do understand that you are in Baghdad, right? You do understand that you do not work at the fucking Avis counter at LAX, right?"

The disinterested bureaucratic voice on the phone was unimpressed. "Sergeant, these vehicles are leased through KBR, and they are the property of KBR. I will not give them back to you, and I will not issue you any new vehicles."

Though I knew it did not matter to this guy—I was certain he had never left the Green Zone—I nevertheless was compelled to tell him, "You know that if you do that you will be shutting down the only security team CMATT has. You know we have, at the express desire of KBR employees, provided escorts for your convoys as a favor to cover your guys' asses. Now you tell me you are not going to give me any more vehicles. Let me talk to the staff sergeant there."

Reed answered, "What do you want us to do, Top?"

"Just c'mon back, Huggy. We will figure out something. I will get Colonel Thomas to call over there and see if he can pull us anything."

I hung up the phone and asked Colonel Thomas to intervene on our behalf with KBR. To no avail. He, too, was told that KBR would not issue us any more vehicles. Not only was he rebuffed, but so, too, the new ops officer, Captain John Wheeler USN. Wheeler had recently replaced Colonel Beemer, when Beemer was moved to another section within the palace. Wheeler was a naval aviator who had flown P3 Orion missions during the first Gulf War, something he never grew tired of reminding the team. I think it was his way of saying, "Hey, I am just like you guys, living life on the edge." He was completely out of his element when he was assigned as the deputy chief of staff for operations. Nobody in the office, neither the Maji nor our detractors, felt that Wheeler could even wipe his ass without help. It was one of the few things we would all agree on. Wheeler was scorned and loathed by all but the most sycophantic among the officers. Colonel Eric Deboda, Lieutenant Colonel Sid Johns, and Major Theodorson frequently buffed the man's ass with their lips. Deboda, a reserve Special Forces officer, had recently joined the operations section and was assigned to plans. He was to have a significant impact on all of us.

To his lasting credit and my eternal surprise, Major Sherman, like Colonel

Thomas and the other marine officers in the section, refused to massage Wheeler's ego.

Following Wheeler's and Hesco's failure to persuade KBR to release our vehicles, I turned to CMATT's C-4 section. They had many vehicles in their lot, but all were issued out. Fortunately, we were able to work deals with the engineer officer, a wonderful naval reserve officer, to use one of his vehicles when it was not in use by his section and with Napier to use the chief of staff's SUV. We were also able to share a vehicle assigned to the intel shop. But we could only use these vehicles when they were available, and the intel section's and the chief of staff's were rarely free. Worse, rarely would both the chief of staff's and the intel vehicles be free at the same time. This half-assed solution left us with only one vehicle we could count on, and that was not enough to get the job done. The attitude to our plight within CMATT was predictable. Colonel Thomas alone worked feverishly to have armored Hummers released to us, but this was taking time. Missions were being canceled because the operations section lacked the resources required to put the security team on the road.

Captain Wheeler seemed content with that. "Well, Top, if we don't have the vehicles, you guys can do more stuff in here. I don't know what to tell you."

Still others, like Vorgang, long a critic of the the evolving mission of the team, seemed to enjoy the whole thing. "If we weren't doing a security mission that we had no business doing, runs wouldn't be getting canceled."

That our mission evolved as the war changed seemed to be beyond his ability to grasp. He had once, and not so long ago, loudly proclaimed the war was over. Vorgang was out of his element doing anything other than sucking the cream filling out of a Twinkie. The team was in a unique position. Through no dereliction of duty or cowardice on our part, we found ourselves without the equipment we needed. Through no fault of our own, we suddenly had very little to do, relieved of the most dangerous duty in Iraq. Captain Wheeler was happy to put us to work in the office. Working in the palace and not pulling convoy security everyday meant that we would survive our tours. Our pay would still be the same and we would get to go home. All we had to do was accept what our chain of command had told us: "You can do more stuff in here." Most people would have taken that and run with it. We had already gone beyond what anybody could reasonably expect by volunteering for the team in the first place. We had hit the road about a hundred times, without armor, with communications gear not worth a shit, lacking corpsmen or crew-served weapons, and yet we were all still alive. Clearly, by the standards applied at the palace, and everywhere in fact but the infantry units of the army and the Marine Corps, we had done more than our part. Maybe it was time to call it a day and quit before we lost someone. All of us fully expected May and June to be worse than April, so why not ride it out in the safety and comfort of the palace? Without vehicles we simply lacked the means to continue laying our lives on the line. Most people in that position would have donned shorts, grabbed a beer, and headed for the pool. Most people. I mulled all this over when I gathered the team together to explain that, officially, we had exhausted all means of getting vehicles. I looked around at my team as they shuffled in around me and took their seats. Just as I knew what I was going to say, I knew how they were going to respond.

"We cannot get any vehicles, and nobody else seems to be able to get them for us either. Wheeler says we can just stay here. So we can now live out our days in the palace knowing that we did everything within our power to get the vehicles we needed. We went further and never accepted no for an answer until the last door was slammed in our faces. Now we can all sit poolside, just like these faggots, sun ourselves, and know that we are going home and tell war stories every bit as good as those these palace commandos are going to tell when they get home. You answered the call when I was looking for volunteers. You rode without even the most basic equipment, and you never lost a person or cargo. Most people would call that a good tour and be happy to relax for a while."

I paused as I looked around at my team, trying to size up each person's thoughts.

Continuing, I said, "But I don't think you would have ever volunteered for this duty in the first place if all you came over here to do was punch your ticket. I suspect that all of you are as driven and determined today as you were back in February. I know I am. I do not want to stay in this place, looking at these people, while I slowly become one of them. The war is not over, and there is still a lot we can do. You guys can join the palace pool volleyball team, or we can start looking at some creative ways to get vehicles just like everything else we have had to acquire."

Someone—I do not remember who—asked what we could do.

"Well, Staff Sergeant Reed thinks he can get us two vehicles that we would own. He and Del think they would be good to go. We just have to borrow them."

The substitution of the word "borrow" for "steal" was not lost on anyone. In the old Corps this activity was referred to as a "moonlight requisition."

"Hey," I said, "we haven't decided anything yet. Officially, you guys have been told that nothing is available, and I am not going to tell you to do something illegal just so you can stay on the road. Just like before, this is voluntary. What do you guys want to do?"

Del spoke first.

"Shit, I didn't come all the way over here just to hang out with you ass-holes. I say we go for it. What the fuck can they do to us anyway?"

Bo was next.

"Top, you already know the answer. We're all in, so just tell us what we gotta do."

"Yeah, Top, tell us," Algarin added.

I turned to Reed, who with Meggison had thought up the plan.

He addressed the team. "Well, there are a couple of Nissan Patrols that used to belong to some Iraqi government agency, but nobody has used them since the invasion, but they do belong to someone and they will not give them up. Now I have checked them out, and they run really good, but one is miss-ing the doors and the radio, but other than that they are perfect. Since they do not belong to KBR we can also do anything to them we want. We can tailor these things to our mission."

He turned to me, and continued.

"Now I will tell you, Top, we might have one problem and that is getting fuel for them. The military fuel points will only refuel military vehicles, and the KBR refuel point will only refuel vehicles that have a KBR trip ticket, and obviously we do not have those."

"How can we get them?" I asked.

"Well, Top, I think we might have to make them."

I thought about the potential repercussions of "making" trip tickets on top of "getting" vehicles and how we had already acquired most of our heavy weapons. My unit was turning into a criminal enterprise, and with the "mak-ing" of trip tickets we were branching out into forgery.

I answered, "Okay, make them. What about spare tires and parts?"

"We can get those the same way we got the vehicles," Reed answered.

I asked Reed, "What do you need?"

"Well, Top, Del, Fudd, and I could use some help getting the vehicles over to the house and then some help working on them."

"Do you need people tonight?"

"No, it doesn't have to be tonight, Top. Tomorrow after morning chow would be fine."

Satisfied with Reed's answer, I turned to the Maji. "Okay you guys, last chance to bail."

In the fading light I could see that they were all smiling. I had not seen them smile that way in a long while. As I looked at them, I thought about what had just taken place. All of us had begun to wonder if we were going to make it home. Every time we left the gate we were acutely aware that the next mile might be our last, and we all accepted that not all of us would make it home alive. Then, out of the blue, we had been offered a reprieve. Salvation was ours to take! There would be no dishonor in simply doing what we were told to do. We had exhausted every official option open to us, and so, one could reason, we had done our best to stay on the road. We had done our duty.

A strange word, "duty." A man can stay at Quantico when a call goes out for volunteers to serve in Iraq, telling himself that he is doing his duty. I have heard more than one man say, "If they need me they will ask for me; if not, obviously I am more needed here." A man sent to Iraq, either ordered to go or as a volunteer, can arrive and find himself with a job that keeps him relatively safe and spend his tour content with knowing that he is doing his duty. Very few are the people who will volunteer to go to places like Iraq. Fewer still are those who will see the war, the suffering it brings his countrymen, and actively seek a way to do his duty, not as defined by his military occupational specialty or his duty assignment but by his own sense of duty.

We call these people heroes. Looking around at the faces of these soldiers and marines, my men, my family, I was reminded every day that it was my great privilege to serve in the company of heroes. As I considered how truly blessed was the United States of America that it could call these young men and women its own, I was reminded of something that I had read about long ago.

In November 1943 U.S. Marines of the 2nd Marine Division stormed the Japanese bastion of Betio Island in the Tarawa atoll. Many marines were to be carried ashore in Higgins boats, a vessel of very shallow draft. Tarawa was surrounded by a reef, in some places going out to eight hundred meters off the beaches where the marines would land. General Holland "Howlin' Mad" Smith, the marine commanding the landing forces, was concerned that there would not be enough water over the reef for the boats to clear it. The navy brass, safely tucked beneath layers of armor on their battleships far out to sea, assured him there would be enough draft.

There was not. In the face of murderous machine gun, mortar, and artillery fire, many marines found themselves going into the water when their boats ground to a halt on the reef. Under continuous fire, these men waded in through a half mile of chest-deep water. In seventy-two hours, nearly a thousand marines were killed in action. Of the Japanese garrison of over five thousand men, only seventeen survived.

After-battle photos show a beach littered with dead marines and wrecked amtracs and tanks. In some places the dead were stacked so thick as to remind one of a Civil War battlefield. In this scene of absolute human carnage, something caught the eye of two marine generals who were walking the beach. Crumpled by the seawall where he had been killed was the body of a marine. One of his hands extended to the top of the wall, and in it was clutched a beach marker flag that was planted so that follow-on waves would know where to land. The act of planting that flag had taken tremendous courage. The seawall had been swept by fire; dead marines lay all along it. Any man who stuck his head up was likely to be killed. The water behind the marine would already have been littered with wrecked vehicles and dead marines when he waded ashore; a warning to him! Yet this marine and others like him did raise their heads above that wall, and this marine, like so many others that day, died while planting that simple marker. Looking at this lifeless, mute tribute to duty and courage, one general, tears welling in his eyes, said, "God, where do we get such men?"

Sixty-one years later, I could not have answered the general's question, but I could share in his amazement and thank God that wherever we got them then, we are getting them still. At a time when at least one army convoy had mutinied and refused to carry out a mission due to the lack of armor and the poor state of its equipment, I could not help but feel proud of my team.

At about 1000 the next morning, following chow and the morning ops meeting, I asked Hesco if he would like to accompany me to the team's compound.

"Your 'compound'? What is *your* 'compound,' and how did you get it?"

"Well, sir, we worked a deal with the guy who runs property in the Green Zone. Think of him as this war's Sergeant Bilko. Anyway, we had something he wanted and we made a deal for the compound."

Hesco smiled and shook his head. The compound consisted of a walled area across the street from the parking area of the Presidential Palace. Within the walls of the compound was a single-story building that had one central great room with many bedrooms off of it. The floors and ceilings of this building were very opulent. There was some trash strewn on the floors, and there was no power. Outside the main entrance to this building was a portico that connected the building to a smaller cookhouse just twenty feet away. Beyond the portico were swings and benches clustered around two outdoor fireplaces. Running parallel to the house was a soccer field and, beyond it, a large paved area around what was left of the Baath Party headquarters.

The headquarters had been completely gutted by American munitions.

From the outside you could see that the building was heavily damaged, but, for the most part, the façade remained intact. The interior of the building, however, was a mess. All the walls had been blown out, leaving the building a shell. But deep within this building was a complex bunker system that survived in spite of the heavy pounding by American aircraft. The bunker was now a popular attraction for Americans stationed in the Green Zone. Next to this building was a large tower, Iraq's version of Seattle's famous Space Needle. The tower bore the scars of American heavy machine-gun and tank fire but it remained intact and was, in fact, sturdy enough to allow people to walk to the top where the view of Baghdad was impressive. Most important to us, the compound was only accessible from one point, and this point was protected by a locked gate that only we and the guy who "leased" the property to us had the keys for. This meant that we would have a private place to call our own. Best of all, the property also had several garages that we could lock. This allowed us to secure our vehicles rather than leave them in the common lot where anybody could do anything to them, including booby-trapping them, which was believed to have happened at least once. Two British security men died from burns in that incident. Iraqi witnesses reported that their was a small explosion which set the British vehicle on fire. In spite of their attempts to rescue the two men, both were killed when the Iraqis were driven back by flames. Later investigation of the blast revealed that a bomb had been attached to the underside of the vehicle.

Entering through the gate, Colonel Thomas stopped and looked over at the Baath Party headquarters and across the soccer field to the area we had occupied. Stunned, he asked, "Is this all yours? How the hell did you get it again?"

"Well, it's not really ours, but since nobody else is using it, the guy who controls it has said we could use the place as long as we keep it clean. We're going to keep the vehicles secured in those garages," I said, pointing to the garages nearest the portico. "And we will have our nightly socials over there by the house."

Hesco, still not quite able to believe what he was seeing, exclaimed, "You gotta be shitting me."

Then he grinned at me and said approvingly, "Man, I love you guys."

We moved on to where the boys were busy working over our two new vehicles. Since we could alter these vehicles in any way we chose, the team was busy tearing them apart. One vehicle would be assigned to lead, the other to rear, or 3. The team pulled off the rear hatches, which allowed the trunk monkeys to more easily employ their machine guns. With the hatches removed, these weapons and their gunners could cover a much greater arc more effectively than had been the case before. By making these vehicles lead and rear, we also ensured that any impact damage would be incurred on a vehicle we owned and not on one we had borrowed. Of course, rank does have its privileges, and that included having the best vehicle assigned as vehicle 1.

Vehicle 1, a.k.a. All Star One, had a radio and doors with functioning windows. While we traveled with the windows down, it was always nice to roll them up, once we had reached a safe area, to rest and enjoy the air-conditioning and the tunes. All of our KBR-supplied vehicles had functioning windows, AC, and radios. But of these two, only vehicle 1 had all of those luxury items. Vehicle 3 had AC but lacked doors and a radio. The team found replacement doors by going to a destroyed-vehicle park and pulling four doors off of a Nissan patrol that had been destroyed by a VBIED. Naturally, the doors were a mess. They were caved in, and it was difficult "molding" them to fit. Eventually they did fit, and well enough to allow the doors to be opened and closed. But the doors lacked window glass, which made the AC all but useless. As soon as Boeringer and Algarin realized this, they were pissed.

Boeringer started it. "Hey, J, you see this shit? We get this fuckin' thing with these ghetto doors, no radio, and no fuckin' windows. You might as well take the AC out and put that in the rear of vehicle one, and we all know it's all about vehicle one."

Algarin quickly added, "It's because I am Puerto Rican, isn't it, Top."

"No, Algarin, that's not the only reason at all. It's because you're bald *and* Puerto Rican," I answered.

"See, J, what I tell you about Top?" Boeringer intoned.

Reed walked over to Hesco and asked him what he thought of our chop shop.

"Are you kiddin' me? This is awesome. I don't even want to know how you guys got the vehicles, but I am really proud of all of you. This is awesome."

Reed thanked Hesco, and added, "We have a few more things to do to them before they are road ready, but we have our own stuff now."

Hesco looked at the guys as they continued to work on the vehicles. It was obvious that he was very proud of them and maybe even found it a little hard to believe that men would go to such extraordinary lengths to stay in the fight. Hesco understood. He would have done the same thing. Still, watching it happen was something that reminded Hesco of what he and all of us took for granted, America had sons and daughters of whom she could be justly proud. Many of them made do with plywood armor and patched together weapons and vehicles and did their duty every day. Their names never made it in the media. That "honor" was reserved for the very few who disgraced themselves in simple-minded pranks captured on film and for the men and women who refused to drive one mile because they lacked mission-essential equipment. Hesco smiled and shook his head slowly as he said, "Incredible." He stayed for a while talking to the team, which was something he never felt like he got to do enough. To us, Colonel Thomas was something like a big brother. He would always be there for us, and he would always support us. Though he did not know it, he was critical to us.

After Colonel Buchanan left, Hesco was the only officer in operations who gave a shit what happened to the team and was in a position to help us. As we walked back to the office, Hesco talked about how impressed he was with the determination of the team.

"That's what I will miss when I leave here, Top. It's the only thing I will miss about the Corps when I retire. We get these young guys and they can piss you off so bad with the stupid shit they get themselves into, but when it counts they are awesome. I am going to miss that."

May turned out to be a lot quieter than anyone had expected. Nobody knew why, and the sudden dissipation of violence caught us as much by surprise as did the eruption in April. In an effort to "lure" or "generate" more business, depending on the point of view, I had started using other convoys as bait. In the past whenever we saw our countrymen leaving the Green Zone as if they were still back in the States, windows rolled up to preserve the nice AC, talking to each other as if they had not a care in the world, and weapons stowed away, we would link up with them in an attempt to provide them some measure of security in spite of their foolishness. Eventually, though, I saw this as a lose-lose proposition. If we kept bailing them out by providing them with the look of a hard target, which every private knew was the best way to avoid becoming a victim, how were they ever going to learn? Besides, it was not as if we could protect every potential victim on Iraq's roads. Protect one and the enemy just waits for a less vigilant target and claims his quota of fools anyway. *But* if instead, we shadowed the potential victims, then maybe, just maybe, we could ride up on them being ambushed and kill their attackers. If we were lucky we would kill the attackers before any American lives were lost. Some people would find this very cold, but in fact it was a perfectly logical decision. It was not my job to convince other soldiers that we were at war; if they could not see that, then whatever happened to them was their own fault. But by using them as bait, not sending them out, mind you, but just following them and letting them make their *own* mistakes, then maybe we could make the route safer for everyone—fools and all—by killing those who would continue to feed on the less intelligent among us.

The tactic was simple enough in its execution. We would pull up just inside the Green Zone and wait. I would stand outside my vehicle and watch the convoys roll by. Those having two vehicles drew immediate attention. If the only soldiers in them were not acting like men at war, alert and menacing, but were instead behaving as if they were on a date, exchanging sideways glances while running their yaps, no weapons at the ready, and windows firmly rolled up, then they were my bait. Once they drove by, I would hit my stopwatch and time two minutes. When the two minutes elapsed, we would roll down Route Irish in a low profile. By low profile I mean we made every attempt to look nonthreatening. We would cover our trunk monkeys as best we could and keep our own weapons out of sight as we departed the safety of the Green Zone. In other words, we were doing our very best to look like victims ourselves! We would maintain this posture for one mile, until we had passed the nearest good points for enemy observation of traffic leaving the Green Zone.

For some time it had been believed that the enemy used spotters along the route to alert prepositioned enemy forces of the departure of American convoys, particularly those that looked weak. While baiting or dangling the willing victims, as some called it, did not produce the desired results, and May remained comparatively quiet, the team's missions nevertheless continued to grow in scope and frequency.

One of the new missions we pulled in May was providing escorts for New York City police officers sent to Iraq to train the new Iraqi police force. The New Yorkers were mostly retired officers, and most of them were great guys whom we enjoyed supporting. We would pick the police officers up at a hotel in downtown Baghdad not far from the police academy and then run them to the academy. Before running our first mission for them, however, we had to conduct some route recons.

On 13 May we conducted route recons to both the hotel and the police academy. We quickly discovered that, regardless of the route we selected, traffic was going to be incredibly heavy. While the traffic was congested, the first few runs went without a hitch. By 18 May we had already conducted several escort missions for the police officers. Some days we made as many as four runs for them. The eighteenth started with an early run to their hotel. We ate an early breakfast and were in the lot for our premission checks and briefs by 0645. Will and Facemyer, as was now becoming customary, were arguing about whose gear was on whose side of the vehicle.

"Facemyer," Will said as he shoved Facemyer's gear across the seat they shared, "your fucking stuff is on my side again. Move it."

Facemyer, always lower key and less stressed than Will, would piss Will off more by not moving fast enough and being largely dismissive of Will's complaints.

"For fuck's sake, man, you've got plenty of room, but go ahead and move my shit over a few millimeters so you can get that extra elbow room."

"Fuck you, Facemyer."

Facemyer, egging Will on, said, "Awww, now he's all butt hurt."

Will took the bait. "What the fuck does that mean, anyway? You always say that, and it's always stupid. 'Awwww, he's all butt hurt.' Fucking Facemyer."

Eventually, Will and Face would settle their border dispute, but the rest of us in the vehicle—Reed, Meggison, and I—enjoyed these displays. Reed said it was like taking bickering siblings on a long trip in a hot car with no AC. Whenever Will or Face bitched about room or the lack of AC in the rear seats, Meggison would quickly remind everyone within earshot that his small corner of hell, in the rear cargo area, lacked a seat, was more cramped because of the rockets, machine gun, and ammo, and that no AC ever reached that far back, having long been gobbled up by the 130 degree heat of a Baghdad summer. Will and Face, putting aside their petty fight, would then attack Meggison.

"Fuck you, Meggison. Before you joined the army you didn't even know what AC was."

Will quickly supported Face in his counterattack on Meggi. "Yeah, fuck you. You have plenty of room, and you get all the air you could need. You don't even have a door, fat-ass."

As we departed the Green Zone at 0715 for our 0800 linkup with the NYPD, I was surprised by how cool the temperature seemed. I was not sure that it was actually cooler than normal and wondered whether I was simply getting used to waking up with the temperature above 100 degrees before 0700. Whatever the reason, I was thankful for the relief. As we neared the gate I got on the radio, "Remember, guys, it's all about how we live the next fifteen minutes."

We crossed the bridge and cleared the traffic circle with no problem. The traffic was lighter than it had been on our previous runs to the police academy. But once we hit the market area the road became very congested. This was caused by a temporary barrier around a building just off the right side of the road. While it was not clear what this building was, the heavily armed

American security detail left no doubt as to who had caused the traffic delay. We crossed the road into the oncoming traffic and then made our way to the back of the hotel, where we hit a neighborhood that was protected by a single roll of concertina wire stretched across all road entrances. We had made note of this on our recon, so finding the concertina across our path did not cause us any alarm. Many neighborhoods in Iraq had something of a neighborhood watch. These always consisted of some sort of barrier to vehicle traffic, and often these barriers were guarded by heavily armed men. There were no guards for this barrier, however. We dismounted, with Will and Face watching my back as I pulled the wire out of the way. This was repeated when we cleared the other side of the neighborhood on our way out. We turned right onto a busy road and were less than five hundred meters from the hotel. The hotel itself was surrounded by Texas barriers. These barriers were large blocks of concrete that fit into place, side by side, forming a protective wall around the hotel. The barriers protected the ground floors from small-arms fire and RPGs, but their primary purpose was to keep people out and, more important, to protect the hotel from attacks by VBIEDs.

Just outside the hotel, and directly in front of us, was a busy intersection. We cleared the intersection very easily. We just slipped into the right-turn lane, turned right, and entered the serpentine barriers that slowed traffic entering the hotel's parking area. The barrier was covered by numerous Iraqi security guards armed with AK-47s.

Less than ten yards past the barriers was a PKM machine gun positioned so that it could fire on any unauthorized car attempting to wind its way through the barriers.

"You know, Top, if one of these guys sneezes, it's on."

Looking around at the six heavily armed men backed up by the PKM, I knew what Facemyer meant. Entering places like this was always tense for us, just as I was sure that it was for the Iraqis. Any threat perceived by us would be quickly and lethally dealt with. Of course, once one shot was downrange there would be no stopping it until there was nobody left to kill. A misunderstanding in these situations would be very bad. The Iraqis understood this and, most often, were very good about keeping their hands where we could see them and away from their weapons. This trip was no exception. Once we had cleared the barriers, we entered an open area, the far end of which was blocked by a car. Here our vehicles would have been searched for explosives had we not been a U.S. military unit. The Iraqi guard in this area merely asked us why we were there, and once we told him, he waved at the Iraqi seated in the car that blocked our way to the hotel.

The Iraqi moved the car and we proceeded past the barriers and to the parking lot, where we met with the police officers who were lining up their convoy. While the police officers got an accurate head count, I walked over to their dog handler. His job was not only to help train Iraqis in how to use a dog, he also checked incoming vehicles for explosives. I really loved his dog, and every morning I would bring him something to eat and just pet the animal while the police officer told me what it was like being in the canine unit. The dogs I saw in Iraq always reminded me of home, and most of us went out of our way to feed and care for them. I do not think that we were unique in this. I have seen several pictures of German soldiers holding, feeding, or playing with dogs or cats during World War II. One of the most memorable is of a puppy that looked like Bengi sitting on the commander's hatch of a German tank while the crew serviced the vehicle. For the Western fighting man, these animals had long represented a connection to home. As I petted the dog I thought about my own dogs and cats. I thought about my family and my home, and I wondered if I would ever see any of them again. For the few minutes it lasted, this dog was mine, and I was home.

Algarin interrupted my thoughts. "Top, they're up."

"Okay, Starsky," I answered as I patted the dog one last time.

I stood up and walked back to make sure that the police officers were in our convoy where they should be. I found the senior officer and asked him how many personnel and vehicles he had.

"Four Suburbans with nineteen officers," he answered.

I counted the four Suburbans and ensured that they were tucked in behind me with my number 2 and 3 vehicles behind them. I climbed back into my vehicle and we started to roll. We cleared the barriers and turned left to approach the same intersection we had cleared when we came to the hotel. The traffic was very heavy. We quickly dismounted and stopped all cross traffic and oncoming traffic that was turning left, across our direction of travel. After that, we remounted and pushed through until we hit a second large intersection less than a thousand meters from the one we had just cleared. While the rest of the team got out and pulled security around the vehicles, Facemyer, Williams, and I raced forward to the intersection.

I hated this place. The traffic here was always so backed up that we were on the ground far longer than I liked. Face, Will, and I were also dangerously exposed in these crowded streets as we were several hundred yards ahead of the team. We could get popped, and it might be a while before the rest of the home team knew what was happening. Upon reaching the intersection, we quickly stopped all traffic as we had earlier and waved through the vehicles in our lane. Iraqi drivers who had been stopped by us hated it, but those who were frantically being motioned forward were very happy for the suddenly clear path. Once our vehicle pulled up, we quickly remounted and cleared the intersection.

I keyed my handset. "Two and three, are you up, and have you cleared the intersection?"

As I waited for an answer, I looked in my mirror to see that the convoy was still intact.

"This is two. Up on packs and clear," responded Del in her best airline pilot's voice.

"Stonewall, Starsky, Rear D is up on personnel, and we have cleared, over."

Once we had cleared this intersection we were largely home free. Turning off the paved road we drove through a large manufacturing area of some type, and then we were in a large open area. The police academy was visible less than five hundred meters away. The trip from the hotel to the academy had taken less than ten minutes. We dropped off the police trainers and scheduled a pickup time of 1300.

On the way home we took the highway and were able to avoid most of the heavy traffic until the very end of our trip, but even this was light compared to the traffic going out. Once we were back in the Green Zone, we conducted some immediate-action drills at the Crossed Sabers before knocking off for noon chow. We were all back in the lot by 1215 and ready to roll by 1230. It was over 110 degrees when we cleared the gate.

We had wanted to take the highway, but the traffic through the market area leading to the highway was not going anywhere, so we turned right, using the same route we had used in the morning. While I did not like using routes more than once in a day, it seemed like a better choice than the market road or the highway since the market between us and the highway was at a standstill. In hindsight we would have been better off just taking our chances with the traffic in the market. Taking the alternate route turned out to be no better than going through the market. We quickly became stranded in a sea of stopped vehicles. Dismounting, Will, Face, and I raced forward to clear a way for the convoy. Most often, we would have to run less than fifty meters forward of the convoy; on bad days we might have to push as many as two hundred meters forward. This was a very bad day, however. We had not been running for very long when we realized that traffic was backed up for several hundred meters.

We pushed on, the heat baking our brains within our helmets and our flak jackets crushing and smothering us as we labored for each step. The weight of our gear and the heat, the ungodly heat, seemed to hold us in place. No matter how hard we tried to force our legs to move faster, we seemed unable to move forward. The heat in Iraq sometimes seemed every bit as sinister as the men trying to kill you. It seemed alive, and it seemed all-powerful. It tried to crush and bake the life out of you. Finally, heads throbbing and chests heaving, we reached the intersection we needed to clear. We immediately began directing traffic, but we were so far forward of the convoy and the traffic was so heavy, it would still be several minutes before the team reached us. As I pushed vehicles through, Will and Face scanned the rooftops, passing cars, doors, and windows for potential threats. We were well aware of how alone and vulnerable we were so far forward of our team. But we could not dwell on that. My job was to move traffic, not worry about potential threats. That was Will and Face's problem and I trusted both men with my life. If the unfortunate did happen and I was shot by a sniper, or my heart simply said, "Fuck this, it's too hot," and quit on me, I knew these two would not leave me lying in the street. They would do whatever they could for me. Strangely, considering how isolated we were, a little American island in a sea of hostile faces and crawling cars, I felt safe, almost invincible. I trusted Will and Face that much.

"Man, this is so fucking dangerous."

"Yeah, I know, Will. Hopefully we will not be here too long."

I kept directing traffic, but occasionally I would glance up at a rooftop or at a window or darkened doorway. "Was that door open before?" Your mind could conjure up all sorts of evils lurking about. Our primary concern was snipers, and it was very easy to imagine that these waited behind every window and in every doorway. During those long lonely minutes it felt as if all the eyes in Islam were upon me, waiting for the moment I was not paying attention or, maybe, the moment I became distracted.

That moment occurred a thousand times a day, but if it occurred at the wrong time, I was dead. No matter how alert we were, the enemy could strike at any moment and disappear back into one of the hundreds of doorways, windows, or passing cars without having ever been seen. Maybe all three of us would be killed; maybe just one.

Life and death in Iraq, who lived and who died, was often simply a matter of being in the wrong place at the wrong time. If those two random things fell into line, then you had a very good chance of being killed or maimed. Anytime you were stopped in Iraq, outside of a FOB or other secure area, you were in the wrong place. Now the element that needed to fall into place for you to have a shitty day was the timing. If the wrong people saw you, you were in danger of being killed. Maybe you would get drilled by a sniper who was simply driving by when he noticed you or maybe you ate a VBIED. Anything could happen, and the longer you stayed in one place, the more likely it was that *something* would happen.

Finally Reed pulled up and we jumped in. Scrambling for a water bottle, Facemyer simply said, "Fuck's sakes, man."

"Oh man, Chris, I have never been so glad to see you."

"Was it hot out there, Will?" Reed asked.

I answered. "Hot and too fucking long, Huggy."

"Well, Top, next time send Waters. He could use the exercise," Reed teased.

Waters, large and new to Iraq, was clearly having trouble with the heat, but he was trying. He was on the team solely because he had medical training in advance of what any other member of the team had. Or so it was thought at the time. Ultimately, it was decided his medical qualifications were no better than our army-trained combat lifesavers', and Waters, always a poor match for the team anyway, would soon be reassigned to a desk job in the palace. After clearing hell's very own traffic jam, we had smooth sailing and easily made our pickup time. The trip back to the hotel was trouble free. After dropping off the police officers I debated which way we should take back. I had wanted to take the highway, but as we drove over it on the overpass leading to the hotel, it was obvious that traffic on it was going nowhere. Besides that, the market area where we would exit the highway was always bad. That left us one route, and that was the one we had taken in. While traffic on our side had been heavy coming in, it was not at all that bad on the side we would take on the way out. Though we had already taken that route today, I made the decision to take it again. It was to have dire consequences.

We left the hotel, and while the traffic was heavy, it was not nearly as bad as that on the highway. Just when I was about to pat myself on the back for my "wise" choice, things started going sideways on us. We were only three hundred meters short of the traffic circle that would take us home when we noticed that all the traffic to our rear had stopped. Cars were stopped in the road as if they were sitting at a red light, but there was no red light. In fact, there were no traffic lights anywhere in Iraq. The only other time we had observed behavior like this was on 8 April when we had killed the Mahdi. Whatever the reason for the odd behavior, we all knew one thing, when something out of the ordinary occurred in Iraq, it was frequently a precursor to death. As I questioned the wisdom of taking this route yet again, I tightened the grip on my rifle.

"Huggy, cut around to the right," I ordered.

When we tried to cut around the traffic to our front, a large truck swerved in front of us, blocking our way.

"*Top?*"

Reed was asking me what we should do. For a few milliseconds, everything seemed as quiet as the awkward moments following an Al Franken joke. Before I could answer, the silence was shredded by a long burst of machine-gun fire. Trapped in the canyon walls of the city, the sound was louder than it otherwise would have been, and it reverberated. I could feel it hammering against my spine. Immediately, I thought that my rear vehicle had been engaged in an ambush. There was another blast of machine-gun fire followed by the echo. I thought we were in serious trouble. Move, move, move! Move faster! I urged my body into action, but it seemed reluctant to obey. My training and my experience told me that the inside of my vehicle was a coffin on wheels, but my body wanted to stay inside, where it believed was safe.

I reached for my door handle. As soon as my hand touched the handle, my one dominant thought was that I was still *alive*. I had survived initial contact. I thought, "I am still here and now someone is going to die." We had always told ourselves that, no matter what happened, if we made it out of the vehicle, the enemy was going to have more of a fight on his hands than he wanted. He would either break contact and disappear back into the shadows or he would surely die by our hands. He was not going to win. I had been afraid until the moment my hand hit the door handle, and then I knew, no matter what happened, I was going to make it. We were going to kick ass.

Once we dismounted, all the blood spilled that day would be Muslim. Nothing to worry about now except not reaching my bag limit for the day. I dismounted and knelt behind the rear fender of a parked car. I looked left and saw several Iraqis diving for cover in a small café. More fire could be heard to the rear of the convoy. A lot of it was PKM fire, long blasts that dominated the smaller, slower fire of AK-47s and the precise *pop, pop, pop* of M-16s, all of it mixing together and bouncing off the walls of the buildings around us in a chaotic and somewhat familiar and therefore comforting way. Looking over my right shoulder, I spotted Facemyer, just behind me and smiling ear to ear.

"Let's go," I shouted.

There was now an incredible volume of fire pouring out, with very little or none coming in. I reached the rear of the convoy to see an Iraqi cab slowly rolling up behind the convoy. Pieces flew off of the cab and the windshield was spider-webbed by multiple impacts. I dropped to a knee using a parked Iraqi vehicle for cover and opened fire on the cab. Will and Face, flanked to my left, made sure that our rear and left were secure. Under the relentless hammering of 5.56 mm rifle fire and the crushing blows of Josleyn's PKM, the cab seemed to be disintegrating as it slowly rolled to a stop. It looked like the bus in the Clint Eastwood movie, *The Gauntlet*. Every square inch of windshield was shredded by a bullet. As the cab came to a stop, the two men who were in it were no longer visible and, looking at the shape of their car, I assumed they were dead or on their way to being dead. Seeing no additional threats, I ordered a cease-fire.

"Cease fire, cease fire," I screamed while at the same time giving the hand and arm signal for cease-fire.

I scanned the area again for any threats and then began to move toward the cab to see if there was anything we could do. There wasn't, and we quickly remounted. The traffic that had been to our front was gone. As I entered the vehicle, Reed keyed his handset, "All stations, let me know when you are up."

Only one vehicle answered.

Pissed that we did not yet have a head count I said, "Stop the vehicle, Huggy."

I keyed my handset. "All stations, we are not going any fucking where until you tell me you are up."

Each vehicle replied that they were up, and we rolled. The last thing any of us wanted to do was leave a guy behind. Amped up as we were, that was a distinct possibility, and we had to make sure we had all of our people back before we rolled. We moved forward and reached the traffic circle with no problem. Once in the circle and very near our exit, an Iraqi police officer attempted to stop traffic for us but was not 100 percent successful in doing so. An Iraqi vehicle, disregarding the police officer's directions, darted in front of us. Reed wasted no time reducing the vehicle to junk. He collided with the right front quarter panel and rode up on the hood crushing the suspension. As this was happening, I was on the radio with the boys trying to make sure the team was calm and focused. The younger guys like Dann found this comforting. Old vets like Gunny Josleyn just wished I would shut up.

Once we were back in the Green Zone, we celebrated being back and congratulated Gunny J on his quick and decisive action in engaging the cab. In fact, Gunny Josleyn had put 165 rounds of PKM into the cab. Josleyn was a marine sniper, and their motto is One Shot One Kill. I could not help teasing the gunny.

"One hundred and sixty-five shots and two kills. You suck."

The team congratulated the gunny as he slid out of the cramped cargo area of his Ford Explorer. Expended cartridge cases littered the floor of the cargo area. Josleyn, all smiles, clearly relished having his first chance to get some since he had been in Iraq. Looking down at all the brass, he said "Well, it's not as accurate as an M-40 [marine sniper rifle], so I had to use a lot more ammo, but she does get the job done."

Boeringer walked up and looked in the cargo area as well. Patting Josleyn on the shoulder, Boeringer gave him his first nickname.

"Hey, Top, I think it's Gunny Get Some now."

Staff Sergeant Libby, who had been riding with us, was elated.

"Man, I never thought I would ever get to do anything like that. I love this place. That was a rush."

Noting Libby's warriorlike spirit and contrasting it with what was the norm in the air force, I said approvingly, "Makes you one of a kind in the air *farce,* eh, Libby?"

Not everybody enjoyed the "rush" however. In addition to Libby we had one other guest with us. He was a U.S. Army captain who had just joined CMATT that week.

"Colonel, is it like this every day for these guys?" the shaken captain asked.

Hesco, who was also with us for the run, answered, "No. I mean it's always intense, but this is one of the few times they have killed anybody."

The captain looked on as the boys continued their wild celebration, shook his head, and walked off.

"Hey, Top." It was Reed, and he had his arm around Delacroix's shoulder.

"She closed out some fuck out there, and I just wanted to tell you. She is fucking awesome."

I looked at Del and smiled. All of us had known for some time that Del was a great addition to the team, and her actions that day were nothing more than a reflection on Del as a warrior. She was such a seamless fit with the whole, I admired her just as much as I admired my boys. I was very glad she had stuck up for herself and challenged me when I had not wanted her on the team. I could not even picture the team without Del. Baseball had its Jackie Robinson, and in the small world of Jack Lynch, women in the military had Del. As we walked back to the palace I realized that I felt powerful and invincible. I loved being the guy who led the convoy security team, a lethal and perfectly balanced weapon that functioned so seamlessly, with each part fitting perfectly into the whole. In fact, I loved the war. I loved my part in it, and I dreaded the day I would have to leave. Combat was addictive. Combat was seductive, and it was especially so when you did the killing but were lucky enough to not have to deal with the harsher truth of war, which is that war kills and maims your friends, too. Eventually, the team would have to deal with that reality, but in May of 2004 that reality was still a lifetime away.

After seeing Major Drury, who conducted our debrief, I went back to ops and answered more questions posed by some of the officers in the section. Shortly before we took off for chow, Sergeant Major Zelaya stopped by to tell me that my section would have armored SUVs by 27 May. This became a hot topic of debate at chow.

"You mean, we stole all that stuff and now they are going to give us shit we should have had all along? Do you believe them, Top?"

I answered. "I don't know, Starsky. We were supposed to have M-4s and real radios long ago, but we don't. Still, the sergeant major seemed certain we would have them."

"Oh, what the fuck does he know, anyway? He doesn't know anything that the chief of staff or Napier does not tell him he knows."

Will continued. "No, it's the same fucking thing we have dealt with since we started this. A lot of empty fucking promises, and then when it comes time to deliver, they fuck you, and when you ask them where it is or what happened to it, they give you some dumb fucking look. The only thing any of them cares about is themselves."

I conceded. "You might be right, Will. Sure as shit the past does not bode well for us. But if they do not have them, that is okay because we own our own shit now anyway."

"Listen to them, J, bitchin' about armor, and we don't even have AC."

Algarin answered, "Yeah, Bo, and if we get armor, you know Top is going to take the best one for himself."

Boeringer continued his rant. "Fuck yeah, he will. Fucking vehicle one will have more armor than an Abrams, big fuckin' rims, CD, DVD player, and a bar, and what the fuck will we get, J? We will get their old vehicle *after* they take the AC out so they can mount it on the floor of Top's vehicle so his nuts can be blown without Huggy having to take his eyes off the road and then they will armor our shit with cardboard and tin foil . . . the fucks."

"I would just be happy with windows, Bo," Algarin answered.

Del added, "Well, I don't think any of us are going to have to worry about it. Nobody here gives a shit about us, and if they are getting armor, we will not be getting any."

Reed agreed. "I am with Del, Top. No way we see any of that shit even if it does get here."

Most of us left chow feeling certain that there would be no armor, but we held out hope just the same.

The following day, the long simmering dispute within the operations section about the role and conduct of the team boiled over. It reached its boiling point when an officer new to CMATT joined the operations section. Lieutenant Colonel Sid Johns was 6'1" tall and possessed an ample midsection, the byproduct of a comfortable life serving in the air force reserve and working as a full-time lawyer in the real world. The most remarkable aspect of his appearance, however, was his milky white skin and silver white hair. Sid, or Sidney, as we derisively referred to him, had a face that reminded us of a mole, which frequently caused us to call him Sidney the Mole Man or simply the Mole Man. While he looked like a pale version of Morocco Mole he lacked that character's intelligence. In fact, Sidney lacked all the finer qualities that defined a man, which was rare, even among our critics, as they all possessed something of virtue. One of the things Sidney lacked was assertiveness; he made suggestions and observations while talking to you like you were a dim-witted client. Being new to Iraq, new to war, and safely tucked deep within the reassuring walls of the palace, he knew absolutely nothing about what the roads in Iraq were like. His opinions on combat escorts, QRFs, and security missions were based solely on the opinions of men like himself, men who, for the most part, never left the palace. These opinions were formed, developed, and made into unassailable "fact" in the minds of those who shared them. They were based on observations made from afar about what things "sounded" like. To these men, the tactics employed by the team always "sounded over the top" or "too aggressive." Sidney quickly fell into line with these men. Like Sidney, these men had two things in common, a deep and abiding desire to stay locked behind their desks, hiding behind words like "duty" while at the same time offering up any number of opinions on what my team should be doing. Knowledge and experience were not required of anyone who wished to voice loud opinions within the ops, and Mole Man was quick to share his. Frequently, as the team would mount up, Sidney would loudly ask pointed questions, such as, "Top, why do you guys carry so many weapons? Why do you take so many people?"

Most often, I would answer the Mole Man respectfully but in way that made my contempt obvious. "I don't know, sir, but I think it has something to do with the war and stuff. You know, not everybody in Iraq wants us here, and some, from what I see on the news anyway, even want to kill us."

We took lots of people because I was a big believer in General Nathan Bedford Forrest's tenet, "First With the Most." In other words, get there first and with as many men as possible. Still, no matter how many people I took, I knew we would always be outgunned. The numbers simply meant we would have a fighting chance. Maybe Johns should have been asking questions about why we did not have armor or American crew-served weapons. Maybe he should have asked why I had to "find" two old Russian machine guns instead of having American weapons issued or why we did not have radios that worked beyond one hundred meters. But to ask those questions you had to actually give a shit about what happened to the team. I sometimes wondered whether Sidney asked the questions he did in the hope that someone in authority, with balls, and agreeing with him, might actually suggest that our numbers and weapons, such as they were, be reduced. While it was easy enough to find people who would agree with him, finding one with balls was quite difficult.

The first inkling of how wide the gap between those of us on the team and the majority of the staff had grown came when Colonel Deboda pulled me aside and questioned the attitude of the team. "There has been a lot of talk around here about your conduct and that of the team. Some people think you guys are too eager for a fight. Some even think you go out looking for one."

I was stunned. I sincerely believed that it was our obligation to do everything we could to win the war. To me that meant "closing with and destroying the enemy" as so eloquently stated in the mission of the marine rifle squad.

Not even making an attempt to hide my loathing for the staff, I responded, "Well, sir, we are. Fuck these people. Isn't that what we are supposed to do, look for and kill the enemy? What am I missing here?"

"Well, you can think it, but I wouldn't go telling anybody that. You guys are on really thin ice. Look, Top, I am on your side, but you guys need to be careful."

As soon as Colonel Deboda said, "I am on your side," I should have gone to medical to have the knife removed from my back. It would be a few weeks, but eventually we would discover that Deboda was just a shorter, fitter version of the Mole Man.

The following day, Patterson approached me when we returned from a convoy. "Top, I need to talk to you."

I knew it was not good.

"What now, Pat?"

"Fucking Johns, Theodorson, Deboda, Sherman, everybody, was talking shit about you guys today. I don't remember all of it, but Johns said that you better watch yourself. They said you guys were too aggressive and unprofessional and that they were going to do something about it. Major Sherman kept calling you guys the 'Lynch mob' and said that they [the team] were your private army. Then First Sergeant Bret Bowman [U.S. Army] got into it because he said you guys did not give him a ride back to Kirkush. Sherman then said, 'Yeah, nobody goes unless Top says they go.'"

While hearing that Johns, Theodorson, Deboda, and Sherman were busy wagging their tongues, I was surprised to hear Bowman's name mentioned. "Bowman, he was bitching, too?"

Pat nodded his head.

"That sorry fuck was late, and we don't wait for anybody."

Pat was nervously smoking a cigarette, "I know, Top, I know."

"What else?" I asked.

"Well, then it was like Major Sherman noticed I was there, and he points at me and says, 'They never even take Staff Sergeant Patterson. All they ever do is fuck with him while he works on their fucking awards.'"

Sherman never said these things to us. When he saw us, he always said, "Hey, guys, how ya doing?" In fact, he said it so frequently that Will took to repeating the words whenever he saw Sherman. That we were the topic of such negative conversation, while we were out, and that none of this criticism was put in a professional forum but instead passed around like schoolgirl gossip [by school girls I might add] infuriated me. But what Patterson told me next positively bordered on criminal.

"Top, before I tell you anything else, you gotta promise you will just talk to Lieutenant Colonel Thomas about it."

"Oh man, is it that bad?" I asked.

"Yeah, Top, it is."

I set my helmet on the ground and sat on it. I rested my head in my hands and said, "Go ahead."

Patterson continued, "Top, don't count on getting the M-4s Captain Jones ordered for you."

Pat hesitated, waiting to see if I would say anything. I didn't. I just looked up at him, and Pat continued. "Major Sherman was talking about that today, too. He said, 'Master Sergeant Lynch made some fucked-up drug deal to get them M-4s, and I'll be damned if I let him get those.'"

I was shocked. This was beyond comprehension. Captain Justin Sherman was a tanker in the Marine Corps. He had extensive time on Iraq's roads, and he knew, just as well as we did, the value of the M-4 for combat escort missions. The full-sized M-16 has greater range, accuracy, and lethality than the M-4, but it is cumbersome by comparison and difficult to employ from within a vehicle. It also takes longer to dismount a vehicle with the M-16.

While the difference was not great, Sherman should have known that potentially it could mean the difference between life and death, and yet he was actively seeking a way to divert the one weapons system I had been able to actually get on order. Was the personal hatred for us within the operations section so great that people would even stoop so low as to block our acquisition of weapons that were critical to our mission, thereby making it *easier* for people to kill us?

That these statements could be tossed around an office filled with senior officers and enlisted men of all grades blew me away. Of course, things like this were never said in front of the team or Colonel Thomas. But so confident were our detractors, they freely said all of this and more in front of the new deputy J-3 (with the arrival of General David Petraeus the sections had been redesignated from C-1, C-2, C-3 to J-1, J-2, and J-3) Lieutenant Colonel Heathcliff Woolsley Toddington of the Australian army, and in so doing seriously overplayed their hand. We had worried about what the next deputy might do to curtail the team's operations. Those who opposed the team had obviously used the time that we were on the road to their advantage in attempting to influence the new deputy. They had now had the first word. When I got back to the office, I noticed that all of the palace ninjas seemed upbeat. Had someone cut their tours short? Had the enemy made a promise to stop mortaring and rocketing the Green Zone? Mole Man Johns, Theodorson, Deboda, and Sherman were the happiest of all. In fact, each greeted me more warmly than they had before. Their greetings were meant as a taunt, and I knew that. Then one of them said something that was obviously meant to be ominous, "There are going to be a lot of changes around here now, a lot of changes." The obvious glee was almost childlike.

Hesco came up to me as I stowed my gear in the wall locker. "Hey, Top, c'mon out here for a second. We need to talk."

We walked into the hallway. Hesco turned to me, saying, "Look, I don't want you to go blowin' your top, and I don't want you to say anything to anybody in that office. Apparently, there are a lot of people in there that want to break up the team and change the SOP. We have a meeting tomorrow morning with the new deputy, just you and me, none of the other guys."

"Who else, sir?"

Hesco answered, "Lieutenant Colonels Deboda and Johns, and Major Theodorson and Major Sherman. Top, I don't want you worrying about this. Let me do that. Just don't say anything to these people, and don't lose your cool tomorrow. The new deputy seems like a fair man and I think if we present our side of things, in a *rational, coherent* manner, like I know *we* can, we might win this thing. One thing he has made clear is that tomorrow will be the last of the BS he is going to tolerate."

I went to chow with a heavy heart. My job on the road was filled with stress. While I liked it, that did not make it any less stressful. But the added stress of dealing with all of the childish backbiting and second-guessing that I endured in the palace was getting to be too much. Sleep that night did not come easily.

We met in the operations section secure room at 0730 the next day. Lieutenant Colonel Toddington had us form our chairs in a circle. Seated clockwise from Lieutenant Colonel Toddington were Sherman, me, Hesco, Theodorson, Deboda, and Johns. Toddington started the meeting.

"All right then, we all know why we are here, so let's get started. All I want from any of you is what you see as the problem, and let's keep it professional. I don't want to hear any personal attacks, as I have heard enough of those in the short time I have been here."

Major Sherman, who had called my team the "Lynch mob" and the "Lynch militia," spoke first. "I just think that the team's missions have grown beyond the original intent, and I just think we need to reexamine what our mission is."

For a guy whose mouth was a running sewer when we were on the road, his comments were surprisingly brief. He added, "I question why we sent thirteen people to escort four going to An Numiniyah?"

Looking at Sherman, I said, "That's it, sir? I think there's more to your side than that."

Sherman glared at me. I looked at Toddington and continued.

"Sir, Major Sherman has said much more than that in the past, and I am surprised that he is not bringing the same issues up now, in a professional forum, where we can get some resolution, but I will stick to the issues he *did* raise. Our mission has changed as it has for the whole of CMATT. When CMATT was first established they were looking at building an army in a relatively secure operating environment; obviously, that has changed dramatically, and with the increased violence we have had to create a dedicated convoy security and QRF team where there was none before. We also only created the force protection cell since Major Sherman arrived. [The force protection cell was Sherman's.] Lots of things have changed, and our mission is no exception. We took a heavy escort to An Numiniyah because we were going to be more than three hours outside of Baghdad, and we needed to make sure we took enough to fight and win. In addition to escorting four of our guys [Sergeants Balan and Shenk and two soldiers new to ops] who were being moved to An Numiniyah, we were escorting forty thousand dollars, several hundred AK-47 rifles, and thousands of rounds of ammunition. The escorts provided by the First Cav run, they have done so more than once, and we were not going to entrust the safety of our friends to them."

Next Hesco spoke, and it was obvious he was pissed.

"Not one person in this room, other than Lieutenant Colonel Deboda, has ever even been on the road with these guys."

Pointing at each in turn, Hesco added, "Not you, you, or you, none of you. You don't know anything about what they do or how they do it, so you should shut up and stick with what you do know. Instead, you guys sit around the office and take shots at them all day. These guys are risking their lives every day in the most stressful environment I have ever been in, and then they get back here and have to put up with this petty shit. I am tired of it. Every other combat escort team in the country has armor, crew-served weapons, radios, and medics. These guys have none of that. Every other team in this country came over here as a team. These guys were put together from spare parts, and I think it's amazing that they are able to do what they do with so little help. Instead of talking about this, we should be trying to figure out how to get these guys the things they need."

Next it was Theodorson who spoke. In the open, under the blazing lights of the stage, Theodorson withered. "We just need to examine the mission."

Mole Man, being the lawyer and not even playing the warrior that his uniform suggested he might be or at least should be, said, "Well, everybody had good points. We all just need to work together."

He then nodded to Hesco and me and smiled. As I looked at him, I thought about selling him to the terrorists. Supposedly they would pay fifty to seventy-five grand for a captured American male, double for a woman. Given his physical attributes and his metrosexual demeanor, I felt certain I could get the female rate after a suitable knockdown for ugliness and lack of camera presence. Lieutenant Colonel Toddington wasted no time.

"All right then, if there's nothing else, I have made my decision."

He paused and looked around the room. Given the vociferousness of the opinions that had been expressed by these men before, I found it a little surprising that when offered a chance to have their grievances heard in a forum where something might actually come of them, these guys had so little to say. Toddington continued. "Now, before I tell you what my decision is, I have some things I want to say. I have only been here two days and I have to tell you gentlemen that the amount of fucking shit, and I am calling it that because that is what it was, that I heard in that office, about other members of the operations section, sickened me. It was so bad I thought it was a joke. I mean, I really thought it was a joke. I thought you guys were playing a joke on the new deputy. But it just went on and fucking on, and I realized it wasn't a joke. These people were fucking serious. Gentlemen, that shit comes to a bloody fucking halt now. From this moment forward, all members of the section will be treated with respect. If you have a problem with anyone in the section, you will bring it to me, not to Captain Wheeler, to me. I will not tolerate a dysfunctional section. If there is anybody here who cannot operate under these rules, well, then pack your belongings, mate."

It was obvious who the majority of these remarks were directed toward. As the team had not even been in the office when things reached critical mass, Toddington could only be talking about those who sat in the office and berated the team while it was on the road. Given Toddington's reaction, I am sure that things were far worse than I dared even imagine they were. The expressions on Theodorson's, Mole Man's, and Sherman's faces said they knew the game was up. Yesterday's joy was gone, and the look on each man's face was priceless.

"Now we have all had our say. When I announce my decision the debate is over, and we move forward from here as a team. I don't want to hear anybody winging [pronounced "win ging," a term Aussies used to describe bitching] about it, is that clear?"

"Yes, sir," we answered in near unison. Toddington continued.

"Before I came to this meeting I took the liberty of talking with other people both in the section and in CMATT as a whole. This included the J-2. The team will continue to be led by Master Sergeant Lynch, who will report directly to me or Lieutenant Colonel Thomas. If you're not one of those two people, you have nothing to say to Master Sergeant Lynch about how he handles his team. If you have a problem with him, you bring it to me or Lieutenant Colonel Thomas." Turning to me, Toddington said, "Master Sergeant Lynch."

"Yes, sir."

"You will continue to operate per your own established procedures until and unless I or Lieutenant Colonel Thomas tells you otherwise, is that understood?"

"Yes, sir."

Turning his attention to the assembled officers, Toddington asked, "Now does everybody understand where we are on this?"

Again, everyone affirmed that they did, with one exception. Sherman glowered at me when Toddington asked him if he understood.

Toddington did not miss it. "I am waiting on you, mate. Do we have an understanding or not?"

"Sir, I think that, no, sir, we do not," Major Sherman stammered.

"Well, let me rephrase that then. You had your say and you said you had nothing more to say. Now I have told you how we will proceed from here, and now I am asking you, mate, and I will not ask again, do you understand?"

Sulking, Sherman answered, "Yes, sir."

We left the room and entered the office, where Sherman wasted no time confronting me.

"I don't like that fucking poster," he said, pointing to the large poster of the team's insignia that I had hung on the wall behind my desk. "It does not represent me, and I don't like it."

Enjoying the moment, I answered, "Ummm, you're not on the team, so you're right, it does not represent you. Isn't this something you should have brought up in the meeting, sir?"

Hesco told Sherman, "Knock it off." When Sherman persisted, Hesco called him out into the passageway.

"Major, with me right now, and don't say another fucking word."

The childish display, in such an open setting and in front of so many people, spoke volumes about the major's character. I sent Patterson to go and get the team so I could pass the word to them. Now it was my turn to gloat.

"Pat, go get the team and tell them I have fantastic news."

Pat wanted to ask me how things had gone but knew now was not the time or place. He quickly grabbed his cover and went to go fetch the team. As I waited, I looked around the office at all the people who thought that I was a bloodthirsty murderer.

The thought that we killed people could not have been what made them hate us so much. After all, I remember observing them as they watched camera footage of an air strike in Fallujah. In the fuzzy image you could clearly see several, maybe as many as thirty, people running from one building and out into the street. You could not see any weapons on these people. The palace commandos watched as several bombs were guided onto the fleeing men, obliterating them. The pilot celebrated his kill as he should. The peace-loving "warriors" in the office, men like Vorgang, had also celebrated. They loved the video, calling it "motivating." So what was different? These people were comfortable watching a man blow apart thirty unarmed men and yet, somehow, I was a barbarian. Maybe the difference was that they did not have to look at the people who died eyeball to eyeball? Neither did their killer. The pilot killed from a few thousand feet up, not fifteen meters. That we killed face to face, and enjoyed it as much as the pilot did, was what bothered them. They were just squeamish about violent death up close. It was okay from afar, it was even okay to enjoy it from afar, but up close, "Man, those guys are sick."

To some people, we were simple thugs, little better than the enemy, while the pilot was the knight of the air. We were Joe Pesci's character in *GoodFellas* while the pilot was Robert De Niro's character, lethal but charming. For the record, I loved the video and consider the pilot a hero. He wasted as many as thirty men who surely would have been waiting for the marines when they hit Fallujah again.

While most in the operations section hated us we did find friends in unexpected quarters. Major Abbas, of the New Iraqi Army, was one such man. He had the build of a warrior, 5'9", well muscled and proportioned. Abbas wore a thin mustache similar in size to Hessen's. He was a professional and dedicated officer. When I first met him, Abbas had already paid a very heavy price in the war. An insurgent rocket attack on his home had killed his infant daughter, blinded his mother for life, and wounded him. Yet he continued to come to work knowing that he ran an awful risk, much higher than that run by any American serving in Iraq. On a bad day, American soldiers and marines risked their lives, but we never placed our families in jeopardy. Officers serving in the New Iraqi Army did that every day simply by pulling on their uniforms. Abbas stopped me one day and said, "Lynch, I want to thank you for all you are doing here in Iraq."

I tried to tell him that was okay, but he continued.

"No, my friend, my brother, I am grateful to you, and the Iraqi people are all grateful. It is the terrorists that are making things bad for all of us. We have to kill all the terrorists; *you* must kill them all. There will be no new Iraq until they are all dead. They do not want a new Iraq for the Iraqi people."

I listened to Abbas as he continued to talk about the enemy within. I noticed that one of his hands was heavily bandaged. When he paused, I pointed at his injured hand and asked him what had happened. He explained that he was with the leader of the Governing Council when his convoy was attacked with a VBIED. Several, including the leader, had been killed. Abbas was fortunate to be alive.

"Damn, sir, I did not know you were on that detail. I am glad you are okay. What are you going to do now?"

"I am going home, my friend. I will see you tomorrow."

As we parted, I thought about what Abbas had said: "I will see you tomorrow." He was going home, a home surrounded by hidden enemies who wore masks when they murdered the families of Iraqi army officers, and all he said was "I will see you tomorrow." It was just another day for him. While attacks like the one he had just survived weakened the resolve of the safe, the protected, and the ignorant thousands of miles away in cities like New York and Los Angles, it did not weaken the resolve of the men fighting the war, men like Major Abbas. As I watched him leave, I wondered if I would do the same thing in his shoes. Risking my own life was child's play compared to risking the lives of the ones I loved.

The support of men like Abbas was sorely needed. The constant sniping within the J-3 was taking a toll in May. How many times can men be called Nazis, killers, and thugs before they start taking a second look at themselves? I was growing concerned that the near constant second-guessing of our actions by the palace elite was going to cause someone to second-guess himself when he should have pulled the trigger. Before Colonel Toddington's intervention, the harassment of the convoy security team was reaching epidemic and childish proportions. Photos of the team, taped to the lockers of team members, were defaced. Words like "Nazi" and "Fascists" were scrawled on some, while still others were simply drawn over. Sergeant Williams was a favorite target of our unseen "prankster." We would return from the road to find that one of the palace pussies had taken some time out of his busy and dangerous day to deface or remove a picture from Will's locker. Coming in from the road, all we wanted to do was unwind and enjoy the fact that we had cleared yet another mile. The last thing we wanted to do was put up with childish bullshit. One day Will had enough. I was shoving my flak jacket in my locker when Will showed me a picture of the team that he had taped to his locker that someone had defaced.

"Top, look at this fucking shit. Some sorry-ass fuck keeps fucking with my shit, and if I find out who the fuck it is, I'm going to kill them."

The remarks were intended for and loud enough for everyone in the office to hear.

"Well," I said, taking the picture, "since you don't know who did it, that would mean killing an awful lot of people, Will."

"Yeah, well, it's not like we don't have the ammo for it, and *they* know we have the ability."

Staff Sergeant Reed was standing with us. Taking the defaced picture, he said, "Top, this is how people get hurt. The team has had enough of it, and something should be done soon, before it gets out of hand."

I looked around the office. Everybody was busily engaged in their work, faces hidden behind monitors, hands typing away, but it was obvious that they were listening.

"Well," I said, "don't kill anybody *yet,* Will. Let me pass it to the deputy [Toddington]. I think he will fix it."

Will stormed off. "Fuckers."

"Top, you going to chow with us?" Reed asked.

"Yeah, Huggy. Let me finish securing my shit."

I finished stuffing my wall locker and headed to chow with the team. As we walked to chow, Will continued to fume about having his shit fucked with by some faceless candy ass. Algarin added, "Yeah, Top, that's fucked up. Can't they just leave us alone?"

Boeringer was more direct.

"Fuck that. I catch one of those people in my shit, I am gonna fuck' em up. I think we should just shoot the lot of 'em, Top. I mean, what the fuck they gonna do to stop us, *beg?*"

Reed quickly chimed in. "I get Mole Man Johns."

Will quickly laid claim to a victim of his own. "You can have him, Chris, but that fat fuck Waters is mine."

"Oh man, Will, can you imagine that shit? All that fat and all that blood and his high-pitched bitch scream. Ahhhhh, no Willliaammmss," Facemyer encouraged.

"Oh man, I would so shoot him in the man tits," Will answered.

"You can have him. Just leave me Ricks and Vorgang," said Meggison, taking a long drag on his cigarette. He appeared to be deep in thought, with the faraway look of a man celebrating his orgasm with a postencounter smoke.

"Damn, Meggison, was it that good? What did you do? Shoot them with Prom Date?"

"No, Del," Meggison answered. "It's not that. I was just thinking about what I was gonna do with Ricks first."

Though jealous that everyone had claimed a kill and left none for me, I quickly chimed in anyway.

"You know, guys, this is how bad shit starts. First, it's just a joke and then it's a fantasy, and bam, before you know it, we're all standing over a bunch of bullet-riddled corpses, chests heaving, sweating heavily, smoke pouring out of barrels and empty magazines and casings littering the deck and looking at each other and wondering how it happened and what to do with the bodies."

Someone answered, "Well, Top, it's like Staff Sergeant Reed always says: 'After this tour we are all good for one PTSD-related killing when we get home.' Here, home—what's the difference?"

It was all a joke, of course. While at least one staff officer had voiced the belief that we all deserved to die, we would, in fact, have died for them. Not that we cared about them, but we valued our professional reputation as war-riors more than we hated our detractors. As to the PTSD, some at home might view us as maladjusted, permanently scarred war vets too ashamed to admit that we had it. After all, the American people expected that their vets were ticking time bombs in need of help. War was, to them, a debilitating experience that left neither victor nor vanquished, just the dead and the men-tally and physically broken.

Already, the military was being accused of underreporting the cases of PTSD. We all knew that was bullshit. In most wars there is a winner and a loser. We also knew that most veterans, though not all, returned home when the war was over and made a life for themselves. Most Vietnam vets had done this, but you would not believe that if you watched the news or read the paper.

For us, joking about killing our fellow citizens when we returned home and then copping a PTSD plea was a stab at the public perception of warriors since the war in Vietnam. We settled in for chow and said very little more about killing our own.

After chow I ran into Chief Master Sergeant Vorgang. Vorgang was get-ting ready to go home and he was having a drink with Gunny Hessen and Corporal Napier. Vorgang was talking about the team and how aggressive he thought it was and how he would have done things differently if he had been the operations sergeant major. It was obvious that all three were surprised to see me standing in the hallway that connected my trailer to Hessen's and Napier's.

"What the fuck would you have done differently?" I demanded.

Vorgang, who only moments before was talking about how he would do things differently, now suddenly found himself void of the specifics as to what, exactly, he would do differently. "I don't want to get into that now."

"You wanted to get into before I walked in. Still pissed that Colonel Bu-chanan did not even look at you for that job? Still pissed that I didn't hang out with you like Jackson? What is it? You didn't like the tactics I employed, the missions we took, or the people I picked?"

Vorgang defended himself. "You know I don't think we should be doing all the security stuff you guys do, and I think you guys could do it differently."

"Yeah, you said that before, but you never said who should do it instead," I challenged.

"Anybody, Master Sergeant Lynch, anybody."

Not willing to let the matter rest, I continued. "Well, why didn't you fucking think about that before I got here and recruit yourself a team of crack air police officers? Oh, that was because you thought the war was over, remember? And how would you do things differently? What is the maximum effective range of an RPG-7V against a moving and a static target? How about the maximum effective range of the RPK, the PKM, or the AK? Do you know any of that basic, mundane crap? Name me three insurgent TTPs used in convoy attacks, you know so fucking much, c'mon."

"Top Lynch, you know I'm not an infantryman, but I do know I would have done things differently," Vorgang answered.

"Yeah, and you would have done them with who? Who else, other than yourself and Captain Ricks, would have given you a team to lead? Colonel Buchanan, Thomas, and Roddington, all with combat arms backgrounds, never even looked twice at you to run the office. You think *anybody* was ever going to give you a combat mission, and if they did, do you think any soldier or marine would ever have listened to a fucking thing you had to say?"

Vorgang responded. "Hey, you know what, I have my opinion and you have yours, so we are just going to have to disagree and leave it alone. I know one thing, I am not taking any chances when me and Stacy leave here tomorrow. I hooked us up with the Brits, and they are taking us out under armor." (Stacy was Captain Ricks; I learned in Iraq that in the air force enlisted men can call officers by their first name.)

I did not say anything, but I wanted to kill Vorgang before he could go home. Here he was, a career tech man who spent most of his four months in Iraq behind a desk, telling me how he would have conducted convoy escorts differently. Yet he was not taking any chances on his last ride out. By that time my team and I had made over a hundred runs without armor, and this candy ass wasn't even going to the airport unless it was under armor. It was now clear how he would have done things differently if he had been in my place. Considering that he was unwilling to make this *one* run without armor, I assumed he would have scrubbed most or all missions until he had armor. Our hero! I did not ask Vorgang how he had been able to get armor, the most precious of assets in Iraq, for Ricks and himself. I did not ask whether he had attempted to pull the same strings for my team.

No, I just wished him luck, saying, "You have a safe trip, you and Stacy."

Later that night, as I sat in my trailer I thought about ambushing Vorgang's and Ricks's convoy.

On May 29 we learned that the police officers we used to escort to the MOI had been ambushed on the BIAP road. Their two-vehicle convoy had been lit up in a drive-by ambush that killed one and wounded three. We really liked some of those guys, and war being what it is, I was sure those hurt and killed were among the finest. (True enough, we later learned that the man killed was one we all considered a friend. Worse, he and his wife had recently lost their daughter. I grieved for his wife.)

My guys continued to hit the road every day among mounting losses across Iraq. In fact, for the most part they seemed to revel in the harsh new reality of the war. But they also prayed. They passed out candy and food to children or purchased fifty-cent melted candy bars from them for a dollar. And they loved their comrades with a selfless love so deep that they would die for each other. Though they may have believed in the war, or not, they loved their country and were certain that what they were doing in Iraq was somehow making home, wherever that was, safer. They were among the finest men I have ever met, and I would do anything to get them home. Looking ahead, that seemed to be iffy at best. In anticipation of increased violence, all but the most critical runs out of the Green Zone were being canceled by higher. Where did that leave us? On the road, of course. On 30 May we were to escort six tractor trailers loaded with 7,500 AK-47 rifles and two million rounds of ammo to Tadji. In the hours before the premission prep began, I entertained myself watching and listening to the team as they cleaned their weapons.

Gunny Josleyn joined the weapons cult with Meggi and First Sergeant Tyvela. Tyvela, an old army guy and Vietnam veteran, was a loyal friend of the team. As the master of property within the Green Zone, he was also a valuble friend. Watching Gunny J, also known as the "Gate Keeper," and Meggi work long hours into the night, fixing and cleaning the PKMs and making working 1911 .45 caliber pistols from parts, was like watching two old Swiss watchmakers. These two guys knew the weapons, no matter how exotic, inside and out. Without them, we would not have had two working PKMs, nor would we have had 1911s or Browning High Powers. While I enjoyed watching their expertise in action, what I most enjoyed was just watching the interaction and camaraderie of these two very different men. While both were in their late thirties, that is where all similarity ended. But as they handed parts back and forth to each other, asking questions of themselves and sharing their own expertise, it was quite clear that neither man felt the need to best or one-up the other. Gunny was always very serious and most often very quiet. Meggison, on the other hand, was always making fun of something or someone or laughing at someone else's joke. But when Meggi and the Josleyn were working on some new weapons or just cleaning their own, Meggi was just like Josleyn, quiet and professional.

Their interaction was seamless, and they were a joy to watch. Their mutual respect and affection for one another reminded me of the relationship between my maternal grandmother and her sister, Nan. Both women were widows when they decided to live together, and both were as different from each other as were these two men. But their relationship, like that which Josleyn and Meg enjoyed, was built of a sincere and mutual respect. Gunny and Meg were also our machine gunners, trunk monkeys, and both men quietly enjoyed the responsibility and respect that came with their jobs. In all probability, neither man had ever seen, let alone used, a PKM before coming to Iraq. Now, though, both were experts in their care and cleaning. Better still, both men were as deadly with the weapon as was any American soldier or marine in Iraq with his U.S.-issued weapon. They were certainly better with the weapon than our enemies, who affectionately called the PKM the "Reaper." In the hands of Gunny and Meg, the PKM lived up to that name, easily harvesting souls. In the hands of an insurgent, the name Reaper was a bit much. That was akin to Richard Simmons introducing himself as a cage fighter. While Josleyn and Meg frequently helped each other to finish cleaning the other's PKM, Will was interested only in his highly modified AK and the RPG. Vehicles 1 and 3 each carried an RPG, and Will was designated primary gunner on vehicle 1's RPG. Mostly, though, he was interested in his AK. The AK can be fed by thirty- or forty-round magazines, or seventy-five-round drums, with thirty being the standard. When we got two seventy-five-round drum magazines, Will attempted to cop both for his rifle, "Crazy Ivan." Boeringer was the first to notice Will's less-than-generous nature.

"What the fuck, Top? You gave Will both seventy-five-round drums?"

Of course I had not, and Will was forced to give up one. Will defended his greed, saying that he only wanted the best for Crazy Ivan. So in love was Will with his rifle, he would sometimes break into verse. Holding his weapon aloft he would say, with a heavy Shakespearean accent: "And it shall be the most bad-assed weapon in all Majistania, and I, only I, shall possess it, and it shall be called . . . Crazy Ivan."

While all of us named our weapons and took great care of them, nobody but Will had speeches for his weapon. The most interesting feature of Will's rifle was the three small Punisher skulls, each adorned with the green headband of the Mahdi army, that he painted on Crazy Ivan's buttstock.

"Let me see that thing, Will," I asked.

"Okay, Top, but be careful with him. He does not like strangers," Will said as he handed me his weapon.

I looked at the three Punisher skulls. "You know, Will, you get two more and you will be an ace. If you were a pilot, you would get a DFC for that."

"What if I just get a couple of our officers instead? Does that count the same?"

"I think two of those would get you life. Here you go." I handed his weapon back to him. "The Beast [I had named my own weapon the Beast of Baghdad] is getting jealous. Fudd, let me see your weapon."

Specialist Brackin carried an M-16A2 service rifle, as did I. He also carried a Browning High Power.

"Which one, Top?" asked Brackin.

"The rifle."

Brackin handed me his rifle, which I broke down and examined. Brackin was a good soldier, and I knew his weapon would be clean, but these opportunities gave me a chance to talk to my individual soldiers and marines in a semiprivate fashion. It allowed me to check their mind-set and let them know that while they were a part of a team, they still counted as individuals, too.

"You're doing a lot better with this thing than when you first got here, Fudd."

"I would have been better, Top, if I had gotten to fire her as much in the States as I have here. I can shoot, Top."

"I know you can. Now all we need to do is get a skull or two on this bad boy."

Brackin smiled at the thought. "You think we will get more chances, Top?"

"I hope so, man. They keep telling me June is going to be really bad, so we will just have to see. Just remember, this is a two-way rifle range, Fudd."

"I will, Top, you can count on me. I ain't gonna forget that shit."

As I handed Brackin his rifle, I asked if he had named it.

"No, Top, not yet."

"How about Black Beauty? Given your taste in women."

Brackin looked at me and smiled.

"Del, let me see yours."

Noting the potential sexual connotation of my request, Meggison was quick to advise Del to file sexual harassment charges against me. Del ignored the remark and handed me her bolt carrier group and upper receiver.

"You know, Del, when you got here, you were easily the worst shot on the team. You do really well now, and I love watching you shoot—you and Pat."

"Thanks, Top. Thanks for being patient."

"No problem, Del, and thank you for being persistent."

Del smiled at the reference to her insistence that I give her a chance to prove herself. One by one my soldiers and marines began putting their weapons back together. Mindful of the time, they rarely needed to be told when to wrap up some premission activity.

Our first weapons run to Tadji was easy except for the multiple route closures due to the heavy IED and VBIED threat. Other than that, the most difficult aspect of the run was keeping Iraqi vehicles out of the convoy and making sure that the contract drivers did not miss a turn or take a wrong turn. To my surprise, these runs became a daily event. They were also a real grind. While we were a lucrative and vulnerable target, we made no contact with enemy forces. In fact, most of Iraq was quiet and nowhere near the violence of April was occurring anywhere in the country. June was looking a lot like May, and not at all like what we had been told to expect.

Still, Baghdad remained a very dangerous place. A VBIED left five soldiers dead and wounded four more. Another attack near the MOI killed one and wounded three. The insurgency had grown more lethal in that the attacks produced more casualties than before and more randomly; it seemed to thrash about with no thought to a higher purpose other than to simply kill Americans. The careless or the unlucky became victims. Soon, however, things started picking up.

The end of the first week of June saw a dramatic increase in attacks on convoys in the Baghdad area. Six soldiers were killed and four wounded in two attacks, one taking place near the MOI yet again, and on a route we used. While deadly, these attacks were nothing, in terms of skill and lethality, when compared with the attack on a Blackwater convoy, on June 5, on Route Irish, the road to BIAP.

The convoy consisted of two vehicles, one armored and one not. Not far from the Green Zone, the convoy was attacked by as many as twenty men in as many as seven vehicles. Three vehicles may have sped past the convoy on its right, spread across the traffic lanes, and stopped, blocking the Blackwater convoy. A second element of as many as three vehicles may have then pulled alongside while a third element blocked the rear. The enemy then poured intense automatic weapons fire into the convoy from no more than fifty meters; at least one PKM machine gun was used. With no rear gunners, the convoy was easy meat. The attack killed four and wounded three. The wounded survived by running across the median, taking an Iraqi's car, and driving back to the Green Zone. These men reported that they had no ammo left when they broke contact. They also said that the men who hit them appeared to be more skilled than the average insurgent, and many were speculating that the attackers were Chechens.

The survivors reportedly said that part of what made them think the attackers were Chechens was how incredibly fast these men were able to change a magazine. I was not so sure. We timed Iraqis changing magazines when we trained their personal security details and we found them to be very fast; some could pull a magazine out of a pouch and have it in the weapon and the weapon back in their shoulder in less than three seconds; as to whether the attackers were Chechen or not, I could not say. Regardless, Chechen or homegrown, it was obvious that some new players were targeting convoys on Route Irish, and they were very good at executing fast, mobile small-arms ambushes.

Mobile ambushes, along with more traditional fixed ambushes, IEDs, and VBIEDs, made the 5.4 miles of Route Irish between the airport and the Green Zone the deadliest stretch of road in Iraq. As to the Blackwater convoy, I could not understand how anybody out here ran out of ammo. Small convoys are extremely vulnerable to complex attacks by significant numbers of men; you had better carry enough ammo to cover your ass. We carried twenty magazines per rifle and ten for our pistols. Add all the AT-4 and RPGs and PKM ammo, and we would be hard pressed to run out of ammo unless we were in Mecca during the hajj.

Attacks like this one validated the tactics we employed, contrary to the bitching of our critics. No vehicle would ever be allowed to pull alongside, let alone pass our convoy. Given that we had two rear-mounted PKMs, by the time a vehicle pulled abreast of mine, it would be a flaming wreck once our faithful and lethal trunk monkeys were done with them. Then the crematorium on wheels would eat more lead from those of us firing out the side windows. We never allowed vehicles in front of us to slow down, let alone stop. We created a "bubble" around ourselves, and anything entering the bubble was subject to increasing levels of force, culminating, when necessary, in lethal force.

Our most important protection against the kind of attack that destroyed the Blackwater convoy was our rearmost trunk monkey, Gunny Josleyn. It was his job to let his vehicle commander know that a high-speed target was closing from the rear. It was the vehicle commander's job to pass this to the rest of us. In this type of attack, I would then have the team spread out and take all three lanes; this would allow my trunk monkey to support Josleyn's fire by engaging additional targets or pouring more fire into Josleyn's target. We would then stop, blocking the enemy in as Iraqi civilian traffic closed in on him from the rear, and we would feed our attacker PKM, M-16, AK-47, AT-4, and RPG rockets until we had killed him. The last thing any goat fucker wanted to do was try to pin us in and attack us as he had the Blackwater convoy. That was a sure ticket on the pain train to torment town. This was not mere after-the-fact boasting. We practiced this maneuver frequently as part of our SOPs. We went to the range frequently and practiced speed drills for multiple target engagements. I can honestly say that while we feared IEDs, we longed for the type of attack that had eliminated the Blackwater team. You train for how you will fight, and you fight the way you are trained. We worked hard because we wanted to stay alive, and we wanted to win, and we certainly wanted to put our training to the test.

Whoever hit the Blackwater convoy appeared to be experienced and dedicated and to have numbers similar to ours. They would be perfect trophies for us. While I hoped that it was our destiny to meet these diaper heads, I did not think they would be that stupid. They seemed adept at finding and feeding on victims. For their purposes a few victims would do just fine. All they had to do was kill a few Americans and we would start scrubbing missions in an effort to avoid contact. The day after the attack on the Blackwater convoy we were to pick up more weapons at BIAP and run them to Tadji. That mission got axed as nonessential.

While I agreed with the decision to cancel a large, slow convoy hauling weapons and ammo, I could not agree with the decision to have us all simply hunker down on our FOBs. Instead of having the team hide in the Green Zone, we should have been put out there, without the large, slow, vulnerable trucks and their critical cargoes, trying to draw the enemy out and into the open so we could kill them. We could not kill anybody sitting on our asses in the Green Zone. Killing was all the war was about then. There were no cities to capture, no armies to crush, just a bunch of people to kill. The war was a test of wills, as all wars are, but this one was stripped of any means of breaking the enemy's will except by killing him.

You could not break his will by capturing strategically critical objects or symbolic cities important to him. You could not break his will by maneuvering his army into a position where it could only surrender or be destroyed. No, the only way to break the will of this enemy was to kill enough of them, and we were not doing that in the Green Zone. We allowed the enemy to repeatedly close Route Irish, the most important 5.4 miles of road in the country. Why we could not control this vital artery remains a mystery to me. IEDs, VBIEDs, complex static and mobile ambushes, you name it and the enemy was able to do it any time he chose to. While not as bad as April, Route Irish remained deadly, and it should not have been that way. In an effort to destroy the enemy on Route Irish, I asked for permission to run up and down the route as a rolling QRF or as bait. I also asked if we could set in ambush teams along the route at night so that we could detect and kill IED teams attempting to set in their deadly weapons. Incredibly, these ideas were rejected as too risky. I did not see it that way. It was far riskier to roll down a route that had no security, as nothing more than a target, than it was to be proactive about making Route Irish safe. Besides, war is risky by its nature, and when you start looking for ways to avoid risk, you are looking for ways to lose, whether you know it or not. We were surrendering to the enemy the cities and the arteries that connected them. It was insane, and I grew more pessimistic about our chances to win.

As I left the palace that night, Libby walked with me and told me that a VBIED had hit the gate at Tadji. While I questioned the wisdom of not cutting us loose, I had to admit that I was glad our mission there had been scrubbed. As I said earlier, death in Iraq was often about being in the wrong place at the wrong time. On 6 June 2004 the gate at Tadji was the wrong place, and we had been scheduled to go there. I didn't give that too much thought, though, as *almost* being at the wrong place at what *might* have been the wrong time was as significant as almost being pregnant. Still, June started looking like it might get as bad as everyone feared.

The attacks at the end of the first week of June seemed to spread from Baghdad and across the country. But it was nothing like April, and only Baghdad seemed to be seeing a lot of activity. For the rest of the month Route Irish and indeed much of Baghdad remained very deadly, with attack levels near what they had been in April. Much of the rest of Iraq remained strangely quiet.

The first week of June also saw the departure of CMATT's commander. General Eaton was going home after having built CMATT from nothing. His replacement was Lieutenant General David Petraeus, whom we had picked up back in April. Everybody in the palace worried that Petraeus would make life miserable for us. I did not know why. For the team, our only concern would be a directive from the general ordering a change in our tactics. This possibility was discussed with the team and Colonel Thomas. We had no intention of changing anything. We would keep doing what kept us alive, and if told to change, we would not. When it came to staying alive, the end always justified the means. Besides, it was not like guys on the general's staff would be riding with us. Quicker than a Muslim cleric issues a fatwa condemning someone to death for a cartoon, our SOPs were the subject of a review, but that review was not directed by General Petraeus.

With the pending arrival of the new general, I was called to a meeting with Captain Wheeler. It was not a meeting about the convoy team, just a J-3 meeting. I hated these meetings because they frequently consisted of groveling officers trying to win favor with the impressionable captain Wheeler. The worst of these was Major Theodorson followed closely by Johns and Deboda. These guys had their heads so far up Wheeler's ass they might as well have been turds. Colonel Buchanan would have crushed these bootlickers. Unlike Wheeler, Buchanan knew what was going on. You could not blind him with bullshit the way these men did Wheeler. Wheeler was asking what should be briefed to the general. Though inept, Wheeler knew enough to be worried about his job security, which he clearly was. Theodorson and Johns, not content to tell Wheeler what they were going to brief the general about *their* jobs, instead focused on the convoy security team. Theodorson spoke first.

"Sir, I've been looking at the way we provide the convoy escorts, and I think we can make some minor changes there that will keep us out of trouble with the general."

This bootlicking ass was concerned that the general, whom he had yet to meet, might have problems with our tactics because so many other people did. Rather than risk a possible problem, better to change what we were doing, even if it put us at greater risk, just so long as we didn't do anything that might bring some heat to operations. I also wondered what Theodorson meant when he said that he had "been looking at the way we provide convoy escorts." Since he had never, not once, even done so much as show up in the parking lot as we mounted up, let alone ride with us, just exactly how was he looking at what we did? Was he remote viewing? Johns, sensing that it was safe and that he had a receptive ear, and possibly not wanting to be outshone by Theodorson, quickly added, "Sir, I've looked at this, too. I have gone out to the staging area and I have even talked to some of the other teams, and I really think we could curtail the amount of people we are sending, and I think we need to look at the weapons."

What the hell! Neither Theodorson nor Johns had so much as sat in one of our vehicles, let alone gone anywhere with us. After all, it was safer to form opinions from the palace. But their offering advice on how we should operate was akin to Sean Penn writing a book on foreign policy. Worse, Johns actually seemed to believe that by wearing his beret (his personal trademark) and seeing us off at the staging area, he was a combat vet with an opinion to be valued. Besides, what teams did he talk to? First Cav's? Many of their teams had only one goal, avoiding combat.

Turning to me, Wheeler asked, "Top Lynch?"

"Sir, I think any change is potentially lethal. I have no idea what Major Theodorson is talking about because he did not say anything specific, but even so, since he has never even made it to the staging area, I do not know on what basis, other than the same shit we have gone over before, he would have for suggesting any change."

I looked at Theodorson and asked, "Do you have anything specific, sir?"

Theodorson did not. He just looked at me with a dazed and confounded expression that seemed to say, "Doesn't he know I am an officer?"

I was not done. "Lieutenant Colonel Johns actually seems to believe that by walking out to the staging area, watching us prep and go, and talking to other teams he has a basis for an opinion."

I had been in Iraq long enough to lose any concern about being blatantly disrespectful.

Turning back to Wheeler, I finished by saying, "I don't think we need to make any changes, sir."

Wheeler nodded his head. "Top Lynch, I think that you should be there when we brief the general."

I left the meeting and went looking for Colonel Thomas. I told him that, contrary to what had been established at the meeting with Lieutenant Colonel Toddington, Johns and Theodorson were again pushing for changes in our SOP. Colonel Thomas was pissed that these two sorry sacks of spineless crap had not bothered to mention their ideas to him, as he was the current operations officer and, as such, was the officer responsible for the team's actions. It was more of the same. It never seemed to dawn on any of our critics that we lacked armor, decent radios, and corpsmen or medics. For a time we even lacked machine guns; shit, we even lacked vehicles. Half of my guys still had to carry Russian weapons, and none of us had been trained for this mission prior to our arrival in Iraq. Considering what we lacked I thought it was a testament to our SOPs that we had yet to suffer a casualty. We had only recently acquired American crew-served weapons to replace our Russian-made PKMs. Our trunk monkeys were now armed with the superior 240 machine gun. Additionally, we were able to get three M-249 SAWs, which gave each vehicle an automatic rifleman. These potentially lifesaving weapons were acquired by the team in a way that, while outside the norm, was far more effective than waiting on our command. Fittingly, given how things worked at CMATT, the weapons came without ammo. One of the CPA staff officers, Kelly Hudson, came to the rescue here and put me in contact with one of the security contractors whom she thought could help. She explained: "They have a lot of ammo for their American weapons, but I know they are in constant need of other things, like ranges and an escort to get them there. Maybe you guys can work something out."

The contractor, a retired Navy SEAL, said he could get me 50,000 rounds of 5.56 mm for the SAWs and 25,000 rounds of 7.62 mm for the 240s. In exchange he asked me for an MP-5 with ten magazines. Knowing what his duties were, I understood his desire for a weapon of nearly pistol-like size but far greater firepower. I told him that would be no problem but asked that he keep the details of our deal to himself; I was not at all sure Kelly would have approved of my less than standard practice in obtaining what I needed. He agreed, and a deal was struck. True to his word, the man delivered the promised ammo a few days later. If not for Kelly, we would never have gotten the ammo so critical to us. But unlike many of our superiors, she saw a problem and did what she could do to help. For our part, we never took no for an answer, and we did everything we could, including running the risk of incurring the significant wrath of legal, just for the privilege of fighting.

Our critics within CMATT never seemed to realize just how much effort we expended simply to stay on the road. They also failed to realize how heavy our workload was compared to that of other teams. Most amazing of all, they never once asked why my team, operating with so many handicaps, had suffered zero casualties! There were a lot of teams in Iraq that could not make that claim. Did my critics think the enemy avoided us because of our impressive armor and heavy weapons? Being that we lacked both, that was unlikely. Did they think our survival was purely a matter of luck? They never dared consider that our survival might have had a lot to do with our SOPs and the brutal nature of my team. We certainly did not owe our survival to our state-of-the-art weapons, communications, or armor. But to actually acknowledge the obvious would mean to acknowledge that what we did worked. To acknowledge that meant accepting that they actually knew nothing about the complex and potentially lethal operations I and my team performed almost every day. It was far easier and less damaging to ego to simply harass the shit out of us with an endless stream of childish BS like defacing team photos or making nonsensical suggestions that we change what was obviously working!

These people were never going to leave us alone, and, lest they be forgotten, neither were the insurgents. Later that night, at 2207, we took some mortar fire. One round was quite close and shook the walls of my trailer. Unlike the round that seemed to land on top of us a few weeks earlier, this one did not cause me any duress. Incoming never bothered me as long as it did not wake me up. Anyone who has ever been annoyed by an alarm clock can appreciate, just a little, the abject terror of being awakened by incoming mortar fire. It sucks worse than a Michael Moore documentary, and I never wanted to experience that again. While I was not overly bothered by this attack, it always felt very odd to know that someone had just deliberately tried to kill you. Not "you" personally, but just you or any other American he could get. I found myself imagining these men running their mortar out to a firing position, setting it up, dropping a few rounds down the tube while they chanted "*Allah Akbar,*" and then breaking the mortar down and fleeing into the night hoping that they had just sent some American devils to hell. Tomorrow, in honor of the fact that Allah had not answered their prayers, I will eat some pork sausage at morning chow.

Sergeant Jason Algarin *(From the collection of Jack Lynch)*

The following morning, after I had eaten a hearty breakfast that included both bacon and sausage, Colonel Thomas told me that he would cover the brief to the general for me. That was fine by me. Hesco always had the team's back, and I was sure he would do right by us. He did. That was no surprise, but the man who came up big for the team was Major Drury, Colonel Sarna's replacement as the intelligence officer. Major Drury, having been briefed by Sarna, Libby, and Garate, prepared a detailed brief on the evolving enemy threat. He then went on to stress the importance of allowing the convoy security team to continue operating as it had. Major Drury went so far as to guarantee the general that what had happened to the Blackwater convoy on Route Irish could not happen to our team *because* the tactics we employed were expertly designed to thwart known enemy tactics. Against this forceful argument, backed up by the facts that the intelligence officer had concerning attacks on American convoys all across Iraq, and Hesco's own brief, Theodorson and Johns did what I would expect; they briefed only their own small and insignificant piece of the operations pie. Both seemed to forget that just the day before they had some really keen ideas about the convoy security team that they were just dying to brief to the general. That Theodorson, Johns, and Deboda were terrified of Hesco, I had no doubt. But what really killed their motivation that morning was Major Drury, the wild card, turning out to be a great friend of the Maji. The intel section, which knew the most about enemy tactics, techniques, and procedures, would prove to be the best friend the Maji had, from start to finish.

Major Drury did not look like the stereotypical intelligence officer. Of medium build and standing 5′8″ he had the face of a teacher. He looked like

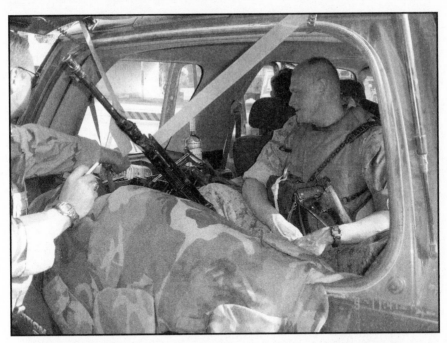

Corporal Kelly Meggison and Gunnery Sergeant Robert Josleyn. Note the old-style flak jackets used as "armor" for the gunner's station. *(From the collection of Jack Lynch)*

a quiet, passive guy. He was not. He was intelligent, ruthless, and absolutely dedicated to crushing the enemy in Iraq. Like Colonel Sarna before him, he understood the war from the ground. He did not give a shit what we did as long as we stayed within the ROE and brought all of our people home.

Later that evening, General Petraeus made the rounds through his new command. He dropped in on the operations section. Mole Man, Theodorson, Deboda, Toddington, a battle captain, and I were all present. Mole Man was not a man to miss a chance at some face time with the general. After I called the office to attention, Mole Man beat out the other suitors (Theodorson and Deboda) for the general's hand and quickly introduced himself. He then introduced the battle captain before bringing the general to where I stood.

"This is Master Sergeant Lynch, the operations sergeant major and the leader of our convoy security team."

The general smiled. "Stand at ease, Master Sergeant. You don't have to introduce me to the Top. He picked me up at the airport back in April and made sure I was safe. Master Sergeant, they tell me that what happened to the Blackwater convoy could not happen to your team."

"Yes, sir, that is true."

The general responded, "Well, Top, whatever you're doing, keep doing it, and don't change a thing. Tell your team I appreciate what they are doing over here."

Mole Man shook his head effusively in agreement, and Theodorson just smiled meekly. They both knew that I knew they wanted to drastically change what we did on the road as they had consistently said, and in fact had advocated just twenty-four hours before. Now all they could do was agree with the general as if they actually shared his beliefs. They shook their heads and smiled because they had no choice. Career officers who were in Iraq to punch a ticket were not about to disagree with a general.

I smiled back. "Yes sir, we weren't planning on it."

CHAPTER 11

Heroes, Villains, and Rockets
With Your Fruit Loops

They're like Lay's chips—you can't kill just one, can you, Will?"

"I have three kills, Top," Will answered.

"I don't know about that shit, Will," interjected Staff Sergeant Reed.

"I'll give you the one, and maybe even two, but three is pushing it," said Reed, continuing his attack on Will's claim to three kills.

Will was so beside himself that he stumbled in his reply, which only left Reed another opening.

"Use your words, Will, your W-O-R-D-S, just like we talked about."

Reed, Face, and I laughed, and Will told Reed to kiss his ass. Will was not the only victim of Reed's teasing. Next Reed turned his attention to me.

"Don't feel bad, Will. I am pretty sure that everything Top shot had already been shot at least once."

In truth, I envied Will his three kills, and my not having them reminded me of a story Tug once told me. He knew a sergeant who was part of a hunter-killer team in Northern Ireland. They spotted a target, and one of the men asked for permission to engage. The sergeant told the commando to wait—and then proceeded to shoot and kill the man himself. Needless to say, the trooper was upset that his kill had been stolen. Unprofessional though it would have been, I certainly had had more than one occasion to think that maybe I should have done the same.

"You calling me the T. rex of kills, Huggy?" I answered, in a play on the growing belief by many that the Tyrannosaurus rex, contrary to its fearsome reputation as a killer, was nothing more than a large, loud scavenger. Obviously, I was also poking fun at my own reputation within the walls of the palace.

"No, not at all, Top," Reed said. "I'm just saying is all."

"Well, I don't know about you white devils, but I know I have two," Facemyer chipped in.

"Nobody can take those from you, Face. I saw those," Reed said. As if on cue, Will met the challenge, "Oh fuck you, Chris, you're just saying that to piss me off."

I did not think about it at the time, but I am sure some people would be deeply disturbed by men arguing over who had killed who.

When I did think about it, after I returned home, I was not bothered by what we had said or by what it revealed about us. Man is, by nature, a killer. While I have heard many men say that killing was not easy and that they regretted it, I did not believe that is universally true. Warfare is competitive, and man likes to record his achievements and measure them against other men's. The world has lauded the greatest air aces since the first plane was shot down in flames. Richard Bong, they will say, is America's greatest ace, having shot down forty Japanese aircraft. As with any other ace, Bong had his picture taken in front of his aircraft, an aircraft emblazoned with forty Japanese flags marking forty victories over Japanese aircraft. Civilized folk back at the air base or in the States would share in the grinning aviator's glory and conveniently ignore the fact that those forty aircraft were not flown by robots. Bong's victories came with a human toll, too. The men in those planes were either torn apart by the hammering of Bong's heavy guns or incinerated in their machines. But celebrating those victories and decorating a man solely because of the number of kills he has is a time-honored tradition. Somehow, though, when killing is stripped of the guise that a machine is the target, it is not to be celebrated, and the killer is not to be decorated solely for having killed. With the exception of the sniper, the man who does his killing face-to-face is supposed to be ashamed and feel guilty about having killed.

Will walked around the palace with three skulls painted on his rifle and people looked at him like he had just left his kid brother with Michael Jackson. But let some pilot, with three little flags painted on the side of his aircraft, land at BIAP and everybody would treat him like he won the war. To hell with that! None of us was going to feel bad because we had killed. We reveled in it. Maybe, if our enemies had been someone else, a civilized and honorable foe, then maybe we would have regretted the necessity of killing them. In this war we killed out of necessity, but it was a pleasure as well, a guilt-free pleasure. We were killing animals who would kill a man, a woman, or a child just because they were not Muslims or maybe because they were not the right kind of Muslim or not Muslim enough. We were fighting an enemy who thought it was God's will to strap bombs on retarded women, send them into crowded markets, and then detonate the bomb. It was very easy to see why the boys, fighting such "men," would argue about who killed whom.

Heated conversation aside, we completed the run, another weapons and ammo mission to Tadji, uneventfully. We pulled into the lot, secured our vehicles, weapons, and gear and went to chow. Our evening ritual complete, I returned to the office alone. I turned to the roster and looked at the scheduled departure dates for the team. For some weeks now I had been concerned about what would happen to my team after I left. While most were scheduled to leave within two weeks of my own scheduled departure, Dann and Del were not slated to leave until late in October. For some time I had been debating whether I would ask for an extension of my tour. I loved my job, and I believed in the war; I believed my part in it was important. I also hated my job at Quantico and most of the self-serving SNCOs and officers that populated the place. On the other hand, I missed my family a great deal, and I wanted to go home. But above all, I wanted to see that my people made it home. If I left, I would worry about Del and Dann until they, too, had made it home. I would feel as if I had abandoned them. They already had enough to worry about without getting a new leader who would not look out for them. Maybe my replacement would be a great guy, maybe he would be better than me, but it was at least as likely that he would not be. Would he lead and make sure Dann and Del got home, or would he always just say go and do and never say follow? Would he know anything that would get them home, or would he be a clueless ticket puncher? While I thought about my family, I did not give them much consideration, and what little I did was outweighed by my sense of obligation to Del and Dann. Of course while I knew Colonel Thomas would approve my request, I suspected my bosses at Quatico would be less than happy. As I left the office I stopped by Hesco's desk and told him that I wanted him to go ahead and formally request that my tour be extended. He was not surprised.

"Are you sure it's what you want to do? Have you told your family?"

I answered, "No, I have not, and I really don't know how I will tell them, but I am sure. I want to stay until Dann and Del leave."

"Top, I'll let Captain Wheeler and the Commandant's Office know."

Hesco then looked at me funny and smiled.

"What, sir?" I asked.

"Nothing. Go on, get out of here. I will see you tomorrow."

As I walked back to my trailer I thought about what I had just done. I worried about being killed after I should have been home and the impact that would have on my family, but I was certain that I was doing the right thing. This was my team. These people had joined, in part, because of what I had told them. They had faithfully followed me where I led and I could not leave them just because my tour was up. Besides, by extending I would only be doing what I had already asked, and what Will and Face had already done. It really did not matter now. The choice was made, and I believed that I had made the right decision. That would be my consolation if anything bad did happen to me after what had been my scheduled rotation date. There was still a lot of work to be done, and I was determined to do my part.

The following day we made another weapons run to Tadji.

The run passed as most did, without incident. The days were just a blur, and before I knew it, it was the tenth of June, my twenty-third anniversary as a marine.

I can remember cleaning a locker room when I was on maintenance duty shortly after arriving at Parris Island for recruit training in June of 1981. In an open locker I saw the uniform blouse of a Marine Corps gunnery sergeant, the sleeve decorated not only with the man's insignia of rank, but with four service stripes as well, representing sixteen years of service. On the chest were eight ribbons, including the Purple Heart and Vietnam Campaign ribbons. As I looked at that uniform I wondered if I would ever be a hardened combat veteran as I imagined that man to be. I wondered if I would spend as long in the Corps and if I would go as far. Considering how far I had come, I was very thankful for my career. I was amazed that the years had gone by so quickly. Yet as happy as I was to have had the career I had, I was also saddened by the realization that it would soon be over. I knew that no matter how long I stayed in the Corps, this would be my last time to lead warriors in combat. So whether I stayed on until I hit thirty years or retired at the end of this enlistment mattered little. My career would end when this tour was over. It seemed so unfair. Yesterday I was a recruit admiring the accomplishments of a man I did not know, and now I was contemplating the end of my career. It was almost as if I had gone from boot camp to retirement with no stops in between. I envied the young marines just starting their careers.

They were doing at eighteen what I did not get to do until I was forty-one. They were fighting a war I had wanted to fight since 1979, and they would spend their entire careers fighting this war. My service, by comparison, seemed to be largely wasted, having consisted, as it did, of nearly meaningless combat forays in Panama and the Gulf and a lot of BS before, between, and after those less than glorious operations. It was a painful realization.

The big issue facing me, of course, was not the value or merit of my career, it was simple survival. In May all the intel had indicated that getting killed was not going to be too hard to do once June started. But June had gotten off to a relatively quiet start, and though attacks had increased as the month progressed, the number was nowhere near as bad as I had expected. Much of the "combat" that did occur was of the political variety. The big news was a memo that Democrats charged laid the ground for the prisoner abuse at Abu Ghraib. The soldiers involved in that, dispshits like that model of feminine virtue, Lynndie England, could not even read the word "memo" let alone read the memo. Most of us in Iraq, enlisted and officer alike, believed that the freak show at Abu Ghraib was nothing more sinister than a bunch of inbred rednecks having a good time.

All of us were shamed by their actions. But worse than that, we were endangered by the tremendous amount of attention the incident got. You had Democrats producing memos that they claimed showed the whole thing to be President Bush's fault. I was convinced that much of the Democratic Party wanted to see us lose the war. In the run-up to the 2004 elections they saw each casualty as a small gain on the president in the polls. They and their media allies touted "grim milestones" as our casualties rose. These were the same people who in another war had decried the use of body counts. Unless, or so it seemed, anyway, the body count was that of U.S. personnel. During the Vietnam War the media and the antivictory crowd had ridiculed the U.S. military for placing any emphasis on the enemy body count. They had claimed those numbers, no matter how high, were meaningless to the outcome of the war. Now they breathlessly reported each death of a serviceman, whether killed in action or simply died of natural causes, as if each represented a major battlefield defeat for American arms. (In fact, this would reach such ridiculous proportions that in July 2008, when the United States lost six men killed in action, then the lowest toll for any month of the war, the big news on CNN's Web page and elsewhere was "Another Grim Milestone Reached With the 100th Death of a Female Service Member." Pushing past the grim headline and reading the rest of the story, however, you learned that the woman died of natural causes. Hell, for that matter, one of the dead listed for that month had been injured in 2005 aboard an aircraft carrier and the death clearly had nothing to do with the war in Iraq.) Like that previous war fought in Asia, the hard-won victories of this war were being thrown away by a media and a political party that kept telling our enemies, in essence, "All you have to do is stay in the fight until the elections and we will give you the victory."

These people were either fools or traitors; there was no third option. They were, by their words of comfort to the enemy, killing us just as surely as were the IEDs. They sickened me. I wished that the allegations being made were true. I wished that the president would authorize torture, as a matter of policy, in the interrogation of terrorists. We should be extracting every ounce of info we can from those people, no matter what we have to do to them to get it. I have often heard opponents of the war ask, "How do you stop a man who is willing to die anyway?" A suicide bomber kills, in part, because he believes he will have a reward in the afterlife and because his family will be taken care of. His family will be heroes because they gave Islam another martyr. The suicide bomber is comforted in the knowledge that his sacrifice will be honored by his family, friends, and neighbors. His family may even be paid for his selfless act of courage. But what if, instead, he knew that his family would be hunted down and slaughtered? What if he knew his neighborhood would be destroyed and his neighbors and friends killed? I suspect that if a suicide bomber knew that his homeland, the land that spawned him, would be reduced to a howling wasteland populated by the broken bodies of everyone who ever knew him, he might think twice about driving his car into a convoy. If not him, I am certain his neighbors, friends, and family would not be as willing to sit by and cheer him as he departed on his mission of jihad. They would turn his ass in.

Torture, humiliation, and death, applied as a matter of policy, controlled by the Department of Defense and our intelligence services, would be a powerful weapon in this war. These people already hated us (there was no Abu Ghraib before Iran, Pakistan, Beirut, *Achille Lauro*, Khobar Towers, Somalia, USS *Cole*, East Africa, and September 11), so who gave a shit if we actually gave them reasons to hate us? Like they didn't already? We needed to give these people reasons to hate and *fear* us. We needed to make what we did to Japan seem like a small misunderstanding between good friends by comparison.

In modern history only one people, the Japanese, have ever shown a true willingness to fight and die to the very last man, woman, and child. And even they found that there was a limit. Now, as then, it is simply a matter of helping the enemy realize that there is a limit. To me it means, just as it did in

World War II, killing on a scale and in a manner that convinces these animals that we have the means and the *will* to do whatever it takes to win this war. If that means that we kill them all or just one, the choice is theirs. War is a test of wills. Because of the lack of will on the part of the American people, and not because of any weakening of the resolve of those of us actually fighting the war, we stood a very good chance of losing. Abu Ghraib, nothing more than a redneck prank going global, was made into *the* story because it supported the defeatist agenda.

On 12 June we picked up some FBI agents at BIAP. While we were as-signed as the escort, a group from DynCorp actually drove the vehicles carry-ing the agents. The G-men had to travel under armor, and since we lacked armor, someone else had to actually carry the agents. DynCorps provided big black armored Suburbans for the occasion. I wished that was all they had pro-vided, but the Suburbans also came with their own drivers and shooters, and they sucked. The overpaid hired help treated our brief like it was a waste of time. After all, at some time they had been Special Forces or Seals or some such bullshit and we were simply army and marine grunts of low skills and even less intelligence. They were so *special* that they needed us, in our unar-mored shit cars, to pull security for them! That was a trend in Iraq we were all starting to notice. While we did not have any first- or even second-rate equip-ment, we were more and more often being called upon to act as a human shield for people who considered us beneath them. Once on the road, the DynCorp's drivers, having not listened to the brief, failed to keep a proper following dis-tance between vehicles. They stayed right on the ass of my number 2 vehicle and on each other's asses as well. If my 2 had gotten nailed, the following vehicles were going to pancake into him and each other at about 90 miles per hour. Five casualties in one destroyed vehicle would have instantly become more than a dozen casualties in several vehicles. Some guys are so "special" they just can't learn anything, and following simple directions is a basic skill that escapes them. Many of the contracted security details in Iraq thought that training meant taking steroids (a significant and unreported problem with many contractors working in Iraq) and sitting poolside getting that nice Iraqi tan, and these guys were no different. I was glad to be done with them when we pulled into the Green Zone.

The following day I was eating a late breakfast with Gunnery Sergeant Josleyn. As was our custom, we sat around for a few minutes talking about nothing in particular as we nursed our cups of coffee. It was getting late in the morning and the conversation was starting to lag when I asked, "Are you ready to go?" Before Josleyn could answer, there was a powerful explosion that sounded like it had come from within the palace and not too far from the chow hall.

For a millisecond after the explosion there was a dead silence, and then people began to scream and cry as they dove under their tables. Still others, assuming positions of importance and authority beyond their deskbound world, began shouting commands, useless commands. Most of these chow hall heroes were civilians.

"Everybody get under a table and take cover. Stay here and don't move," shouted the wannabes.

I did not know which I found more loathsome, the sheep diving under tables as they wailed and moaned or the "heroes," standing amid the "horror of war," calmly directing others to take shelter. We got up and headed to the operations section. At first I even carried my coffee, but I soon realized, given the panic-stricken flight of many of my fellow diners, that I had a better chance of wearing the coffee than drinking it, so I threw it away. As I turned the corner, however, and looked down the long hall that led to CMATT, all I could see was a dense cloud of dust rolling toward us. Now I began to feel the first twangs of panic as I thought CMATT might have been hit by a suicide bomber. My friends were down there. Gunny and I began to run toward the cloud. Remembering my first mission to the Baghdad Recruiting Center, I dreaded what we might find on the other side of that cloud.

When we reached the wall of dust, we could see that it was localized. To my right was a shattered window that looked out on a courtyard. Crumpled next to the window, and crying hysterically, was a woman who had been walking past the window when it was shattered. While she was not injured, she had come close to death, and her hysteria was easy to understand. A man was kneeling with her, offering words of comfort. I was struck by his genuine and empathic concern for the woman whom I believed he had never met before that morning. Looking into the courtyard I could see that it was littered with debris. It now seemed as if a mortar or rocket had hit the palace and caused minor damage. Gunny and I quickly climbed through the window and checked to make sure that nobody had been hit. Except for tools, the courtyard was empty. As we headed back toward operations, some of my guys came running up to me.

"Man, Major Sherman told us he had just seen you guys in the chow hall and he sent us down here to check on you."

"Really?" I answered in more than mild shock. "Gunny and I thought you guys had been hit."

"No, not even close," Dann answered.

Still not able to believe what I was hearing, I asked, "Major Sherman sent you guys after us?"

"Yeah, Top, and he seemed genuinely concerned about you guys," Del answered.

I did not know what to say. I still do not know what to say. Later we were able to determine that a rocket, had landed about twenty-five meters from the chow hall. If the rocket had had a delayed fuse and it had functioned properly, it might have been able to penetrate to the chow hall before exploding. Had that happened we would have suffered quite a few casualties, possibly even Josleyn and me. (Many months later, insurgents would again hit the palace with a rocket. This time the warhead did not detonate upon impact. Instead, the rocket penetrated the outer wall of the palace and two inner walls before cutting an American woman in half, bouncing off the floor, and taking off the head of an American naval commander. The men who launched that attack, and no doubt many others on the Green Zone, were observed by a drone and subsequently captured. I have wondered if they were the same guys who hit the palace while we were at chow).

While the rocket that hit us that day caused no casualties, the panic did. In the mad dash to escape impending doom, a new arrival had left his suitcase in the chow hall. When the case was discovered, it was duly reported to explosive ordnance disposal (EOD) as a suspicious object left unattended. Not wanting to take any chances, EOD blew up the suitcase, scattering smoldering clothes, including underwear, all over the place and knocking the chow hall out of action for lunch. This was the most effective attack on the palace during my tour.

CHAPTER 12

Where Is the Enemy?

On the fifteenth of June we conducted our first live-fire and maneuver attacks on the convoy range at Kirkush. This exercise put our marksmanship and quick-kill training to the test. In live-fire maneuver training, you do not fire from a line as you do on a traditional range. Instead, elements of your unit, such as fire teams at the squad level, move forward in rushes, while other fire teams engage targets to cover the movement. If enemy fire becomes more effective, individuals will rush forward, allowing more men to cover those moving. Once the team or men moving have reached a covered position, they engage targets so that the men who had covered their movement can now move forward. In other words, this type of training involves some people firing their weapons while others move ahead of them, to their left and right. Consequently, it is very dangerous and requires careful attention to detail. But the training is critical to teaching men how to move forward with rounds going past them. It teaches them to trust the guy next to them. The training was similar to the scenario training we did at the Crossed Sabers except now we had targets to shoot at. For the first run, a vehicle would start at a stationary point. Once they were ready, I would yell, "Targets," and the men would dismount their vehicle and lay down heavy fire while they moved toward cover.

We did a "dry fire" (no shooting) walk-through and then a dry fire run-through. If that went well, we then had the team do a full-speed live-fire attack. It was critical that the men quickly clear their vehicle and move to cover. As they were moving, the vehicle's machine gunner would lay down suppressive fire on the enemy. Once the rest of the crew in his vehicle was covered and laying down suppression, the machine gunner would move to their position. Each vehicle went through the same exercises.

By the early afternoon, all three teams had conducted one live-fire attack. It was exhausting. Temperatures were over 120 degrees, and by the time we completed one run-through, we were nearly spent. The culmination of the training was rerunning the same drills but with all three vehicles at the same time. It went beautifully. The teams quickly dismounted their vehicles and immediately laid down a heavy volume of suppressive rifle and machine-gun fire. Quickly, the dismounted riflemen and SAW gunners made it to covered firing positions and immediately engaged targets at the cyclic rate so that they could cover the temporary loss of machine-gun fire as the gunners dismounted and moved to join the rest of the team. Once we had gained fire superiority over the "enemy," I had my rocket men launch a salvo of three rockets. Shock and awe thus obtained, I led the team in the assault on the enemy position.

It all went very well. The months of scenario training with immediate-action drills and the numerous ranges had paid off. We had taken marines (two infantrymen, one cannon cocker, two logistics types, one brig guard) and soldiers (two rangers, one special ops, four infantrymen, two mechanics, and one admin NCO) and made them into an effective unit. I was very proud of my team. Live-fire and maneuver ranges are difficult even for infantry units, and men are frequently killed. For a collection of misfits from so many diverse backgrounds, my team had performed very well.

Drained, but satisfied, we loaded up our vehicles and headed back to the headquarters building, where we would pick up some Brits and Aussies who were going back to the palace. It was a large convoy. Up front were two armored Hummers. Behind these were the Brit and Aussie vehicles. These were followed by my vehicles. Most of the trip was dull. The runs to and from Kirkush were hated now. Long gone was the excitement we once felt at making any run anywhere. As we neared Baghdad, the traffic, as was always the case, grew heavier but was not as heavy as normal. Though welcome, it was always a cause for concern whenever anything out of the ordinary, even something that had positive aspects, occurred in Iraq.

Ahead of us I could see several cars parked on the shoulder of the road.

This was not unusual, as Iraqis frequently parked alongside the roads. Sometimes it was so they could shop at roadside stalls or sometimes they just seemed to park and gather to talk with friends. But every time I passed a car parked along any Iraqi road, I knew I was taking my life into my own hands. I knew that when it came to a static car bomb or a roadside bomb, I would not survive because I was good. I survived because I was lucky, nothing more, nothing less. A bomber might watch ten convoys roll by before deciding to blow up the unlucky bastards in the eleventh convoy. Luck was not something a person could cultivate or build; it was either good or bad, and no matter what it was, sooner or later it was going to change. But here, once it went from good to bad, you were screwed. Bad luck meant you got hit, and getting hit meant you were very likely either dead or horribly wounded. We had been very lucky so far. We had been in Iraq for over four months and had been missed by two IEDs already. But sooner or later, luck always changes. As we sped past the parked cars, maintaining about a hundred meters between our vehicles, an Iraqi car suddenly shot from the side of the road and pulled out in front of us, between my vehicle and the British one in front of me. An Iraqi vehicle had gotten into our convoy!

This was a potential death sentence. The Brit, maintaining the speed he had before the convoy was broken, quickly pulled away from us. We were forced to suddenly slow behind the Iraqi vehicle. The convoy was now dangerously separated. Frequently, insurgents would separate a convoy by detonating a VBIED in the middle of it. This not only separated tail from head, allowing each section to be engaged and destroyed piecemeal, but the blast also killed many of the men in the convoy. It was the insurgent version of shock and awe. The Iraqi driver appeared to be frozen, hunched over his wheel with his attention riveted ahead. As we closed on him, Reed flashed his high beams and honked, but the driver remained motionless, like a statue. "Damn," I thought, "I can't believe this is happening." I could envision his car suddenly flying apart as a powerful explosion tore through it before engulfing my vehicle. I thought about climbing out my window and shooting him, but the car was too far over for me to be sure I could even engage him.

Everything seemed to play out in slow motion, but it was only seconds. In a few more seconds, maybe even less, I was convinced we were dead unless we did something about it. Reed was apparently thinking in time with me. "TOP?"

"Take his ass," I answered.

I watched as Reed gunned our vehicle forward. Ignoring my sector of fire, my eyes remained glued on the vehicle in front of us. Nobody said a word as our vehicle shot forward and quickly closed on the Iraqi vehicle. It was like being unarmed and rushing a man armed with a pistol, hoping you can get to him before he can level his weapon at you. Suddenly, almost imperceptibly, I felt a slight bump. While the impact with the Iraqi vehicle barely registered with me, the results were catastrophic for the Iraqi. Reed had expertly pitted the vehicle. As soon as the Iraqi's left front tire hit the curb, the vehicle went airborne, Al-Qaeda-to-the-moon airborne. The vehicle leapt over eight feet into the air. As we passed it I looked over my shoulder, suddenly worried for Del's and Algarin's vehicles. I worried that either driver might panic and over-react to the wildly flying vehicle in front of them or that the vehicle would be detonated by a secondary triggerman.

First Del's vehicle, and then, to my complete relief, Algarin's, cleared the destroyed Iraqi vehicle. Slumped over the wheel was the driver, who I assumed was dead. Face and Will erupted into wild cheers and patted Reed on the back.

"That was fucking awesome, Chris," Facemyer said.

Will was almost impressed beyond words. "Man, Chris, I think you killed him with the fucking car."

"What the hell! Vehicle one, you fucking killed the guy," Boeringer radioed. Reed, though, was not as animated as he normally was.

"Man, I was sure that fucker had us. I was sure."

Reed looked at me in a way he had not done before nor would ever do again. He looked at me like he was scared, like he was surprised to be alive.

We will never know if the man we hit that day was a suicide bomber. If he was a suicide bomber, our lives may have been saved by the Brits. One of their vehicles was equipped with a device that jammed signals used to detonate IEDs and some VBIEDs. These jammers had a limited range, and as the British vehicle pulled farther and farther away from us, we were rapidly losing the coverage it provided. While a jammer did not always work, we felt certain that on this day it had, giving us enough time to destroy the threat.

After that the trip passed without any problems, but I could not stop replaying the incident in my mind. I was sure that I had made the right decision to protect the lives of my men as well as my own, but I did not like not *knowing* that the man we had, in all probability, killed was a threat. Had I sentenced an innocent man to death with a few words? While I wanted to know that he was trying to kill us, I did not *need* to know. My friends, people who trusted me to do the right thing when their lives were at stake, were still alive. Ultimately, the only justification I needed was in the sounds of their voices.

I knew that no matter what the future held, I was always going to make the decisions I thought most ensured the survival of my people. If I had to kill a thousand a day to do that, fine, I could do that. I kept my doubts about the man's guilt to myself. My guys were smart enough to know that we just might have killed an innocent man, without my giving those doubts added weight by sharing my own. That might make them hesitate when they needed to act, and maybe the next time something similar happened we would lose five of our own in a blinding flash. I did not want them worrying about what I was going to think when they needed to take action based upon their own judgment.

In Iraq, you were quick or you were dead. Sooner or later you were going to run into someone who wanted to kill you. Their attack would come suddenly, and violently. The attacker would not wear a uniform. He would instead rely on the populace as cover and your desire not to kill unless necessary to get close enough to you to strike. He wanted you to wait. For his attack to be successful he needed you to hesitate. While we might eat an IED or lose some of our own in a gunfight, we would never eat a VBIED because we had hesitated. That would never be allowed to happen. For me, it was far easier to deal with the consequences that came from not having the emotional security of *knowing* the guy had been a threat than it would be to say to the parents of any one of my own, "I am sorry." I would always make the decision that I believed most ensured the survival of the soldiers and marines on my team.

Interestingly enough, I did receive some support from an unexpected quarter. The Brits whom we were escorting had observed the whole incident, and they applauded our actions as being "spot on." Considering how reluctant the Brits were to use lethal force, their words were surprising and comforting. Returning to the office, I shoved my gear into my wall locker and collapsed into my chair.

"Pat, where is everybody?" I asked Patterson.

"They are going to the Chinese food place, Top."

"You wanna go to KBR then?" I asked.

"If you don't mind waiting, I will be ready in about ten minutes."

Patterson had become my most frequent dinner companion because he and I had duties that sometimes kept us in the palace past the time the rest of the team was willing to wait. Most often, our conversation was about Pat's loathing of his job and how much he wished he could hit the road more often. Pat also used these opportunities to fill me in on all the office politics. For whatever reason, every one of our critics within the operations section felt they could say whatever was on their mind in front of Patterson and that the words would not get back to me. Could they be that stupid? Did they mistake my harsh harassment of Pat for genuine hatred? Were they that dumb? Apparently they were. Rarely would Pat ever reply to my hazing in front of anybody. With the rest of us it was open season when we were not in the office, but not with Pat. Pat would only retaliate to my hazing when it was just the two of us. I was never sure why this was so, and I at first chalked it up to how he was raised. Be respectful of your elders etcetera. But eventually it became very clear that Pat looked up to me. That Pat looked up to me as something of a big brother was obvious, and not just to me.

Part of the reason for this may have had to do with his feeling that he was somehow not the equal of other members on the team. He was, after all, an admin NCO and a reserve one at that, on a team that had marine grunts, a sniper, and rangers on it. Pat may have felt that way about himself but nobody else on the team did. Pat earned his place just like the marines, the rangers, and the spec ops soldier. Nobody on the Majestic Twelve gave a shit about résumés. Being on the team and staying on it was all about what you did in Iraq, and Pat always pulled his weight.

"How did it go today, Top?" Patterson asked.

"Reed wasted some dude with the car. Other than that, you did not miss much, man."

Pat looked over at me as if to say that he would beg to differ. He merely said what he had after missing the fight on April 8: "I hate you fuckers."

As Pat continued to finish up his work, we talked about our homes. There were two things Pat missed about home, one was his wife and the other was his dogs. I always enjoyed these quiet times with Pat. He was a great friend and a loyal comrade.

Following chow, we held our daily debrief. Considering my own concerns about what had happened on the road, I added something to the end of the debrief.

"You all know this already, but after today I wanted to remind you that no matter what happens when we are on the road, I will support your decisions. If you pull the trigger or smash some guy's car, you will never have to look over your shoulder and wonder if I am going to hang you out to dry. You cannot hesitate out there, you all know that. If some guy is closing on the convoy, a guy who has failed to stop even though you have given him verbal warning, hand signals, and pointed a weapon at him, then shoot his sorry ass. He was either stupid, very stupid, or he wanted to kill us.

"I wish you could have the satisfaction of knowing, the psychological protection of knowing, he was a threat, but you most often will not get that here. But don't hesitate, because if you do, and the guy you gave a pass to is a suicide bomber, then we are all going to know it, because he is going to take out a vehicle and waste five of *us*! You think about that for a minute. Look around and pick which five of your friends you are willing to risk for any one of these people? Five of us are not worth giving some guy a pass just because you were not sure. I will always support you, no matter how I might think I would have done something differently. I will never second-guess you, and you need to know that. You need to never second-guess yourselves. Leave that to the faggots inside these walls; believe me, they do enough second-guessing for all of us, I hear it every day. Months from now or years from now, when you are safe at home, you may forget how dangerous this place was and ask yourself if you really had to do everything you did. That kind of debate is for people who watch, observe, and judge; it is not for those of us who have to make life and death decisions every day over here. When and if you ever start to feel that way, don't. That's the best way I can put it, just don't. Instead, try to remember what it was like, what you thought, at the time. And if you are at home, try to remember that it was your actions that got you there."

We then shifted to other things, including the plan for the following day. After all essential information had been passed, I opened it up for questions.

"Anybody have anything they want covered?"

Meggison answered first. "Yeah, Top, I have something."

"What is it, Meg?"

Meggison continued saying, "Well, I think we got a real serious problem with one of the guys on the team, Top. I mean this guy is supposed to be one of us, and he can't even properly identify a weapon."

I looked around the group and back at Meg. "Which sorry bastard is it, Meg?"

"Well, Top, seems like Staff Sergeant Reed, ol' Huggy Bear, can't tell the difference between a PKM and an RPK. Now, Top, if you got a guy who can't tell the difference between those two weapons, do you really want him driving your vehicle? For that matter, do we, any of us, want a guy like that shooting a weapon anywhere near us? In the strain of combat he might think we all look like towelheads." Meggison was referring to an incident on the way to Kirkush in which Chris had identified a man on the roof armed with a machine gun.

Reed jumped to his own defense. "Top, you know that's bullshit. The first words out of my mouth were RPK, and before I could correct myself, Meggison was all over it like a fat kid on a chocolate bar. Look at the man's glasses; he can see into the future with those things, so it makes sense he would ID a weapon before I would."

Meggison's glasses were indeed thick, so thick that the team had, some time ago, decided that he could see into the future.

I had to agree with Reed. "Yeah, he probably saw the thing last week, Huggy. Sorry, Nostrodumbass, but I think I will keep him as my driver."

Reed continued. "Hey, Meggison, I bet you didn't see me pitting that vehicle the way I did, did you?"

In a play on his reputed ability to see into the future, Meggison answered, "No, Chris, I didn't see that, but you should be more worried about what I *do* see happening to you next Thursday."

The levity is sandwiched between dealing with the stress of daily convoys and the accusations that assail us from every darkened corner where fobbits lurk. So it was no surprise when, after the debrief, Captain Wheeler asked me to see him. Most often when an officer wanted to see you, it was a tossup. Maybe the guy had something good to pass, or maybe he was about to shit on your pillow and wipe his ass on your sheets. Knowing the nature of the beast as I did however, I knew this could not be good. Wheeler had been growing more confused with each passing day, and the only time he wanted to talk with me it was about some new concern with the tactics employed by the team. Other than that, our interaction was nil. Indeed, Wheeler seemed to be completely isolated, even from the staff.

When I sat down, Wheeler handed me a four-page missive written by one of the officers we had recently taken to the Water Palace, Captain Dale Lewis, United States Navy. Captain Lewis suffered from the same problems many sailors and airmen did: He could not stomach the reality of war from ground level. As a naval finance officer, Captain Lewis, a tall, fat man with red hair, had never had to worry about making life-and-death decisions. Not only had he been spared the brutal reality of command on the ground, but his cushy job also meant that he lacked the infantry training and experience required to have an informed opinion about the tactics employed by the convoy security team. Intelligence was the last barrier between his opinions and his mouth, or in this case pen. That barrier was to prove flimsy at best. Like many other officers in the palace, Lewis was supremely arrogant, and certain that his status as an officer of the United States Navy not only entitled him to an opinion, but made that opinion factual. Lewis, in Iraq for two weeks and on the road twice, once in an armored bus, submitted a four-page manifesto documenting what he found to be the deplorable conduct of the convoy security team.

Not only were the standard complaints about the team being too aggressive in the missive, but there were some new observations as well. Chief among these, Lewis felt that the team was disrespectful toward officers. While we hated most of the officers at the palace, for the self-serving, ticket-punching, second-guessing "warriors" they were, I was not aware of any overt act of disrespect. Still, I knew that such strong feelings could not be completely hidden, and I had to acknowledge that it was possible these feelings did manifest themselves in some overt ways. So what if they did? Respect, at least in infantry units, was earned; it was not given to anybody, SNCOs and officers included, just because of their rank, and we were a provisional infantry unit.

It was not our job to make people like Lewis feel better about themselves just because they happened to be commissioned officers. Maybe, though, to be fair, there was more that qualified Lewis to have an opinion. Maybe he had seen a few Steven Seagal movies and taken notes. Maybe he had passed a SEAL before. "Great, sir, you're an official American samurai!" I finished reading the letter and looked up at Wheeler.

"So, Top, is it true?" Wheeler asked.

"Which part, sir?"

"Well, let's start with the tactics you employ."

"Sir, we lack armor, and jammers, which would offer us some protection from IEDs and VBIEDs. That means speed is our only protection from these threats. I know that Captain Lewis does not understand that, given that he is new here and his background as a finance officer has given him little exposure to combat in any form."

There were other issues that Lewis had raised, but we did not get into them. My remarks about Lewis could be equally applied to Wheeler, and he knew it.

"You don't like officers, do you, Master Sergeant?"

"Sir, I have met many fine officers during my twenty-plus years of service. In fact, I can only think of five or six that were useless, until I got over here. Here most of the officers seem to be very self-serving, and many are lethally incompetent. I have tremendous respect for Colonel Buchanan, Lieutenant Colonel Thomas, Lieutenant Colonel Sarna, and Major Drury. It seems like those guys, all infantry officers or intel officers, get it. They understand the war and what is required to survive, and they do everything they can to help us, while most of the people here do not give a shit about any of that stuff so long as we are respectful and don't do anything that might offend them."

Wheeler looked at me, and it was obvious he was pissed. Maybe he was pissed that his name was not among those of the officers we (the Maji) deeply, almost reverently respected. By omission he knew what group I cast him in. I expected him to ask me what my opinion of him was. He did not.

Instead, he simply said, "Top, you can leave now."

As I dismissed myself I wondered what the repercussions of our conversation would be. It had been obvious that Wheeler was concerned about the issues Lewis had raised, many of which I was sure he agreed with.

Now Wheeler had this candy-assed fellow yachtsman as a key ally should he decide to attempt to force changes in our SOP. Of course, we were not going to change anything just because some guys who sat in the palace thought we should. Do your jobs, I thought; get us some equipment and then maybe we will listen. As it was, what could they do, send us to Baghdad and make us run convoys without armor, medics, or radios? Shit, they could not even get us ammo. Were they going to not issue us vehicles or critical weapons like rifles and machine guns? Done and done. Were they going to send us home and find other people to volunteer for the job? No. In short, there was nothing they could do to us. They could screw with us in the palace because that was their world, but out on the road it would always be, regardless of what anybody else said, business as usual for us. There was one final accusation in Lewis's missive. This one was new. Specifically, he had accused the team of making "catcalls to women." This appeared to be a lie, plain and simple, a bald-faced lie told by an officer and a gentleman, a man of integrity. However, knowing that Lewis was a man of limited intelligence, I had to give him the benefit of the doubt. Maybe he was not lying. Maybe what he thought were catcalls was nothing more than the intervehicle banter, from man to man, about women. It may come as a shock to most of America, living safe and sound in a PC world, but men, real men, not the ersatz variety that passes for men today, talk about women. They talk about their natural attributes and sometimes they get vulgar, especially when they are in places like Iraq. This kind of frank discussion among men would rightly be found to be insulting by most women if said to them or in their presence.

But there were no women involved. These same guys would bend over backward to open a door for a woman because they do desire *and* respect them and because they are traditional men. It was a bitter irony that Lewis was Smythington's replacement. How did DOD find an ass of equal stature to replace the departed Smythington? One was English and the other was an American, and yet the two were soul mates. I had seen the Joint Manning Document (JMD), which listed every billet within CMATT and who, by rank, service, and nationality, should fill it, and nowhere in that vast document was there a line number for a Dumb Fat-Assed Bastard. Try as I might, I just could not find it. Maybe DOD meant to send Lewis somewhere else. As it was, Lewis was nothing more than the latest in a long line of critics. I seriously doubted that anything would come of his complaint, but I hated having to deal with all the petty crap from men like him. I had far more important things to do than to keep looking over my shoulder to see who was standing behind me with a knife. On the road things had finally started picking up after the slow start.

Things got even hotter in the Green Zone. On June 17 we started taking more fire in the Green Zone. I had just fallen asleep when, at 0048, we were hit by a single mortar round. While I did not like being awakened this way, the round was not nearly as close as the first such attack, which had kept me awake weeks before. Falling back to sleep was easy. At 0533 we were hit by multiple mortars, four or five to be exact. It was a little harder falling back to sleep after this attack. Part of that was because I had to get up in an hour anyway. Lying there, I realized that this was the first time we had received two indirect fire attacks on the same day. As I drifted back to sleep I had no idea that the two failed mortar attacks were but the start of an exceptionally violent day in Iraq.

After waking, we rushed off to chow and ate as a team, which was rare for us at breakfast. After chow we turned to weapons and vehicle maintenance. At 0905 Colonel Thomas received a phone call telling him that the Baghdad RC had been hit by another suicide car bomb. Hesco did not know if we would be needed, but I had the Maji stage anyway, which Hesco thought was a good idea. As I watched the team hurriedly throw their weapons together, grab their gear, and move toward the staging area, I thought back to my first day in Iraq, when the Baghdad RC had been hit the first time, killing forty-seven men. I contrasted what was happening now with the situation then.

In February the operations section had to scrape together a team and had even been compelled to throw two guys on the mission who had been in Iraq for less than twenty-four hours. That team lacked training and cohesion and was at best a stopgap measure. Four months later we had a highly trained, motivated, and cohesive team staging in case it was needed. I felt proud of what we had been able to accomplish. I threw on my body armor, which with each passing day seemed to be getting heavier, grabbed my rifle, and headed to the lot. As I did so, I glanced at the sheep in operations. They looked at me as if they were genuinely amazed that anyone could so enjoy the work we on the convoy security team did. One of the captains told me to have a good time and be careful. As a jab at our antagonists in the section, I could not help but answer, "Oh, you know, we will, sir, especially if we get to kill more than just time."

When I reached the staging area I gathered the Maji around me and I gave them the standard brief that preceded all of our runs. Then I added something. "Listen, this is the first time you will be pulling security at a site after it has been hit. Our first concern once we are on the ground is to quickly clear the gate and get into position. Follow-up VBIEDs will be our primary threat."

I reminded the team of the previous day's intel, which stated that numerous VBIEDs were believed to be cruising the Baghdad area looking for American convoys to attack, especially near the gates to the Green Zone. Within minutes Libby had come out to the lot and briefed us about what little he knew of the attack. Hesco showed up and told me to mount up the team; we were rolling as soon as we were ready.

We raced to the RC. The run was accomplished in almost record time. While horrible, the scene was nowhere near as bad as it had been in February. This new attack had killed seventeen people, not the forty-seven wasted in February. The barriers and security procedures put in place following the first attack had done their job and prevented a greater loss of life. Still, it was a lot to take in. An Iraqi man walked past us carrying a large pail filled with hands, feet, and severed fingers. Dann, walking ahead of me, stared into the gore-filled bucket with fascination. At the gate, where we had pulled security no fewer than ten times, was a small crater and the smoking remains of the suicide bomber's car. While little of the car remained, there was enough left to show that the bomb had been in the trunk. Lying not far from the shattered remains of the car were several 105 mm artillery shells, which the suicide bomber had evidently used as his weapon. One of these shells had been thrown about ten meters to the right by the blast, where it detonated, causing yet more casualties. Looking above the gate I could see that shell fragments peppered the guard tower where Napier and I had assumed our post the last time we augmented security at the RC. The large, jagged hole, dead center of the tower, made it clear that had the attack occurred while Napier and I were there, we would not have survived. Looking at the tower I pondered what it would have been like to be there when it was hit. The last time Napier and I had stood watch there, we had done what we always did, look out across our front at the abandoned zoo or down the street which ran across our front between our position and the empty zoo. We would talk about both the serious and the nonserious as we scanned our area for potential threats. We later learned that one man had been killed in the tower, the life of his friend having been spared when he left the tower to get water for the two of them. I could not recall how many times Napier or I had gone to get water on the days we manned the tower. But I know on this day, this same seemingly insignificant act determined who lived and who died.

One man lives, another dies. The Iraqis are attacked instead of us. All a matter of chance. Right place, wrong place; right time, wrong time. Sometimes it was much better to be lucky than good. While we did not know the guard killed in the tower, another guard whom we did know had also been killed in the attack. Radiating out from the gate from, just a few feet away to as far as twenty yards were several destroyed cars, vehicles of innocent passersby. These sad wrecks were peppered with small, jagged holes torn into their sides by the shrapnel thrown out by the blast. Looking inside these wrecks I saw bodies shredded by the jagged steel fragments of the 105 mm shells. In still others I saw great pools of blood filling seats and splashed against shattered windshields and torn upholstery, the victims having been already removed. Whereas the primary cause of death in February's attack had been blast, which literally tore apart anyone in its path, shrapnel was the main killer in this attack. Shrapnel, while no less deadly than blast, at least kept the bodies more or less intact. Looking at the demolished gate, I thought back to how many times my team had pulled security there, and I was so thankful that we had not been doing so on this day. Surveying the carnage, I wondered how many of my guys would have been lost had we been there.

Blowing around the scene were numerous pieces of blood-splattered paper. One of the Iraqis whom we knew was reading them.

"What does it say?" I asked.

The Iraqi waved his hand as if he was finding it difficult to comprehend what he was reading, not the language, just the reasoning.

The Iraqi finally answered. "He says that he is a Baath Party man and because of that he cannot find a job in the new Iraq. The Americans will not allow him in the police or the army and he cannot provide for his family. He says that in the old Iraq he had to join the Baath Party just to get anywhere in the army, and now it is a bad thing? He does not understand."

Other Iraqis were gathering more pages. Some were hopelessly covered with gore and blood. I had heard enough anyway. This man had killed people he did not know simply because he could not get a job in the army or the police. It didn't make much sense, but little in Iraq did at times. Will *seemed* just as stunned by the lack of reason behind the slaughter.

"What a shame, Top. What a shame."

"Yeah, Will, I know," I answered.

"All these perfectly good dead people, and we didn't kill one of them. What a waste."

Will being Will. Classic entertainment.

I laughed. "You know, when you put it that way, Will, it really does change your perspective. Now I feel sorry for us. C'mon, let's get in the gate."

Inside the inner wall that protected the recruiting building, we met a small child and his mother. The woman worked at the recruiting center and had just cleared the gate with her child when the suicide bomber struck. While the child still appeared to be in some mild shock, he was very friendly. The boy was eight, and he clung to his mother's hand with one hand while in the other he clutched a simple "toy." The toy was an aluminum door handle. Dressed in light blue shorts and polo shirt adorned with kittens and wearing a denim cap, the child was every bit as innocent and sweet as my own. He was a poignant reminder of the conditions under which the children in Iraq were growing up. I could not look at him without feeling great pity for both him and his mother while at the same time thanking God that my children were Americans. This child had witnessed horrors that mine would never see, I hoped. I was keenly aware, looking at this broken child, that my own children could face the same horrors if we lost this war. None of us in Iraq would let that happen, for we knew what the price of defeat would be. But I also knew that no nation wasted the blood of brave men and walked away from more victories than did the United States. I hoped that this would not be a repeat of the forfeit in Vietnam.

As we gathered up those members of the American staff who would be going back to the palace with us, an Iraqi man who worked at the RC came over to us. At first the man made small talk, then he looked around as if to make sure no local ears could hear. He looked in the distance and spoke slowly.

"Iraq . . . Iraq is a country of thirty million people. Most Iraqi are good people, but a few, a few of them are bad guys."

It was obvious that he was talking about more than the day's suicide bomber.

"I hope," I said, "we can make this work for the rest of you. A terrible price is being paid, and this place should be a monument to those Iraqis paying it."

The Iraqi man looked at me and smiled before thanking me for all we (the United States) were doing to make Iraq better. The man looked toward the demolished gate, shook his head in disgust, and walked away.

The ride back to the palace was quieter than normal. After lunch we learned that some children had been killed in the attack. Staff Sergeant Reed said that one was a little girl who used to always come out to see us when we were pulling security at the RC. The children had been selling Cokes to the men waiting to enlist. I remembered seeing an abandoned pushcart filled with Coke bottles sitting forlornly among the debris of the morning's suicide attack. It made me sick to remember it.

We were truly fighting a great evil, and while the consequences of losing the war were clear to those of us in Iraq, it did not seem that many outside Iraq saw them as we did. Listening to all of the stuff being spewed by former generals, Democrats, and the media made it clear that many of those at home just did not get it.

The former generals talked about a flawed war plan and slammed the president for sending us to war without the proper equipment. I could think of no perfect war plan. Abraham Lincoln managed to lose more battles than any president ever has and along the way appointed a selection of buffoons to command his armies and, oh, by the way, lose the lives of over 300,000 of his soldiers. Woodrow Wilson saw more than 50,000 American troops killed in five months of warfare during World War I. Franklin D. Roosevelt allowed Pearl Harbor to be lulled to sleep and then attacked with devastating results. He looked the other way when Admiral King stubbornly and foolishly refused to adopt the proven British convoy system, almost costing us the war and certainly costing us many unnecessary casualties among our merchant mariners. I wanted to know what Roosevelt knew and when did he know it! Roosevelt also lost Wake, Guam, and the Philippines, and was powerless to help his allies as they, too, were swept from the Pacific. Then Roosevelt sent troops into battle with tanks that were hopelessly outclassed by their German counterparts and allowed American bombers to enter the war using tactics that were to prove costly failures. Harry Truman suffered humiliation at the hands of a North Korean peasant army which swept the U.S. 8th Army into a tiny perimeter only to have victory snatched from the jaws of defeat by a marine brigade, the very men Truman had derided as merely the navy's police force.

Of course, Lincoln did not lose those battles and he did not kill the soldiers who died in them and the American people understood that and re-elected him in 1864. Likewise, Wilson did not lead troops in the Great War. Roosevelt did not lead troops in World War II, nor did Truman in Korea. Those wars were fought with the best equipment, tactics, and men available. Rumsfeld had tried to explain as much to the media and the American people when he said, "You go to war with the army you have," only to be hammered for it. The generals make the plan and the generals select the equipment. The United States has invested great sums of money in highly technical weapons. Any taxpayer can see them at the Norfolk Naval Shipyard or any air base; and while they are critical in a war with China, Iran, or North Korea, and even in the invasion of Iraq, they are designed for a different kind of war, and are of little use in the war we find ourselves fighting. The army and Marine Corps do not have enough money to have every piece of equipment for every possible conflict.

How all of this fell on the president was beyond me. Maybe as the governor of Texas it was George Bush who decided to buy B-2s, ballistic missile boats, and unarmored Hummers. It had gotten so that I could not stand to see the news. So much of what was said were defeatist lies. I wondered if the United States could have won World War II with the defeatist attitude that permeated the media and the Democratic Party. We certainly could not do so in Vietnam, and I feared this war was going in the same direction. I guess none of that really mattered, though, as it was all out of our hands. We still had a job to do regardless of how the war was being reported or perceived at home.

The day after the attack at the RC was a light one for us, weapons maintenance and vehicle preventive maintenance. The guys got to do laundry and get haircuts, mundane things that are often neglected in the day-to-day operations of the team. For one of us, the day had a tragic turn. Most of the team had already turned to work on their weapons when Will walked in, the obvious victim of a bad, a very bad, haircut.

"What the hell, Will, you get a haircut or prepped for a lobotomy?" I asked.

"Huh, huh, very funny, Top. Stupid Arabs."

"Stupid Arabs? Your doctor is an Arab, Will?"

Will was not in a laughing mood and dismissively answered, "Funny, Top!"

Continuing, I said, "You need to wrap your head in some yellow crime scene tape, Will. Your haircut is a crime against humanity."

"Okay, Top, I get it. Shitty haircut, ha, ha."

Facemyer could not resist piling on.

"Fuck, Will, what you do, kill the guy's brother or something? You look like some Chinese orphan with a bowl cut. You got a ponytail coming from the back of your head?"

"Oh fuck you, Facemyer. At least I didn't pay for it."

Boeringer defended Facemyer. "Ummm, that's because haircuts here are free and none of us pays for them and, besides, you're paying for it now."

"Fuck you, Boeringer. At least our AC works and my vehicle has windows."

"Well, damn, Will, I didn't pay for mine, either, what with haircuts over here being free and all," Reed added.

Will went back at him. "Hey, Chris, at least mine will grow back without scientific intervention. Can't say that, can you, Chris?"

Reed feigned being hurt, rubbing the top of his balding head and pouting. "You mean I've lost all this hair *since* you got your haircut, Will?"

To make matters worse, Patterson walked in and was obviously caught off guard by Will's pathetic haircut.

"What happened to your head?" Pat asked innocently.

"Hey, fuck you, *Fatterson.*"

"Will, that remark would really hurt me if I were still fat, but"—Pat, rubbed his stomach—"no, I am still trim, and your haircut will look like shit for the rest of the month."

Williams always had a short temper, and only a limited ability to laugh at himself.

Facemyer reminded Will that he often praised things that were free by repeating his mantra, "Just remember, Will, 'Best of all, it's freeeeee.'"

It was a long day for Will.

The following day, Hesco told me that my extension had been approved and that I would be leaving Iraq at the end of October instead of early August. I was glad but more than a little worried about how I would tell my family that I would not be coming home in July as expected. After our debrief later that evening a marine from the Commandant's Office said he had something to show me. Corporal Henry had recently been assigned to the Commandant's Office as one of their numerous admin bitches. He was a good marine, and the team already liked him. Anyway, for many weeks there had been a cat meowing pitifully from somewhere within the palace and nobody seemed to know where the noise was coming from. After a while the noise just stopped and we assumed the cat had found its way out of wherever it was stuck or it had simply died. As I walked with Corporal Henry he commented on my obvious love for our furry friends.

"I have seen you feed the cats after your debriefs, Top, so I thought you would like to see this."

Henry led me into the media room located next to CMATT's conference room.

The mystery of the crying cat was now solved. There, in a small space behind the wall, was a momma cat with six small kittens. Henry gave me a key to the room so I could make sure that mom had food and water. The kittens reminded me that there was still some innocence in the world. I had always been an animal lover, and I was no less so in Iraq. These kittens were special, though. They reminded me of my cat, and that reminded me of my home. The last pet Denise had brought into our home before her death was a black and white fur ball of a kitten. The kitten was a "rescue kitty" adopted from a man who sheltered homeless cats until he found them a home. The black and white patterns in my cat's fur had reminded Denise of cows, an animal which she had developed some affection for after our son fell in love with one when he was just two. Named Jo Jo, Denise brought the cat home against my wishes. To her eternal chagrin, however, the cat and I ended up being inseparable. With Denise's death, Jo Jo became very special to me. He was a small reminder of how caring she was. I used to get so mad at her for bringing stray animals into our home or feeding every kid in the neighborhood or giving my pineapple upside-down cake to the maintenance man. But those were some of the things that made her special to me.

Kittens aside, the war ground on. On 21 June we had two runs to BIAP. The first was to take Commander McAvoy to her flight home. Erin McAvoy, though a naval officer, had always treated each of us like we were normal people and not murderous animals to be shunned. Attractive, intelligent, and always upbeat, she was a pleasure to be around, and while we were happy for her, she would be missed by many of us. Our second trip to BIAP was to pick up Gunny Hessen, who was returning from what amounted to emergency leave. Hessen was easily one of our best drivers, and he had been with me from the start. He had helped build the team when the team consisted of the two of us. Eventually his duties with force protection would take up all of his time, and he was no longer able to serve with the team, a severe blow.

Of more immediate concern that day was the infighting within the palace. In an incredibly unorthodox move, two commissioned officers approached me and said that they really needed to speak with me in private. Once we were alone, one of the officers spoke up.

"Top, I do not normally get involved in the politics of this place; all I want to do is finish my tour and go home. But sometimes I hear shit that just makes my skin crawl. Yesterday Lieutenant Colonel Smith and I were sitting at chow with Captain Lewis and some other officers from his section. I do not know how we got on the subject but at some point you and your team became the subject. Lewis said that he was going to make sure he did everything in his power to see that you were relieved. He said that you and your team were completely unprofessional and that if he worked in that office things would change. We don't want our names being brought into this, but I really felt you deserved to know about the incident. I do not pretend to understand what you guys do. I am a communications officer, but I know enough about leadership to know a good leader when I see one. Top, I think you guys are doing a great job, and I appreciate it. I just wanted you to know about this."

It took me a while to respond. Very rarely do commissioned officers ever go to senior enlisted with a warning about the intent of fellow officers. It is almost unheard of. The fact that not one but two officers felt the need to see me left no room for doubt as to the serious and egregious nature of whatever it was Lewis had said.

"Sir, is it all right if I pass this to Colonel Thomas and let him address it? I will not pass who passed it to me, but I would like to have him handle this."

"Top, that's okay, and if it comes down to credibility, then you can call us in, because this is bullshit."

I answered, thanking both officers, "Thanks, gentlemen."

Fuming, in a blind rage, I went to find Colonel Thomas. This issue had been addressed weeks before. If people had a problem with the team, they were to take it to Colonel Toddington or Colonel Thomas, but this human muffin in a uniform had decided that a better course of action was to take shots at us from afar.

Lewis could not detect that maybe, just maybe, his two breakfast companions that morning did not share his views as he spewed on. I seriously wanted to kill him. I did not tell him how to load ships or wedge his fat ass into his uniform, and I did not need him telling other people how he was going to fix what was not broken. I hated the politics of the palace. I hated having to deal with people like Lewis just because he was an officer and could therefore run his mouth without fear of being called on it. If he were in "that shop," he would not fix anything; he would sit in a quiet corner and pray, as they all did, that Colonel Thomas didn't reach his bullshit threshold and start kicking ass. Or that I did not reach mine and just start killing off some of the home team.

I found Hesco and told him what had been said. He went ballistic and stormed over to Lewis. You could hear him yelling at Lewis all over CMATT. Lewis, given a perfect opportunity to start fixing "that shop," said nothing. He was no longer as talkative as he had been at breakfast. At some point, Lewis's boss and like-minded friend came to his defense, and things got uglier. Eventually, Lewis and his boss went to the chief of staff. Colonel Henry, in a dark foreshadowing of what was to come, sided with the two officers. Colonel Thomas was ordered to apologize to Lewis for what he had said. Captain Wheeler even warned Colonel Thomas, "I am seriously considering relieving you, and it wouldn't be the first time I have done it."

Wheeler was so lost that everybody, even those in the office who most manipulated him against us, knew he was useless, and yet he was threatening to relieve Hesco? You could see that Hesco wanted to use Wheeler in a human anatomy class. What of Lewis's own remarks, which at least two officers had found so objectionable as to call me aside just to tell me about them? When I asked Wheeler if I would be getting an apology from Lewis, he told me to drop the matter and never mention it again. It did not matter that both of the officers who had approached me about the incident outranked Lewis. All that mattered was that we not offend. I really hoped that Lewis would ride with us one more time. We had used our chain of command and gotten nothing from doing so.

But Lewis and friends were not done just yet. Lewis had won the support of at least Wheeler, and that was evident next day when Wheeler told me he wanted me to attend a meeting with Colonel Thomas, representatives of the intelligence section, and himself. He had requested the meeting, he said, to address the concerns Lewis had outlined in his letter and that were highlighted by the previous day's incident. Wheeler then said, "I don't want any finger-pointing or shouting. I just want you to present your SOPs and then explain them. I want the two to give me an opinion on what you are doing. They are an outside source, and I think they are in the best position to fairly evaluate what you are doing."

Normally I would not have worried about this at all, as the two had always been a key ally of the Maji, but things had changed recently. Colonel Sarna and his equally supportive replacement, Major Drury, were gone. Now Colonel Danelle Scottka, U.S. Army, in Iraq less than three days, would judge our SOPs. Knowing nothing about her, I was worried. Colonel Thomas did not seem worried at all. Wheeler asked if we had any questions, and as we had none, he dismissed us.

Hesco told me to get a brief ready and to maintain my composure no matter what happened. "You can't win any friends if you can't be friendly, Top."

"Yes, sir, and you cannot properly kiss ass without a close shave and without knowing a little about the person attached to that ass."

I went and found Libby and Garate and told them what Wheeler had just told me.

"We know all about it, Top," said Libby. "She [the new colonel] asked us what we knew about you guys and told us she wanted us to be there. Now listen, I won't be there, but Garate will, and I am telling you, Top, it doesn't matter. The colonel is on board. She is smart, and you can count on her just like you could Sarna and Drury."

I looked at Libby and asked how he knew that.

Garate answered. "Top, she is all about being proactive and protecting yourself, and believe me, Libby and I have been prepping her ever since we got wind of this. You're gonna be fine."

I left the two feeling reassured but still not certain how the meeting would go.

Next day, 23 June, I reported to Captain Wheeler for our meeting. Thomas and Scottka were already there.

Captain Wheeler started. "Colonel, this is Lieutenant Colonel Thomas and Master Sergeant Lynch. Lieutenant Colonel Thomas is the current operations officer and oversees our escort missions. Master Sergeant Lynch runs the team, and that is why the two of them are here."

I waved and nodded toward the colonel while Hesco got up and actually shook her hand as he introduced himself to her. Wheeler seemed annoyed by the gesture.

"Well, the reason we are all here," Wheeler intoned, "is because several people have raised a few issues, nothing serious, about the tactics employed by the convoy security team. Some people are concerned that the team may actually be too aggressive, and I just want us to make sure that we are doing the things we need to do in the right way. Colonel, I know you're new here, but as the two, I felt you could give us a good reading on what the convoy security team was doing right and what they could do better. I'd like Top to explain the makeup of the team, its personnel and equipment, and explain his SOPs, and then I'd like your opinion on what they are doing. So if nobody has any questions, Top, why don't you start by giving the colonel some background on the team."

I felt like I was sitting in the principal's office explaining why I had gotten into a fight. Wheeler would have been a much better host for a children's program, but unfortunately for all of us, we were stuck with him.

As Wheeler spoke, I looked at the colonel, trying to figure out how to read her. She was very cool, and nothing in her expression gave a hint of what she was thinking. Did she have an open mind or had she already made it up in our favor after having been "prepped" by Libby and Garate? I was certain she had heard more than a small amount of the negative crap floating around the palace. While her expressions revealed nothing of her inner thoughts, Garate was all smiles. First, I explained to the colonel the background of the team. I spent very little time on this before jumping into the real reason we were all there, the SOP. I carefully explained the SOP to Colonel Scottka, who listened patiently. When I was done, she asked if she could ask a few questions.

"Yes, ma'am," I answered.

The colonel then asked a series of questions that were scenario based. I answered each question in accordance with the SOP. Regardless of the prep work Libby and Garate had invested in her, the colonel's questions were very well thought out, and they were clearly her own. She was nobody's puppet.

As I listened to her questions, I knew that the two would continue to be our greatest ally in the palace. When I finished answering her questions, the Scottka turned to Wheeler.

"Captain, I have read numerous after action-reports, as well as briefs on enemy TTPs, and it sounds like the team has very sound SOPs. Given their lack of *proper equipment* I think they have done very well to have come this far without sustaining any casualties. That fact alone is the best evidence that Colonel Thomas and the Top have put in place the best SOPs under the circumstances."

I looked over at Wheeler. Contrary to what I expected, he did not seem at all disturbed by this and simply asked, "So you would not recommend any changes at this time?"

Any doubts about why we were there were erased with that question. I doubted that Wheeler really cared about SOPs, about what worked and what did not. Wheeler was a survivor, and he knew how to cover his ass. Against mounting criticism he could now say if, at some time in the future, something went horribly wrong, he had asked an independent, yet qualified, source to examine the SOPs we were using.

"No, I wouldn't change anything at this time. We can always reexamine things if the situation changes, but I don't expect that will happen anytime soon."

Wheeler thanked her, as did Hesco and I.

That was the last time our SOPs were seriously challenged. People would continue to bitch, but they would never again gain any traction. I can only imagine how bitterly disappointed people like Lewis must have been. Three times within a month, starting with the arrival of Lieutenant Colonel Toddington and again with that of General Petraeus and now, our critics had launched serious efforts to change the way the team operated. Each time they had failed.

The day only got better. Later, the office held a formation to present Captain James, one of our battle captains, with his end-of-tour award. Captain James was a Marine Corps pilot and, like most pilots, very laid back. During all the months of political intrigue, he had never said anything, and I never knew where he stood on the issues. After being presented with his award, Captain James was given the floor. He spoke about how much he had enjoyed his tour, and that while he had enjoyed his time, he was glad it was over. He thanked Hesco and even thanked the long departed Colonel Buchanan. Pointedly, he did not thank Wheeler. Then, turning to me, he said, "Top, you have taken heat, a *lot* of heat, for the way you run your team. I just gotta tell you, you were what the office needed, a marine master sergeant to get in here and fire things up. I believe that you train your guys hard and that you are all very good at what you do, and I believe that is why you are all still alive. Thanks, Top."

While I sincerely appreciated what James said, it was made better still by the looks on the faces of Johns, Deboda, Thedorson, and Wheeler, priceless! But Johns, ever the weasel, nodded in agreement and thanked me for all I had done. Mole Man was good at surviving, too; in mixed company he was everybody's friend.

At about this time, the team discovered that we had another supporter but in the last place we would expect to find him. Lieutenant Colonel Laroach was a U.S. Air Force officer, and a vocal supporter. He was a tall man, of medium build, who looked like an Italian mobster from the old sixties television show *The Untouchables.* Though he was new to the palace, Laroach said that he had heard enough, both pro and con, to form his own opinion. Furthermore, he said, many people, including most of the officers, were solidly behind us. He once relayed to me a conversation he had had with an officer who was complaining bitterly about the surly attitude of the team and its aggressive nature. A second officer, an apparent supporter, acknowledged that we might be rough around the edges but then, according to Laroach, asked the other man who he would rather have covering his ass, our critics or us. The critic acknowledged that he would ride with us, rough edges and all.

As June wound down, all of us waited for the other shoe to fall. The transition of power from the CPA to an interim Iraqi government was drawing near. There had been very little violence compared to what we had expected. Nobody knew why, but one theory that had seemed to make sense to all of us was that the insurgents were saving what they had for fantastic attacks just before the transition, which represented the formal transfer of sovereignty from CPA to the Iraqi interim government. While there was little increase in insurgent activity, there was a significant increase in the activity of American army units on the BIAP road. Most often, the road was patrolled by Iraqi army units if it was patrolled at all. The American army contented itself with manning the gates at Victory and the Green Zone while throwing a rare checkpoint on the road itself. These checkpoints, consisting of a Bradley or two, were not actually on the road; they were well off of it and appeared to be there only to provide observation. Their value was doubtful. But as the transition of power drew closer, the army increased its activity along the route. This was a welcome sign for those of us who traveled it. June was bad, but not as bad as May had been.

CHAPTER 13

The War at Home

CNN reported that eighty-nine Coalition troops died in May, making it the second-deadliest month of the war. After April, I had expected May to be even deadlier and June to be far worse. But by 25 June Coalition losses stood at twenty-nine killed for the month, far fewer than May, and obviously less than we expected. We had no idea what to make of the drop-off in enemy activity, and higher was just as much in the dark. It made little difference to us. We still made runs almost daily, and we knew that any of those could be our last, good month or bad.

The good news also had very little impact on the perception of the war at home. According to CNN, 73 percent of over 200,000 respondents to a poll felt that we were losing the war. That worried most of us. With the media hammering away at Abu Ghraib and Democrats screaming that the president had "lied" us into the war, it was easy to see why many sound-bite–fed Americans might think we were losing. Increasingly, those of us at war were keenly aware that it could all be lost, all the pain and suffering made meaningless and the victories hollow, because the American people, almost completely unaffected by the war, could decide it was time for us to come home.

The thought sickened me. In 1968 the American people, naive and as self-absorbed then as they are now, allowed their own media to steal defeat from the jaws of victory when they portrayed the smashing American victory over the North Vietnamese Army and the Viet Cong during the Tet offensive as a defeat. There was no parallel in history for such pessimism following such a clear and decisive victory. Tet was a disaster for the Communists from which they should never have been able to recover, and yet they did. Of course, that recovery was aided by defeatist attitudes not on the battlefield but on the home front. Those attitudes were nurtured by a treasonous media. More than thirty years later we found ourselves fighting a war far more important than that which we fought in Vietnam. If we lost this war the results would be catastrophic for the West. The media, with no battlefield defeats to breathlessly report, looked to those stories that could still undermine support for the war. Abu Ghraib fit that bill nicely, as did the "Bush lied" theme.

In spite of the dire predictions made by intel and the equally dire reporting of the war, June was winding down with a whimper, not a bang. There were reports of new threats, however, indicating that the enemy was preparing for Tet-style attacks across Iraq in the days before the transition of power. On 26 June, intel went further, stating that at 0000 on 28 June the enemy was expected to launch heavy rocket and mortar attacks against Coalition facilities across Iraq. These attacks would be concurrent with more limited sapper-style attacks on police stations like those that had taken place in April. Daylight would see heavy attacks on American convoys with IEDs, VBIEDs, and traditional ambushes. There was fresh reporting that VBIEDs were again circling the Green Zone and other Coalition targets, like sharks waiting to pounce on convoys as they departed and arrived at Coalition bases.

There was even some reporting that the Green Zone itself might come under ground attack. I asked one intelligence officer what he thought of all the new threat reporting. I respected the man, and his opinion carried great weight with me. "Well, Top, if I had to bet, I would bet that we do not have a clue, but the prudent part of me knows that it does not hurt to take the reporting seriously."

I had to agree with him. It seemed highly unlikely that all of this would happen as intel said it might, and that was important to remember. Intel never said the enemy *will* do this or that, they merely said that a *possible* course of action had materialized based on some observed or reported event, trend, and so on. Force protection took the reporting seriously enough to pass on instructions that if the Green Zone was attacked, everyone was to remain in their trailers. That did not sit well with us. I did not like the idea of cowering under my rack hoping that I would be defended by some guy who was more

Tower 2 at the Baghdad Recruiting Center after the car bombing in June 2004. Note the multiple holes in the tower made by shell fragments. *(From the collection of Jack Lynch)*

concerned with his own survival. To make sure we did not find ourselves in that position, we coordinated with the MP unit based at the palace. The MPs had the secondary duty of defending the trailer park; the marines from FAST Company would defend the palace. My team would serve as a provisional rifle squad and be integrated into the MP unit's defensive plan.

I explained all of this to my team. Like me, they were very skeptical, but they understood that, no matter how many times intel was wrong, you could never afford to ignore it, despite the temptation to do so. Making the fantastic reporting a little harder to believe was the fact that while intelligence frequently cried wolf, they had not so much as whimpered in the days before deadly April. Taken together, the rumors of attacks that never came and the whiff in April, many officers and men had decided to simply ignore the reporting. While my guys thought it was all crap, they still took the proper precautions. True professionals that they were, they still felt that it was a good idea to be ready, just in case, and there was no bitching about planning and being prepared should the attacks come. As things turned out, our extra preparations were not necessary. The massive attacks that intelligence thought were in the offing never materialized.

We did take increasing mortar and rocket fire in the last days of June. These attacks most often took place, as they always had, in the early-morning hours. They were not effective or particularly frightening, but they did make us think about what could happen. What if that had been closer? What if the next one, already in the air, was a direct hit? More than once I had imagined my own death as these things dropped on the Green Zone. I also looked at these as live-fire tests of courage, minor and almost safe, like training, but with the knowledge that we could be killed, even if the chance was very remote. Passing the test only required that we ignore the incoming, keep reading or writing or working. Passing the test only made us better prepared to face what might happen on the road, where real and sudden terror lurked at every mile and every turn. The mortars and rockets were just practice for the nerves required to go on the road. But that was only the case if we were awake when they hit. Being awakened by them was something else. Being awakened by a near miss was something no one ever forgot, and it could be terrifying.

While the mortar and rocket fire increased in volume, their effectiveness did not. The insurgents were terrible shots with these weapons, so much so, in fact, that I was thankful for every one they launched. Every miss meant one round less that could be used to make a far more deadly IED. While we found these attacks to be largely nothing more than an inconvenience, other people were being "prudent," sleeping in the palace basement, which was safer than being in a trailer. When rear echelon folks give up the comfort of their quarters for the safety of a basement, you know, no matter how bad his aim is, the enemy has actually accomplished something.

Increased mortar and rocket attacks aside, life changed little for us as the team continued to make runs daily. It was following one of these runs that I first took note of something I had seen many times, but had never really paid much attention to before. Whenever we returned from a convoy, the team, as all teams were, would be mobbed by children selling Iraqi chocolate bars. Even under the best conditions, these bars left much to be desired. In 130 degree heat they were little more than a lumpy milkshake. We always bought whatever the kids were selling, even if it was melted, and while the price was fifty cents a bar, we paid most often with a dollar bill even if we had fifty cents in our pockets. "Friend, friend, I have no change" would be the child's reply.

To these kids we were an easy mark. On this day what stood out most was Will. He gave each child a Pepsi. That might not seem to be a big deal, but the rest of us could scarcely believe it, for Will had a well-deserved reputation as being very guarded with his stuff, any stuff, but nothing more so than his Pepsis.

Facemyer had asked if he could grab a Pepsi out of Will's fridge. "Fuck no," Will said. "You get paid the same as I do. You were at the exchange at the same time I was, and you watched me pay for mine, so if you wanted one you should have bought your own then."

Will was not kidding, and Facemyer ended up drinking a Coke that Fudd offered him. But here was Will, giving these children something that he would not share with a friend.

Hesco had pointed out this seeming contradiction before. "You know, Top, people talk about you guys like you would kill your own mothers for fun, but they never ride with you and they never see you guys give the father with his head up his ass the benefit of the doubt, even though he could kill you, just because his wife or kid are in the car with him. They never see you guys feeding the kids at the RC or waving to and talking to kids during a security halt, and it just pisses me off the way they talk about you guys."

Our hearts went out to the children because they were innocent. It was not their fault that they lived in a man-made hell populated with crazies. Will gave children Pepsis, and I fed cats and kittens. That may seem like a contradiction, but it is not. Warriors are among the most compassionate people on earth. We enjoyed freeing souls but we felt protective of the weak and the innocent. These children were both.

Killing Islamic militants did not make us lose our humanity. It made us look for ways to express it, to stay tied to it, in spite of what we did and how ruthlessly we did it. The children and the animals reminded us of a world outside Iraq. More than once I had seen one of my guys threaten to kick the shit out of a local for mistreating a child or a dog. Yet at the slightest provocation these same guys could kill without remorse, enjoy doing so, and even joke about it. We left the lot with lighter pockets but feeling a little more human for it.

After storing our gear I decided that I would take a nap. It had been a brutally hot day and the earlier run had proved taxing, so I was more than ready for a siesta. My head had not been on my pillow for fifteen minutes when I heard what sounded like a very large bee directly overheard. This was no bee, however, and it was with more than mild alarm that I realized I was in the flight path of a rocket or mortar.

I lay in my rack as the buzzing sound grew louder and more intense and faster as the weapon began its descent. *BuuuuuzzzzzzZZZZZ!* I did not know what to do. There was nothing I could do. Run? Run where? To a bunker I would never make it to anyway? Under my rack so that I could later be found dead, under my bed when I should have been at work anyway? Too embarrassed and afraid to move, I just lay there for what seemed an eternity and listened to the sound of onrushing death. The sound continued to grow in intensity right up until the very moment of impact, which, contrary to what I expected, actually landed about three hundred meters away from my trailer. After the impact, I quickly grabbed my cover and my rifle and headed to the other trailers just to make sure none of my guys were hit. Within fifteen minutes we had everybody accounted for, and I went back to my rack to sleep away the hours before chow. I did not know it at the time, but that would be the last attack before the transition of power.

On 28 June the Coalition pulled a fast one on the media and us and the insurgents when they restored power to the Iraqi people ahead of the scheduled date. It appeared that this move let all the wind out of the insurgent's sails, in the short term anyway. Now there could be no front-page-grabbing attacks on the eve of the transition as the world watched with bated breath. While this did not mean the remainder of June would be easy, it did mean that the transition of power had been successful.

While we were all glad that the transition had gone off so well, there was bad news. Al Jazeera was showing pictures of a U.S. Marine, blindfolded, with a sword over his head. Islam's version of missionaries were threatening to kill the man. The story of how the marine was captured made no sense, and I smelled a rat, a big fat rat. The "marine," identified as Corporal Wassef Hassoun, was a Lebanese Muslim, and I did not buy anything his so-called kidnappers said. The militants claimed that they had infiltrated the marine's base and kidnapped him. That was obviously crap. It was beyond belief that a bunch of Iraqis could infiltrate a base crawling with marines who wanted to kill them and then kidnap a marine and make it off of the base. If they had a team of men that good, then there were far more important men to be kidnapped, and those men were located in places far more vulnerable than a marine base, all over Iraq. Of course, the fact that the kidnapped marine was a Muslim only added to my doubt about the story. But the element that really drew my attention was when the marine went missing. According to the Pentagon, the marine "went missing Monday, a week ago." It was odd and inexplicable that the towelheads waited so long to show a video and that the Pentagon had waited so long to report the marine missing. A week later we had this marine doing a guest appearance on Al Jazeera. Many Muslims in the United States were members, as far as I was concerned, of a fifth column that everyone—the Pentagon, the media, and the American people—wanted to pretend did not exist. Before the war even began, Sergeant Akbar, U.S. Army, had killed two comrades out of loyalty to his faith, Islam. Others had been arrested for plotting to disrupt operations or sell classified gear or plans to our enemy.

There was a reason Japanese American soldiers were not allowed to fight in the Pacific Theater during World War II. Units composed of Japanese Americans fought in Europe and did so with great distinction. In very rare cases individual Japanese soldiers did serve in the Pacific but it was the rare exception. Frequently these men served in intelligence where their knowledge of the language and customs of the enemy made them valuable. In this war it did not seem prudent to allow Muslims to serve. After all, I would understand it if we were at war with Ireland and I was assigned anywhere but Ireland; nothing personal, just prudence. While I did not have proof of what I suspected, one thing was clear. The United States Marine Corps, which had suffered its share of casualties, had not had a single man fall into the hands of the enemy until Hassoun was captured. (Still true as of September 2009.) Something about this whole story did not seem right. I shared my thoughts with the operations section.

Colonel Toddington was not impressed. "I don't know if you've seen the latest intelligence, mate, but he is on Al Jazeera with a sword over his head."

"Yeah, that's a lot of shit, sir," I answered. "They will not do a damn thing to him, mark my words. He will either just disappear or, even if they do kill him, it will be because he served his purpose. I know that guy is dirty."

Toddington was dismissive of my opinion; he should not have been. Hassoun would in fact survive his captivity and be released unharmed. After being released, Hassoun turned up at the American embassy in Lebanon on 7 July 2004. A preliminary investigation concluded that he had deserted. In December 2004 he was, incredibly, allowed to go on leave and he deserted a second time, and is believed to be in Lebanon or Syria.

The Marine Corps quickly killed the story. I do not know if the story survived long enough to make it to Australia, but if it did, I am sure Toddington thought back to our conversation about the story when it was still new. Hassoun was a traitor, and he had no place in my uniform. While I knew it was not fair, I really did not think it was wise to put Muslims in places where they could hurt us. If that was unfair, too bad; they had only themselves to blame. (Years later I would work with Muslim American translators. Their hatred for Israel and opposition to our involvement in Iraq was breathtaking.)

June ended without any widespread or large-scale attacks by the enemy.

The Baghdad Recruiting Center after the suicide car bombing in June 2004.
Left to right: **the author, Lieutenant Colonel John Thomas, and Sergeant
Jason Algarin.** *(From the collection of Jack Lynch)*

Intel had been wrong again, and that served to illustrate just how bad our
intelligence in Iraq was. We never seemed to know what the enemy was going
to do. In part, this was because our intelligence sucked, but it had a lot to do
with the nature of our enemy, too. While the media routinely made it sound
like the enemy was a cohesive and skilled force, it was not. They were lethal in
the way that a homicidal maniac wielding a shotgun in the mall is; they could
kill lots of people and grab headlines, but beyond that, what were they
achieving? The insurgents had few effective weapons. They had mortars and
rockets, but were not very good with them, with the exception of some of the
guys out in the Al Anbar. By far their most effective weapon was the IED or
VBIED, but after that the enemy had very little else he could count on. Beyond killing Iraqis by the score and attacking American convoys, the enemy
had shown himself to be completely unable to conduct anything at the opera-
tional or strategic level. In fact, his wanton killing of Iraqi civilians showed a
total lack of strategic thought. The enemy was often a murderous Islamofas-
cist who flailed wildly about like a violent psychopath, killing the unlucky or

the unwary here and there, but to what purpose? It was this very random, uncoordinated, and frequently senseless killing that made it so difficult for intel to get a grip on what was coming next. Intel looked at our vulnerabilities and maybe even thought back to the Tet offensive and thought what they would do if they were the enemy. Looked at from that perspective, the reporting made sense. If I were the enemy, I would have launched attacks just like those that we expected. So what if my men were cut down like wheat? That had happened to the North Vietnamese and the VC during Tet, and they still won, based solely on how the events were reported to the American people. As the transition drew near, the eyes of the world had been on Iraq, waiting for Tet-style attacks that never came. The reporting which was sure to accompany such attacks would have sealed the fate of President Bush in the November elections and guaranteed our defeat. Of this I had no doubt.

Long before the war in Vietnam we fought a similar war against an enemy every bit as PR savvy as the North Vietnamese. From 1899 to 1905 we fought an ugly war in the Philippines against Philippine insurrectionists. One of their early war aims was to influence the American presidential election in 1900 in hopes that the antiwar candidate, William Jennings Bryan, would win the election and withdraw U.S. forces from the Philippines. And this was in the days before instant mass media, the Web, and TV! Our current enemies were just as media aware as had been the Philippine insurrectionists and, after them, the NVA. And yet they were completely unable to launch any attacks of any significance. That, combined with their obvious awareness of the instant nature of today's media, with its endless twenty-four hour news cycle and its impact on the American psyche, spoke volumes about the enemy's limited capabilities for anyone interested in more than a sound bite.

CHAPTER 14

Hummers for a Week

July dawned bright for the Maji. After four months of tireless effort, Hesco had been able to get the team the most critical piece of gear we lacked, armor. On the last day of June we went to BIAP to take possession of four armored Hummers. I viewed these as critical pickups. The armor meant that we now had a chance of surviving an IED or VBIED attack, which we all knew was highly unlikely in our current vehicles. The Hummers also meant that we could now mount our .50 cals and Mk-19s, which had been acquired by us in the same deal that got us the 249s and 240s. Unlike those lighter weapons, these larger weapons required mounts and structural reinforcement that our little SUVs lacked. The addition of these weapons meant that if we found ourselves locked in a firefight, we would be far better able to inflict grievous losses on our foes than had been the case. These powerful weapons provided almost as much comfort as the armor. I really felt almost euphoric. When I had arrived in Iraq, I said I wanted to rewrite the SOP, and we did. I wanted to get crew-served weapons, and we did. I wanted rockets, grenades, and tons of ammo, and we got all of that. I wanted M-4s, and they were coming. I wanted armor, and now we had it. I felt like we had delivered everything we had promised these guys. We were safer now, and we had weapons that we only dreamed of in

July 2004 at the Baghdad International Airport. **Standing,** left to right, **are Corporal Kelly Meggison, Sergeant Melissa Garate, and Staff Sergeant Edens, USA; Sergeant Edward Boeringer, USMC; Sergeant Jones, USA; Staff Sergeant Daniel Libby, USAF; the author; Specialist Isis Delacroix, USA; Sergeant Jason Algarin; and Sergeant Jason Williams. Sitting on the vehicle** left to right **are Sergeant Kevin Facemyer, Specialist James Brackin, and Gunnery Sergeant Robert Josleyn. Kneeling** left to right **are Lance Corporal Charles Dann and Staff Sergeant Chris Reed. Johnson and Edens were the first of two replacements for departing members of the team. Garate and Libby were intelligence specialists who frequently supported the team.**
(From the collection of Jack Lynch)

February. It was an extra that these Hummers also had air-conditioning, which in the heat of a Baghdad summer was worth almost as much as the armor. We would be as comfortable in these as we had been in our old vehicles. Well, most of us would be.

As Algarin checked out the Hummers he noticed that two of them had Blue Force Trackers. These systems had GPS mapping. Thus one of these vehicles was destined to be mine. I had no preference as to which one I got until Algarin called me. With Boeringer standing next to him, Algarin yelled, "Hey, Top, the AC in this one works."

"Thanks, Starsky, I'll take it." Turning to Reed, I continued, "Huggy, go check that one out."

Boeringer, who had long bemoaned the fact that his vehicle lacked both AC and windows, immediately registered his displeasure with what he saw as Algarin's betrayal of their mutual best interests.

"What the fuck? Jason, man, those guys have had working AC since we got these shit cars, while we are riding around without AC, or windows, and we have dead people's doors on our shit." (The doors on Boeringer's and Algarin's vehicle had been pulled off of an Iraqi vehicle that had been destroyed in an IED attack that left four dead.) "Then you go and tell Top which fucking Hummer has working AC. You are a total buddy fucker, man. You are a Blue Falcon. Seriously, man, that's what I am going to start calling you because you are such a buddy fucker." A Blue Falcon is something of a superhero buddy fucker, a guy who can always be counted on to screw his buddies, no matter what the situation.

Algarin protested. "Bo, c'mon, you know it's not like that."

"Don't give me that Bo shit." Boeringer was not willing to let his friend off the hook just yet. He turned to me. "Hey, Top, let me tell you what kind of buddy fucker, what kind of Blue Falcon, this guy is. A few days ago on a trip to Tadji, you had just called a suspicious object in the road, in the left lane. Your vehicle and vehicle two both go over to the far right because you've got it that way, Top. Your driver takes care of you. Del did the same for her guys, passing the thing on her side. But not our fucking vehicle. You want to tell him what you did?"

Algarin smiled. "No, man, why don't you go ahead?"

"Damn right I will, you fucking rat. Top, this Blue Falcon goes in the *median*, the median! Lewis and Clark here decided he would blaze his own trail, and he made sure that trail put my side on the side of this potential IED, didn't you?"

I was laughing so hard I had tears in my eyes.

Later, I would have tears in my eyes for a different reason. The feelings of increased security and power were not to last long; in fact they lasted less than two weeks. The Hummers were every bit the lemons the AMC Gremlin had been. On our initial run with these vehicles one went down. That was okay, because with three left, we still had enough to keep running with the Hummers. At first we also hoped to quickly get the down vehicle back up. Surely it was a minor repair.

It was not. It was a complete write-off. In fact, in short order all four vehicles would be rendered useless to us. In spite of the best efforts of Colonel

Thomas, it would be less than two weeks before we were back in our old vehicles. Of our eventual total of over 220 runs, only 8 were made with the benefit of armor.

The team celebrated the Fourth of July by nearly getting into a firefight with a British contract security team. It started when the Brits, traveling in unmarked vehicles, attempted to overtake our convoy. It was Boeringer who alerted me to the problem.

"Top, Gunny [Josleyn] has two vehicles trying to overtake us, and he thinks they might be contractors, but he can't tell."

"Three, do not let them pass, check?"

"Roger, Top," Boeringer responded. "He is holding them in place, just passing the word up."

Contracted security guards were a growing problem for the military. Many of them believed they were superior to uniformed service members doing the same job with less and for much less money. It did not matter whether the guard was a Brit or an American, the attitude was almost always the same. Apparently the Brits did not like the fact that Gunny kept his 240 trained on them. When we pulled up to the Camp Victory gate, they pulled in behind us. That was incredibly foolish, but as with a Blackwater detail that had allegedly pulled four soldiers from their vehicle and then forced them to lie facedown in the street as they trained their weapons on them, contracted security guards in Iraq, fueled with steroids and an overblown sense of power, felt they could bully uniformed service members. Often that was true, but not with our team. Most of us were more than willing to drill a contractor or two.

"Top," it was Algarin, and there was an edge in his voice, "we have a serious problem back here."

I dismounted, and as I did, so, too, did my team. As we dismounted, so did the Brits, and things quickly degenerated. Two groups of heavily armed men, separated by mere feet, were shouting at each other, and it was getting worse by the second. The Brits were extremely upset that they had not been allowed to pass our convoy and that Gunny had kept his weapon trained on them. The fact that they wore beards, in a deliberate attempt to look more like locals, should have at least clued them in to the fact that overtaking an American convoy was going to be dicey at best. I carefully watched their hands, and I am sure we all were doing the same thing. An army MP was going nuts. He kept shouting for everybody to return to their vehicles.

"Get back in your vehicles. Get back in your vehicles now!"

Then, over all the commotion, I could hear him on his radio. "Get the lieutenant up here. These guys are getting ready to kill each other."

I thought we were getting ready to reenact Lexington with live ammo.

The MP became more frantic. "Get back in your vehicles *now!*"

Somehow it worked. Simultaneous with my efforts to get my guys back in their vehicles, the Brit team leader did the same with his guys. Later that same day we actually ran into the Brit team in the palace. The team leader apologized, but added, by way of explanation, that his team was agitated because we would not let them pass and our rear gunner was pointing his machine gun at them.

"We had a U.S. Army convoy shoot us up once, mate, and my guys didn't want to go through that again."

Though I did not say it, I understood why they got shot up. Running up on the rear of a convoy was a very good way to get shot. Refusing to keep your distance, even when a weapon is pointed at you, was an even better way to ensure you got lit up. These guys were very lucky that the older, more mature, and rock-steady Josleyn was on our rear gun instead of some young private. The Brit and I parted friends, having both expressed our mutual regret at the unfortunate and nearly deadly incident. It would have been extremely difficult to explain how we got into a firefight with Brits and why they were all dead from multiple gunshot wounds. Besides they seemed like decent guys. Brackin, who had witnessed the mutual apology, could only say, "I still think we should have shot 'em, Top."

"We can't kill everybody, Fudd, and if we ever decide we are going to start doing shit like that, we are going to start in the three."

Boeringer did not see it that way. "I don't know, Top, those arrogant pricks looked like a good place to start to me. Fuckin' pricks."

Boeringer would never get a post at the United Nations. A few days later, on a trip to BIAP in our old, yet reliable shitmobiles, I fired my weapon for the first time since 18 May.

It was another routine run to pick up personnel at the airport on the now infamous Route Irish. As we passed under an overpass, a car suddenly shot off of a ramp and closed rapidly on my vehicle from the right. As the vehicle rapidly devoured the time and space between us, the time and space between life and death, my mind began to evaluate what I believed my options were. First I swung my rifle over in the direction of the approaching car. The driver clearly saw me, but everything was happening so fast, I honestly did not know whether the gravity of the situation registered with him, and I did not care. While still separated by two lanes, I fired two rounds into the engine of his car; that was the only break he was going to get. If his car did not immediately alter course, I was going to kill him. This guy was living on borrowed time and so, too, maybe, were we. The car immediately veered hard to the right and away from us. Had he been a suicide bomber, he would not have veered off; he would have continued on toward us. The problem with using an M-16 to stop a car is that it can't; the 5.56 mm round can only get the driver's attention.

A .50 caliber fired into a car will disassemble it and stop it in its tracks. In reality, I had given this man too much of a chance. If I had been forced to kill him, he would have been that much closer, so close, in fact, that had he been a suicide bomber he would have killed or maimed us anyway. That was the problem with the war on Iraq's roads. You wanted to give these guys the benefit of the doubt; you wanted to know that when you took a man's life it was because you had to. But the enemy relied on that natural hesitation to kill a man who only *might* be a threat. That hesitation had cost the lives of scores of soldiers and marines. The stress of making these life and death decisions, several times a day, every time they were on the road, was a lot to ask of our young men and women. Was it any surprise that a young soldier had nearly killed our Brit contractor friends? Our guys were being asked to weigh the *possibility* that a guy was a threat against the *possibility* that he was just an inattentive driver. Nothing was certain except for the consequences of hesitation if in fact what you were facing was a jihadist bent on your destruction. If you hesitated at that moment, then you were guilty of the greatest of crimes in a combat unit; you had let your friends down and they were going to die. They were going to die because you did not want to kill a guy who you could not tell for certain was intent on killing you. For most of us, the decision to kill an errant driver was never an easy choice to make, but it was also not a choice that any of my guys hesitated in making or one they moped about later. They just couldn't, not if they wanted to make it home.

We made it to Camp Victory without any additional excitement. Camp Victory had the largest exchange in Iraq and we could buy almost anything there. Our guys always bought junk food and then hit the Burger King. Reed had recently been talking to me about a larger, "special" world beyond the mind-numbing drudgery of duty as the operations chief at Quantico.

As I sat in my vehicle eating my Whopper, Reed mentioned again that he felt I would be a good fit with either his unit or the CIA, and he added that he knew one of the officers within the palace was a recruiter for the agency. I was flattered, but I saw nothing in myself that made me think I had a future with the CIA, and I knew nothing of Reed's unit.

"Man, Huggy, I am honored, but I gotta ask, why me?"

"Look around, Top," he said. "When you got here, there was no team, no SOP, no nothing. You had a significant part in building something from nothing; in a forward-deployed combat environment you adapted and overcame. I know that is a cliché, but it fits, man. We look for people who can operate with little or no support and who can make difficult decisions under duress. I'll be honest with you, Top, I was impressed when I met you. It was obvious that you were intense and dedicated, and you were a great leader, but your in, at least with me, the thing that completed the picture, was April 8."

From the point of view of being recruited for bigger things, I did not understand why anything on that day would have stood out, other than our having killed a bunch of people.

"What about it?" I asked.

"Top, this is a bet-your-bars environment, and I know you knew you were going to be in for a lot of grief if you made the decision to engage that day. The easy thing would have been to follow the Cav, drive on, and live to fight another day. You knew what the potential consequences were, and you did what you knew to be right anyway. You know that is not as common as it should be."

Not knowing what to say, I indulged in male camouflage, in other words, bravado. "Does that mean if we kill twenty more I can be a director or something."

Reed, always sharp enough to take any opening, quickly answered, "Well, Top, *you* gotta get one first, then maybe you can reach for twenty."

"I said if *we* kill twenty, smart-ass. Besides, one was mine."

Meg, who may have been listening the whole time, just laughed his sinister laugh. "Huh, huh, you guys."

Frequently, quietly tucked away in his cave, we would forget that Meggison was nearby. We would only be reminded of his presence when he would suddenly interject himself into a conversation, take an opening left by someone else, and verbally insult or berate his unfortunate victim. In that way he was very much like something of a monster, rarely seen but always lurking, ready to strike. Sometimes Meg would just laugh and shake his head and say, simply, "You guys." The way he laughed was sinister; dark and creepy by itself, but when he added the "you guys" it was positively evil. None of us ever quite knew what ol' Meg was thinking. All of us were glad that the insurgents gave Meggi plenty to kill; it kept him from looking at us as potential victims. "C'mere, you Muslim hooka, and let ol' Meggi kill ya," was something we did not want to hear Meggi say to us. Meggi was a very different character, and he knew it. But all of us were odd in our own way, and in the Majestic Twelve we had all found a home.

Our happy home was about to lose the one member who did the most to keep us happy. Colonel Thomas was rotating home in July, and all of us wondered what would happen to us once he left. A few members of the team thought that everything would be fine as long as Colonel Deboda was still there. Most of us had long ago recognized Deboda for what he was. As things would turn out, Hesco would be gone less than twenty-four hours before Deboda fully revealed himself as the petty, small, and insecure man he was. There were other goodbyes in July as well. On the ninth we took Schroeder to the airport, his four month over. I did not step in to stop his early departure. He had given us what he could and he was spent.

Later that same day, we got tabbed to make another run to BIAP to escort a busload of soldiers bound for the palace. On the way out I opened up on another car. As we passed an on-ramp a vehicle shot from the ramp and, while behind us initially, rapidly caught up with us and drew slightly ahead almost before I noticed it. Less than two hundred yards ahead was an off-ramp. Because there were three men in the vehicle I was not concerned that this was a VBIED as it would be extremely wasteful for the enemy to blow up three suicide bombers when one was far more economical. I also knew that at that point in the war no more than two men had ever been observed in a VBIED.

However, their driving and the location of the ramps, as well as the position of the Iraqi vehicle, all indicated the *possibility* that they were going to do a drive-by on us. Typically, when a drive-by attack occurred, it was reported that the attacking vehicle would suddenly appear adjacent to the target vehicle, after the target passed an on-ramp. As the attacking vehicle pulled alongside the target vehicle, the occupants of the attacking vehicle would open fire on the target. Before the target could respond, the attacking vehicle would speed forward and take an off-ramp, which typically was located twenty-five meters away, but could be farther out. The sudden appearance of the attacking vehicle followed by a sudden and violent ambush and then a quick getaway on the next off-ramp, left the target no time to respond.

In our case there were two other factors that greatly diminished our ability to defend ourselves. First, we were in a Hummer, and the Iraqi vehicle was so close to ours by the time I noticed it that it would have been impossible for Facemyer, who was manning the fifty, to depress his weapon and engage this threat. Since the driver's first duty was obviously to drive, Williams was seated behind him to provide that side of the vehicle with a set of eyes that could look for threats rather than watch the road as the driver did. Second, firing a full-sized rifle such as my M-16A2 from within any vehicle was a chore, but doing so from within the tight confines of a Hummer with its small window was extremely difficult. By the time I noticed the vehicle, my engagement window was rapidly slipping away.

I fired immediately and sent three rounds through the center of the back window. The occupants immediately threw their hands out, letting us know they were not a threat, but that was only the beginning. Because of the width of the Hummer was its small windows, Sergeant Williams never saw the men throw out their hands. Having heard my shots and not knowing for sure the nature of the threat, Will screamed, *"Get him, Face!"*

In slow motion, Reed (who saw the men's hands go up) and I listened as Facemyer disengaged his turret ring lock, allowing him to bring his .50 caliber heavy machine gun to bear on the threat. We listened in disbelief as the powerful weapon swung over to the defenseless Iraqis. Click, click, click. Each click of the revolving turret ring brought Face's fearsome fifty closer to the "threat." Reed and I both screamed, "Noooooooooo, Faaaccceeeeeee, *noooooooo!"*

It was like a slow motion scene leading up to some regrettable tragedy. Noooo!!!! I imagined Face cutting lose with hundreds of half-inch-wide slugs on a car less than eight feet away. *Chunk, chunk, chunk,* followed by the sound of empty brass raining down on hard pavement followed by screams and still more shooting. It does not take a ballistics expert to figure out what a .50 caliber armor-piercing bullet does to the human form at a range of less than eight feet. Arms and legs are torn off, and skulls are turned into soup bowls. It does not take a psychiatrist to figure out what the reaction to this sudden fire would have been in the vehicles behind us. Everybody on the right side of the convoy would have opened up. The result would have been a scene of such total carnage a Hollywood special effects artist would be envious.

Fortunately, Face heard Reed and me and did not fire into the vehicle. It all happened very quickly. It was only by the grace of God that nobody was killed. I could not resist the temptation to tease Will. In my best girl voice, I cried, "Get him, Face!"

Reed laughed. "Top, you smell that?"

Sniffing the air, I replied, "Yeah, smells like Will shit himself again."

Will laughed at himself. "Fuck, man, I didn't know. All I knew was Top is shooting at something, so it seemed like a good idea to get Face on it."

I frequently teased Will, and when I did, it was most often his courage that I attacked. Making fun of a coward would not be fun at all, but Will was no coward. Besides, he was so easy to spin up, and his responses were the stuff of comedy legend.

About a month before this incident, we were being interviewed, over dinner, by a female air force reporter for the Armed Forces Radio and Television Network. She was surprised to hear that we were all volunteers and that we did not exist as a unit until we were assembled in Iraq.

The reporter asked, "How do you guys do this without medics, armor, or radios? I do not think there are a lot of people who would volunteer for your jobs even with the right equipment."

"Well," I said, "not all of my guys are happy about being on the team now that they have realized how dangerous the job is. Take Will here."

As soon as I said it, Will rolled his eyes and just gave me an evil stare as he put down his fork. In the past few weeks Will had gotten used to me introducing him as a cowering slacker. As the reporter looked Will over, I explained. "Will reached the end of his rope on April eighth. While everybody else was dismounted and engaging the enemy, this guy was lying on the floorboard, thumb in mouth, and muttering, 'Please take them, you can take all of them, but spare me,' as he wallows in his own waste. The guy shits himself so often he, no shit, has to wear a diaper when we are on the road."

Will said nothing. Incredibly the reporter actually believed what I had told her. Worse, instead of being repulsed by the "coward," she felt compassion.

She soothed, "Well, that's okay. Not everybody is cut out for what you guys do."

Will was sick with rage. "Okay, okay, you're gonna tell her the truth, *right?*"

Will later told the boys what had happened. "This guy," he said, pointing at me, "is telling this reporter, a fucking reporter, that I am a cowering guy who needs to wear a fucking diaper just to get in a vehicle *and she believes him!* I bet if I hadn't said anything, Top would have left that story the way he first told it and I would be famous as the only soldier in Iraq wearing diapers."

CHAPTER 15

Deboda and Friends

In mid-July we were given another duty. When I first arrived in CMATT, back in February, I immediately developed, implemented, and supervised a training program for shooters and drivers. Many other E-8s and E-9s must have recognized that these programs were needed, yet not one section thought it necessary to train its own people. That ended in July when Sergeant Major Zelaya, no visionary himself, directed that I train any CMATT personnel whose duties might put them on the road. That was a long list. A part of me loathed the senior enlisted within CMATT. Not one of them, with the exception of First Sergeant Fullard, ever did anything to train their people in how to survive. Long before the sergeant major made it policy, First Sergeant Fullard was sending his people to me for training.

Though CMATT thought the training was critical, few people would ever find the time to be trained. Those few who did most often went to one range and that was it. One range was not training. It was an introduction to weapons usage, and that was it. I tried to explain this to Captain Wheeler, who thought our training CMATT was a great idea. He dismissed my concerns about the limited value of the training by saying that it was better than what they had before, and that itself made the people we trained better able to survive. While it was better than nothing, it was not nearly enough. I believed that the real purpose of the training was to allow people like Wheeler and his superiors to say that they had done everything possible to train their people. While I thought they could have and should have done more, I had to acknowledge that they were doing more than had ever been done in the past. It was a start. The training would commence on 13 July when we were to take ten soldiers, sailors, and airmen to Tadji. We never made it. Our gun trucks that day were led by Second Lieutenant Carl Felcher, U.S. Army. Things went downhill as soon as he opened his mouth at the premission brief.

"Our mission today is to safely get from here to Tadji; that is our objective. To ensure that we are successful in that, you will, at no time, engage enemy forces."

It had long before ceased being a secret that many of the 1st Cavalry units providing support to CMATT convoys had no interest in getting into a fight. While most of their briefs were crafted in such a way as to make it difficult to engage the enemy, this was the first time it was so blatant. All of us stood there with our jaws open in stunned, mute surprise.

I spoke up. "So if we see Mahdi army guys running around with RPGs and severed heads, we are not going to kill them? What if they are setting up an ambush for a follow-on convoy?"

The lieutenant stuck to his "run first, last, and always" school of warfare. "We will not, unless fired upon, engage any enemy forces, armed or otherwise."

That was shortsighted, and did nothing for us in the long run. Sure, by avoiding combat that day, we would survive that day, but what about the next day or the next week? What about our comrades in the convoy behind us? To say that many of these soldiers cared only about seeing the end of their tours was not unfair; it was true. This lieutenant, this "warrior" was no exception. The very sight of him and those like him sickened all of us. He continued: "Iraqi vehicles will be allowed to pass the convoy. Any vehicle that breaks down will not be towed; it will be abandoned."

Many units allowed Iraqi vehicles to pass their convoys. They did that until they ate their first VBIED, and after that they did not allow Iraqi vehicles to pass them anymore. Even these sorry asses had been very good about not allowing Iraqi vehicles to cut into or to pass our convoys. Now Felcher seemed to be making up his own rules. This was one of the few days my guys had Hummers of their own. Felcher saying that any vehicle which broke down would be left behind was a direct shot at us, as we had towed two of them already, and he knew that. Further, he certainly would not abandon any of his own vehicles, as his battalion commander might frown upon that.

Naturally, I took exception to his decision to abandon any vehicle broken down. Certainly, General Petraeus would, too. Leaving an armored Hummer to be looted and destroyed by the locals because it had a ruptured radiator hose would not set well with any general. After the jackass finished his brief, I asked for some clarification. I asked the hardened killer if he knew what the ROE was.

He answered, saying, "I know what my ROE is. What is yours?"

Disgusted and making no effort to hide my feelings, I said, "First, it's not *my* ROE. It is the commanding general of CJTF-7s ROE, General Ricardo Sanchez, U.S. Army, and the FRAGO in which it came out stated that it was not to be modified by *any* subordinate units for *any* reason."

I added, "Tell me how you can write your own ROE? Show me the subsequent FRAGO which gives you or your unit that authority, *lieutenant!*"

The lieutenant stuck by his guns and refused to acknowledge that "his" ROE was in direct violation of the CJTF 7 ROE. Knowing that I could achive nothing, I decided to pull all CMATT personnel off of the convoy. That included not only my own team but those CMATT personnel we were escorting to Tadji.

Felcher was obviously pleased with himself. Now he knew that no matter what the provocation, so long as they were not shot at, there would be no combat that day. The prospects of his immediate survival thus brightened, the lieutenant beamed happily. The homicidal maniacs would not be going with him. He was safe!

I gathered my guys around. "As soon as you get your crap put away and before you do anything else, I want statements from each of you as to exactly what you heard and saw starting with that fucking brief."

"Listen, everybody, that brief is the big deal. That brief represents a clear violation of CJTF-7 ROE and cannot, in any way, by anyone of any rank, be justified. These people would do anything to stay out of a fight."

As I walked back to the office I was fuming. I could not believe the brief Felcher just gave. He would abandon any vehicle that broke down for any reason, no matter how minor? He would not engage enemy personnel under any circumstances unless they first fired on us? I was certain that not only would my chain of command have serious issues with this, but even Felcher's own must surely have some problems with the brief he gave.

I was wrong on both counts.

My own chain of command, seeking to avoid embarrassing fellow officers, directed Colonel Thomas and me to meet with Felcher's battalion commander. I argued that the matter should be referred to CJTF-7 since it concerned a serious violation of the standing ROE. That would not happen. Nothing would be done. Felcher was an officer and I was just a master sergeant. Right or wrong did not matter so much as *who* was right and wrong. Officers could violate standing orders and that was okay. Officers, it seemed, were only wrong when they crossed a superior officer.

Next day, Thomas and I went to go see Felcher's battalion commander. After introductions, I repeated to the battalion commander the brief his lieutenant had given, highlighting both the ROE and the abandonment of CMATT equipment. The battalion commander said that his lieutenant was wrong in how he briefed the ROE in that it was never in their ROE to first let people shoot at them before they could themselves engage enemy forces. However, the battalion commander would not comment on the aggressive ROE CJTF-7 had put out concerning some insurgent elements because his battalion was not going to follow that ROE. That a battalion commander in the U.S. Army could just make up his own ROE seemed incomprehensible. That nobody would pass this up to CJTF-7 seemed criminal. The battalion commander went on to say that his lieutenant was also incorrect when he briefed that any CMATT vehicles that broke down were to be abandoned. That, he said, only applied to Iraqi army equipment. He defended his lieutenant by saying that the young officer must have confused the two. The battalion commander added that he would address the ROE and the abandoning of CMATT equipment with the lieutenant. As to the tactics to be employed, in particular, allowing Iraqi vehicles to close on convoys, the battalion commander said that his lieutenant was correct in how he briefed their SOP.

Their commanding general had decided that now was the time for a change, a change the battalion commander explained that "would make us less intrusive on the Iraqis." The battalion commander acknowledged that this would increase the risk to those in convoys but it was "a risk the general is willing to take." A risk *the general* is willing to take! I am sure it was, and why not? *He* would not be the one taking the risk. Of the two thousand plus lost in the war, the only KIA rarer than an airman, sailor, or marine first sergeant or sergeant major was a general. In fact, there were no general officer casualties. What the general was really willing to do was write a check and cover it with our asses. While I understood that there might well come a time to modify our tactics, it had not yet arrived. Having accomplished nothing, Colonel Thomas and I thanked the battalion commander as we left.

Before we departed, however, the battalion commander made what to him was merely an observation, but to Hesco and me amounted to a startling reve-lation. "Dealing with marines, there is no doubt in my mind that you guys are born and bred to kill from the first day of boot camp, and the army is just not like that."

Nothing could be truer or more tragic. But what applied to the army did not necessarily apply to all soldiers as I well knew.

When we got back to the office, Toddington was waiting for me.

"I have some bad news, mate. As of today, there have been no replace-ments identified for the convoy security team. With the exception of Gun-nery Sergeant Josleyn, who has a replacement, the rest of you simply do not."

Toddington went on to explain that he needed the team to extend by two months. I could not believe it. At a time when we were increasingly finding ourselves scrutinized for one reason or another, the very people who were our critics had identified a need for us to stay beyond the time we were due to ro-tate. I had already extended, but that was for my guys. Doing it for these people made no sense. We did not owe them a damn thing. It was a sure bet that the officers would rotate on time. Why in the world should I ask my guys to stay for these ungrateful bastards?

Toddington was frank. "I pride myself on my ability to judge people, and knowing something about group dynamics, I know I would have better luck pushing a turd up a hill with a fork than asking anyone of them to stay if you weren't behind it, mate."

I hated him for even asking. I hated the people who asked him to ask even more, because it was those very same people who were our loudest critics. They would not have given a damn if any of us were killed. I also hated words like "duty" and "honor." Because I believed in those words and despite what I be-lieved about most of the officers in CMATT, I knew, as soon as he asked, that I had no choice.

My country was calling. I would ask my guys to go one more mile, but we would want some things in exchange for staying.

"I will ask, sir, but I want something if we stay. We will want to rotate out on the same day, together, just like a unit."

Toddington did not think there would be a problem with that, and I told him I would ask the boys after evening chow when we held our daily debrief. As I sat at chow, I thought about how I would ask my guys to stay, especially in light of recent events and the pending departure of the respected and be-loved Colonel Thomas.

When the time came, I started with a history lesson. "When General Lee surrendered his army after four years of bitter fighting, he could call less than thirty thousand men to the colors. The rest had been killed, wounded, or captured or had simply left for home in the war's final months. A select few, a very few, had been in the fight from first to last. It has always been that way. A select few will endure everything when their country calls and any of their countrymen are locked in battle. They just feel obligated to share in the burdens and hardships of their countrymen. One more day, one more mile, and one more hill, these men simply gave everything asked of them until they were wounded, or killed, or the war was over. We have now been asked to stay. They do not have replacements for us, and while they will not force anyone to stay, they are asking that we stay. I am going to stay. I am not staying for them. You guys know what I think of these people. I am staying because I am obligated to stay. If a guy can stand at the final roll call of the Army of Northern Virginia, then I can go one more mile here. I do not expect any of you to stay and nobody even has the right to ask you to. You have all already done more than most people, even those in a uniform, will ever do for their country, and nobody has the right to expect more from you. Most, if not all of you, volunteered to come to Iraq in the first place. All of you then volunteered for the team even though you knew what that meant. All of you except Meggison, anyway; he may have been too stupid to know any better."

There was some laughter, and then I continued.

"I know you all are fed up with this place and these people. But I am asking you to put that aside and to stay with me. The war is not over, and we are still needed over here. Aside from the obligation, there is one benefit if we stay. If we stay we get to rotate home as a team so long as we stay to 15 October. So, what do you guys want to do?"

It was quiet for a little while, and then Face spoke up. "Well, fuck, I've already done it once, so I guess I can tell the wife I will be coming home a little later. That's why they make batteries."

Everybody laughed and then, when they had settled down, I went around the circle as we had so many times before, but this time I asked each man in turn what he was going to do. Without exception, they would all stay. We had been derided as cowboys, murderers, undisciplined, and disrespectful, and yet when called, we were all, one more time, volunteering for the most dangerous job in Iraq. While it was our command that had asked that we stay, that was not why we did it. We were going to extend because we were, more than the ticket-punching officers who needed us to stay, professional soldiers and marines. We were warriors at heart, and we would stay because our country needed us and because this was our calling. We would stay because other soldiers and marines were depending on us to do so. We were men and a woman called to arms. More than any love of country, that was why we would stay. In the end, we really had no choice. Once asked we had to stay. We could not change what we were even if we wanted to, and we were warriors. Even if every fiber of our being screamed, "Hell no, I am not staying here in this fucking circus working for people who are trying their damndest to get me killed." None of that mattered. We were what we were, and we would stay.

I notified Toddington of our decision and he said he would pass it to the chief of staff, Colonel Henry. Toddington did not seem surprised that we had elected to stay. The following day, almost as if on cue, a VBIED hit Baby Assassins' Gate leading into the Green Zone. Baby Assassins' had long been recognized by those of us on the team as the most dangerous gate to leave from or come in through. Because Baby Assassins' served as the main entrance into the Green Zone for Iraqi pedestrian and vehicular traffic, it was always crowded with people and vehicles waiting to be searched before being passed into the Green Zone. While completely necessary, the process created long lines and delays. Our biggest concern was the gaggle of Iraqi vehicles parked at the gate. They numbered as many as two dozen or more on some days. As we crept past this long, immobile line of parked vehicles, we could not help but wonder which one might be a VBIED just waiting for a convoy, any convoy, to come pulling into the gate. If you were at the wrong place at the wrong time, you were simply going to die.

To provide us a small measure of protection, I had started having our convoy pull up about fifty meters off the gate. We would dismount and stop traffic, keeping a bubble around our vehicles. When the gate entrance lane, next to the search lane, was clear, I would have the team quickly mount up and the drivers would gun their vehicles past the Iraqi vehicles waiting to be searched. While the search lane was never free of a throng of Iraqi vehicles, sometimes we got lucky and the entrance lane would be clear of traffic and we could just race right in. Still, we knew we were highly vulnerable coming into the gate. Less than a week before, Reed had remarked on how dangerous it was. I had agreed with him, saying that it was only a matter of time. Today, time was up for ten Iraqis, who just happened to be at the wrong place at the wrong time. That was how a lot of people died in Iraq.

A few days after the bombing at the gate, Colonel Deboda told me that he would be making some changes in the convoy security team once Thomas left. I did not know what those would be, but I had seen enough of Deboda to know I would not like them. It made me seriously wonder if we had done the right thing in extending. We had certainly not extended to have this clown, or any of them for that matter, screw with us.

Maybe if the officers were as dedicated as my guys, they would have set the example and extended first, before asking us to do so. But in the palace, officers were only as dedicated as their orders told them to be. They would do their time, get a medal, and go home as soon as possible. They sure as shit were not going to raise their hand to extend their tour or do anything that might get them hurt, but they had no problem asking others to do what they would not. Leadership by example was unheard-of among many of the officers within the palace. As the day of Colonel Thomas's departure drew nearer, it became obvious even to the most optimistic among us that life would change the minute he left. It would not change for the better, and it would not change because anyone really gave a shit about us and wanted to instill some (from their perspective) much needed discipline. For Deboda it was all about power. What Deboda never understood is that leadership and the right to lead are not given simply because of your rank. You earn it, and he had not, nor would he. Thomas and Buchanan had long ago earned not only our respect but our admiration. They were both no-bullshit men of action who demanded results and did not want to hear excuses about not having this or that.

No other officer within the three commanded the respect these men did. Deboda did not. The only thing his rank did for him, in our eyes, was get him a bigger check. A crack whore can with five kids gets a bigger check from the government than a crack whore with three, so even that wasn't saying much.

On July 17 it was our sad duty to escort the beloved and deeply respected Lieutenant Colonel John Thomas, our "Hesco," to the airport on his last ride in Iraq. It was a somber trip and much of the premission banter was missing. Most of our thoughts centered on what would happen after he left. We knew that things would be different, but we did not know how much so. We spent about thirty minutes at the terminal with Colonel Thomas. Each member of the team said goodbye and got a picture taken with him. Also leaving with Colonel Thomas were Gunny Hessen and Corporal Napier. They, too, would be missed. After all the goodbyes were said, the team mounted up and headed back to the palace.

"Well, now what, Top?"

I knew what Reed was asking.

"I don't know, Huggy," I answered, "but I am sure it is going to suck. We don't have any friends now, and Mole Man Johns, that candy britches The-

Lieutenant Colonel John "Hesco" Thomas departs Iraq. Note the three
skulls painted on the buttstock of Sergeant Jason Williams's modified
AK-47. *(From the collection of Jack Lynch)*

odorson, Deboda, Wheeler, and Sherman are all still there, so I am sure life
will indeed suck."

Will quickly added, "And don't forget that fucker Toddington. I am telling you he is just like the rest. I was right about Deboda, and I am right
about him."

There had been a time when some members of the team had really respected Deboda. Will had never respected or trusted him, but Will did not
trust anybody he did not really know. While much of what Will's mother
had tried to teach him about being civil had clearly not registered, everything she said about "stranger danger" had more than stuck. As for me, I
simply did not know what to make of Toddington then. He had supported
us when he checked in, but how much of that was due to the influence of
Hesco? Before the day was over, I would have to admit that Will had nailed
him right.

No sooner had we arrived at the palace than Deboda wanted to see me.
Deboda told me that he and Toddington thought that we were taking too

many people on our runs. They felt we could get by with a lighter escort and that was what they would eventually put into place. When I protested, Deboda said that they had carefully examined the pros and cons and that they were convinced we could get by with fewer people. Besides, they really needed help in the office. The officers were pulling extra duty, and they needed us, as a largely untapped resource, to pull more weight there. Eventually, they, not I, would decide who would be going on the road and who would be reassigned to the office. Deboda said that there would be no change; the decisions made were final. He was very smug.

"It will not be as big a deal as you might think because eventually the only runs you guys will make will be to BIAP. All other runs will rely on the escort provided by the First Cav."

Now it was obvious that some time before, and behind Thomas's back, Deboda had talked with the 1st Cav about pulling us in. We made the Cav nervous because we did not avoid combat, and they did not want us on the road. I asked Deboda for clarification. "You mean you are going to entrust the safety of our assets and people to the same guys who have abandoned trucks loaded with ammo and weapons? Buses loaded with our own people? And how are they going to do that? They can't cover all the runs now."

I knew that the 1st Cav lacked the resources to cover every run out of CMATT, which had been renamed Multi National Security Transition Command—Iraq (MNSTC-I) by General Petraeus. Like it or not, these fucking clowns were going to need their own dedicated security team. (In fact the next team was both much larger than mine and far better equipped, illustrating just how shortsighted Deboda was.)

Deboda replied that that was exactly what he meant.

I responded, "Okay, sir, cancel our extensions. My guys are not staying here so they can be reassigned as clerks while some are left on the roads with a diminished capacity to protect themselves."

Deboda seemed to have expected this. "Well, Top, if that is your intent, I can pull the JMD [the JMD, Joint Manning Document, was the document that carried each person's rotation date], and we will find a way to extend people."

"You do that, sir, so long as everybody is held to the same standard. You guys have already let Schroeder, Hessen, and Napier leave early, so if things are so critical, why was that allowed to happen?"

"They did not leave early."

"Yes, sir, they did," I answered. "Schroeder got here weeks after any other member on the team. Hessen and Napier arrived the same day I did."

Deboda replied, "Well, I can't change that, but I am going to fix the JMD."

Deboda was going to go out of his way to screw with the boys now that Hesco was gone. Deboda, true to his word, did check the JMD against my own roster, which reflected each team member's rotation date.

Having found no discrepancies between the two, he then attempted to change the long-standing policy within CMATT/MNSTC-I that started a man's tour from the day he checked into his processing center stateside. Most of the orders stated that a soldier or marine would be assigned temporary additional duty (TAD) for a period of 180 days. Further, the orders stated that this period of TAD started from the time the soldier or marine checked into his processing center. The orders did not say that the soldier or marine would be TAD, on the ground in Iraq, for a period of 180 days. Deboda fought long and hard to push the start date for tours back to the date the soldier or marine actually checked into MNSTC-I. But this went nowhere fast, as it would have had to be applied to all MNSTC-I personnel and not just the convoy security team. Officers in MNSTC-I were not about to see their tours extended just because Deboda wanted to screw with us. Deboda then tried to apply the rule more selectively. Only those personnel whose replacements had not yet been identified would need to be extended. If that were the case, the only people in the three who would have their tours extended would be those of us on the convoy security team. But the change would have an impact on just enough people outside the three that this idea was killed as well.

Having failed twice, Deboda, as petty as he was stubborn, attempted to have the start date for tours pushed back to the date the soldier or marine arrived in Kuwait. The difference could be as little as ten days and as much as three weeks. Still, it would have to be applied to all, so this initiative was also killed.

This went on for weeks and it drove the personnel officer nuts. The personnel officer was a crusty old marine chief warrant officer. "Who the hell is this guy? He thinks he is going to change your dates but not the rest of MNSTC-Is. I am telling you that MARCENT will have a fit." MARCENT is the marine component of Central Command.

In the end, not through any lack of trying, Deboda failed in his repeated attempts to involuntarily extend the team. I had to admit that Will was right about Toddington. Having watched Deboda kiss Colonel Thomas's ass for months, when he obviously had serious reservations about how he let us operate, I was certain Deboda would not have proposed such sweeping changes without first having gotten the support of Toddington. Wheeler was a nonfactor, as he just sat behind a desk and never knew what was going on. The real power in the three rested with Toddington.

As all of this was playing out, Lieutenant Colonel Deboda had a word of warning for me. "Top, you are on thin ice with your superiors."

I was not sure what prompted the warning, and I did not care. Big deal. When hadn't I been?

Should it bother me that these useless clowns thought I was a problem? Deboda had not waited an hour after Thomas left to start screwing with us. He attempted to extend our tours, and now he was threatening me with my "superiors." I did not have any superiors among the officers left in the three. I had ranking officers, but they certainly were no more my superior than the diminutive man standing in front of me. After leaving the office, I went to see the sergeant major. I told him what had happened between Deboda and me and I asked him, knowing that the commanding general was concerned about the pending loss of the security team, if he or the chief of staff had been made aware of our offer to extend. The sergeant major was stunned.

"Well, Top, I didn't know that, and I am almost certain that the chief didn't either. And what do those people want to use you guys for?"

I repeated what Deboda had said. The sergeant major said he would get to the bottom of it. After giving the story time to grow, I told Colonel Toddington about my conversation with the sergeant major, pointedly telling him that he and I believed the chief of staff had not been made aware that the team had offered to extend. Toddington seemed genuinely taken aback and more than a little surprised that I had gone to the sergeant major.

Though Toddington said nothing at the time, he had plenty to say fifteen minutes later when he called me over to his desk.

"I do not want you telling anybody that you are all willing to extend just yet, mate. I want to make these people do their fucking jobs and get your replacements in here."

I believed then and believe now that what he really wanted was for no one to know that we were willing to extend. The officers in the three seemed to be willing to put a reduced and improperly trained team on the road and reassign significant numbers of the team to the office. I believed that this was a misguided attempt to curtail our ability to take offensive action. It seemed as if they viewed us as a greater threat than the enemy. Of course, their plans would also greatly reduce our ability to defend ourselves. But that was okay with them. After all, putting a vulnerable team on the road was not going to get them killed. But putting up with us might drive them to suicide. Though I had already extended, I now, for the first time during my tour in Iraq, looked forward to going home and leaving this place far behind me. It was not the war and the stress of the road I looked forward to leaving. It was the palace with all the politicians, the ticket punchers, in uniform that I looked forward to leaving behind.

To my surprise, Deboda had still not dropped the idea of extending our tours. Accordingly, on 25 July, Wheeler, Toddington, and Deboda went over the JMD until 2200 that evening in yet another attempt by Deboda to find something, anything, that would allow our officers to extend our tours.

Deboda wanted me to, again, ask the Commandant's Office if the policy was that a soldier or marine spent 179 days TAD or actually on the ground in Iraq.

"I have already done that."

Deboda, not very bright, said, "Well, do it again, and if you don't get the answer I want, then I will ask them myself."

"Well, *sir,* why don't we avoid wasting the time and you just go ask them now?"

Deboda, still not getting it, replied, "Because I want you to make them give us an answer."

Was Deboda as deaf as he was stupid? They had already given us an answer, and no matter how many times we asked the question, the answer would be the same. The Commandant's Office had no intention of extending our tours because they knew that they would then have to extend everyone's tour and that would never happen. Perhaps sensing failure on one front, Deboda and friends moved on to another. For whatever reason, the conversation suddenly turned to awards. They wanted to know who had been put in for what. I told them that Colonel Thomas had not told me, which, for the most part, he had not. I had seen Delacroix's award package. Though she had been put in for a Joint Service Commendation Medal with combat V, the board, made up of officers, had bumped her award up to a Bronze Star with V.

Del's was the first award they took aim at. Wheeler, Toddington, and Deboda felt that it was excessive, and even though General Petraeus had already been signed off on it, they would not award it to her. But they did not stop there. They wanted to downgrade all of the awards, though Colonel Thomas had written them, and every one of them had already passed a review by Toddington before being forwarded to Wheeler for his signature. In fact, no award left the three that Wheeler did not sign off on. But that was only the start of the process. The award was then submitted to a board comprised of senior officers from throughout MNSTC-I. The board could recommend that the submitted award be approved as it was, upgraded, downgraded, or simply disapproved. But the board's actions were still merely a recommendation. The final stop was the commanding general's desk. The general could sign off on the board's recommendations or upgrade, downgrade, or deny the award. Now, for some reason, Deboda and friends were seeking to downgrade the awards that *they* had already approved and forwarded, awards that had already passed the board, and in many cases had already been signed off on by the commanding general.

That was unheard of! The reason for this extraordinary action was, to me, transparent. Our meeting that night had been about extending the tours of the convoy security team. Having failed in that, they were making it clear that they would retaliate. Deboda said that it was his team now, and he would put the team in for what he felt we rated! Never mind that this miserable little shit would have us for about three weeks when Colonel Thomas had written his recommendations based on his observations of five months. Of course, the only awards that would ever be downgraded were those of the convoy security team. No officer or enlisted office person had their awards downgraded. Far from it. Meggison, who returned to MNSTC-I, for subsequent tours, would later tell me that both Deboda and Wheeler left with Bronze Stars with the combat V device! But that would not be the case with the convoy team's awards. Not only would awards not yet approved be downgraded before they even went to a board, though Wheeler had forwarded them; those awards already signed off by the general would also be downgraded. Using their rank, the senior officers of the three had decided to take away medals earned by the team because they could do nothing else to them.

They could not force them to extend or pull them off the road, but they could beat them in the palace. The palace was their home and we were just the visiting team. They were officers and we were enlisted, and nobody in the chain of command gave a fuck what they did to us, regardless of how dishonorable, wrong, and loathsome. On 28 July, I informed Toddington that I had requested permission to speak with the commanding general of MNSTC-I. Toddington, visibly pissed, slammed his hatch, saying, "You do what you have to, mate."

That I would, though I doubted that anything would change. The closer I got to the end of July, the more aware I became that my tour would end shortly. My own request for an extension had been denied by MARCENT, who wanted me home immediately. I did not know what to read into that at the time. Later I would learn that MARCENT had grown disgusted with

MNSTC-I's handling of personnel. The haphazard way in which personnel were requested and assigned had begun to grate on the commands supporting MNSTC-I. Still, I was able to push back dates of departure for me and Gunny Josleyn to 8 August. That meant I had little more than a week left in Iraq. I could not believe the tour had flown by so quickly, and I thanked God that none of us, thus far anyway, had been killed or wounded. Those thoughts led directly to a dark fear that resides in every combatant, the thought of being killed just before going home.

It was a fear that lurked in all of us. I felt it then, in my last days in Iraq, during the down times between missions. Every time I shaved on a morning that we had a mission, I would look at my face and seriously wonder if this was my day to die. I would study each detail of my face as if trying to paint a mental picture vivid enough to last for eternity. I would tell myself how I would fight and die that day if it were to be my last on earth. I would look into my own eyes and wonder what God would see in me when the time came for our face-to-face meeting. As I got closer to leaving, I would linger just a little longer in the mirror. But nothing changed on the road. When I led an escort, every part of me remained focused on the mission, and there was no time to dwell on the tour winding down and on how badly it would suck to be killed or maimed in the last part of my tour. I knew that it sucked equally, whether you were hit on your first day or your last, but it *seemed* worse if you were nailed shortly before you rotated out. I also knew, as we all did, that you were no more likely to die in your last week than you were in your first. Death was not that purposefully cruel.

Above all this, I worried about the fate of my friends. By the time I left, Boeringer, Algarin, Napier, Hessen, and, of course, Schroeder, would all be home. Meggison, Delacroix, Reed, Facemyer, Williams, Dann, Patterson, Joselyn, and I were all that was left. Williams, Face, Joselyn and I would all be leaving on the same day, which left Reed, Meggison, Dann, Patterson, and Delacroix. How would I handle being home while they still toiled under the threat of death they faced on the road and the pettiness of the MNSTC-I officer corps?

On 29 July we were tasked with taking a British brigadier from CPATT to the Baghdad Police Academy. CPATT operated out of the Presidential Palace, one floor above us. CPATT trained the Iraqi police just as we trained the Iraqi army. The request was not written as normally would be the case. At about 1000 that morning, the leader of the brigadier's PSD (personal security detail) came to see me in my office. The Brit asked if we could take the brigadier to the academy. The request struck me as odd, given that a PSD team existed solely to provide constant security for their principal, in this case the brigadier. Curious, I asked the man why he would not be able to provide the escort himself.

"We just have too many missions going, mate, and we need you to take the mission if you can."

Again, I could not understand what other missions they might have, given that the brigadier was their mission. Authority to execute missions now rested with Deboda, and he had stated he wanted to curb the runs we did. But Deboda, ever eager to please someone who might drop a good word or two about him, immediately said that we would take the mission. I looked at a map and asked the Brit to show me the objective and any known routes to it. The academy was located one block off of Haifa Street, which was so deadly and violent that it was frequently closed to all Coalition traffic. When not closed, movement was restricted to only critical missions. A naval intelligence officer had once warned me against ever taking Haifa Street under any circumstances, given our lack of radios, corpsmen, and armor. Not surprisingly, Haifa was restricted that day. I said as much to the Brit.

He responded, "Yeah, I know, mate, not an easy one this is."

I immediately suspected that they wanted us to take the brigadier because Haifa was closed. Looking back, I realize that the weeks under siege at the palace may have made me paranoid.

When I asked the Brit if he knew of any way other than Haifa Street, of getting to the academy, he said that he did not. After the Brit left, I spent forty-five minutes looking for potential alternate routes to the academy. That was difficult, for most of the maps were old, and none of them, new or old, reflected all the barriers and closed routes that had sprung up after the invasion. Baghdad was a maze. After a bit of study, I thought I found a route that would work and marked it on my map. Our departure time was set for 1400, and I had the team in the lot earlier than normal, at 1230.

I went over the known route, Haifa Street, with the team, and then we covered the alternate route I thought would work. It would take us on the freeway and past the Baghdad Recruiting Center, to our left. The alternate route was almost entirely on the freeway, and therefore both faster and far safer than Haifa, which was critical, given the importance of our passenger.

After agreeing that the alternate route was definitely worth a shot, the team checked their weapons and gear. This time the ritual was different, though. Something about the team's attitude was very different, and at first I did not recognize it. It was not long, though, before I realized what was different. They were, for the first time, fatalistic about a pending mission. The banter and carefree happiness that had always been there was still there, but now it seemed stilted, almost forced, and not at all sincere. The team then became as giddy as Japanese schoolgirls. It was the most bizarre premission behavior I had ever seen. They took up a large amount of money and sent a couple of runners over to the 7-Day Store (military 7-Eleven) to buy the most outrageous amounts of candy, soft drinks, and snacks. They looked like navy chiefs in a candy store. Rarely, a guy or two may get a soft drink and maybe something small to eat before a run, but even that did not happen often. When guys did buy soft drinks and snacks, it was most often once we reached our objective. Now they were going nuts, and it seemed to me that it amounted to something of a last meal. We all knew that this mission could be dangerous, but that was true of any run, so I was not certain what it was about this run that seemed to so bother the boys.

But whatever it was, I felt it, too. When the brigadier showed up, he had a major with him. I showed the major our proposed route, and he said yes, it would work. In fact, that route was the one he always used himself. While I was surprised that the PSD leader did not know about the alternate route, when it was his job to protect a general, I did not dwell on it for long. A run down Haifa might be a great idea without the brigadier, but with him it was a very bad idea. While we most often did, as our critics asserted, go looking for a fight, we never did so when we were providing a combat escort to any officer of the rank of colonel up, or when providing security for large convoys loaded with weapons and ammo. Some things were just too valuable to risk, and while we never felt that way about our own lives, we were certainly aware of the importance of such men as the brigadier. The trip to the academy went exactly as expected and took us less than ten minutes.

To my surprise the academy buildings and grounds were very well kept. The buildings in which classes were taught, and officers and students billeted, were white, with blue roofs and a broad blue stripe about eighteen inches high along the bottom of the buildings going down to the ground. There were numerous trees and even some grass on the grounds. It was one of the nicest places I had seen in Iraq outside the Green Zone. The gate into the academy compound sat under the watchful eyes of over a dozen Iraqi men who appeared to be doing nothing more than drinking coffee, smoking cigarettes, *and* noticing who came and went.

We were not safe there at all. Still, we did not worry about our surroundings too much while at the academy, but we did make note of the fact that this was not a FOB, and in fact no more secure than any other place in the Red Zone. We found a place to park under some trees that provided welcome shade from the noon sun. Here, unlike our practice at places such as Kirkush and other American facilities, we did not remove our body armor. Looking around, I could see that we did not have the shade all to ourselves. Lying nearby were four dogs, and these drew our immediate attention. As I petted the dogs, Lance Corporal Dann thought my dual personality worth noting.

"Fucking Top and his animals. Puts together a team of hardened killers and melts at the sight of a dog or even a cat."

Algarin added, "I think his call sign should be Doctor Dolittle."

Without even looking at Algarin, I replied, "And yours should be Doctor Do Less and Bo's should be Doctor Do Nothing."

Facemyer, never gracious enough to let a poor rejoinder die a quiet death, mimed hitting drums and said, "Top tells a joke. Take two."

"Hey, Top, how come you never rub me behind the ears like that? Looks like it feels pretty good," teased Algarin.

"If you had hair, any hair at all, just enough so that I could pretend you were a dog, I might, Starsky, but petting you behind the ears, as things are now, would be like stroking a bald rat."

Far too soon, the brigadier finished his meeting and we had to mount up, leaving our new friends behind. Though these dogs, unlike every other dog or cat I saw in Iraq, were obviously well cared for, we still left them with fresh water and MREs.

As we pulled out of the gate, we made note of what the crowd standing outside was doing. It had not grown, and they appeared only mildly interested in our going. That did not mean they had not called friends and set up an ambush for us just down the road, but at least it appeared that we would clear the gate. The trip back went as smoothly as the trip out had gone. Once we were back within the Green Zone, we quickly stowed our gear and secured our vehicles before rushing off to chow.

At about 1845, while we were still eating, Deboda, who had come to power saying he would curtail our runs, called my cell phone to tell me that we were needed back at ops right away.

"What's going on, sir?"

"I need you guys to make a run to BIAP and meet a J-4 crew already there. They are off-loading weapons that I will need you to escort to the North BIAP warehouse."

I quickly looked at my watch and asked for a phone number to the senior guy on the ground at the airport. Deboda gave it to me and I called the man, a lieutenant colonel. I told him that he had to be ready to roll by 1930, as force protection rules and MNSTC-I policy forbade us from conducting night operations without prior approval by both entities. The colonel assured me that he would have his people ready by 1930. I told him that would be great, but if, for some reason, he did not have his people and cargo ready by 1930, we could meet them in the morning and make the run then.

The colonel did not like that idea because it would mean that he would have to spend the night at BIAP, away from his air-conditioned cable TV and refrigerator-equipped trailer. That was a price he was simply unwilling to pay. War was hell, wasn't it. The colonel assured me that they would be ready on time.

We departed the Green Zone at 1900 with Deboda in tow. The team arrived at the airport at about 1915 and had effected a link-up with the J-4 by 1930. They were not ready. Looking at the massive cargo plane in front of me, an old AN-12 of Russian design, I concluded it would be some time before they were. The colonel had either lied to us just so he and his people would not have to spend the night at BIAP, or despite having graduated from college and risen to the lofty rank of colonel, he was so stupid as to believe that his six-man working party could unload the massive jet in the time allotted by us. I did not like being lied to. While the Ukrainian crew unloaded the plane, Iraqis loaded the weapons, 4,500 AK-47 rifles, on waiting cargo trucks.

Daylight was leaving us in a hurry. I told Deboda and the colonel that we should scrub the run for now and pick up the escort in the morning. After all, these weapons were just going to be shoved in a warehouse, so there was no mission-critical reason to make the run now. I also reminded both men that we did not have any night optics and that our night training was rudimentary at best, except for those of us with infantry backgrounds. Furthermore, I reminded both officers of MNSTC-I and force protection policies and procedures and stated that we would be in blatant violation of both. Deboda disregarded all of that and said that we would make the run that night. Finally, I asked Deboda, "Well, sir, have you coordinated this run with any of the units operating in the area?"

Given the half-assed nature of how this was being executed, I was sure he had not. Driving through the operating areas of other units at night was never something to be taken lightly; you could get killed by friendlies even if the movement was coordinated. Failing to coordinate that movement with those units was a *very* good way to get killed—as an Italian journalist and security detail learned all too well. Less than a year later, on 4 March 2005, just outside Camp Victory, Italian journalist Giuliana Sgrena, who had just been released after a month of captivity in insurgent hands, was seriously wounded when the vehicle she was riding in failed to stop at a U.S. checkpoint. The shooting wounded her and killed an Italian secret service agent who had secured her release. The soldiers manning the checkpoint had no idea that the people in the car were Italians, as their movement had not been coordinated with U.S. forces. As faulty as the Italian coordination had been, and as tragic as the results of that failure were, our coordination was worse. We were a dozen heavily armed men, some with Russian weapons, driving around at night in vehicles that looked anything but American. In fact, they were just begging for some friendly fire. It was Custer-at-Little-Big-Horn stupid! Coordination of this type was something that every infantry unit leader understood the importance of.

Deboda was an infantry officer, and he surely must have known this. Maybe he just did not like the idea of staying in BIAP any more than the colonel did. Sure, war was hell, but why make it any harder than it had to be? Deboda decided that we would make the run. While he had said he wanted to limit our missions, he had no problem putting ill-equipped people at risk to simply move weapons to a warehouse and in violation of written policy. Deboda, if he was convinced for some reason unknown to me that the run was critical, should have called force protection and asked for permission to make the run. He chose not to. Had he done so, I am certain force protection would have said hell no. The lack of coordination also meant nobody would know we were on the road. If we got hit, it would be several hours before anybody, other than a unit stumbling over what was left, would know about it. I should have called force protection myself. That I did not go over Deboda and the colonel is unforgivable, and I regret not having done so.

I fell victim to my own ego, and by so doing I was risking the lives of my men because I was not going to go over the heads of these officers to get a mission killed. To me, no matter how screwed up I knew the run to be, going outside the chain of command to kill it struck me as somehow cowardly. By not doing so, I was as guilty as Deboda and the colonel, though for very different reasons.

I called my guys together and briefed them on our unusual situation and made sure that each man understood the importance of ensuring that everybody, even the J-4 shits, was accounted for if we were hit. We would go nowhere, no matter how hot it got, until we were sure we had everybody.

Brackin asked, "Does that go for Colonel Deboda, too, Top?"

I thought about that. I must admit that the thought of Deboda wearing an orange jumpsuit in his very own video did appeal to me. I decided that, yeah, it went for him to.

"Yes, Fudd, him to."

While I sincerely did not care whether Deboda was killed, leaving him was something that would have rightfully disgraced us all, so even at the risk of life and limb and in spite of what we all felt about him, even he would not be left behind. Still, I hoped that if we were hit, he would be the one paying the price for his own stupidity, not one of my guys.

As things turned out, people would pay for Deboda's foolishness, but neither he nor any of us would be picking up the tab. At 2320 the last of the weapons were finally loaded and we were ready to move. It was a full three hours and fifty minutes later than the colonel had said they would be ready. We left BIAP for the North BIAP warehouse.

This trip would normally take five minutes, but since the movement was not coordinated, the gate leading directly from BIAP to the warehouse was closed. That meant we would escort four semitrailers on a circuitous course through Baghdad. Crawling at forty kilometers per hour and escorting a fat target, we were easy meat for IEDs and VBIEDs. While many of Iraq's roads lacked lighting, large parts of the route we would travel were well illuminated. We would be very easy targets for ambush in these places. While we would be clearly visible to our attackers, it was unlikely we would see them, bathed in light as we would be. Those parts of the road not well illuminated presented another problem. Iraqi drivers were notoriously inattentive even under ideal circumstances when they could clearly see what we were and know that they should avoid us. Under these conditions, the lack of visibility and our slow speed, it was a certainty that vehicles would close on the ass of the convoy at high rates of speed without knowing what it was they were closing on until they were on top of us.

It now became obvious that the lack of proper marking on the rear vehicle for a night run had robbed us of something we depended on to help ensure our survival and that of innocent Iraqis. In daylight or with vehicles properly marked for night operations, we could present a posture that said to the locals, back off, stay away, or you could get shot. Our posture was like a rattlesnake's tail: It was designed to warn off the unwary before more violent action was required. Anything that ignored the warning immediately became the subject of greater scrutiny. Are women or children present in the vehicle? If not, how many males are there? Two or less and you started getting ready to use lethal force to defend against a potential VBIED. But if women or children were present in the vehicle, then no matter how provocative, no matter how threatening the driver's actions seemed to be, you gave the guy a pass. Thus far in the war the enemy had not used women and children in their VBIED attacks. We were all thankful for that! But now, robbed of sunlight, we could rely on none of that, and everybody, the locals and ourselves, were in greater danger than would have been the case had we just waited a few hours to dump the shit in the warehouse! Because of my sincere desire, contrary to what my palace critics thought, to avoid killing the innocent, I issued an order that I had never issued before.

"Do not fire, I repeat, do not fire on any vehicles approaching the rear of the convoy unless you are positively certain that you have no choice. These poor bastards have no idea who we are. Over."

Vehicle 2 answered up and affirmed that they both copied my order and understood. Vehicle 3, at the rear of the long convoy and therefore about five hundred meters from my vehicle, never answered. I knew that was because our radios were useless. My instructions were really nothing more than the legalese double-talk of the very people I loathed. How could you be *positively certain* of anything in Iraq? The enemy did not wear uniforms, and he relied on our sincere desire to avoid killing the innocent to let him get close enough to kill and maim our friends with a VBIED. My instructions, as well intended as they were, would have been of little value to vehicle 3 anyway. In spite of his seniority, Gunny Josleyn had been placed in the rearmost vehicle as a machine gunner because he was the most experienced person I had. I relied on his superior judgment and maturity to make sound decisions with little or no input from me.

Gunny, realizing that the cars closing in on him could not possibly know how much danger they were in, went so far as to turn on his light and illuminate himself and the long barrel of his 240 machine gun in a vain attempt to warn off vehicles closing from the rear. The Iraqis were not used to the Americans moving semis escorted by unmarked SUVs at night, so they were even more inattentive than was normally the case.

The senior man in Gunny's vehicle that night, the vehicle's commander, was Deboda. Deboda gave orders that were counter to mine. Deboda was now the current operations officer, and therefore my immediate superior. He was not merely a passenger; he was in command.

Vehicle 3, with multiple high-speed threats closing from the rear, opened fire. Gunny fired warning shots. That was enough to cause the Iraqis closing from the rear to back off. What were they to do? They had been placed in an impossible position by the very man who was now telling them to open fire. I can only imagine the stress they were under. No night vision gear, no communication with anyone outside their own vehicle, and for all intents and purposes "alone" on their little island as our rear guard.

I had no issue with what they did; in fact I would have done the exact same thing, but I had serious issues with the decisions that put them in the awful place they now found themselves in. In that respect it was very much like the incredibly poor command decisions that led to the USS *Vincennes* shooting down an Iranian airliner in the Persian Gulf on 3 July 1988, resulting in the deaths of all 290 aboard. In that incident the captain of *Vincennes*, William Rogers III, put his ship in a position where the only option that seemed available to the crew was to shoot down the unknown target closing on them.

Deboda himself employed, according to those in the vehicle, his own weapon frequently. The blame for this incident rested with Deboda, and even with me. It was my error for not calling force protection or simply refusing to go. I had let pride get the better of my judgment, and Iraqis had paid for that. We were escorting rifles that were going into storage; they were not needed by some Iraqi unit going into battle, and yet Deboda thought the mission so critical that it justified what I saw as a violation of standard operating procedures. There are some things that I will never understand. Deboda was not only our frequent critic, he had even gone so far as to address with me the team's obvious desire to locate and kill the enemy as if that were a bad thing. Yet he had set in motion on this night a series of events that placed many people in great danger. I was the irresponsible cowboy? I was the headhunter?

We arrived at the warehouse and waited while the four secured the weapons and trucks within the compound. At some point, we realized that the four's people had just left without us. Without so much as a word, they just rolled out. Assholes! We packed it up and left by about 0045.

We did not leave a moment too soon. We had just left the compound when we heard the impact of several mortar rounds hitting the complex. The incident reminded me of a discussion I had had with Wheeler a few days earlier concerning attacks at and near the North BIAP warehouse. The complex itself had been taking a lot of mortar fire in the last few days, and this fire frequently coincided with the arrival of Americans at the complex. Convoys leaving the complex had been ambushed, and the theory was that a man inside the complex was tipping the insurgents. Of course, it might not have been as sinister as all that. A guy across the street could provide all the info required to launch these attacks. Regardless, Wheeler and others had considered putting us in the complex to augment security as intel believed that a ground attack against the complex was possible. Now we had very nearly been caught in a mortar attack that could have killed or maimed any number of us. And for what?

We arrived back at the palace without any further problems. The team went to late chow and talked about the night and how foolish the run had been. Over coffee, we wondered aloud what the morrow would bring. All of us were starting to grow weary of being in Iraq. The stress of day-to-day operations was not the biggest reason for this, though it no doubt took some toll. But dealing with Deboda and his friends was getting to be too much, especially if we had to deal with them on the road. It was one thing to put up with the petty and childish actions in the palace, but on the road the interference of men like Deboda was not merely tiresome, as it was in the palace, it increased our risk. As I walked back to my trailer I thought about everything that had happened, and I debated what to do. I doubted that Deboda had gotten permission from anyone to launch his midnight ride, and I seriously doubted that he would tell anyone, let alone file the required after-action report about the convoy in the morning, as I had told him he needed to do. I hoped that he would not, as this would leave him with some additional explaining to do once I dropped the manhole cover on his bare grape. As I lay in my rack, I decided that I would tell Wheeler what Deboda had done, provided Deboda performed as expected and failed to tell Wheeler about the incident himself. I knew I could count on Deboda to do what he felt was in his own best interests.

I seriously doubted that Wheeler would do anything about it, let alone take the matter higher for action in any event. Not because Wheeler gave a shit about Deboda, he didn't. Wheeler cared about Wheeler, and like Deboda, he, too, would do what he felt was in his own best interests. If he felt going to higher would show that he had no control over the operations section, Wheeler would keep his mouth shut. If he felt it was in his own best interest to roll on Deboda then he would squeal louder than a Nixon aide. I really hoped both men would just be silent. That would be great, because then I could go higher and maybe, just maybe, the commanding general would hammer both men. If it came down to himself or Deboda, Wheeler was going to give up Deboda. First, I had to give Deboda a day or so to tell Wheeler what had happened so that he could not later claim that it was his intent to do so, he had just not gotten around to it. If Deboda failed to mention the incident, then I would tell Wheeler all about it. After telling Wheeler and giving him a few days to initiate some sort of action, I would relate the same sad story to the chief of staff. If Wheeler performed as expected and said nothing, the chief would be more than just surprised by what I had to say. Hopefully, he would actually do something. Deboda, in my view, had already violated standard operating procedures, and if all went as I expected, both he and Wheeler would fail to report the incident to higher.

July 30 passed without Deboda having bothered to tell Wheeler what had happened. That served my purposes very well. Later that evening, at 2356, we took some mortar fire and ended the day on a high note.

On 31 July I was awarded the Bronze Star with combat V. Deboda kicked things off by reading the citation. He began, "For exceptional, velorious service." It should have read "valorous," of course, and I felt like Deboda had screwed up the pronunciation on purpose, as if he could not bear to link any of our names with the word "valorous." Wheeler, Theodorson, and Johns smiled while Wheeler looked at Deboda as if to say, "Okay, that was good but . . ." Wheeler had interesting words concerning Napoléon that he tied in to my service in Iraq. The ceremony was bizarre and the honor rendered almost meaningless by the less than sincere presentation. Aside from that, I did not know how to feel about the award anyway. The award was not for a specific act of valor but for combat leadership, much like those officers frequently receive. Most enlisted men got valor awards for specific acts of courage. I had not. Mine was for recruiting, building, and training, equipping, and leading a unit on 210 of the most dangerous missions in Iraq. To my own mind that simply did not equal the lofty award presented to me.

That we had conducted so many missions with crap for equipment was remarkable. That I had trained a team of soldiers, marines, and Royal Marines to fight as one, with weapons from many nations, was certainly a rare accomplishment. That we found our own weapons, ammo, vehicles, fuel, and parts said a lot about our dedication, motivation, élan, and morale, attributes in a unit most often credited to the unit's commander. But I knew, as every leader ever so decorated surely did, that my decoration was earned by my guys. Leading people who want to fight is easy. In fact, leading the team was among the easiest jobs I had ever had. I knew that my Bronze Star rightfully belonged to my team. I was just a small man driving a very fast and expensive car! After the ceremony, I walked back to my trailer and sat on my rack looking at the award. Beautiful, yet simple, almost austere, the medal was the perfect balance of color and form. I thought about my grandfather, his sons, my father, his brother, my brother, and my son-in-law—each one a marine infantryman. Alone among them, my father's brother, my brother, and I had seen combat. My father's brother had fought in Vietnam and had earned a Purple Heart. My brother had served in Beirut, and I had served in Panama and the Gulf. None of us had ever, in over ninety years of combined service spanning nine decades and four wars, been decorated for valor.

I thought of how proud my son would be, but mostly I thought about how much this simple award would mean to my mother. I wanted her to see me wear it. I put the medal back into its leatherbound case and tucked it away into my wall locker.

CHAPTER 16

Bitter End

In spite of Deboda's attempt to reduce the number and types of missions the team performed, he had been unable to do so. The team had escorted everything from weapons and ammo to soldiers, American colonels, and generals as well as British generals and even very senior Iraqi generals. We had escorted FBI agents, police officers, reporters, and mundane things such as toilet paper and other consumables on our KBR missions. We had provided additional security at vulnerable sites such as the Baghdad Recruiting Center and the convention center. We had performed quick-reaction-force missions to both the Baghdad recruiting center and Tadji. Deboda found that while he and the 1st Cav wanted to reduce the missions we ran, they were unable to do so, because demand for our services was very high, and that demand was a direct reflection of the trust placed in us by those we protected.

August was as busy a month as any before. While our mission load had remained somewhat constant, the types of missions we ran were changing. On 2 August we were scheduled to take an army lieutenant colonel, Lieutenant Colonel Vice, to a meeting at the Sheraton, which was located across the river from the Green Zone. It could clearly be seen from the trailer park where we lived. We had not been to the Sheraton before, and we all looked forward to it. Rumor had it that the Sheraton had shops and a restaurant rivaling those at the Green Zone's Al Rashid. At 0730 we were formed in the lot, having already performed all of our premission checks. We had only the brief to give before we departed. We had a problem, though; Vice did not show at the scheduled time. In fact, Vice did not show until 0815, a full forty-five minutes late for a run he had scheduled. Not at all happy about the delay, I immediately got on him.

"Sir, what time did you schedule your run for? You're forty-five minutes late. Do you know what that means?"

Before he could answer, I began the brief. I stressed that traffic would now be very bad in the area around the Sheraton. As I continued the brief, I noticed that Vice was screwing with his PDA and not paying attention to the brief, whose main purpose was to save his life if we were hit. Already livid, I stopped the brief and locked my eyes on Vice. One by one, all eyes moved toward Vice. Suddenly aware of the silence, Vice looked up.

I addressed him. "Yes, sir, we are waiting for you, just like we have been for the last forty-five minutes."

Vice answered me. "Well, Master Sergeant, yours is not the only mission I have; we do have others."

I did not like the flippant answer.

"This is *your* mission," I reminded him. "*You* requested it and *you* even requested the mission time."

His answer reflected an utter lack of understanding of the situation he had placed us in. "Well, I guess we'll just be late."

I had reached my boiling point.

"Just be late? Just be late! I guess you might not go at all as, like you, I also have other missions. In fact, I am about three seconds from killing this one. Maybe the insurgents will cancel it for us. Because you're late, we will be hitting the Iraqi version of rush hour, and we will be dragging ass in one of the worst fucking areas of Baghdad. Because you are late, our chances of eating a VBIED are much higher than they were just thirty minutes ago. Because you can't even pay attention to the brief, your chances of being our only casualty are higher than they otherwise would have been. But, hey, that's up to you, because no matter what happens to you, I will always have other missions to run. Now, if you are ready to pay attention, I can finish the brief."

Colonel Vice was far more attentive as I continued the brief. Once I had finished, Gunny J pulled me aside.

"Top man, you can't just talk to officers like that. They will relieve you."

I knew that would be the case in most situations, but after everything that had occurred over the last six months, I seriously doubted that I would be relieved. Besides, I no longer cared if I were. I would still retire, so what could they do to me? I felt as immune to consequences as any Hollywood star would, whether he was facing charges for having carved up his wife or having shot her. While the road to the hotel and the road in which we killed people on 17 May were one and the same, the trip was insurgent-free, though painfully slow and tense. The hotel was easy to see but difficult to get to because of all the blocked-off roads and barriers to VBIEDs. We wound our way down a warren of Baghdad streets until finally we broke into the clear behind the hotel. We staged our vehicles and looked up at the impressive façade of the hotel.

Del exclaimed, "This place is fantastic. I can't wait to see what it looks like on the inside."

I had to agree with Del. The place looked very promising. The lobby was a no-shit hotel lobby, and it was easily the equal of the Rashid. We were impressed. The lobby, ornate, well maintained, and filled with shops and restaurants, was what one would expect of a first-rate hotel. Like the police academy, the Rashid, and, in fact, anything of beauty in Iraq, the Sheraton seemed out of place in the filth and violence of Baghdad. We explored the shops for a while before taking an elevator up to the top floor, where KBR operated another of its fabulous dining facilities. Rumor had it that this was the best in Iraq and we looked forward to checking it out. We still had about an hour to kill before the facility opened, but we need not have worried about getting bored. For KBR also operated a snack bar and a game room adjacent to the dining facility.

As impressive as the lobby was, it did not compare with the view from the top. One entire wall of the snack bar and game room was a massive multi-paned window from which you could see much of western Baghdad. In clear view, you could see the palace and the surrounding trailer parks. We killed our time enjoying the view and playing pool.

If we thought the view was spectacular, chow was pure ecstasy! While the food at most KBR chow halls was so good I was amazed that we were not fat, it all paled when compared with that served at the Sheraton! This was war? During the Gulf War I slept in fighting holes, without overhead cover, wearing the same uniform and without bathing for eighty-eight days. We ate MREs three times a day for that same period. Now we lived in trailers that would be the envy of any West Virginia family and we were fed better than we were in our stateside chow halls. Incredible! As good as the chow in Iraq was, the company was always better. While the conversation was most often varied, on this day it was about the insurgency and the tactics they employed.

While we all agreed that the insurgents were lethal, we did not feel that they were in any way effective. Will thought he knew why the insurgents were operationally and strategically ineffective.

"They are dumb, lazy Arabs."

Will squinted his eyes and raised his right hand with the palm up and his thumb touching his index and middle fingers, gestures that we all knew preceded Will's imitating a "typical" Muslim.

" 'We will not blow up the church now, for it is too hot and too early. Perhaps we will blow up the church later today or maybe tomorrow, but not now. For now, we rest. Later we will blow something up.' They are dumb, lazy people."

Most of us agreed with Will. We all knew that U.S. convoys were highly vulnerable, and had we been fighting anybody but these useless turds, we would have had our hands full. While we denigrated our enemy for his lack of skill and courage, we were at the same time thankful for it.

Our time in this man-made Shangri-la did not last long though, and far too soon it was time to don the flak jackets and helmets and get ready for the return trip. We picked up Vice, two of his soldiers, and a civilian passenger in the staging area and headed back to the palace. The ride back was what most of them had long ago become to us, easy and relatively stress-free, or so it seemed anyway. After we got back to the Green Zone and unloaded our passengers, the civilian came up to me and said, "Wow, is that the way it is for you guys every day? That was intense." I thought about what he had said and the bug-eyed looks we had gotten from so many other passengers and I realized that no ride was "normal" or "relatively stress-free." You just got used to it. I did not know how a man got used to that kind of stress, but I knew that we were used to it. The civilian thanked me for the ride, gathered his gear, and left. Lieutenant Colonel Vice apologized for being late and acknowledged that it had been unprofessional on his part.

I thanked him for the apology. As I stowed my own gear, one of Vice's soldiers, an attractive female specialist, walked up to me and thanked me for mine and the team's efforts.

"Top, I just wanted you to know that I really appreciate all that you guys do. A lot of us do, and I just wanted you to know."

Being under siege within the walls of the palace we frequently forgot that there were some who sincerely appreciated our efforts. Her reminder was both welcome and needed. I had only a few minutes to consider what the young soldier had said before I was once again embroiled in another round of palace foolishness.

Dented, windowless, beautiful vehicle 3. *(From the collection of Jack Lynch)*

I thanked her for all of us.

After evening chow, Deboda again called me into the office to see him. "Top, I think Colonel Thomas inflated the awards, and I am going to fix them."

How, I asked, would he do that? Deboda had decided to shred the awards submitted by Colonel Thomas, approved by Wheeler and the board, and signed off by the commanding general. In fact, Deboda went even farther, saying that he was going to launch a review of all awards going back to those awarded for the fight on 8 April.

"That seems unfair. Why just the awards to the team? " I asked.

Deboda denied that he was targeting the team, but the date he chose, 8 April, had significance only to the team. To everybody else it had just been another day, one day closer to going home, or maybe it was the day the dining facility served steak and lobster or the feature film had been *Steel Magnolias.* Deboda had decided that since he had failed to mold the team in his image, had not even earned its respect, he would retaliate in the only way a man like him could; he would use administrative guile to take from warriors who daily risked their lives the medals they had earned. Of course, there would be no review of Deboda's own Joint Service Commendation Medal, which was awarded to him for helping set up the new NCO academy. In addition to all of his other faults, Deboda was also jealous.

Reed had already related a conversation with Deboda in which Deboda had said, "I am not an easygoing father figure like Colonel Thomas." That was true, but why had he stopped there? He could have added so much more by way of comparison between himself and the highly respected Thomas. By contrast, Deboda, had destroyed the motivation of a unit that just a month ago had volunteered to extend. No other unit in Iraq, let alone one tasked with convoy security and given shit to operate with, had volunteered to extend. That my team had was a testimony to the leadership and support of Colonel Thomas. Oddly, not less than twenty-four hours before my meeting with Deboda, Wheeler had asked that the awards be upgraded. He felt that Thomas had unfairly applied a marine standard in what was a joint environment. But, as always, Wheeler never knew what was going on in the three, and the chances were, when he did find out that Deboda wanted to shit-can the awards because he felt Hesco had been too generous, Wheeler would sit by and watch him do it. I knew that Deboda would have his way with the awards.

Still I had some options. It was time to drop some dimes. First, I informed Wheeler about our night run. Wheeler's expression was priceless. He had the look of a happily married man who had just been informed by his wife that there was "someone else" and that not only was she leaving him, but she was leaving him for another woman and, oh, by the way, she wanted to be called Fred from now on, *and* she was taking the dog, too! It was classic! As expected, Wheeler had not been informed of the midnight run or the engagement. Not happy at all, Wheeler thanked me for the information. I decided that I would wait until I saw what he did with the information before I went to the chief of staff. Two days should be enough.

CHAPTER 17

Going Home

On 5 August, just one day shy of my last day in country, we ran four missions. All were weapons runs to Tadji. These runs were very risky in that we had established a pattern of picking up the semis at BIAP, escorting them to Tadji, then going back to BIAP and repeating the process. Obviously, I dwelled on just how unimaginably crappy it would be to get blown up on my last day, but I had no intention of not going on those runs. I had admired the gunny who went to the recruiting center on the day it had been hit in February even though he was but days from rotating out. I knew then that I wanted to go out the same way. End the game the way you played it. The following day I had a meeting with the new MNSTC-I sergeant major, Sergeant Major Pafford, USMC, to discuss the night run and Deboda's screwing with the team's awards. While I was waiting for my meeting with the sergeant major, the team drew a last-second mission to BIAP to pick up a staff officer who had just arrived in country. I thought about letting them make the run without me, but I had not gone on 208 runs just to miss any on my last day. I told Huggy to hold the run until I had finished my meeting with the sergeant major.

I met with Pafford and gave him the copies of the original award submissions, complete with Wheeler's signature and the board results. I also provided him with copies of those awards that the general had signed off on. I then added details about our midnight run, highlighting force protection and MNSTC-I policy and the lack of night gear. While the awards fiasco seemed to have the sergeant major's attention, details about the night run intrigued him even more. He agreed to set up a meeting between the chief of staff and me for later that evening. I thanked him and quickly left to meet the team for our run to BIAP.

The team seemed happy that I had made it for the run. I felt invincible both going and coming. I felt invincible and alive! I knew that I was doing what I was meant to do, leading warriors, and I loved it. I had always known that I loved what I did in Iraq, but on this, my next-to-last day in Iraq, I was more fully aware of how much the war and my team meant to me. Painfully, I knew that it would all end soon. I knew that with each passing minute my tour drew inexorably toward its conclusion.

I looked over at Huggy, back at Face, Will, and Meg, and knew that they had all become an integral and indispensable part of me. Leaving them, parting from them, would be like losing a part of myself, and I dreaded that. Realizing how little time I had left with the team, I no longer felt invincible. I felt very weak and very alone. What was I without my team? But my war in Iraq was not yet over, and I had one fight left. Later that evening I would meet with the chief of staff and try to set right everything Deboda had done. I really did not know what to expect. Part of me fully expected that the chief of staff would ignore everything, the medals, the failure to follow established policy, and the engagement that resulted from that failure, combined with the subsequent failure to report the incident to higher.

Deboda, Wheeler, and Toddington were officers, and we, me included, were *just* enlisted guys. As enlisted men, regardless of how long we had been in the service, we lacked the credibility that officers carried. We were, in the eyes of most officers, just thugs, hired help of little intellectual ability and certainly beneath trust. Whereas they saw themselves as professional warriors and leaders, they saw us as guys who were incapable of doing anything other than the menial work of a grunt. A smaller part of me, recalling the honor and leadership of such men as Thomas and Buchanan, hoped that we would get justice. But I had seen enough both in the Marine Corps and in Iraq to know that it was highly unlikely.

Later that evening I met with the chief of staff, Colonel Henry, U.S. Army. Sergeant Major Pafford attended as well. I laid everything out for the chief. I explained the history behind the awards and how Deboda had changed them after Colonel Thomas left. I showed him the awards packages and even the citations for those awards the general had already signed off on. I also told him that our section had offered to extend and the circumstances that caused us to rescind the offer. I asked if either Deboda or Toddington had told him that we had offered to extend, and, as expected, he said they had not.

Saving what I thought would be the best for last, given that it did not involve conflicting opinions or judgments, just cold hard facts, I outlined the details of our night run, highlighting my view that Deboda had made the decision in violation of established policy, and as far as I knew, had not informed anybody of his decision or of the consequences of that decision. The chief listened, but said little, not a good sign. When I finished, he asked if I had anything more. I knew then that *nothing* would be done. Six months of sacrifice and service, six months of risking our lives, and it seemed like none of it meant a damn thing to this guy. We had done everything, even broken the law, just to stay on the road, and none of it had meant anything to anyone but ourselves. I thought about that after I left my failed meeting with the chief. Had our service, heroic and selfless as it was, meant so little? Indeed it had. But so what? Deboda, Wheeler, and Toddington all knew what they were, and no award they could take from us or pin on their own chests was ever going to change that. Each knew his limitations, and so long as any one of us or any warrior anywhere drew breath, they would be reminded that they were not the equal of other men. Deboda and company could take awards from brave men and women, but Deboda and his supporters on the staff would never want to be in a darkened alley with with any of my guys. Deboda, Wheeler, Johns, Theodorson, Ricks, and Vorgang knew what they were and we knew what we were.

Many in our chain of command had, in my opinion, failed in the most basic obligations of command. They had failed to get us armor, blocked our acquisition of M-4 rifles, failed to get us crew-served weapons, and even failed to get us vehicles, fuel, spare parts, working radios, and ammo. But we did not fail! We got everything we needed to do our jobs while they sat on their asses and watched. When they asked us to escort anything from generals to cargo, we answered up, and we never failed. In over 220 escorts neither we, nor the people we protected, sustained a single casualty. We had pulled security at some of the most dangerous sites in Baghdad and did so without loss. In the end we reigned supreme on the road, but within the palace walls we never had a chance. So what if we were a little brazen. The roads in Iraq were not a place for the timid or the weak. In the end it did not matter that our service was held in such low value by our antagonists. What mattered most was how we felt about that service. I knew the men and woman on my team were among the bravest and most dedicated soldiers and marines in Iraq, and nothing could take that away from us.

On our last evening in Iraq Face, Will, and Gunny Josleyn were presented with their end-of-tour awards. All were given a chance to make remarks at the conclusion of the ceremony, as was normal. Gunny Josleyn and Face said nothing, but Will was not as kind.

"Yeah, I just want to say thanks for the fucking award. I might be pissed about my first one having been destroyed, but I didn't come here for fucking medals like most of the people in the palace, and *I got to do what I came here to do and more than once, too.*"

Everyone was stunned. There were some very awkward moments as the officers looked at each other, wanting one of their number, just one, to confront the belligerent sergeant. Shredding awards was child's play, confronting a pissed-off ranger was something far more difficult. Making matters worse from their perspective was Will's reminding them in no uncertain manner that what he came to Iraq to do was kill people, not get medals. The very thought seemed to scare the shit out of the assembled staff officers. Deboda, rather than confront Will, turned to me.

"You had better remind that soldier that he is only an E-5, and he had better watch himself."

By now my contempt for Deboda was such that I simply responded, "I am not going to do that, sir."

Before Deboda and I could really get into it, Toddington called Will, Face, and me over to the side. I do not remember everything he said, except that he did say we were the "three finest combat soldiers he had ever met." It was in sharp contrast to everything I had been hearing about my team for the last six months, and I took it as the supreme compliment. It would have been an insult had he called us the finest soldiers he ever met. Being a soldier, a complete soldier, meant being like the people in the palace, and we certainly were not that. Still, it would have meant a lot more coming from someone else.

My last twenty-four hours in Iraq saw the most mortar and rocket attacks I had experienced since I arrived in Iraq more than six months before. At 2336 on 6 August we took a volley of four to six mortar rounds. Since I was awake, these did not bother me, but still I counted each impact as the rounds landed all over the Green Zone. *Crumph, crumph, crump, crumph!* Some were close while others were distant. I thought it was kinda cool to get a parting shot from the locals on my way out. However, when a few minutes later, at 0007, we took still more incoming I thought it was decidedly uncool. While two attacks so close together were rare, the result was not: some noise and no damage. These guys sucked! As always yes, I was thankful for the attacks as I drifted off to sleep knowing that the enemy had just wasted several potential IEDs. My trip out would be a little safer because of it.

I left my trailer on my last morning in Iraq and went directly to the human resources office and turned in my temporary pass. I did not stop by operations; there was nobody I wanted to see there. I walked out to the staging area an hour before my scheduled departure. My team was already waiting for me. We talked about what a great ride it had been, and as we did so, some old friends showed up to share the good times. At some point that morning, we took more mortar fire and it was closer than usual. I was talking with a first sergeant when the rounds hit, and he flinched. I did not. He looked at me funny and said, "Damn, that was close." I answered, "Happens all the time."

Likewise undisturbed, Will, Huggy, and Face joked about still taking mortars. Del teased those of us going home about being killed before we left.

"You guys are not home yet."

"Well, you're fatttt!" Will challenged.

Of course Del was not fat, but Will was compelled to answer Del's reflecting on the possibility that we could still be killed.

"She does look bloated, Will, but I think that's just the PMS," Face added.

The fun did not last. Deboda made an unwelcome and unnecessary appearance before I gave the brief. I did not know why he showed up, but he and I had an argument. At some point Deboda, unable to emerge from the shadow of Hesco, took one more shot at the departed senior officer, "I do not need to be liked as much as Colonel Thomas did."

I responded, "Colonel Thomas never *needed* to be liked, but he was. He was liked, respected, and admired because he was a sincere, competent, and caring leader."

After Deboda departed, I held my last mission brief. I concluded with a question which I had asked them all before.

"Okay, what is it all about? What constitutes mission success?"

In unison they answered, "It's all about your continued glorification and survival, Top."

"That's right," I answered. "Especially now."

I then asked if they had any real questions. They did not, and we loaded up for my last ride. The trip to the airport was like most of those before it, stressful yet without incident. As I scanned my sector, as I had hundreds of times before, I tried to memorize every sight, sound, and smell. I wanted to make sure I never forgot what it was like going down the BIAP road. While this was the deadliest stretch of road in the world, what did that really mean? Not much. Had the insurgents been half as capable as the media made them out to be, this road would be littered every day with the burnt-out wrecks of American military vehicles.

It was not. This was not World War II, Korea, or even Vietnam. The people we were fighting could not even load the magazines of the Japanese, Germans, North Koreans, Chinese, or Vietnamese. Iraq could be deadly, but it was not nearly as bad as it was made out to be. If you remained alert, paid attention to your surroundings, and projected a posture that made it clear you were not to be screwed with, you had a very good chance of going home alive regardless of the number of times you hit the road. All the armor in the world was not going to save you if your head was up your ass or anywhere other than focused on what you were doing. We were living proof of that.

At BIAP, I handed my helmet, flak jacket, and ammo to Huggy. We spent about an hour there, all of us together one last time, talking about how great it had been to get to work together. At last, sooner than any of us wanted, it was time for the team to head back and for us to report in. We hugged each other and promised to get together as soon as we were all back in the States. None of us could have possibly imagined then the sad occasion that meeting would actually be. As I watched them drive off, I could not help but be aware that they were on the road without me for one of the very few times in the six months I had been in Iraq. I knew that there was no longer anything I could do to protect them. I felt like running after them. Once they had driven out of sight, I turned to Gunny Josleyn, Will, and Face. I could not imagine making the long trip back without them. They were all I had left.

Our flight out of Baghdad was easy, and in no time we landed in Kuwait. From the airport, we were taken by bus to a fantastic hotel on the beach. The chow was incredible, with so many varieties and in such generous portions that it proved to be impossible to eat it all. Then we wandered the grounds to check out our surroundings, just as Gunny J and I had done when we first hit the palace. Face brought some booze, but nobody, including Face, felt like drinking. I did not sleep well, and the morning seemed to come on too quickly. We boarded a bus for the airport that afternoon. It felt so strange to be riding around without weapons or looking for potential threats. It was a little difficult to relax. Many hours later we were loaded aboard a DC-10 for a short flight to Al Udeid Air Base in Bahrain.

The terminal was packed with soldiers, marines, and civilians waiting to fly out. It stank and it was noisy. After what seemed a lifetime, we were finally called to board our flight. I slept some of the flight but sleep was difficult to find, and most often I just stared out the window. If Will, Face, or Gunny J were up, then I would just shoot the shit with them. If not, I would look at my watch, which was still set to Baghdad time, and imagine what the team was doing at that moment. We flew into Germany early on the morning of 9 August. The airport had a great USO and some small shops where we could buy newspapers and magazines. I bought a magazine about World War II fighter pilots and then went to the small restaurant located near the terminal where I ordered a light breakfast and read my magazine. It was not long before it was time to file back into the terminal and wait to be boarded. The terminal was packed with service members returning from the Middle East and families going home from Germany. Families with small children were called to board first. The whole process took a while, but it went smoothly, and we were soon seated and in the air. During the flight I noticed that two of the flight attendants were wearing the rank insignia of some of the people they had brought home. They had air force, army, navy, and marine insignia, but they did not have the insignia of a master sergeant of marines. I pinned mine on the lapels of both women.

When we landed at Baltimore-Washington International Airport, we off-loaded and staged our gear in the USO. Face and Gunny J stayed with the gear while Will and I looked for our connecting gates. It was not long before I was reminded that I was back in the United States where the tin soldier ruled with an iron pen and a miraculously clean, never-used rifle. As we walked through the airport, I caught a man dressed in civilian attire eyeball-ing me as if I had just slept with his mother. I knew immediately what he was and what his apparent problem must have been. I was not wearing any rank insignia on my uniform!

Seeing a marine in an airport without his rank insignia is quite common if that marine is deploying or returning from a deployment—flight attendants collect insignia of rank. Obviously, this sack of shit now eyeing me like I was Gomer Pyle did not deploy enough to know that. Standing around the man were several other, younger men. As Will and I approached, the man tried to get my attention by tapping his collar in an attempt to tell me what the dip-shit surely knew I already knew; I was not wearing my rank insignia. That meant that he was asking me for an explanation as if I owed him one. I did not see it that way.

As loud and as contemptuously as I could, I yelled, "What do you want?"

The man, who turned out to be a marine master sergeant, with the ill-fitting (given his rank) last name of Sargent, was not at all happy with the belligerent question.

"You're out of uniform, and because of the way you challenged me this could have gotten very ugly, but I am not going to go there because you're hard like that, right?"

By "hard like that," I assumed he thought I was not wearing my rank as some sort of symbol of my rebellion against the machine. I looked at him and answered, "Yeah, I am. Go fuck yourself, shitface."

Without even so much as pausing, Will and I continued on our way. Will laughed and said teasingly, "I see you still haven't lost your knack for making friends, have you, Master Sergeant. Damn."

Will commenting on my ability to be blunt was akin to Bill Clinton lecturing Richard Nixon on integrity. Having found our gates, Will and I turned around and headed back to the USO when we walked by Sargent again. Doing his best to appear authoritative and respected in front of his boys, many of whom would later tell me what a complete and incompetent ass he had been in Kirkush, Sargent yelled, "Hey, private," in an obvious reference to the fact that I was not wearing any rank insignia. Louder, and certainly loud enough for his boys to hear, I answered, "Go fuck yourself, fuckface!"

It was amazing that this guy had not been made a sergeant major and given a rifle battalion as he had everything the Marine Corps looked for in the sergeant majors it shit on its infantry battalions. He was not a frequent flyer on the Marine Corps deployment program. He was simple-minded. He was a martinet, and he was not an infantryman, the perfect selection for sergeant major of an infantry battalion.

Will, Face, Gunny J, and I spent our last few hours together at the USO lounge. We talked about what we were going to do when we got home more than anything else. Will was going to spend some time at Face's New Jersey home. Gunny J and I were going home to our families. Too soon, the time came for gunny and me to board our flight to Tampa. We hugged Will and Face goodbye and we all promised to stay in touch with each other. Gunny and I landed in Tampa a few hours later and immediately went to MARCENT to process out, the last step severing all of our official ties to the war in Iraq. Everything went great until the personnel officer, a marine warrant officer, called me into his office. The warrant officer had heard about Deboda trying to rework the tours of marines assigned to MNSTC-I and he was not at all happy about it. He had me write a statement, which he then collected. He took me to meet the senior marine officer at MARCENT and explain to the two of them what had been happening with the rotation dates as well as some other issues.

It was one more waste of time and effort that wasn't going to change anything. I was relieved when the Gunny and I were given our flight dates, which were for the following day, 11 August. We left MARCENT and headed to the Tampa Marriott where I had stayed before leaving for Iraq. We showered and met in the bar for dinner. As we ate, we talked about what we would do next. The Corps had very little left to offer us after the tour we had in Iraq. I did not want to go back to Quantico, and I had no interest in returning to a line battalion just to be the operations chief, stuffed away in a battalion headquarters, while young warriors fought and died. I could not do that. As we talked, I looked around the bar at all the people, including many young men, so completely unaffected by the war. Drinking, eating, and copping a feel where they could, I loathed them for their safety and their ignorance of the price being paid to protect them. I loathed them for not being where other young men of their generation were. While I was in Iraq, I had frequently dreamed of being home. Sitting there that evening I was sure that being home, surrounded by cowards masquerading as men, would not be what I had expected it to be.

After dinner, we went back to our rooms, both spent from the long trip. I quickly fell asleep and did not wake until my alarm went off at 1000 the following morning. Gunny's flight departed before mine. Neither one of us really knew what to say as he got ready to board his plane. We hugged and both commented about what a great tour it had been, and as with Will and Face before, we promised to keep in touch. I never felt more alone than when I watched the gunny's plane lift off and fly out of sight. I went and found a place to sit in the airport bar where I spent the next few hours playing Tri-Towers and thinking about my team, now scattered all over the planet. I was relieved when the time to board my own flight came. I looked forward to seeing my family and my home, which Robin had extensively remodeled during my absence, though the very thought of my reunion with them filled me with the unique anxiety of anticipation. My flight into Reagan National Airport was very relaxing. The flight was not crowded at all. In fact, the big 757 was nearly empty, which allowed a flight attendant and me a good chance to talk.

She thanked me for my service and asked what it was like in Iraq and about my family. We talked a lot about the war, the politics of the war, and about our homes and how much we missed them when we were away. As the plane neared D.C., she wished me well. I buckled myself in and looked out my window at sights familiar to me since childhood. Even at night, maybe especially at night, D.C. is a beautiful city. The monuments, illuminated as they are, stand in stark contrast to the surrounding dark. I always enjoyed coming into Reagan National more than Dulles because of the view! As the flight descended, my anticipation of seeing my family grew just as it did every time

I came home from a long deployment. After we taxied in, I quickly gathered my small carry-on bag, and as I left the plane thanked my flight attendant for helping me to pass the time. I walked down the long corridor leading to the terminal where I knew Robin was waiting for me. I did not know what to expect when I saw her. This was *our* first deployment. Denise had always been the one waiting for me when I returned from my adventures abroad and I knew what to expect from her and I always anticipated those reunions with great joy. I anticipated this one no less, but I was also more than a little apprehensive. Though this was my twelfth trip overseas, it felt like my first. I was very nervous, and I did not know why. I hoped that I would see Robin first so that I held the initiative! As I rounded the corner, I quickly scanned the large, nearly empty terminal. To my left I saw the most beautiful woman in the world sitting in a chair. It was Robin, and she never looked more perfect. We embraced, standing in the middle of the terminal. Robin shook and said, "Oh God, Jack, I can't believe it's over."

I looked down at her and lifted her chin, "It is. It's all over." I did not know it then, but the war would never be over.

I quickly and dispassionately settled back into my duties as the ops chief for Marine Corps Base Quantico. If I had hated my job before Iraq, and I had, I hated it even more now and found it extremely difficult to just show up. Quantico was, even without the war in Iraq, dull on good days. Now it was mind-numbingly dull, and the work—planning and coordinating ceremonies and tracking training—was absolutely unrewarding and without any challenges. Quantico was a haven for senior staff NCOs who had long ago lost all desire to deploy, and they dominated the culture of the base. It had always bothered me that many staff NCOs did everything they could to avoid service in the Fleet Marine Force, but now, with so many young marines fighting and dying, it disgusted me that I had to serve with them. Of course, in their eyes my less than warm embrace of life at Quantico, my less than poster marine image, and my low first-class PFT score said far more about me as a marine than anything I did in Iraq. But that was nothing new. What was new was a heavy dose of petty jealousy on the part of some of the staff officers.

Men like Captain Darvon Layden took every opportunity to make sure I knew how they felt about my tour in Iraq. Layden was overweight even by navy standards, let alone those expected of a marine officer. The guy needed to wear a bra. His chest looked like two baggy, mostly empty coin purses. Much of his time at work was spent on the phone in some animated discussion with his wife about the latest crisis at home. The man was useless, and everybody knew it. So useless in fact that everybody from the base commander to the base sergeant major was left speechless when Layden was promoted to major. Neither his less than stellar career nor his lack of time in Iraq kept him from opining on what qualified a marine as a hero.

"The real heroes in Iraq are those kids kicking in doors, not riding around in convoys."

Captain Daniel Barrett, who had been in Iraq with me and who thought very little of Layden, looked over at me as if to ask "What the hell brought that on?" It was becoming a familiar theme, and I was getting sick of it. While I did not regard myself as a hero, I did not like having some fat office bitch taking shots at me. Besides that, a recent survey found that even among the marines who stormed Fallujah, the most feared and loathed duty in Iraq was convoy or route security. Every time you hit the road in Iraq you knew what could happen. You could be killed or maimed for life. The enemy would almost always have the first crack and it mattered little how good you were if you were in the wrong place at the wrong time. That type of warfare, fighting an unseen enemy who hits and runs, takes a very special kind of courage. *Anybody* who straps himself into a vehicle over two hundred times has bigger balls than some fat-assed staff officer who was content to pass his time at Quantico! Incredibly, Layden had more to say about my tour in Iraq. Layden would tell captains Barrett and Nelson Jerome that he heard from a friend, who had been in Iraq, that I was nothing more than a dangerous cowboy. The friend was a staff officer stationed far from Baghdad, so his opinion was as informed as any Layden could have come up with himself. Jerome and Barrett respected me and told me what Fat Boy had said. When I confronted Layden about it, he said that it was just his friend's opinion and not his. It was a mini version of the palace bullshit all over again. But occasional remarks from Layden and others like him were the least of my problems. My apathy for my work spread to my home life, and my marriage began to suffer. My apathy turned to anger with each passing day, and Robin and I grew farther and farther apart. I just wanted to go back to Iraq, and nothing else mattered. I became more confrontational than I had been before I left, and I knew that I was no fun to be around. I was not aggressive toward my family, but at the slightest provocation with people outside my family I became extremely confrontational. It was getting out of hand, and it was getting to the point that nobody wanted to go anywhere with me for fear of what was going to happen next.

Robin tried to help, but there was nothing she could do. In May 2005, just ten months after my return from Iraq, we were separated. But that was a long way off in the fall of 2004. Worse was to come before then. If I thought that life was as bad as it could get, I was about to get a very abrupt reminder that it can always be much worse.

On 18 October 2005 I received an e-mail from Mr. Berle Sigman, a retired marine master gunnery sergeant and the father of my friend, Staff Sergeant Berle John Sigman IV. I had first met Sigman IV in Panama in November 1995 after I was flown down there to take over as his platoon sergeant following the relief of the platoon sergeant and all the section leaders for Weapons Platoon, Bravo Company, 1st Battalion 6th Marines. With the recent relief of the platoon sergeant and all the section leaders, junior marines had been pushed into leadership positions which, outside of combat, they would not have been expected to fill so suddenly and under such difficult conditions. Of the three sections—machine gun, mortar, and assault—only the assault section, led by then Lance Corporal Sigman, was trying to carry on. Sigman was conducting a countermech (antitank and armored fighting vehicle) class, and it was obvious that he knew his business. I was impressed. Later, when I took over a rifle platoon, I would see to it that Sigman, having reverted back to a team leader, was assigned to support my platoon. He was always there, on time and on target with his rockets. I had once watched as his team put a rocket into a bunker just seventy yards in front of one of my squads, no easy task. When I was moved over to Charlie Company 1/6, I lobbied hard for Sigman to be selected as the assault section leader, and he was. While he was a very good marine, he did have one serious flaw, his name. It was not very long after I met Sigman that I began abusing him for his name.

"Berle John Sigman, what the fuck is a Berle and what the fuck is a Sigman? Berle, Berle sounds like something a redneck would say to his doctor if he had the clap. 'Doc I got berles [boils to the rest of us] all over my dick.' You were named after dick sores."

Of course it did not escape my notice that he was the fourth man in his family so named.

"What really kills me is that your great-grandfather, grandfather, and father, all knowing what a burden the name was, still stuck you with it. Are your parents Catholic, Sigman?"

"No, Top, why do you ask?" Sigman answered.

"Because with a name like that you must have been an unwanted pregnancy, I bet one step away from a coat hanger."

Sigman would always say that his friends and family called him Jack; that in fact he had always been known as Jack; and that the name Berle John Sigman IV was a function of tradition and not how he was identified.

Once, I had asked Sigman how he came to be called Jack. "How the hell do you get Jack from Berle?"

Sigman answered, "I don't get it from Berle. John is my middle name, and Jack is the same as John."

"No, Jack is not the same as John," I challenged. "That is like saying a Yugo is the same as a Mercedes. I will bet your redneck ass does not think a compact Jap pickup is the same as a Ford F-250, do you? Jack is a cool name, a masculine name, and that is why Johns frequently like to be called Jack but you will never hear a Jack tell anyone to call him John. Tell the truth, Sigman, you just like my name, don't you! You want to be me, don't you?"

Sigman denied this. "No, my family called me Jack long before I ever knew you."

"Bullshit! You watched me from afar and said to yourself, 'Man, that guy is so cool, so smart and handsome, I wish I were him.' So you did the next best thing and took my name. I tell you what: I sell a 'Be Like Jack' kit for guys like you. Give me fifty bucks and I will show you how to be me."

So it went for the next ten years. During that time I had met Sigman's family and had grown to admire his heroic father very much, not only for his own service but for raising a warrior son. So it was not unusual for me to get an e-mail from Sigman's father. But this one was different, and what I read left me speechless. Sigman's dad told me that Jack had been seriously wounded in Iraq. I read the e-mail again, almost in disbelief. Sigman had arrived in Iraq shortly before I left, and I cautioned him to be careful and come see me when he got home. I read the e-mail again and replied to Sigman's dad, telling him to call me. In the interim, I contacted one of my former company commanders to see if he had any word as to the nature of Sigman's wounds. As I waited for word on Sigman's condition my phone rang; it was Sigman's father. He told me what little he knew and he asked if I could get any information. The worry and fear in his voice were painful for me, and yet I greatly admired his ability to keep his emotions in check. As we talked I noticed that my inbox had a new message. I opened it.

The message was from my former CO, and it detailed Sigman's condition. My heart sank with fear and dread.

"Left leg amputated below the hip, multiple fragmentation wounds to the arms and abdomen."

The e-mail went on to say that his survival was still in doubt and that casualty assistance officers were standing by for the family in the event that Sigman did not survive. I knew Iraq was dangerous, but I had never really thought about how I would prepare myself for the loss of a friend after I left the place. I had thought about it from time to time, but I always dismissed such thoughts quickly, not wanting to face the possibility that I might lose friends, especially while I was sitting on my ass in Quantico. The e-mail ended with instructions not to reveal Sigman's status to the family as specifically trained people would do so when the time was right. As I read the words, they blurred, and the voice of Sigman's father seemed to get farther and farther away. I wanted so badly to tell Sigman's dad what I knew, to offer him some comfort, but I did not. He kept asking, almost as if begging, for some information as to the condition of his son. I started to cry, and all I could say to this father was that I had to go. I asked that he call me as soon as he heard anything else.

Later that evening my phone rang, and I recognized the number as Sigman's father's. I did not want to answer for fear that the news would be bad just as it had been when my wife's doctor had called the day she died. I stared at the number on the caller ID for several seconds before I answered the phone, expecting the worst and doing my best to be ready for it. As soon as Sigman's father spoke, I knew things were not too bad; his voice was calm and in fact almost formal. Essentially, Sigman's dad passed what I already knew about his son's condition with additional information concerning Sigman's expected arrival at Bethesda Naval Hospital. I thanked him for the update and made plans to see Sigman as soon as he could have visitors.

A few days later I went to see Sigman and his parents at Bethesda. I did not know what to expect, I did not know what to say, and a part of me wanted to turn back and go home. The ward in which Sigman was staying was crowded with wounded marines. Not sure what room my friend was in, I found the marine liaison who told me where I could find Sigman. I walked in and there, horribly wounded by an RPG, was my friend and his anguished parents. Sigman's leg was gone, amputated at the hip, which I knew would make his recovery more difficult than would have been the case if he had lost his leg below the knee. His abdomen, right leg, and both arms had numerous fragmentation injuries, and he was wearing a temporary colostomy bag. He was still dirty and looked as if he had just stepped off of the battlefield. It was a lot to take in, but worse than his injuries was the look of pain, fear, and anguish on the faces of his parents. I dreaded looking at them more than I did Sigman. My own son was fifteen and would be joining the Corps when his time came. The murder of my father when I was only ten and the sudden death of my wife had left me extremely fearful for the safety of my loved ones even when there was no extraordinary cause for worry. I so badly wished that

I were somebody else, a business man, a football player, anything other than a marine dad who had raised his son to be a warrior. Sigman had paid a terrible price to answer the call, and I was certain his parents, particularly his father, were paying it as well. I hugged Sigman and spoke with him and his parents.

"Sig, how are you doing, man?"

"Well, Top, I have been better, much better, but I am okay."

I asked him how he got hit and he told me.

"We had stopped our convoy and I dismounted when this fucking rag head hits me with an RPG. I rolled over and fired like four shots from my rifle before I realized that wasn't going to work. Doc rushed over and did a really good job. Had he not, I might not be here now."

"When did you know the leg was gone?" I asked.

"As soon as I looked down. It was still attached, but barely, and I knew they were going to have to take it."

Sigman then looked at his mom and said, "Mom, Top, taught me everything I needed to know over there, everything except how to kick an RPG away."

He meant it as a joke, of course, but I had already been wondering if I had, in some way, failed to teach Sigman something that would have kept him from being hit. I knew that was silly. You cannot teach everybody everything, and even if you could, some would still be killed and wounded. Though we all laughed, it was obvious that everyone was still just beginning to understand the lifelong impact Sigman's wounds were going to have. Sigman, maybe feeling the awkward silence, quickly changed the subject.

"By the way, Top, you better stop giving me shit about being called Jack. I earned it."

Sigman's parents, and particularly his father, had long known that I gave their son heavy doses of shit for his name, and both had graciously accepted it. I am not sure why his mom did, but I knew why his father accepted the merciless ribbing I gave his son. As a career marine he knew, as we all did, that you never screwed around with marines you did not respect. With them everything was professional. But around marines you respected it was always open season. I am certain that Sigman's dad knew that his son's name made him a high-value, low-effort target. His father also surely knew that I regarded his son as a hero, not for being so horribly wounded but for just being a marine grunt. I left after an hour very glad to see that my friend and his family could still laugh.

On the way home I could not forget Sigman's father. He had raised his son as he should have, to be a warrior, and now his son had paid a fearful price for doing what was right, for doing, as Kenny Rogers once said in a song, "his patriotic chore." I could not help but see myself as I saw Sigman's father. Would my son pay the same price as Sigman had, or would his be heavier still? It was a sobering and frightening thought. My father had been murdered when he was only thirty-two, and my first wife had died at thirty-seven. What right did I have to expect my son to survive a war when just getting out of bed had proven to be lethal to people I loved? I dreaded the possibility that I could be in Sigman's father's place.

I would see Sigman again at both Bethesda and Walter Reed, and I was amazed by the quality of care he received. I do not know where the little corner of hell existed at Walter Reed that was rightly exposed by the media; the wards I saw were incredible, and our wounded were well cared for in them. The last time I visited with him, Sigman was staying in Walter Reed's Fisher House. I was moved by the comfort of these homes away from home, and I was surprised by the volume and quality of gifts showered upon our wounded by both private citizens and corporate America. These men were well cared for in sharp and mind-numbing contrast to the poor warriors left in Walter Reed's hell house.

As Sigman continued his long recovery, my own life further deteriorated. Robin and I were fighting almost constantly, and I was finding life at Quantico growing even more frustrating. Everything since Iraq was boring and dull, and with each passing day I grew more listless, angry, and isolated. I just wanted to go back to Iraq, at a tactical level and not as some glorified staff sissy. Many of my former teammates felt the same way. Jason Williams was already in Afghanistan, but even there he was frustrated by the lack of action in that theater of the war. Sergeant Boeringer was back in Iraq with a reserve sniper platoon. Bo was not suffering from boredom. His unit had already sustained losses and would, by the time their tour was over, sustain the highest losses of any rifle battalion in Iraq. Patterson, too, was back in Iraq, but with a security company. Most of us had little or no respect for the security company. They dressed in khaki, wore Oakleys, and treated soldiers in Iraq like shit they had stepped in. All of us, to a man, advised Pat to can the security idea.

But Pat just wanted to go back to Iraq, and he did not care who he went with. Pat had driven his wife nuts, much as I had mine, and she finally relented when he asked if he could go back to Iraq with the security company. Pat was happy with his tour and with his company, though he wished we were all there together. Pat had never been sure why I finally let him on the team, and his doubts surfaced in an e-mail he sent me. Pat asked if I had finally assigned him to the team because I liked him or because I trusted and respected him. While it was true that I had grown to like Pat a great deal, I would never let someone on the team who I did not trust to pull his own weight. That would require that I risk the lives of many other friends, all of whom I liked just as much as I did Pat, just to make him feel good about himself. That was a heavy risk to run just to avoid hurting someone's feelings. I told Pat as much, and he was happy with that, very happy.

On Friday, 22 April, 2005, I was driving home from Quantico. The weather was a perfect match for my mood, chilly and raining heavily. My cell phone rang and I considered not answering it, as it was illegal to talk on them while driving on base. I looked at the number, and though it was not one I recognized, I answered it, anyway.

"Hello."

The person calling was hesitant at first, but after a short pause spoke. "Top Lynch?"

Now it was I who hesitated. The caller's tone did not promise good news, but rather than feeling any sense of real dread, I merely wondered what the caller could want.

"Yes, this is Master Sergeant Lynch. How can I help you?"

"Top, I do not believe we have spoken before, but my name is Lisa Patterson, Mike's wife. Top, Mike's dead. He was on the helicopter that was shot down."

I swallowed hard and thought about the headline I had read just that morning as I got ready for work. The helicopter, an old Russian HIP troop transport, had been shot down in Iraq. For some reason I had not even briefly considered that Pat might have been on that bird. I thought about his death and the image of the doomed helicopter, which was all over the news, going down trailing smoke and flame. Tears welled up in my eyes, and I thought about how many more people we should have killed when I was in Iraq. Obviously we had not killed enough! But none of that mattered now. Pat was gone, and there was nothing I could do about it.

"I am so sorry, Lisa. I loved Mike very much, and he was a good man."

Lisa thanked me and then asked if I could get the team together for her husband's funeral, which was to be held at the Jacksonville, North Carolina, National Cemetery. She then asked if I would not mind escorting Pat home from Delaware. We exchanged a few more words and some coordinating instructions.

I hung up and started to cry. Pat and I, having spent so much time together under siege within the palace walls, had grown very close, and I knew that I would miss him terribly. He was a good friend, and he was a brave man who never wanted more than to be an equal among warriors. Now he was gone. I got home and called the team. All of us, with the exception of Bo and Will, who were deployed, would be at Pat's funeral. Huggy and I would travel to Dover to escort Pat home, courtesy of the security company, which did a fantastic job taking care of Pat and Lisa.

Within a few days I met Huggy at Reagan National Airport, and we picked up a rental car for the drive to Dover Air Force Base, where we would link up with Pat. We met Pat and his driver just outside the Dover mortuary. We all introduced ourselves and then piled into our cars for the drive to Philadelphia, where we would catch our flight to North Carolina. Once we were at the airport we checked Pat in and were allowed onto the tarmac as he was loaded on the plane. Huggy wore his army class A and I wore my dress blues, one soldier and one marine, accompanying a friend home. I could think of nothing more appropriate and symbolic of our little joint team of soldiers and marines.

While I hate flying and could not imagine a sadder occasion, I enjoyed Huggy's company very much. Huggy and I entertained each other with stories and recollections of our time in Iraq. We talked a lot about Pat and his desperation to get on the team and how well he had fit in.

"Huggy, do you remember him taking all day just to zero his AK with that sorry-ass Chinese optic he bought? Man, Will gave him so much shit."

Reed laughed. "Yeah, and I remember Pat just quietly ignoring the insults being hurled at him. It was like he was in his happy place."

And so it went for the next two hours or so. It was a tonic for me to once again be in the company of someone I had served with in Iraq. In spite of the occasion that had brought us together, it was a good time. We did not discuss the manner of Pat's passing or his wife until we neared Charlotte.

Looking out the window I said, almost absently, "It is hard to believe he died on a fucking helicopter. IEDs and ambushes all over the place and he dies on his first helicopter flight. How long has it been since one of those was shot down?"

"A long time, Top, a long time. I am just glad he was not the guy shot on the ground. As pissed as I am, that would push me over the edge."

Huggy was referring to a widely circulated video in which the insurgents can be seen shooting a survivor as he asks for help. It had enraged all of us, and we had worried for a few hours that the man shot might have been Patterson. By now we knew that Pat had died in the helicopter and that the man killed had been a Bulgarian pilot. Still, we wanted blood for blood, and we wanted a lot of it.

Reed asked, "You worried about meeting Pat's wife, Top?"

"I guess. I just do not know what to say to her."

Reed admitted that he was not sure about meeting her either. "I am worried about that, too, but she seems to be in good shape. I think she is dealing with it."

We said little else to each other the final ten minutes of the flight. All I could do was think about Pat and how he had died. I imagine Huggy was doing the same.

Once we landed and saw to Pat's off-loading we were met by a Department of State security agent who hooked us up with the hearse sent to meet us. The driver of the hearse was an elderly man, and he was accompanied by his wife. They were among the nicest and most compassionate people I had ever met. Since we had a three-hour drive ahead of us, we did not spend the time we would have liked getting to know this warm couple. While Huggy stayed with Pat, I rode back to the terminal to rent a car. I picked up a big black Cadillac SLS. I followed the agent back to where we had left Pat, Reed, and the elderly couple. Reed quickly jumped in and, looking around the spacious caddy, complimented me on my selection. The old man took the lead and we followed.

Reed and I talked the whole way, and as before it was mostly about the team and Pat. It was a great time, filled with fond memories. About two hours into our trip the driver of the hearse pulled into Hardee's.

"I don't know about you fellas, but I'm hungry."

Chatting away, Reed and I had not realized it until the man pulled in to the popular fast-food restaurant.

"We are if you are, sir," Reed answered.

As we sat down, we asked the old guy why he was driving a hearse at his age.

"I had been in the furniture business for forty years when I retired three years ago. That is the worst thing you can ever do. It is like being buried alive, and it was killing me. So I went looking for a part-time job that had hours I wanted to work and would allow me to work with people."

Driving the hearse fit both. His hours where not constant, and the man sincerely enjoyed being able to provide some small comfort to grieving people mourning the loss of a loved one. He and his wife were very gracious and considerate, and it was difficult to imagine better company for our trip. They asked us if we knew the man we were taking home, and when we told them that we did, they asked about him, what kind of man he was, did he have a family and so on. It was nice being able to tell people who did not know Pat how much of a man he was—funny, devoted to the team, and courageous. Then they asked about the war. Did we think we were winning, did we think we could win, and what did we think about the growing antiwar (antivictory) talk in the press and among the Democrats?

"I think they are traitors. We are at war," I answered. "You can argue about how it should be fought, but even that should take place behind closed doors. Once you are at war, you have two choices; either you choose to win or you choose to lose, and anyone who advocates defeat as a course of action is a traitor. They want to make a mockery of all of us."

The old man and his wife agreed, but at the same time they just wished that the war would be over. Unlike the radical antiwar movement who saw dead soldiers and marines as nothing more than props lending their cause a fig leaf of compassion and empathy for those lost, the old couple, like so many Americans, sincerely mourned the loss of so many brave young Americans. That was the real problem with this war, just as it was every war. The people who most loved their country, the people who had the most to offer the Republic, were the very ones dying. Those who had nothing to offer, and certainly had nothing invested in the war, did the bitching. The real tragedy of the war was that it was killing the *wrong* people! The bravery and skill of our young warriors could be made meaningless with the stroke of a pen or a catchy sound bite. The outcome of the war would not be decided on the battlefields of Iraq but in the American media. I was sure it had always been like that, though, the best fighting for the rest.

The conversation ended, we climbed back into our car and followed the old man and his wife another hour to the funeral home where we would meet Lisa Patterson and her mother. Reed and I spoke very little for much of the final leg of our trip, and it passed slowly on small country roads that seemed to be leading nowhere. Directly in front of us cruised the van that carried our friend. Sometimes, when alone in the silence, I would talk to Pat. The conversation was one way of course. I thought about all the times we had shared in Iraq: on the road, the evening socials, and chow of course. Though I did not say so to Reed, I dreaded meeting Pat's wife more and more with each passing mile. I had already brought home a marine who had been killed in action in Iraq, and while that had been difficult, this would be far worse. I did not know what Lisa would say, and I did not know how I would feel meeting her for the first time this way.

Reed interrupted my thoughts. "Top, I think we are here."

Just ahead of us and to our right was a small one-story brick funeral home. There was only one car in the parking lot, a small SUV, and in it, I knew, was the wife of my friend. The old man pulled around to the back of the funeral home to the loading dock. We asked him to wait while we went and greeted Lisa. As we rounded the corner, she was already heading toward us.

"Hello, ma'am, how are you?" I asked.

A dumb question, but I really did not know what else to say.

"Hi, Lisa, it is nice to finally meet you," Reed added quickly.

"It is nice to meet both of you; Mike said so much about you guys, and, Jack, please call me Lisa."

We hugged her, and she moved us to her car, where her mother was waiting, and introduced us.

"How would you like to meet the kids?" Lisa asked.

Pat had as his screen saver a picture of his border collies. Most guys had a picture of their family, but Pat had his dogs, and he always referred to them as his kids. I had never asked how Lisa felt about that, but now it was obvious she felt the same way. They were beautiful and intelligent animals, and it was easy to understand why Lisa and Pat loved them so. After exchanging small talk, I told Lisa that we had some things we still had to do with the funeral home, but I told her we would be quick. Lisa, who up until then had been very cheerful and gracious glanced, to the back of the building, to the place where her husband's body was waiting, and her expression changed to one of dread: "I am not going back there."

I felt so bad for her, and I wanted so much to say the right thing, but remembering my own wife's death I knew there were no right things to say short of an incantation or prayer that would bring the dead back to life.

"Oh, that's okay. No reason for you to do that, but there are a few things Staff Sergeant Reed and I have to do."

We walked back to the old man, who was waiting patiently with the body of our friend. Together we gently removed Pat from the hearse and placed him in the funeral home. Lying before us was the body of a friend. I thought about the last time I had seen Pat as I headed out of Iraq, and I remembered all the times he and I had shared, especially over dinner or in the office when most often it was just the two of us. I loved Pat very much. I admired his determination to serve with the team and his quiet demeanor. He was, by far, the most gentle of all of us, and yet he fit so perfectly with us. He was my friend and my ear within the palace. Because Pat was so unlike the rest of us, the staff sissies within the J-3 thought that they could say whatever they wanted about me or hatch yet another scheme to change the way I and the team operated, all in front of Pat, and that somehow I would never get wind of it. They mistook Pat's quiet and gentle demeanor to mean that like them, he, too, was a coward, longing for the day that Top Lynch and his Lynch mob would get theirs. Of course, Pat was nothing like them. Pat was a man and a warrior, while they were all self-serving men who treated the time within the walls of the palace as a distasteful burden to be fulfilled if their careers were to continue to be upwardly mobile.

Pat, like the rest of the team, looked at Iraq as a place where you could prove your worth among men, among warriors. Still, for whatever reason, his gentle nature, his quiet, almost reserved manner, I always thought Pat would be the last of us to be killed in the war.

"Top, we better get going."

I took one last look at Pat and then headed back to our car. We followed Lisa to a ferry that was the only way to her home. On the boat we talked about funeral arrangements. Lisa was mostly concerned that the team be there, and she hoped that we would be able to come to her home afterward to meet Pat's family.

It was after 2300 when we finally pulled into the driveway of Pat's home, a nice one-story ranch sitting on several acres. There was a very large fenced-in yard where the dogs played, and the open property was bordered by heavy woods. We walked into the home and Lisa showed us the rooms we would be staying in, and then she took us on a tour of her home. The tour ended in what she called Pat's room. Most often you never know what kind of impact you have on a person's life. I knew that Pat and I were close. I knew that the team was very close, but I never fully appreciated just how much Pat's brief tour in Iraq had meant to him. On the largest wall of Pat's room were several pictures of the team. Pat's neck scarf hung on the wall, and so, too, did my last letter to the team before I left Iraq.

I remembered that Pat and Pat alone had asked me to sign it, but I never thought he would frame it and hang it in his home. Lisa asked us to explain where the pictures were taken and under what circumstances—before a mission, during, or after. As we explained the circumstances surrounding each photo it was almost like being back in Iraq with the team and Pat. Now, though, all the memories were and would forever be tinged with sadness. We walked back into the living room where Lisa's mom offered Reed and me a beer. We accepted and sat down. We talked about Iraq and Pat's time with the team. As we did so, Lisa pulled out a box of letters and e-mails that Pat had sent her from Iraq. She handed me one to read.

"Top keeps telling me that the next time they go to a range I can go, too, so I can get the training and maybe get on the team. Well, guess where they are? They are at Kirkush, on the range, and guess where I am? Still in the office! I guess to Top I will always just be the office bitch!"

Reading that now, in front of Lisa I wondered what she must have thought of me. I had been so very hard on Pat. Lisa, maybe sensing what I was feeling said, "You have no idea how happy you made Mike when you put him on the team. He was never happier. When he got back home, all he wanted to do was get back to Iraq but not as an office bitch. He wanted a job like the one he had with you, and he knew that was not going to happen in the army. He used to love to hunt and fish, but he was bored with everything when he got home and we were starting to fight. When he asked if he could go back to Iraq with the security company I was like 'Hell, yes, I will pack your bags for you.' I knew it was the only thing that could make him happy."

I worried that Lisa might feel guilty, but I was unsure what to say. If I addressed it and she had not felt guilty, maybe then she would.

"You know, Lisa, things are the same for me. My wife and I fight all the time. I hate my job, I hate my life, and I do not enjoy anything which I used to. I understand how Pat, I mean, Mike felt. Everything sucks now."

Reed added, "You know you could not have stopped him from going even if you tried. He was going to do what he wanted."

Lisa replied,very confidently, "Oh, I know. Once Mike made up his mind about something, he was going to do it, and nothing could stop him."

Reed and I laughed. "Yeah, I know. I saw that firsthand in Iraq. Man, he would just not take no for an answer."

We talked until about 0100 when we decided we had best get to sleep. Lisa had a lot to do between now and Pat's funeral, set for the following weekend. Reed and I needed to get an early start. I told Lisa that we would stay in touch during the week and I promised her that we would do everything we could to have everyone at Pat's funeral.

The flight back to Virginia was enjoyable. Again, that had a lot to do with the company. Reed and I shared old stories and I realized that I had not been as happy in a long time. While it sucked that it was Pat's death that had brought us together, it was nice to see Reed again. We parted ways at Reed's apartment, which was a few miles from Reagan National. The drive back to Culpeper was a long and sad affair.

In the intervening days between bringing Pat home and his funeral, I busied myself making sure that the team would be at Pat's service. I left for Pat's funeral on the following Friday. Tech Sergeant Dan Libby, one of the intel people who had proven to be such faithful friends, had a beach house rented for the team. Libby, Meggison, and Del's brother were already there by the time I arrived that afternoon. As I stepped out of my white Cadillac I was greeted with a torrent of insults about my "pimp" car.

I walked up the steps and was hugged by Meggison. "Good to see ya, Top."

"You, too, Meg, you, too. How is everybody?"

Libby and Del's brother said that they were doing well and that Facemyer and Dann should be in shortly. Slowly, one by one, the Maji gathered. Only Will and Bo, both deployed, and Algarin did not make it to the house Friday. Those of us who did—Meggison, Facemyer, Reed, Del, Josleyn, Dann, Del's bro, Libby, and Hesco—had a great time. We talked a lot about Iraq and how much we had enjoyed our tour, and we shared a lot of stories about Pat. It was the best time I had had since I left Iraq, and most of us felt that way. The evening ended much too soon, and we knew that the following day would be hard for all of us.

I woke up and made sure that everyone who had stayed at the house was up and getting ready. Dann and Josleyn had returned to their own homes but were to be at the house two hours prior to Pat's service. After I had put my uniform on, I checked those of my soldiers and marines. Like so many premission inspections in Iraq, no detail was missed, and I as looked each one over I knew it would be the last time. We climbed into our cars and convoyed to the Jacksonville National Cemetery just outside the gate to Camp Johnson, which was located adjacent to Camp Lejeune, where I had spent so many years.

Del's brother rode with me. It was interesting to hear his stories about his time in Iraq and about Del and their mother, an army colonel. We pulled into the cemetery and noted the army honor detail standing nearby. The team gathered around me, and we went over our part of the service so that there would be no mistakes. As we did so, Algarin pulled up with his wife and greeted us all with his broad smile. Algarin then introduced each of us to his wife, a beautiful Puerto Rican. Following the introductions Algarin called me to the back of his vehicle as he removed a large picture from it. The photo was a blowup of one taken of the entire team. It was nicely framed and matted, but Algarin pulled it out so that we could all sign it. I also had a large gold team ring which had been shipped to me just prior to Pat's funeral. The ring featured the Maji insignia on its top. On one shoulder was the emblem of the U.S. Army. On the opposite shoulder was a crusader shield, a nod to the fears of our Islamic enemies. The shoulder with the shield also had the year 2004, and above the army shoulder was Pat's nickname from his childhood, HUERO, which meant "white boy." We decided that we would present both items to Lisa during the family get-together later that day. When we saw the army detail take its position, we took ours.

The service was to be held beneath a tent. At the head of the tent was the altar. Pictures of Pat and the urn holding the ashes of our fallen comrade were placed upon the altar. To the left of this was a podium behind which stood my old team and Hesco. Within fifteen minutes of taking our positions a black limo pulled up, and out stepped Lisa. She was crying now, and it was obvious that she had been for some time. There were over a hundred people gathered to say goodbye to Pat. Among them were guards from the prison where he had worked and soldiers from his reserve unit. First the chaplain said a prayer, and then he spoke.

As he did so I thought again about what I would say as I had ever since Lisa first asked me to speak for our team. I did not write anything down as I felt that would be less than sincere, but I had worried about whether the right words would come when it was time for me to speak. Now as the chaplain spoke, I worried that maybe I should have written something down. Next a soldier from Pat's unit spoke, and finally an army major general spoke. When he had finished, he presented Pat's wife with a Meritorious Service Medal. Then it was my turn to speak. I walked to the podium and paused as I looked down. I thought briefly about what I would say, and then I looked at those gathered to say goodbye to Pat.

"I first met Staff Sergeant Patterson in February 2004. I was serving as the operations sergeant major for CMATT and I was putting together a convoy security and quick-reaction-force team when Pat—that's what we called Mike—checked in to be the new admin NCO. Pat heard that I was trying to build a convoy security team and he wanted on the team. I told him no way. I did not see any value in having a career admin guy, a reserve one at that, on my team. He lacked training and he lacked experience, so it was easy for me to tell him no. As all of you who know Pat realize, no was not something he liked to hear. Pat went so far as to give me his résumé, which listed his experience in the prison, but my answer was still no.

"But Pat kept hammering away, and with each passing day I could see that there was more to Pat than his job specialty. So I told him that if he did all the range, SOP, and driver training, then I might let him on the team. Of course, Pat did it all, and still he waited. Eventually he earned his spot on the team, and I never regretted having given him a chance. Still, all the things that had at first caused me to reject Pat out of hand were still valid. The guy was a reservist and he was a career admin guy, so what did he have to offer? Why did I put him on the team? Standing behind me are Pat's teammates. They are wearing the uniforms of the United States Army and the United States Marine Corps. I have served the marines for twenty-three years, my family has served it for generations, and I have always thought of myself as a marine first. But in Iraq I transcended that. We all did. Behind me you see soldiers and marines, but far more important than that, they are warriors. I know a lot of people like to think that everyone who wears a uniform is a warrior, but trust me, they are not. Not one of these men or women joined the military and volunteered for Iraq so that they could get money for college or learn a trade. They enlisted and then they volunteered for Iraq, and then they volunteered for service with the convoy security team because they wanted to fight! They were warriors first, and everything else was secondary to that!

"What does that have to do with Pat? You can teach a man to be many things, but you cannot teach him to be brave. Either he is or he is not. You cannot make a man want to fight; he either does or he does not. Like the soldiers and marines standing behind me, Pat had the rarest of all qualities, courage and a warrior's heart. Pat was a warrior. He wore a uniform, and he had a job title, but in his heart Pat was a warrior the same as each of us. Marine infantry, sniper, brig guard, logistics, artillery; army rangers, infantry, mechanics, and one army reserve admin NCO—thrown together by a mutual desire to serve among warriors and to earn the respect of those we respected. Pat earned our respect and trust. He was a great soldier and he was our friend and we will miss him. Thank you."

I stepped back from the podium and stood at parade rest as the chaplain said his final prayers. After the service, Pat's wife and family went home to prepare for the guests. We took pictures with some of Pat's coworkers and spoke about our time together in Iraq. Looking at Pat's headstone we noticed that Lisa had chosen to have it engraved with our team insignia: the coiled serpents, skull, and sword. Pat had been in the army for eight years and yet his six months with us meant more to him than had all those other years. It was a moving tribute to Pat and the single-minded and tight nature of the team. Eventually we pulled ourselves away so that we could head back to the beach house, change, and then head to Lisa's.

By the time we arrived there, the place was full. It was nice meeting so many people who had known Pat long before he went to Iraq and trading stories with them. After a few hours the crowds thinned out and it was just Lisa, Pat's family and close friends, and us. We told those left that we had some things we wanted to present to Lisa and asked everybody to gather around. Algarin presented her with the signed team photo. It moved Lisa to tears.

"Mike would have loved this. Thank you so much."

Next I handed her Pat's ring and she again thanked us. When the presentations were done, someone asked us to tell the "good" stories that we had not shared with the strangers. We looked at each other and we knew what they meant. Not everything the team was a part of or did will ever make it into print, but most of it was shared that day with the family of our fallen friend. They thanked us for sharing what it was like to serve with Pat and for our honesty about the war and our small part in it. One by one, we said our good-byes to Lisa and thanked her for having us. I drove home alone and with a heavy heart.

Colonel Jeff Buchanan is now a brigadier general serving as the ADC for the 10th Mountain, which is currently deployed to Iraq. His son, Matt, is a second lieutenant in the U.S. Army and will himself deploy to Iraq in the summer of 2009. Colonel Vic Sarna was wounded in Iraq in 2006. He is currently assigned to the Warrior Transition Unit at Walter Reed pending medical retirement. Colonel John Thomas retired from the Marine Corps reserve in 2007 and currently resides with his wife, daughter, and son in Ohio, where he works for General Electric. Major Paul Drury was promoted to lieutenant colonel in February 2009. He is currently serving as a congressional fellow. He lives in the Washington metropolitan area with his wife and two daughters. Robert Josleyn retired from the Marine Corps in 2005 and returned to Iraq as a contracted convoy security guard where he survived numerous ambushes. He currently resides with his wife and two sons in North Carolina. Sergeant First Class Shenk is still teaching when not serving in the National Guard. Chris Reed remained in the army reserve and has since served a tour in Afghanistan. He is now a sergeant first class assigned to U.S. Special Operations Command. Jason Algarin left the marines as a staff sergeant in 2005 and now works in real estate. He lives in Florida with his wife. Kevin Facemyer remained in the army and went back to Iraq in 2005. He is now a sergeant first class, stationed at Fort Bragg, where he lives with his wife. Edward Boeringer stayed in the marine reserve and deployed back to Iraq in late 2004. His unit suffered the highest casualties of any battalion in Iraq. Bo now works as a contractor and in that capacity has been to Kuwait and Liberia and Afghanistan. He currently works and resides in Virginia. Jason Williams deployed to Afghanistan in 2005, and shortly after his return, he left the army. Jason now works as a contractor in Kirkush, Iraq. Kelly Meggison remained in the army reserve and made several more deployments to Iraq, earning another medal for valor. Meggison is now a sergeant serving in Baghdad. Isis Delacroix has stayed in the army and is an applicant for a commissioning program; she will make a fine officer. Sergeant Dave Balan is now a staff sergeant assigned to 20th Special Forces Group (A). Charles Dann left the Marines in 2006. James Brackin remained in the army and is now a sergeant serving at Fort Drum. Schroeder remained in the Marine Corps. His whereabouts are unknown.

Gunnery Sergeant Hessen is still in the Marine Corps and went back to Iraq in 2005. Sergeant Powers was medically separated from the Marine Corps in 2006. He has been back to Iraq several times as a security contractor. He currently works for the navy as a contractor and lives in the Washington metropolitan area with his wife. Corporal William Napier left the Marine Corps in 2007 and currently resides in Maryland. Staff Sergeant Dan Libby is a tech sergeant assigned as the noncommissioned officer in charge of information security for an air force unit stationed at Vandenburg Air Force Base. Sergeant Melissa Garate left the army in 2006 and works as an intelligence consultant. She and Chris Reed are expecting their first child together. Staff Sergeant Sigman recovered from his injuries and was promoted to gunnery sergeant in 2007. My son and stepson are both serving in the Marine Corps and recently returned from Iraq. I retired from the Marine Corps on 1 September 2005 and now work as a contractor to the government. I deployed to Iraq in June 2008 in support of U.S. Army operations in the Baghdad area. I returned in December, 2008.

Appendix one is the signed Bronze Star award for Staff Sergeant Michael Patterson. Issuance of this award, along with the signed awards for Sergeants Jason Williams, Kevin Facemyer, and Specialist Isis Delacroix, was called off after Colonel Thomas's departure when Captain Wheeler USN and lieutenant colonels Deboda USA and Toddington Austrialian Army pulled the accompanying citations and orders for those awards. Lesser awards were issued in their place. As far as I know, only the convoy security team was treated in this fashion.

GLOSSARY

AK-47/AKM

Enemy weapon of choice. The AK-47 rifle is a gas-operated, magazine-fed (30 or 40 rounds) or drum fed (75 rounds) rifle firing a 7.62×39 mm round. The AK-47 is capable of semiautomatic and automatic fire. While crude, the AK is widely recognized as the world's most reliable assault rifle.

C-3

Also know as the operations section, operations, ops, or the three, this is the section within CMATT that ran the organization's day-to-day operations across Iraq.

CMATT

Coalition Military Assistance Training Team. The coalition organization tasked with recruiting, screening, and training men for the new Iraqi Army.

CPA

Coalition Provisional Authority. Body that was Iraq's de facto government until the transition to the governing council in June 2004.

Dragunov

Also known as the Dragunov SVD, or simply the SVD, the Dragunov is a Soviet-era, gas-operated, sniper rifle capable of semiautomatic fire only. The weapon uses a 4×power scope and fires the 7.62×54 mm round.

IED

Improvised explosive device. The greatest threat to roadbound troops in Iraq and Afghanistan is the roadside bomb, a type of IED.

J-3

C-3's new designation once CMATT became MNSTC-I.

M-16A2

The M-16A2 service rifle is a gas-operated, magazine-fed rifle firing a 5.56×45 mm round and is capable of semiautomatic and three-round burst fire. Magazine capacity is 30 rounds.

M-16A4

The M-16A4 is a full-size rifle nearly identical to the M-16A2 except it has the addition of rails, mounts, and optics found on the M-4. It has replaced the M-16A2 as the battle rifle of the U.S. Marine Corps.

M-2

Known as the "Ma Deuce," the M-2 is a heavy-caliber machine gun firing a 12.7×99 mm round which is effective against a wide range of targets, including light armored vehicles. The M-2 is a recoil-operated, belt-fed, automatic weapon that has been in service since 1933. It is mounted on a wide variety of platforms.

M-240

The M-240 is a medium-caliber general purpose machine gun. Though it can be mounted on a variety of platforms, in infantry use the weapon is most often bipod supported. It is a gas-operated, belt-fed fully automatic weapon firing a 7.62×51 mm round.

M-249 SAW

The M-249 is known as a squad automatic weapon. It is a bipod-supported, gas-operated, belt (100–200 rounds in plastic box or soft pouch) and magazine fed (30 rounds), fully automatic weapon firing the same round as the M-16/M-4 rifles. The weapon has a quick-change barrel, and each SAW gunner is issued two barrels, ensuring a significantly higher sustained rate of fire than enemy equivalent weapons.

M-4

The M-4 is a shorter version of the M-16 with both a shorter barrel and a collapsing butt stock. It has largely replaced the M-16A2 in U.S. Army service and is also used by selected units of the U.S. Marine Corps. While many soldiers complain about the weapon's lack of range and lethality, it is extremely portable and ideally suited to convoy security work. Like the M-16A2 it fires the 5.56×54 mm round.

Mk-19

Though classified as a heavy machine gun, the Mk-19 is a blowback-operated automatic grenade launcher firing a wide range of 40×53 mm grenades.

MNSTC-I

Multi National Security Transition Command-Iraq. MNSTC-I was the name given to CMATT when General David Petraeus took command of CMATT in June 2004.

MP-5

Blowback-operated submachine gun firing 9×19 mm rounds in semi or fully automatic mode and fed by either 15- or 30-round magazines. Lacking range and penetration, it has limited military applications.

PKM

Like the M-240, the PKM is a general purpose machine gun. The PKM is a gas-operated weapon fed by 100-, 200-, or 250-round belts. Frequently, however, the insurgents will string together belts of several hundred rounds, making the weapon anything but portable. Hilarity ensues when three assholes attempt to lug the weapon and its serpentine-like belt through the urban combat environment. The weapon fires a larger 7.62×54 mm round and is an insurgent favorite. Unlike the RPK, the PKM does have a changeable barrel.

ROE

Rules of engagement. The rules that outline the conditions under which a soldier or marine can use deadly force.

RPG

Rocket propelled grenade. Name most often applied to the launcher and the rocket it fires. The RPG is a man-portable, shoulder-fired weapon with iron and optical sights. The most common rockets are 40 mm antipersonel or 85 mm antiarmor. Either rocket would destroy an unarmored vehicle while the antiarmor rocket can easily penetrate all but the most heavily armored vehicles.

RPK

Like the SAW in that it is intended for use at the squad level. The RPK functions as the

AK-47/AKM and fires the same round but has a longer barrel and bipods for support. It is fed by the same combination of magazines and drums as the AK-47/AKM. It lacks a changeable barrel, greatly reducing its sustained rate of fire.

SA-7

A Soviet-era man-portable, surface-to-air missile called the Grail by NATO.

SAPI

Small arms protective inserts. The SAPI is a ceramic plate that is inserted into pockets on the front and back of flak jackets. While the flak jacket itself will not stop rifle fire, the SAPI plate will, including multiple impacts from the $7.62 \times 39\,mm$ round at point-blank range.

Top

Slang for a Marine Corps master sergeant. Said to be a carry-over from the days when master sergeant was the senior enlisted rank in the Corps.

VBIED

Vehicle-borne improvised explosive device. More commonly known as a car bomb.

INDEX